ELFQUEST:
THE GRAND
QUEST
VOLUME ONE

ELFQUEST CREATED BY
WENDY & RICHARD PINI

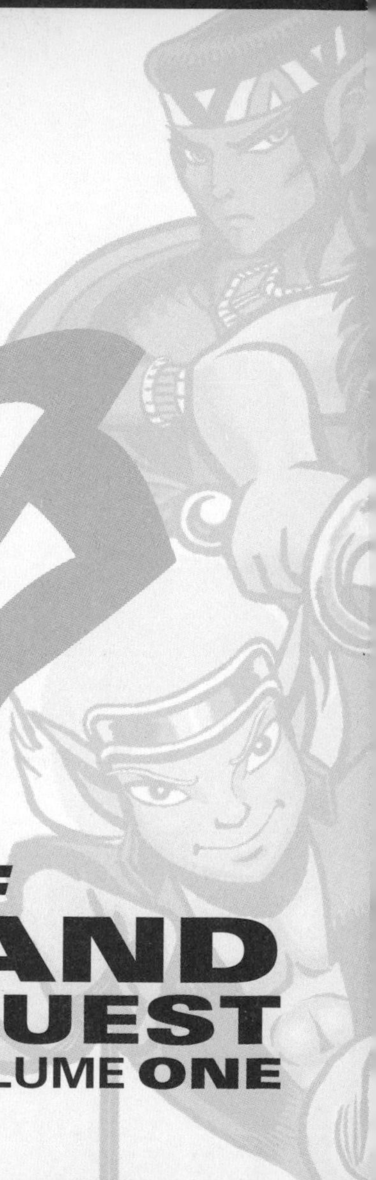

ELFQUEST: THE GRAND QUEST
VOLUME ONE

WRITTEN BY
WENDY & RICHARD PINI

ART AND LETTERING BY
WENDY PINI

ELFQUEST: THE GRAND QUEST VOLUME ONE
Published by DC Comics. Cover, timeline, character bios, and compilation copyright © 2004 WARP GRAPHICS, INC. All Rights Reserved.

Originally published in single magazine form in ELFQUEST 1-5. Copyright © 1978, 1979 WARP GRAPHICS, INC. All Rights Reserved. All characters, their distinctive likenesses and related elements featured in this publication are trademarks of WARP GRAPHICS, INC. The stories, characters and incidents featured in this publication are entirely fictional. DC Comics does not read or accept unsolicited submissions of ideas, stories or artwork.

DC Comics, 1700 Broadway, New York, NY 10019
A Warner Bros. Entertainment Company
Printed in Canada. Second Printing.
ISBN: 1-4012-0136-9
ISBN 13: 978-1-4012-0136-4

Cover illustration by Wendy Pini
Publication design by John J. Hill

The ElfQuest Saga is an ever-unfolding story spanning countless millennia that follows the adventures of humans, trolls and various elfin tribes. Some of the events that occur prior to the time of this volume are outlined below using the very first published ElfQuest story as a benchmark.

0

1,000

2,000

2,000 - 300 YEARS BEFORE

Goodtree, eighth chief of the Wolfriders, founds a new Holt deep in the woods and creates the Father Tree where the Wolfriders can all live. Her son, *Mantricker,* is the first in several generations to have to deal with nomadic humans again.

Mantricker's son, *Bearclaw,* discovers Greymung's trolls who live in the caverns and tunnels beneath the Holt. Bearclaw becomes the Wolfriders' tenth chief.

In the distant Forbidden Grove near Blue Mountain, *Petalwing* and the preservers tirelessly protect their mysterious wrapstuff bundles.

Among the Wolfriders, *Treestump, Clearbrook, Moonshade, Strongbow, One-Eye, Redlance, Pike, Rainsong* and *Woodlock* are born.

4,000 YEARS BEFORE

Freefoot leads the Wolfriders during a prosperous time. Game is plentiful and life is easy.

Freefoot's son, Oakroot, subsequently becomes chief and later takes the name *Tanner.*

3,000

4,000

5,000

9,000 YEARS BEFORE

Wolfrider chief Timmorn feels the conflict between his elf and wolf sides, and leaves the tribe to find his own destiny. *Rahnee the She-Wolf* takes over as leader, followed by her son *Prey-Pacer.*

6,000

7,000

10,000 YEARS BEFORE

Over time, the early High Ones become too many for their faraway planet to support. Eventually groups of these beings travel into space to seek out possibilities on other worlds, bringing along trolls and preservers as helpers. *Timmain's* group discovers the World of Two Moons, but as the crystalline ship approaches, the trolls revolt. The High Ones lose control and crash-land far in the new world's past. Ape-like primitive humans greet them with brutality, and the elfin High Ones scatter into the surrounding forest.

In order to survive, Timmain magically takes on a wolf's form and hunts for the other elves. In time, the High Ones adapt, making a spartan life for themselves. *Timmorn,* first chief of the Wolfriders, is born to Timmain and a true wolf.

8,000

9,000

10,000 YEARS BEFORE

10,000

0

475

600

1,000

2,000

3,000

4,000

5,000

6,000

7,000

8,000

9,000

10,000

6 YEARS BEFORE

The feud between elves and humans ends – seemingly – with the death of Bearclaw. Cutter takes the chief's lock and assumes leadership of the tribe.

25 YEARS BEFORE

Joyleaf gives birth to a son, Cutter, who forms a fast friendship with Skywise. The two become brothers "in all but blood."

475 YEARS BEFORE

Bearclaw begins a long feud with a tribe of humans who have claimed the land near the Wolfriders' Holt. Though both sides suffer over the years, neither can prevail, and neither will give in.

600 YEARS BEFORE

Deep in the desert to the south of the Holt, *Rayek* is born to Sun Villagers Jarrah and Ingen. *Leetah* is born to Suntoucher and Toorah twelve years later.

7,000 YEARS BEFORE

A crucial event occurs during the reign of the fourth chief of the Wolfriders: Swift-Spear goes to war for the first time against the humans of a nearby village. The humans are forced to leave, and he earns the name *Two-Spear*.

Two-Spear has strange dreams of the humans returning and believes the elves are no longer safe. He becomes obsessed by the dreams and tries repeatedly to convince the Wolfriders they must wipe out the human threat for all time. When his chieftainship is challenged by his sister *Huntress Skyfire*, the tribe splits. Two-Spear leaves with his followers, and Skyfire becomes chief of the remaining tribe.

10,000 – 8,000 YEARS BEFORE

In a long diaspora, descendants of the High Ones wander the world. *Savah* and her family settle the Sun Village in the desert at Sorrow's End. Lord Voll and the Gliders move into Blue Mountain and shut themselves away from the world.

Guttlekraw becomes king of the trolls, who have fled to the cold north.

Ekuar and two rock-shaper companions discover the abandoned palace-ship of the High Ones but are enslaved by Guttlekraw. Glaciers force the trolls to move south, tunneling under the future Holt of the Wolfriders.

Greymung rebels against Guttlekraw. Guttlekraw and his cohorts return north, and the three rock-shaper elves escape in the melee. Greymung, now king of the forest trolls, sends a scout to search for the escaped trio.

Winnowill leaves Blue Mountain, finds the troll, seduces him and gives birth to *Two-Edge*. She later kills the troll.

TIMELINE

The ElfQuest saga spans thousands of years and to date has introduced readers to hundreds of characters. At the time of the stories in this volume, these are the major characters you will meet and get to know.

THE WOLFRIDERS

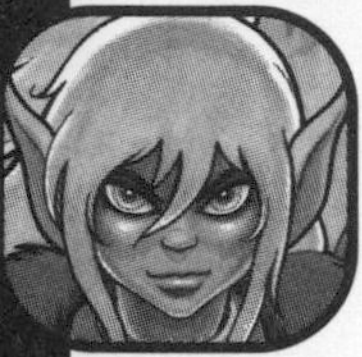

CUTTER

While his name denotes his skill with a sword, Cutter is not a cold and merciless death-dealer. Strong in his beliefs, he will nevertheless bend even the most fundamental of them if the well-being of his tribe is at stake. Skywise believes that what sets Cutter apart from all past Wolfrider chieftains is his imagination and ability to not only accept change, but take advantage of it.

SKYWISE

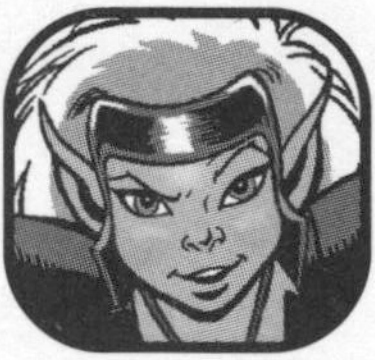

Orphaned at birth, Skywise is the resident stargazer of the Wolfriders, and only his interest in elf maidens rivals his passion for understanding the mysteries of the universe. Skywise is Cutter's counselor, confidant, and closest friend. While he is capable of deep seriousness, nothing can diminish Skywise's jovial and rakish manner.

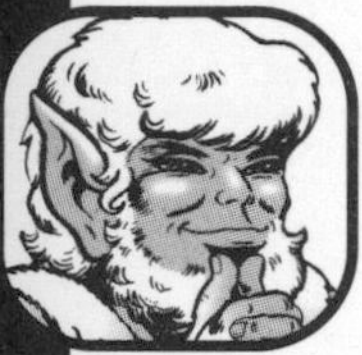

TREESTUMP

Seemingly gruff and no-nonsense, Treestump also has a vulnerable side, especially when it comes to protecting the well-being of his tribemates. More than a thousand years of living with "the Way" has given Treestump a wellspring of wisdom, allowing him to find calm even in the face of great danger. He is something of a father figure to the entire tribe.

STRONGBOW

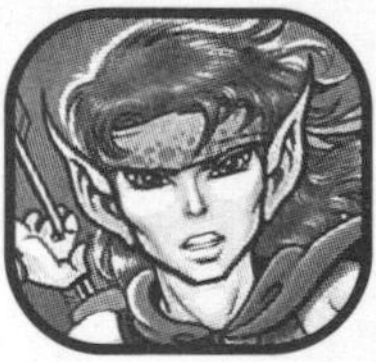

Strongbow is the reserved, silent master archer of the Wolfriders. Ever the devil's advocate, he is often proved right but finds no value in saying "I told you so." Strongbow is extremely serious, rarely smiles, and prefers sending to audible speech. He is completely devoted to his lifemate, Moonshade, and intensely proud of their son Dart.

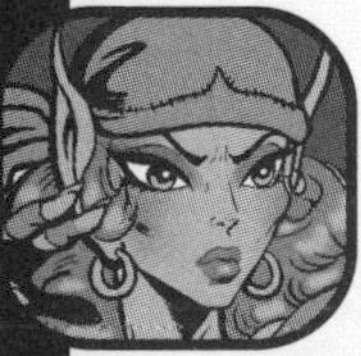

NIGHTFALL

Nightfall is the beautiful counterpoint to her lifemate, Redlance, and one of the most skilled hunters in the tribe. She is cool and calculated, neither vengeful nor violent unless absolutely necessary. The relationship between Nightfall and Redlance is very much one of yin and yang. Nightfall grew up with Cutter and is strongly loyal to the young chief.

REDLANCE

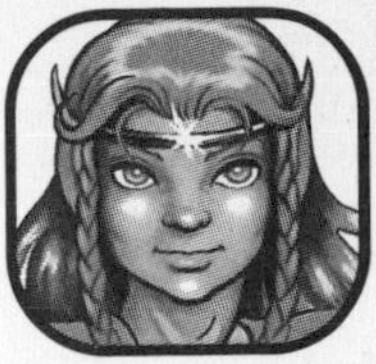

Redlance is the sweet-natured plantshaper of the Wolfriders. Indeed, he will only use his talents defensively to protect the tribe. Redlance is too much a pacifist at heart to do willful harm, and this gentleness makes him a natural to care for the cubs of the tribe. Redlance is a master of the soft counsel, gently prodding other, more headstrong elves in the right direction.

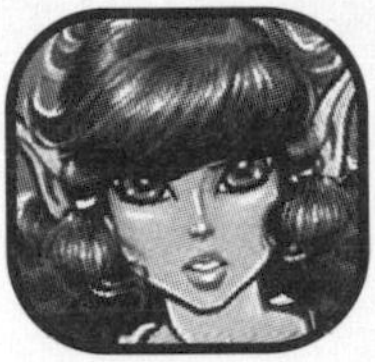

MOONSHADE

Moonshade is the Wolfriders' tanner. Though the process can be lengthy and tedious, she enjoys the quiet hours spent bringing the beauty out of a supple hide. Moonshade, like her lifemate Strongbow, is very much a traditionalist, strong-minded and with unshakable beliefs. Completely devoted to her mate, Moonshade will defend him even when she knows he's wrong.

SCOUTER

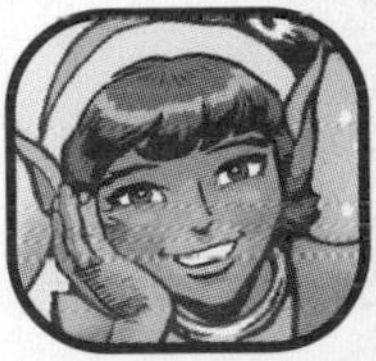

Scouter has the sharpest eyes of all the Wolfriders. He is steadfast, loyal, and often overprotective. He is also extremely intolerant of anyone, tribemates included, whom he perceives as putting his loved ones in jeopardy. Dewshine and Scouter have been lovemates for most of their lives, yet are not Recognized.

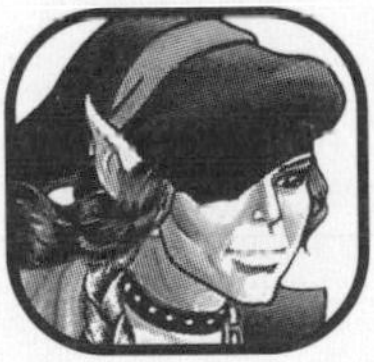

ONE-EYE

Woodhue gained his new sobriquet after his right eye was put out by humans. Needless to say, this seeded a lifelong hatred and distrust of the "five-fingers." Although he still considers Cutter a cub, One-Eye never questions Cutter's judgments; Cutter is chief and that is that. One-Eye is fierce in battle, especially when his cub, Scouter, or his lifemate, Clearbrook, is endangered.

PIKE

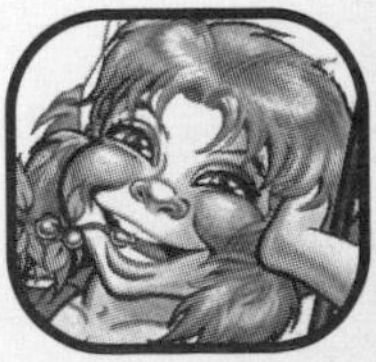

Pike is the Wolfriders' resident storyteller, taking his name from his preferred weapon. The most ordinary and happy-go-lucky of the Wolfriders, Pike has no grand ideals or desires for quests – he is a follower and rarely questions his chief's orders. Fully immersed in the "now of wolf thought" he clings through thick and thin to his two greatest loves: dreamberries and taking the easy path.

THE SUN FOLK

LEETAH

Her name means "healing light" and – as the Sun Folks' healer – she is the village's most precious resource. For over 600 years she has lived a sheltered life, surrounded by love and admiration, knowing little of the world beyond her desert oasis. Though delicate-seeming, beneath her beauty lies a wellspring of strength that has yet to be tested.

RAYEK

Vain and prideful, Rayek is chief hunter for the Sun Village and never tires of boasting of his superior skills. The same age as Leetah, he has spent nearly all those years as the healer's friend – always hoping that she will see him as more than simply that. He is a superb athlete, and skilled in both magic and weaponry.

SAVAH

By far the eldest elf known to either the Wolfriders or Sun Folk, Savah – the "Mother of Memory" for the village – is a child of the original High Ones who first came to the World of Two Moons. Infinitely wise and compassionate, she is the keeper of both history and ritual for the desert elves, yet all her years have not dimmed the twinkle of humor in her eyes.

THE TROLLS

The trolls are the descendants of the ape-like servants of the firstcomers, who, having rebelled at their slave-like status within the palace-ship, caused the cosmic disaster that left them all stranded in the primeval, prehistoric era of the World of Two Moons. Taking to caves and tunnels beneath the land, they adapted over time to grow more massive, uglier and much greedier.

PICKNOSE

His name was inspired by his most prominent facial feature, which resembles the curved business end of a pick. The success of Picknose's interactions with the Wolfriders has been mixed at best, for while he does possess a sort of honor, he is also an opportunist of the first water.

KING GREYMUNG

Compared to the rigors of life in the frozen north, Greymung and his forest trolls have it easy. While he may have shown some grit when he rebelled against Guttlekraw in the distant past, now Greymung has little to do but sit on his jewel-encrusted throne, mistrusting one and all in his underground kingdom.

TWO-EDGE

Two-Edge is the cunning half-troll, half-elf son of Winnowill and a troll named Smelt. An ingenious mastersmith and inventor, he is a teacher to the trolls. Like Timmorn, Two-Edge is unique on the World of Two Moons. Abused as a child by his mother, Two-Edge was devastated when she killed his father and now walks a fine line between cleverness and insanity.

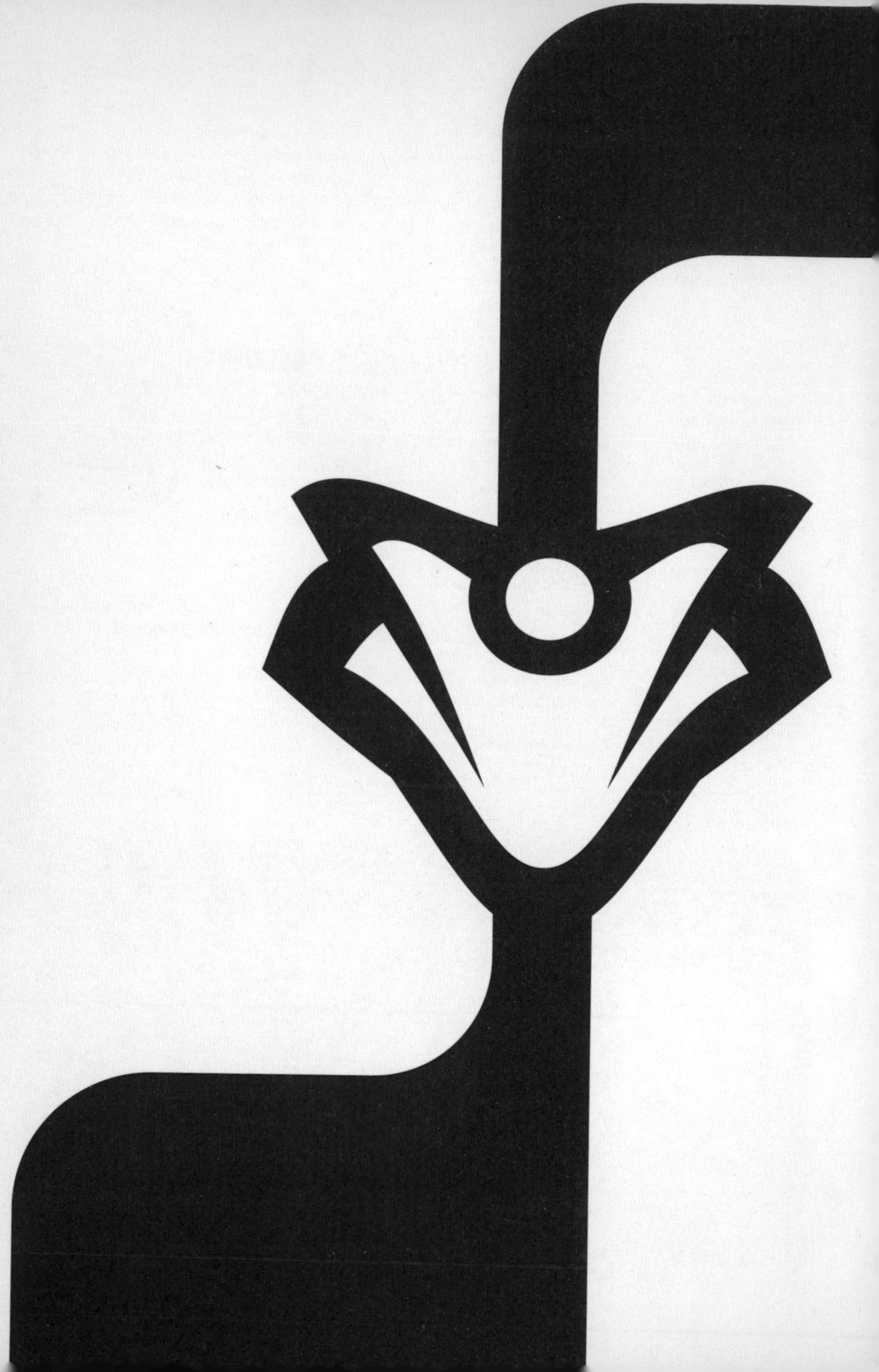

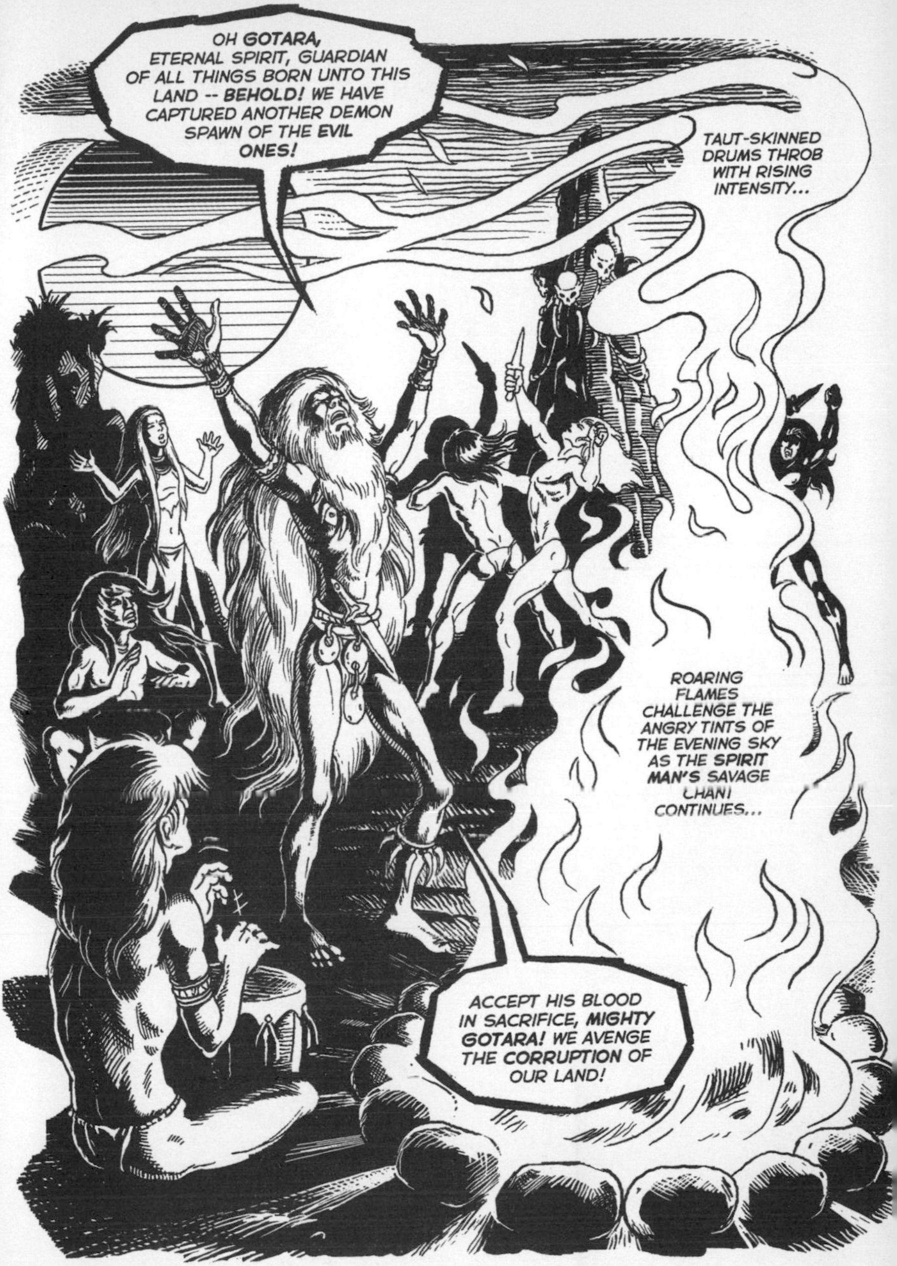
OH GOTARA, ETERNAL SPIRIT, GUARDIAN OF ALL THINGS BORN UNTO THIS LAND -- BEHOLD! WE HAVE CAPTURED ANOTHER DEMON SPAWN OF THE EVIL ONES!
TAUT-SKINNED DRUMS THROB WITH RISING INTENSITY...
ROARING FLAMES CHALLENGE THE ANGRY TINTS OF THE EVENING SKY AS THE SPIRIT MAN'S SAVAGE CHANI CONTINUES...
ACCEPT HIS BLOOD IN SACRIFICE, MIGHTY GOTARA! WE AVENGE THE CORRUPTION OF OUR LAND!

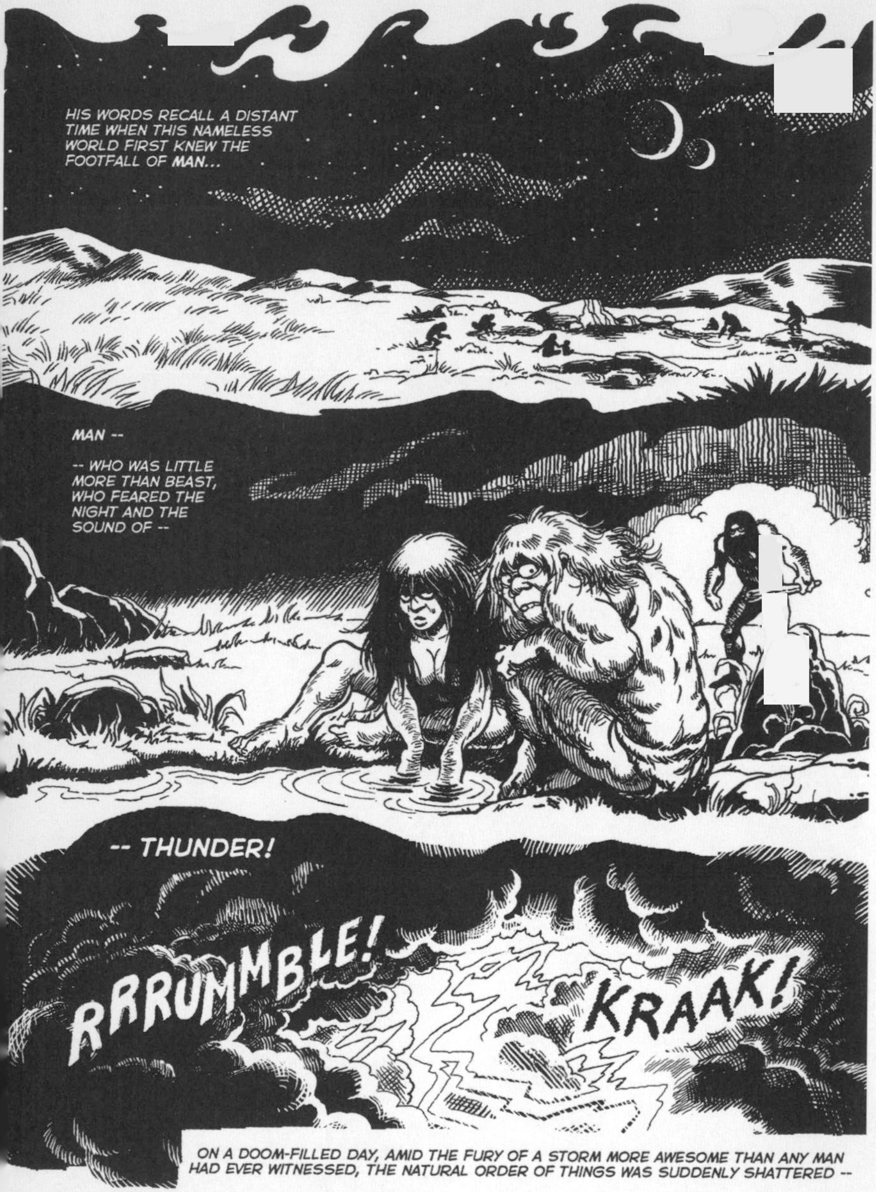
HIS WORDS RECALL A DISTANT TIME WHEN THIS NAMELESS WORLD FIRST KNEW THE FOOTFALL OF MAN...
MAN --
-- WHO WAS LITTLE MORE THAN BEAST, WHO FEARED THE NIGHT AND THE SOUND OF --
-- THUNDER!
RRRUMMBLE!
KRAAK!
ON A DOOM-FILLED DAY, AMID THE FURY OF A STORM MORE AWESOME THAN ANY MAN HAD EVER WITNESSED, THE NATURAL ORDER OF THINGS WAS SUDDENLY SHATTERED --

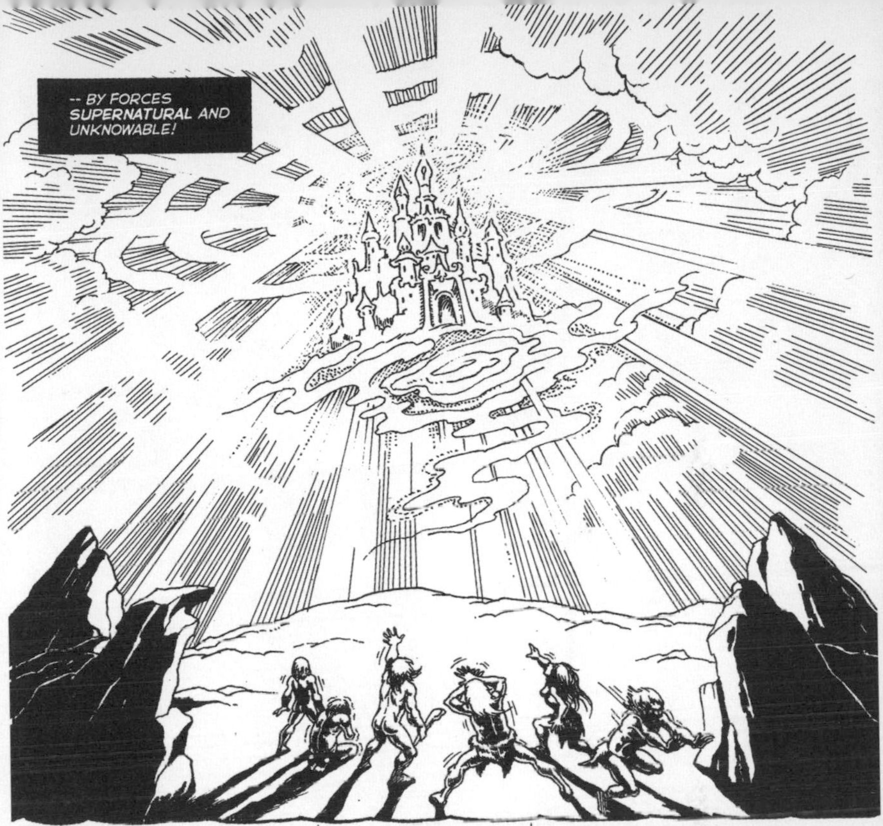
-- BY FORCES SUPERNATURAL AND UNKNOWABLE!

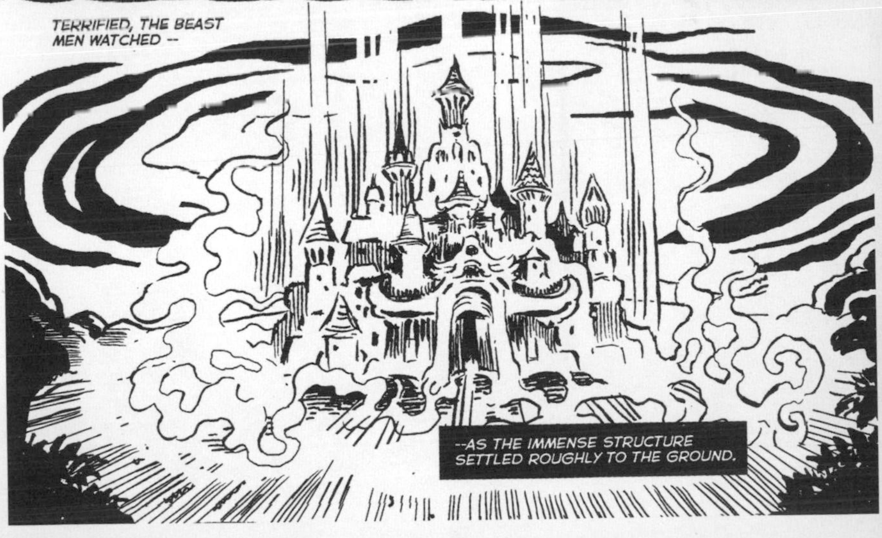
TERRIFIED, THE BEAST MEN WATCHED --
--AS THE IMMENSE STRUCTURE SETTLED ROUGHLY TO THE GROUND.

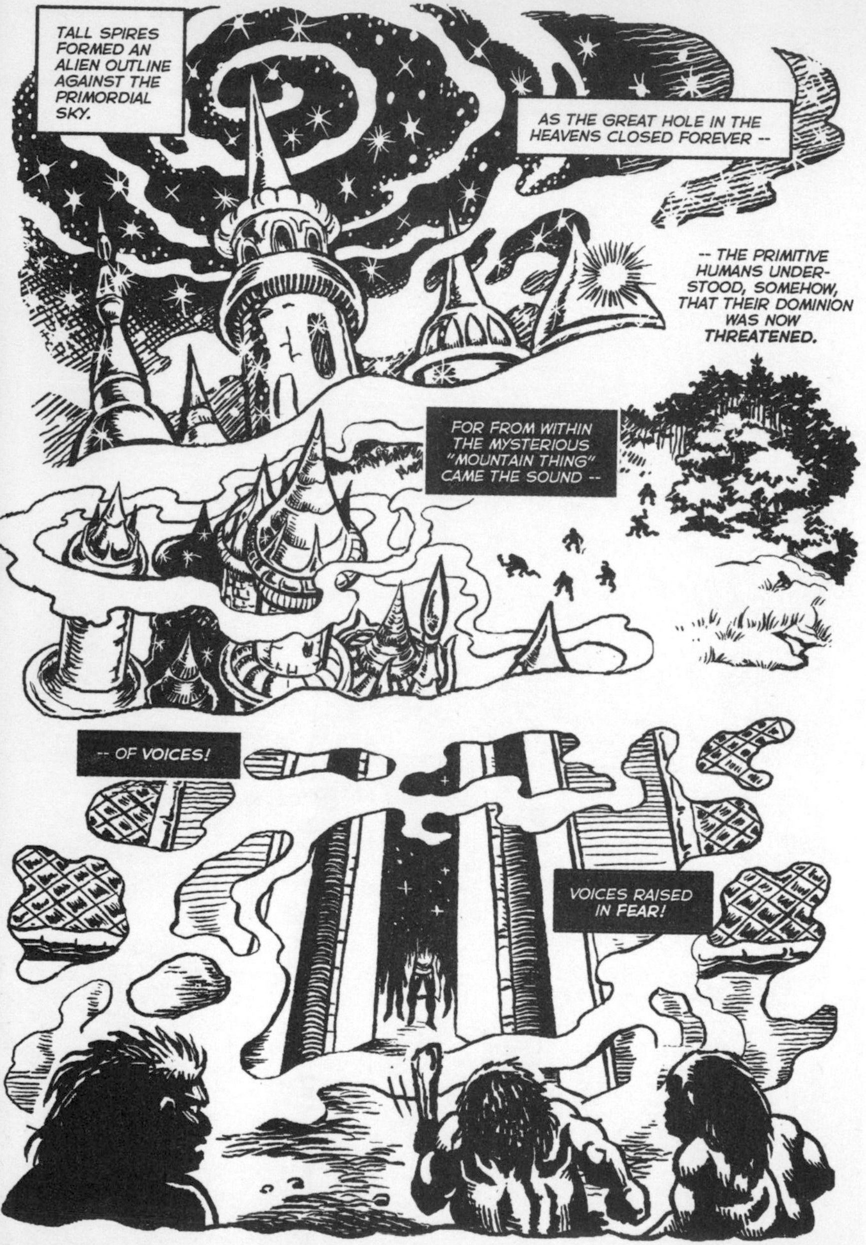
TALL SPIRES FORMED AN ALIEN OUTLINE AGAINST THE PRIMORDIAL SKY.
AS THE GREAT HOLE IN THE HEAVENS CLOSED FOREVER --
-- THE PRIMITIVE HUMANS UNDERSTOOD, SOMEHOW, THAT THEIR DOMINION WAS NOW THREATENED.
FOR FROM WITHIN THE MYSTERIOUS "MOUNTAIN THING" CAME THE SOUND --
-- OF VOICES!
VOICES RAISED IN FEAR!

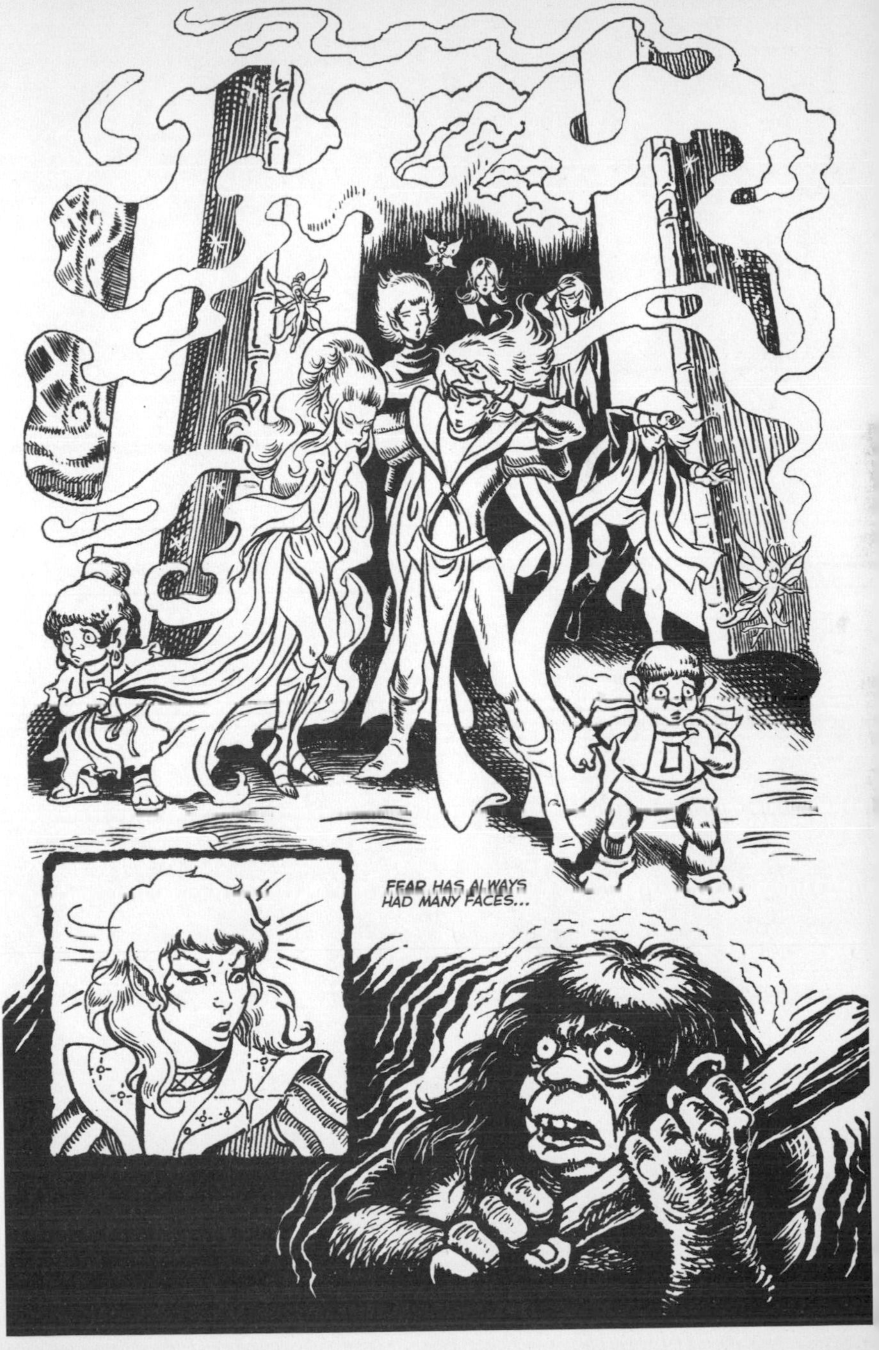
FEAR HAS ALWAYS
HAD MANY FACES...

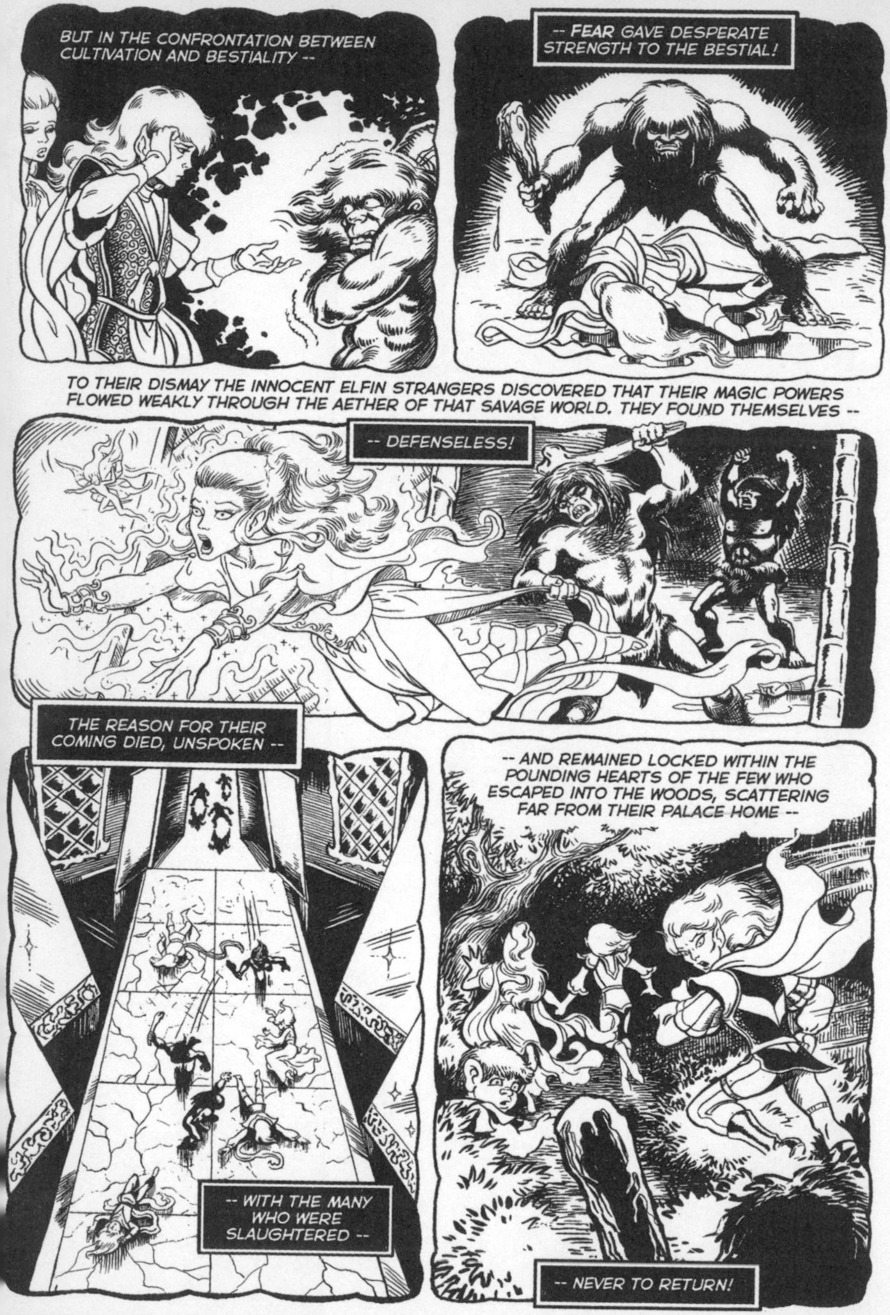

BUT IN THE CONFRONTATION BETWEEN CULTIVATION AND BESTIALITY --
-- FEAR GAVE DESPERATE STRENGTH TO THE BESTIAL!
TO THEIR DISMAY THE INNOCENT ELFIN STRANGERS DISCOVERED THAT THEIR MAGIC POWERS FLOWED WEAKLY THROUGH THE AETHER OF THAT SAVAGE WORLD. THEY FOUND THEMSELVES --
-- DEFENSELESS!
THE REASON FOR THEIR COMING DIED, UNSPOKEN --
-- WITH THE MANY WHO WERE SLAUGHTERED --
-- AND REMAINED LOCKED WITHIN THE POUNDING HEARTS OF THE FEW WHO ESCAPED INTO THE WOODS, SCATTERING FAR FROM THEIR PALACE HOME --
-- NEVER TO RETURN!

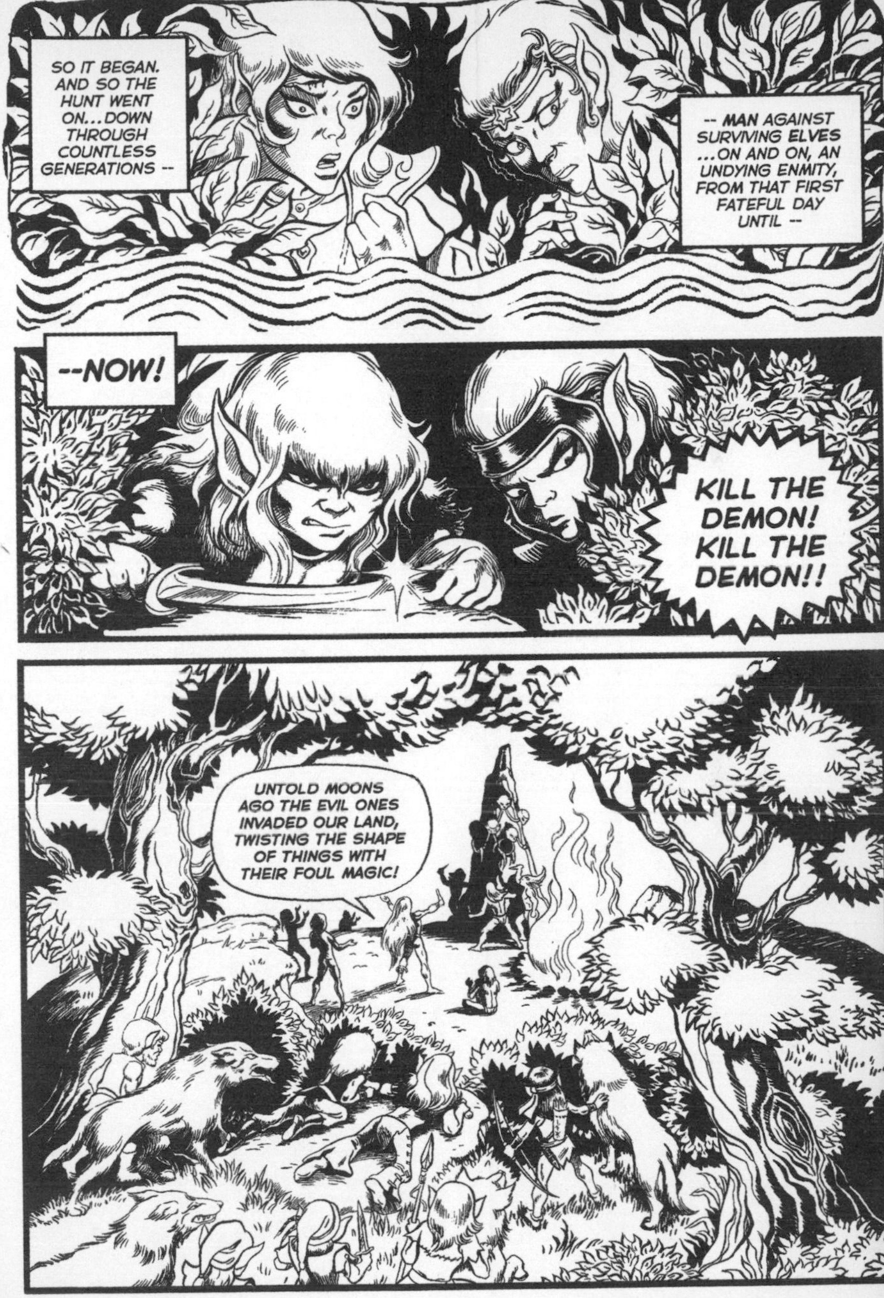
SO IT BEGAN. AND SO THE HUNT WENT ON...DOWN THROUGH COUNTLESS GENERATIONS --
-- MAN AGAINST SURVIVING ELVES ...ON AND ON, AN UNDYING ENMITY, FROM THAT FIRST FATEFUL DAY UNTIL --
--NOW!
KILL THE DEMON! KILL THE DEMON!!
UNTOLD MOONS AGO THE EVIL ONES INVADED OUR LAND, TWISTING THE SHAPE OF THINGS WITH THEIR FOUL MAGIC!

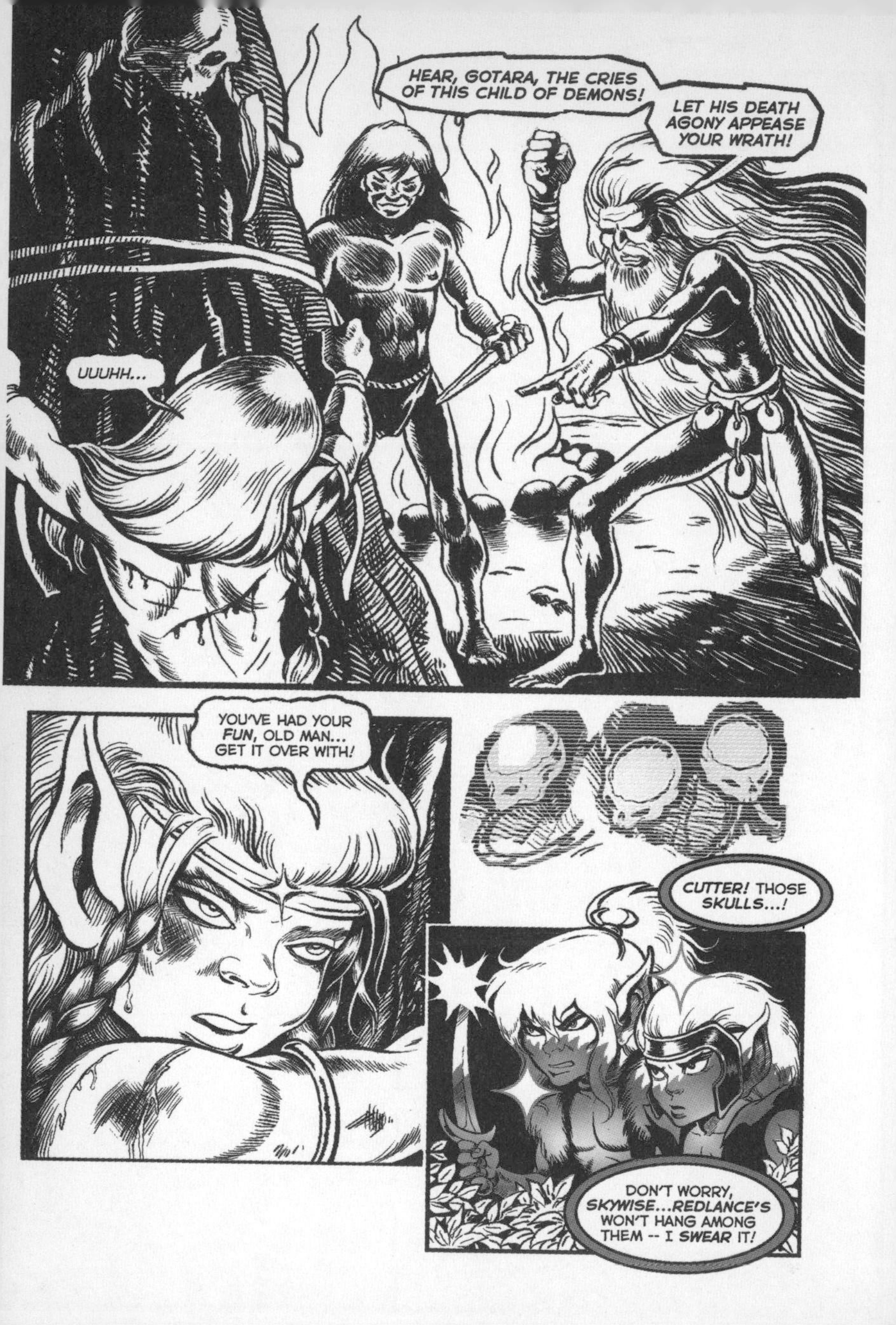
HEAR, GOTARA, THE CRIES OF THIS CHILD OF DEMONS!
LET HIS DEATH AGONY APPEASE YOUR WRATH!
UUUHH...
YOU'VE HAD YOUR FUN, OLD MAN... GET IT OVER WITH!
CUTTER! THOSE SKULLS...!
DON'T WORRY, SKYWISE...REDLANCE'S WON'T HANG AMONG THEM -- I SWEAR IT!

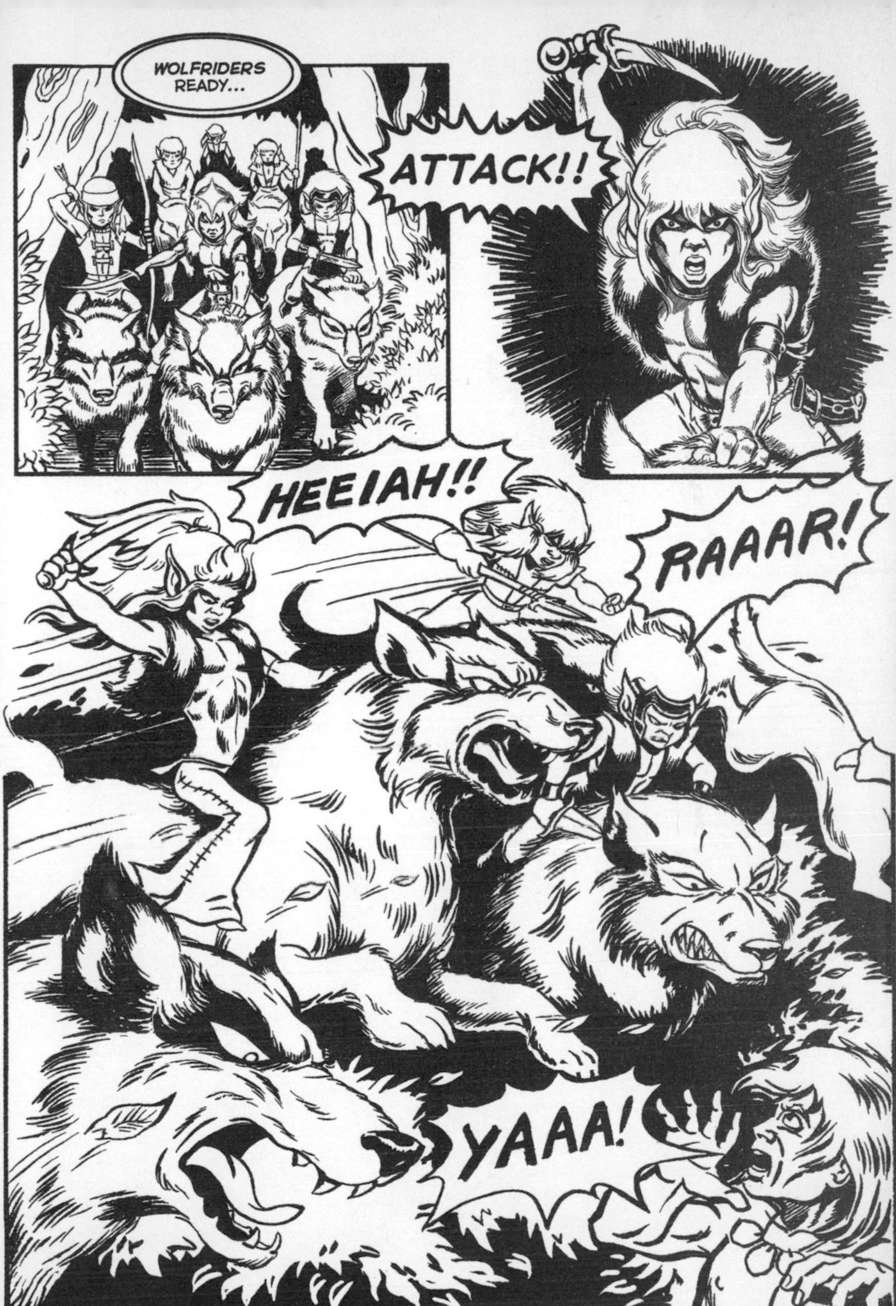
WOLFRIDERS READY...
ATTACK!!
HEEIAH!!
RAAAR!
YAAA!

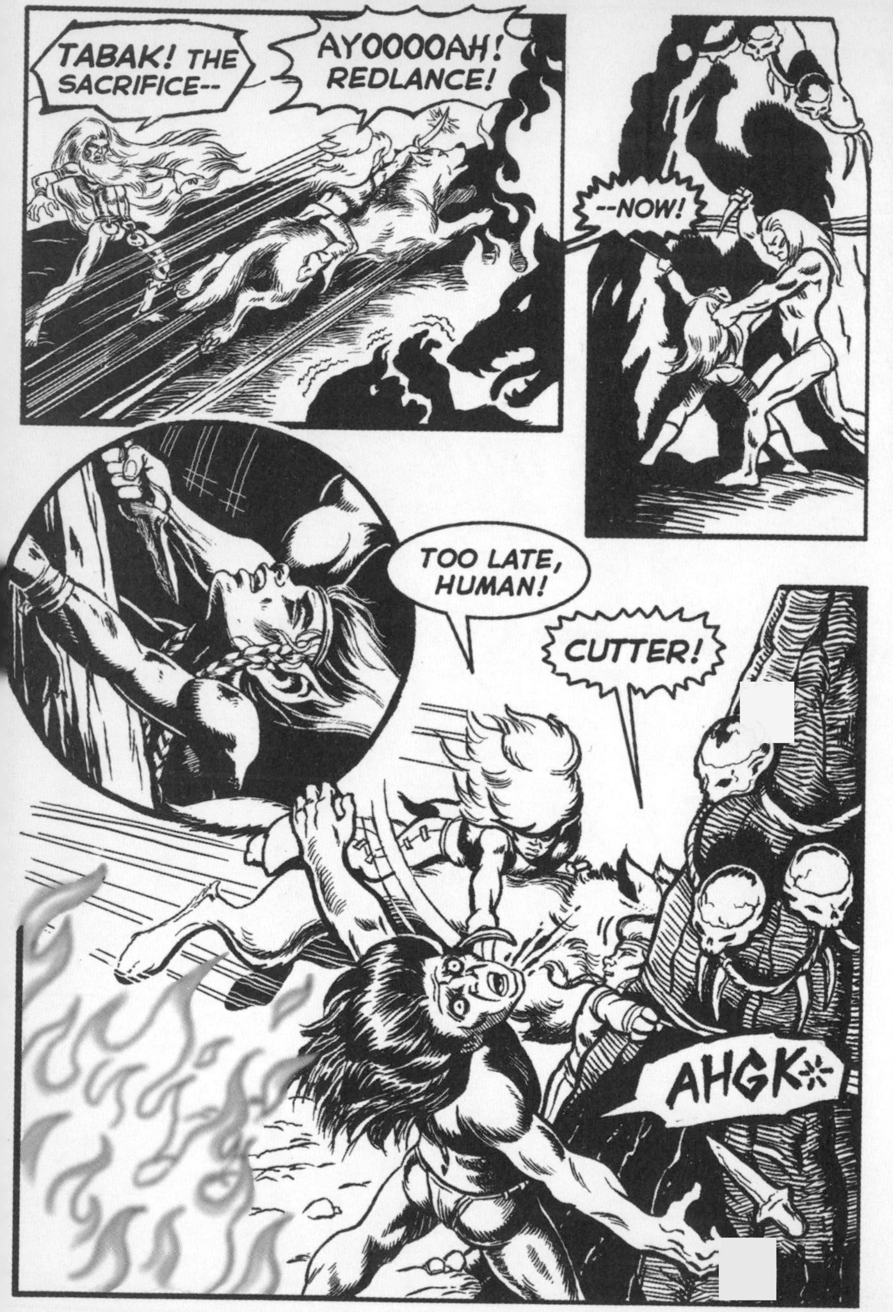
TABAK! THE SACRIFICE--
AYOOOOAH! REDLANCE!
--NOW!
TOO LATE, HUMAN!
CUTTER!
AHGK

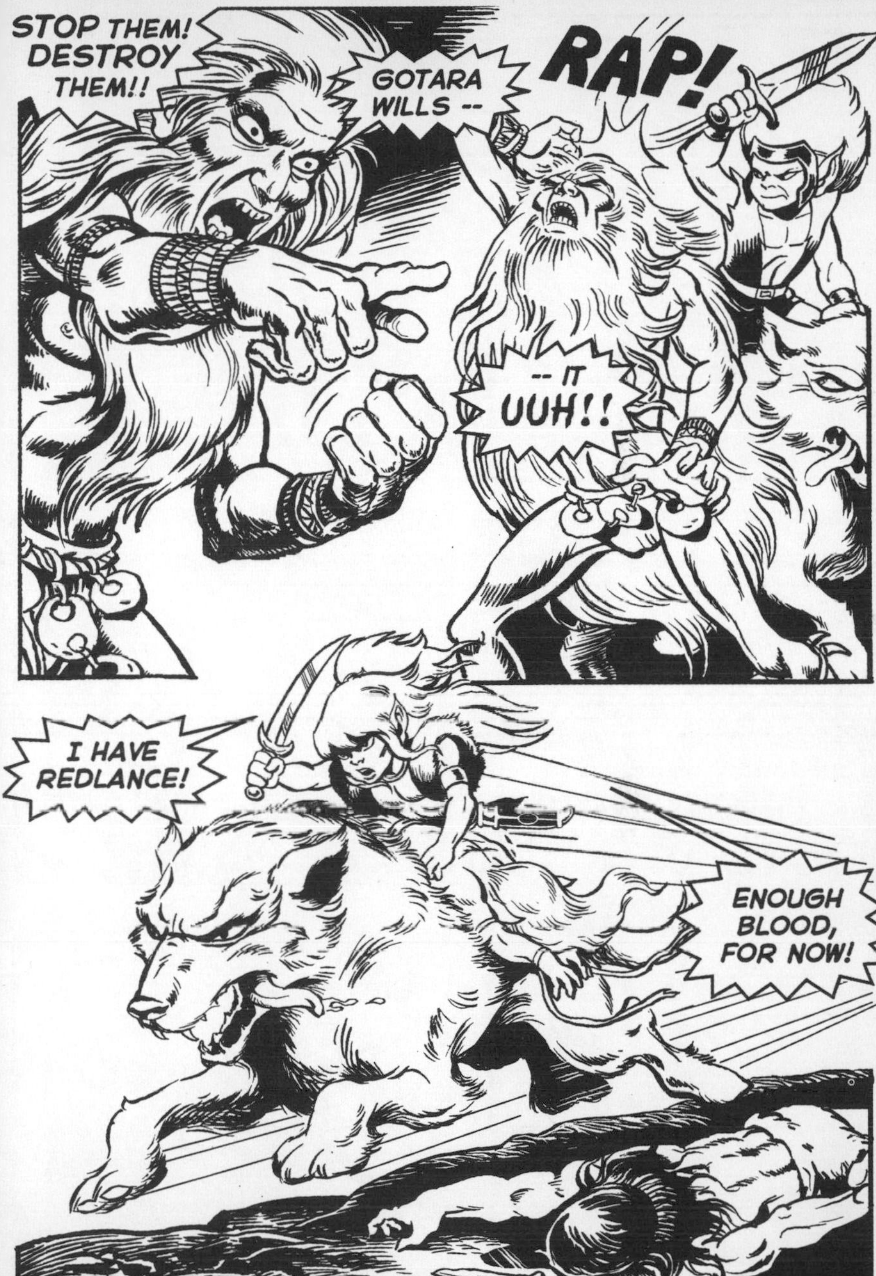
STOP THEM! DESTROY THEM!!
GOTARA WILLS --
RAP!
-- IT UUH!!
I HAVE REDLANCE!
ENOUGH BLOOD, FOR NOW!

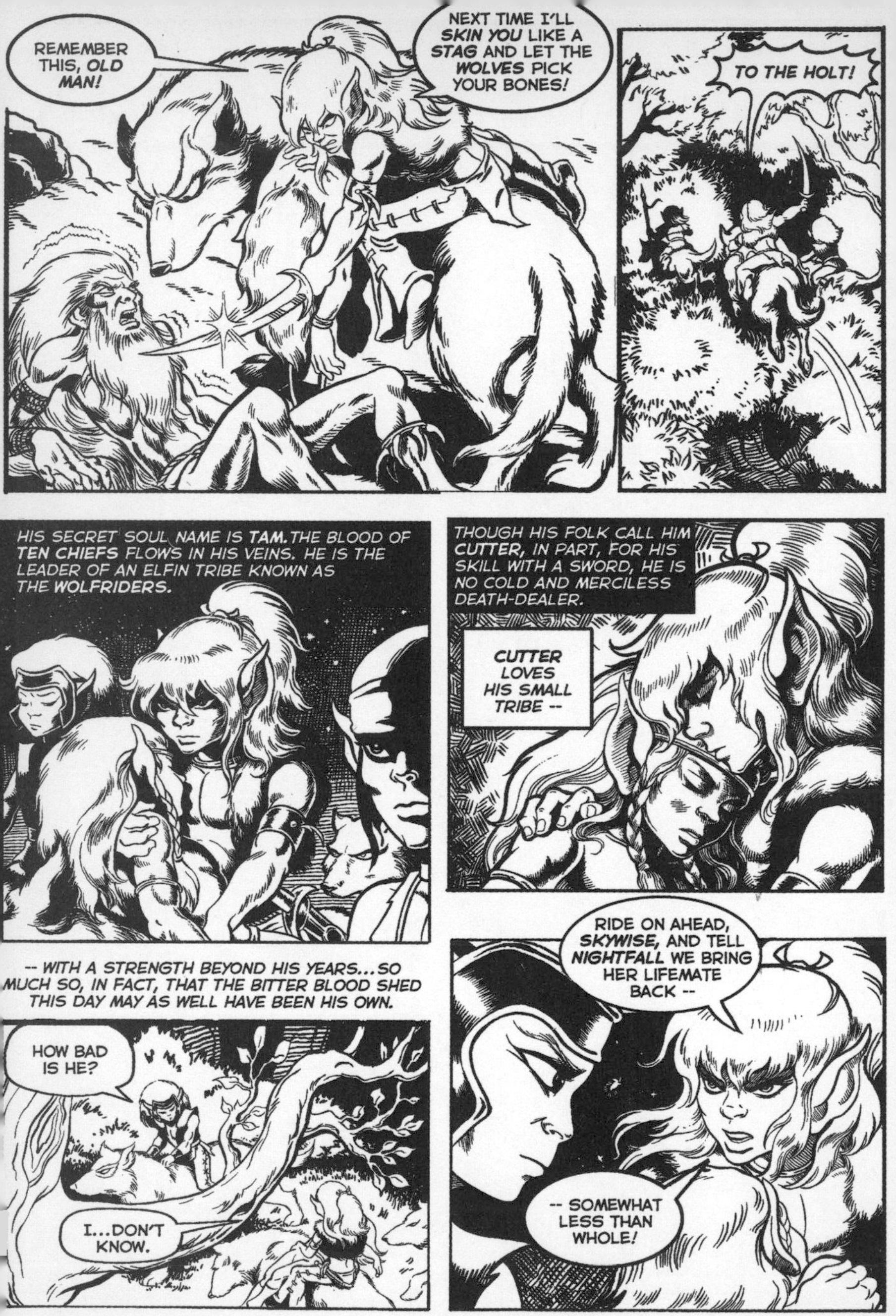
REMEMBER THIS, OLD MAN!
NEXT TIME I'LL SKIN YOU LIKE A STAG AND LET THE WOLVES PICK YOUR BONES!
TO THE HOLT!
HIS SECRET SOUL NAME IS TAM. THE BLOOD OF TEN CHIEFS FLOWS IN HIS VEINS. HE IS THE LEADER OF AN ELFIN TRIBE KNOWN AS THE WOLFRIDERS.
THOUGH HIS FOLK CALL HIM CUTTER, IN PART, FOR HIS SKILL WITH A SWORD, HE IS NO COLD AND MERCILESS DEATH-DEALER.
CUTTER LOVES HIS SMALL TRIBE --
-- WITH A STRENGTH BEYOND HIS YEARS... SO MUCH SO, IN FACT, THAT THE BITTER BLOOD SHED THIS DAY MAY AS WELL HAVE BEEN HIS OWN.
HOW BAD IS HE?
I...DON'T KNOW.
RIDE ON AHEAD, SKYWISE, AND TELL NIGHTFALL WE BRING HER LIFEMATE BACK --
-- SOMEWHAT LESS THAN WHOLE!

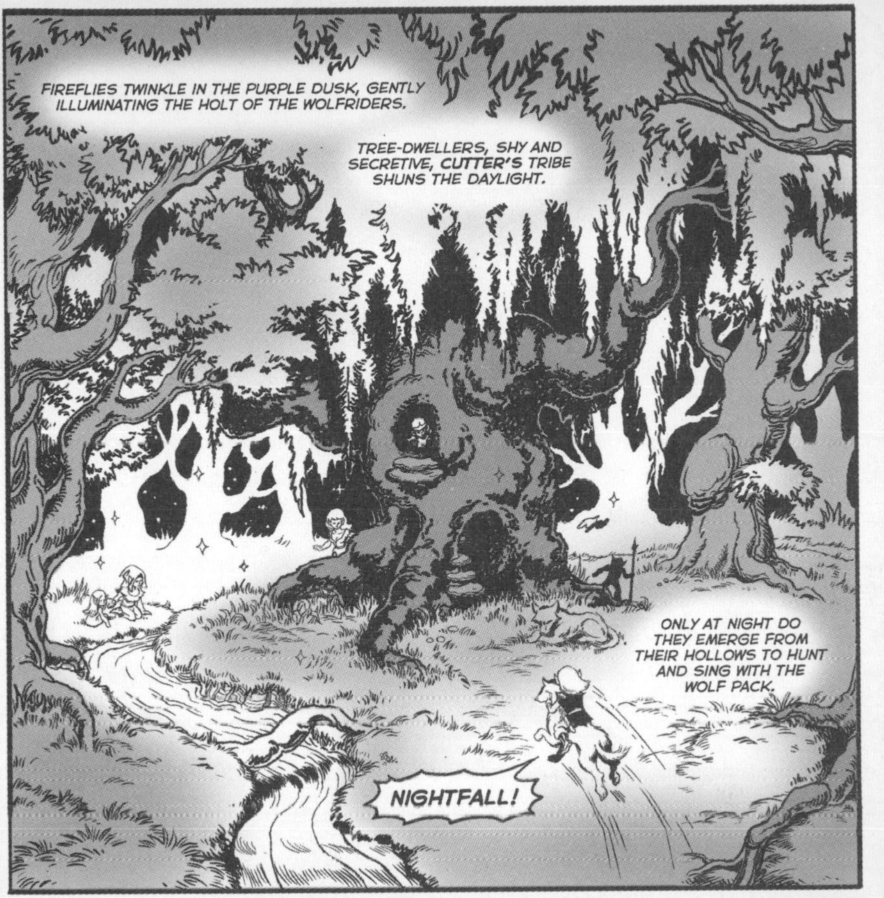
FIREFLIES TWINKLE IN THE PURPLE DUSK, GENTLY ILLUMINATING THE HOLT OF THE WOLFRIDERS.
TREE-DWELLERS, SHY AND SECRETIVE, CUTTER'S TRIBE SHUNS THE DAYLIGHT.
ONLY AT NIGHT DO THEY EMERGE FROM THEIR HOLLOWS TO HUNT AND SING WITH THE WOLF PACK.
NIGHTFALL!

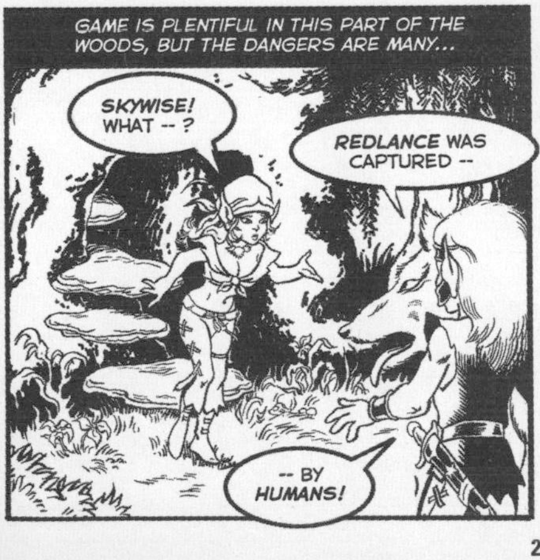
GAME IS PLENTIFUL IN THIS PART OF THE WOODS, BUT THE DANGERS ARE MANY...
SKYWISE! WHAT -- ?
REDLANCE WAS CAPTURED --
-- BY HUMANS!

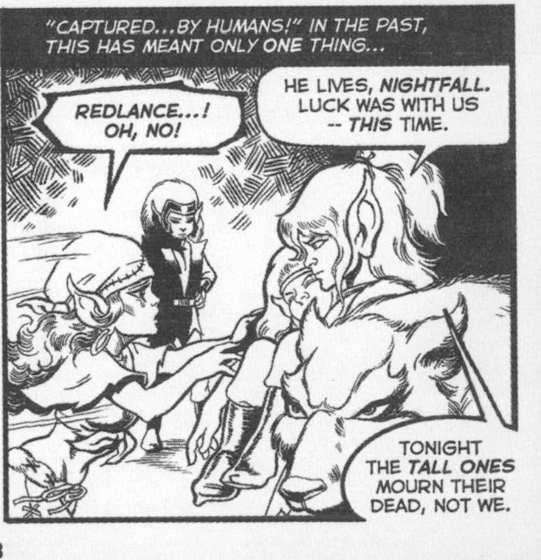
"CAPTURED...BY HUMANS!" IN THE PAST, THIS HAS MEANT ONLY ONE THING...
REDLANCE...! OH, NO!
HE LIVES, NIGHTFALL. LUCK WAS WITH US -- THIS TIME.
TONIGHT THE TALL ONES MOURN THEIR DEAD, NOT WE.

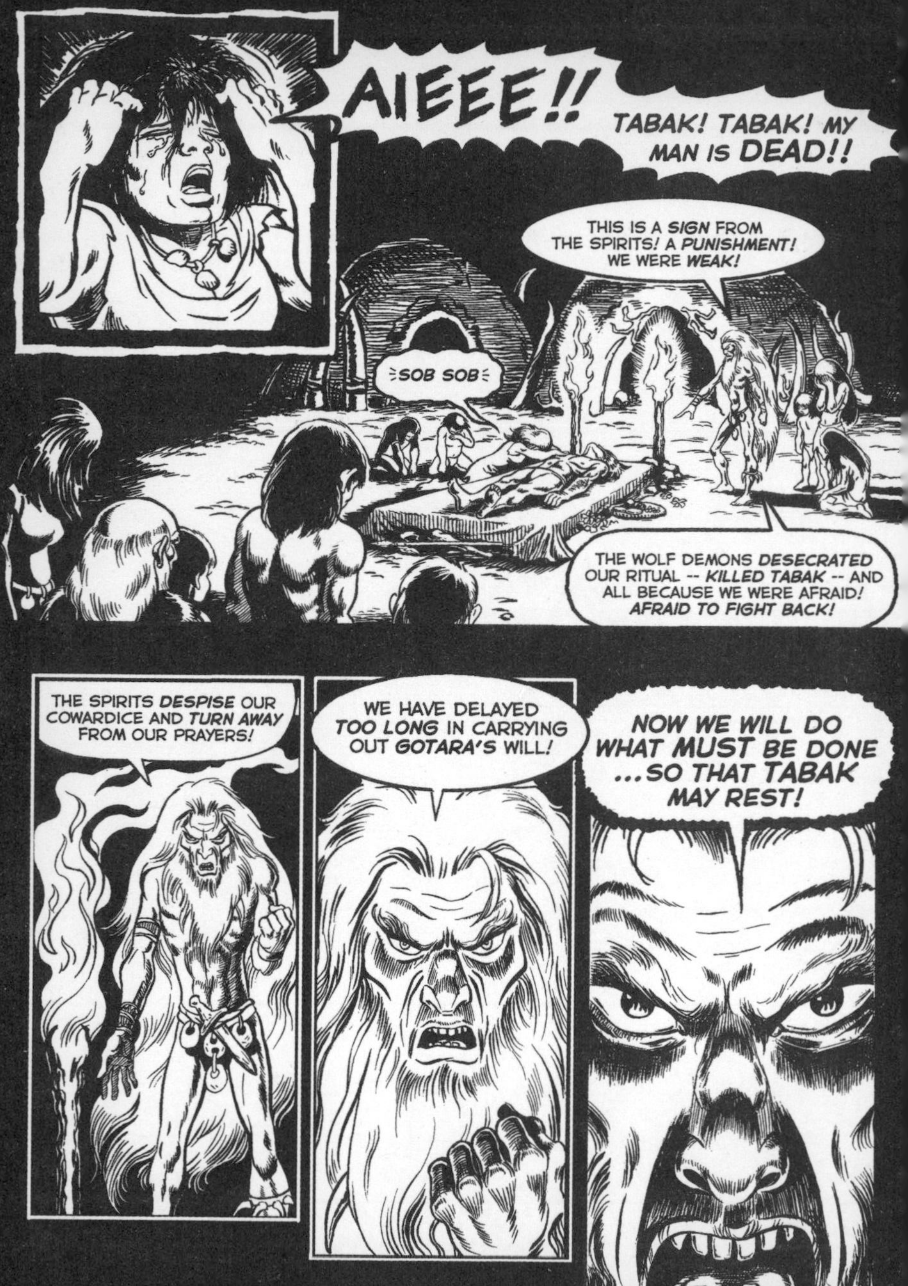
AIEEE!!
TABAK! TABAK! MY MAN IS DEAD!!
THIS IS A SIGN FROM THE SPIRITS! A PUNISHMENT! WE WERE WEAK!
SOB SOB
THE WOLF DEMONS DESECRATED OUR RITUAL -- KILLED TABAK -- AND ALL BECAUSE WE WERE AFRAID! AFRAID TO FIGHT BACK!
THE SPIRITS DESPISE OUR COWARDICE AND TURN AWAY FROM OUR PRAYERS!
WE HAVE DELAYED TOO LONG IN CARRYING OUT GOTARA'S WILL!
NOW WE WILL DO WHAT MUST BE DONE ...SO THAT TABAK MAY REST!

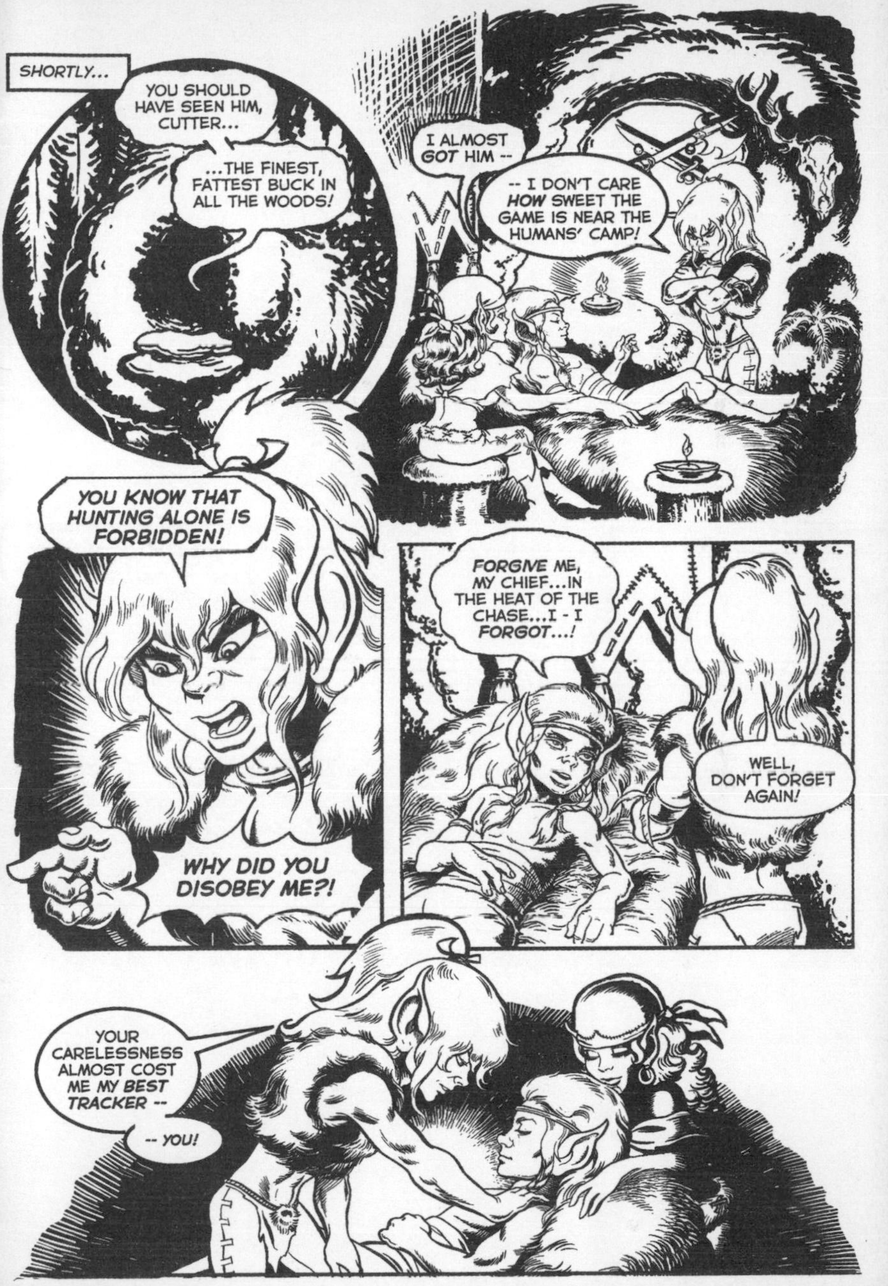
SHORTLY...
YOU SHOULD HAVE SEEN HIM, CUTTER...
...THE FINEST, FATTEST BUCK IN ALL THE WOODS!
I ALMOST GOT HIM --
-- I DON'T CARE HOW SWEET THE GAME IS NEAR THE HUMANS' CAMP!
YOU KNOW THAT HUNTING ALONE IS FORBIDDEN!
WHY DID YOU DISOBEY ME?!
FORGIVE ME, MY CHIEF...IN THE HEAT OF THE CHASE...I - I FORGOT...!
WELL, DON'T FORGET AGAIN!
YOUR CARELESSNESS ALMOST COST ME MY BEST TRACKER --
-- YOU!

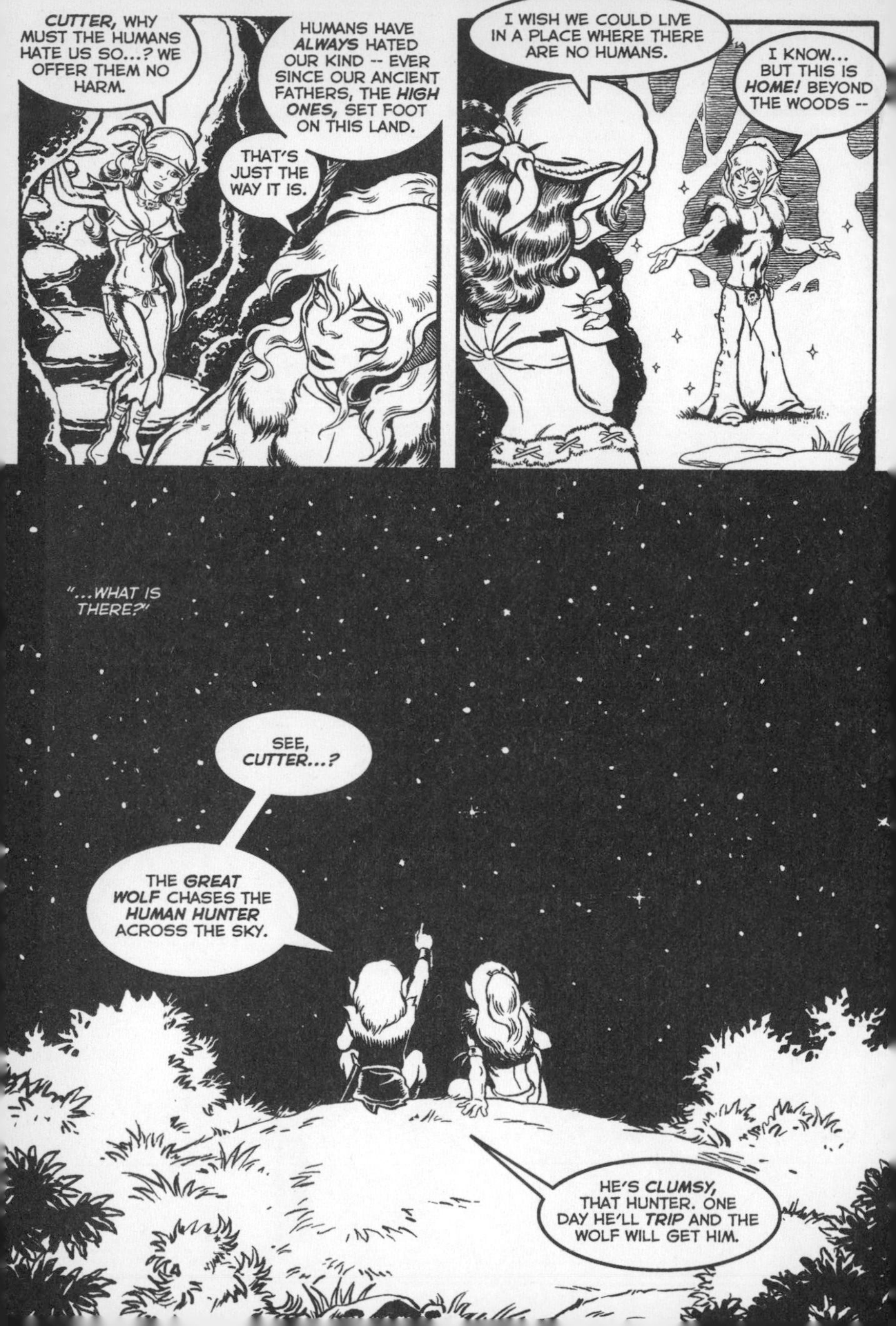

CUTTER, WHY MUST THE HUMANS HATE US SO...? WE OFFER THEM NO HARM.
HUMANS HAVE ALWAYS HATED OUR KIND -- EVER SINCE OUR ANCIENT FATHERS, THE HIGH ONES, SET FOOT ON THIS LAND.
THAT'S JUST THE WAY IT IS.
I WISH WE COULD LIVE IN A PLACE WHERE THERE ARE NO HUMANS.
I KNOW... BUT THIS IS HOME! BEYOND THE WOODS --
"...WHAT IS THERE?"
SEE, CUTTER...?
THE GREAT WOLF CHASES THE HUMAN HUNTER ACROSS THE SKY.
HE'S CLUMSY, THAT HUNTER. ONE DAY HE'LL TRIP AND THE WOLF WILL GET HIM.

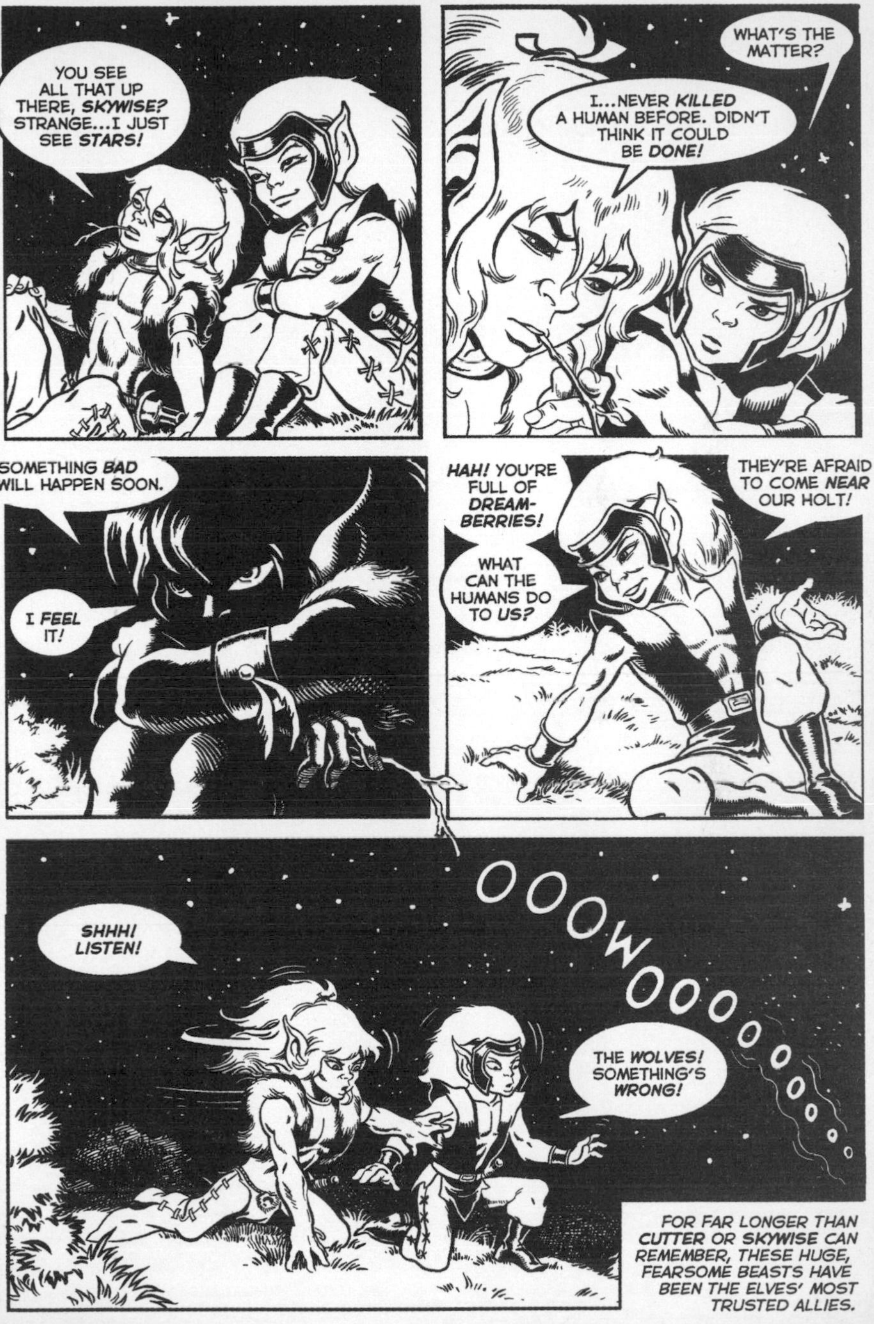

YOU SEE ALL THAT UP THERE, SKYWISE? STRANGE...I JUST SEE STARS!
WHAT'S THE MATTER?
I...NEVER KILLED A HUMAN BEFORE. DIDN'T THINK IT COULD BE DONE!
SOMETHING BAD WILL HAPPEN SOON.
I FEEL IT!
HAH! YOU'RE FULL OF DREAM-BERRIES!
WHAT CAN THE HUMANS DO TO US?
THEY'RE AFRAID TO COME NEAR OUR HOLT!
SHHH! LISTEN!
OOOWOOOOOOOOOOOO
THE WOLVES! SOMETHING'S WRONG!
FOR FAR LONGER THAN CUTTER OR SKYWISE CAN REMEMBER, THESE HUGE, FEARSOME BEASTS HAVE BEEN THE ELVES' MOST TRUSTED ALLIES.

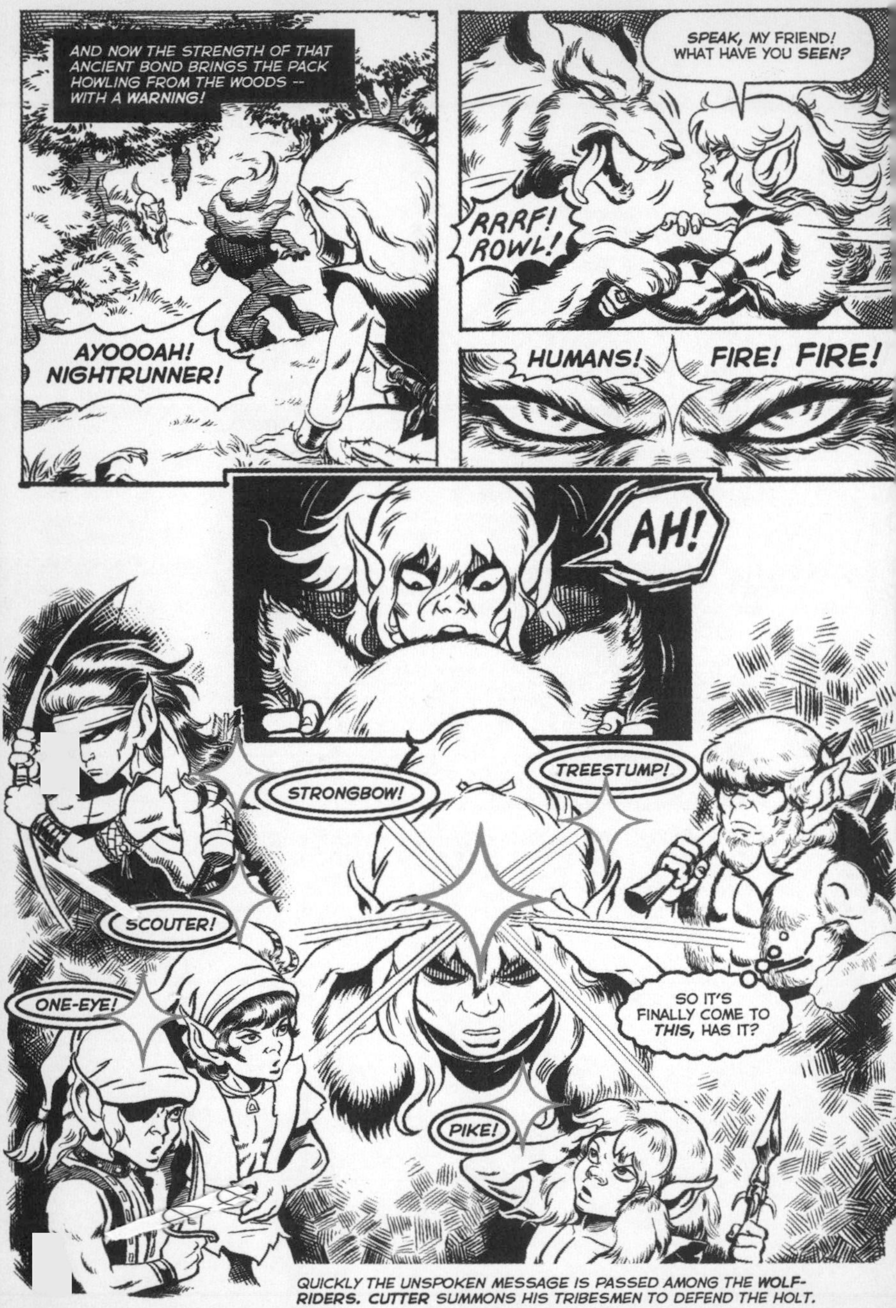
AND NOW THE STRENGTH OF THAT ANCIENT BOND BRINGS THE PACK HOWLING FROM THE WOODS -- WITH A WARNING!
AYOOOAH! NIGHTRUNNER!
SPEAK, MY FRIEND! WHAT HAVE YOU SEEN?
RRRF! ROWL!
HUMANS!
FIRE! FIRE!
AH!
STRONGBOW!
TREESTUMP!
SCOUTER!
ONE-EYE!
SO IT'S FINALLY COME TO THIS, HAS IT?
PIKE!
QUICKLY THE UNSPOKEN MESSAGE IS PASSED AMONG THE WOLF-RIDERS. CUTTER SUMMONS HIS TRIBESMEN TO DEFEND THE HOLT.

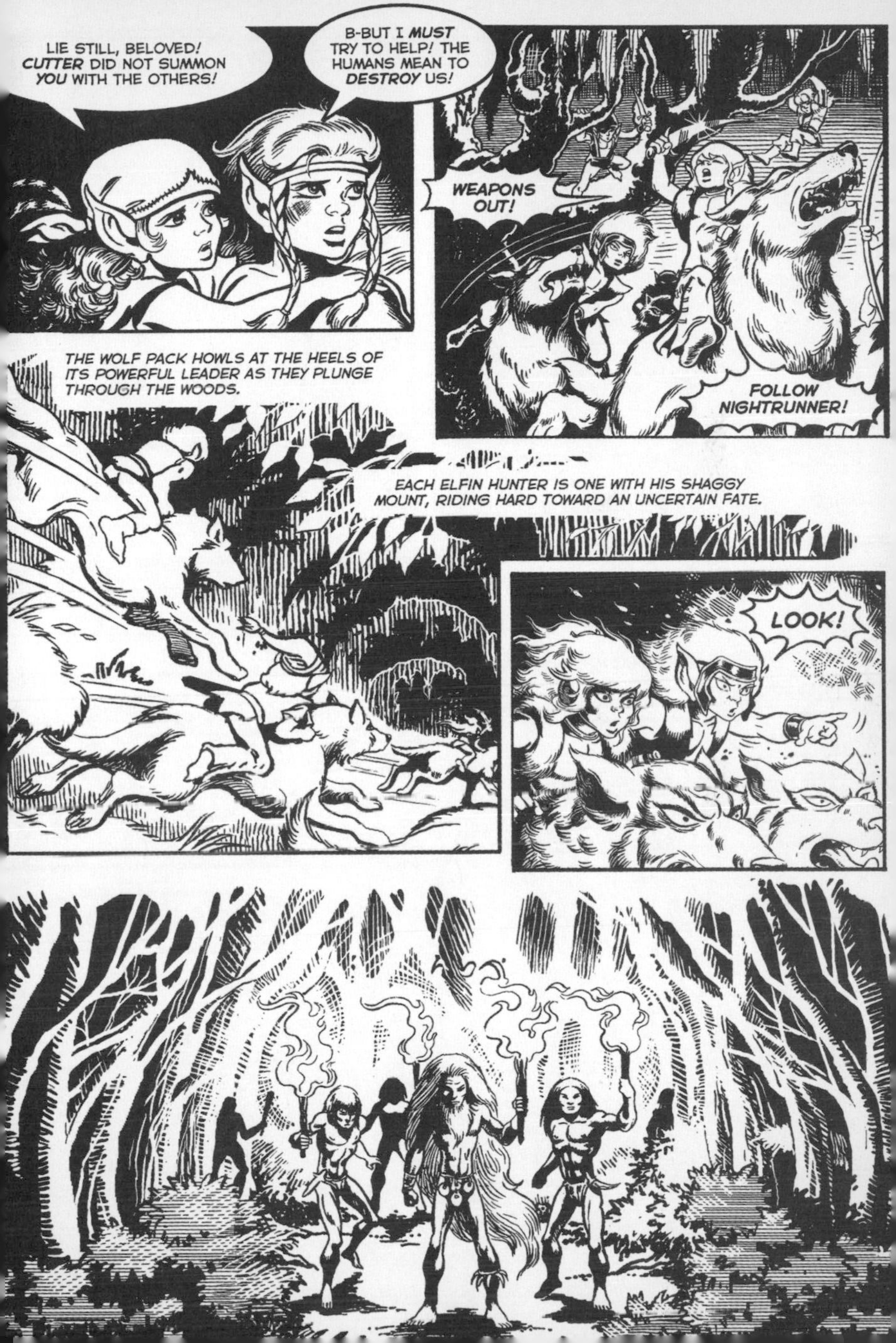
LIE STILL, BELOVED! CUTTER DID NOT SUMMON YOU WITH THE OTHERS!
B-BUT I MUST TRY TO HELP! THE HUMANS MEAN TO DESTROY US!
WEAPONS OUT!
FOLLOW NIGHTRUNNER!
THE WOLF PACK HOWLS AT THE HEELS OF ITS POWERFUL LEADER AS THEY PLUNGE THROUGH THE WOODS.
EACH ELFIN HUNTER IS ONE WITH HIS SHAGGY MOUNT, RIDING HARD TOWARD AN UNCERTAIN FATE.
LOOK!

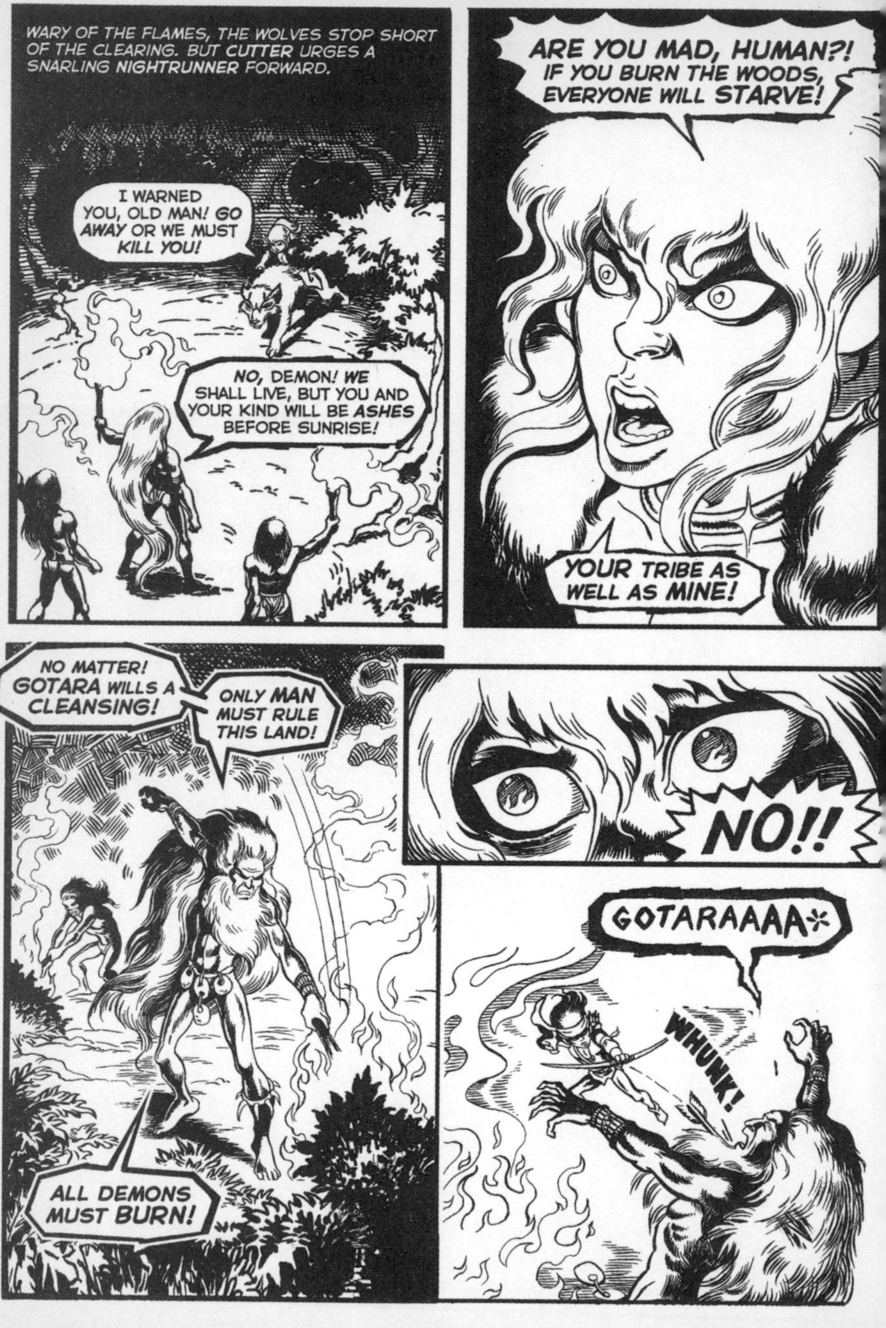
WARY OF THE FLAMES, THE WOLVES STOP SHORT OF THE CLEARING. BUT CUTTER URGES A SNARLING NIGHTRUNNER FORWARD.
I WARNED YOU, OLD MAN! GO AWAY OR WE MUST KILL YOU!
NO, DEMON! WE SHALL LIVE, BUT YOU AND YOUR KIND WILL BE ASHES BEFORE SUNRISE!
ARE YOU MAD, HUMAN?! IF YOU BURN THE WOODS, EVERYONE WILL STARVE!
YOUR TRIBE AS WELL AS MINE!
NO MATTER! GOTARA WILLS A CLEANSING!
ONLY MAN MUST RULE THIS LAND!
ALL DEMONS MUST BURN!
NO!!
GOTARAAAA*
WHUNK!

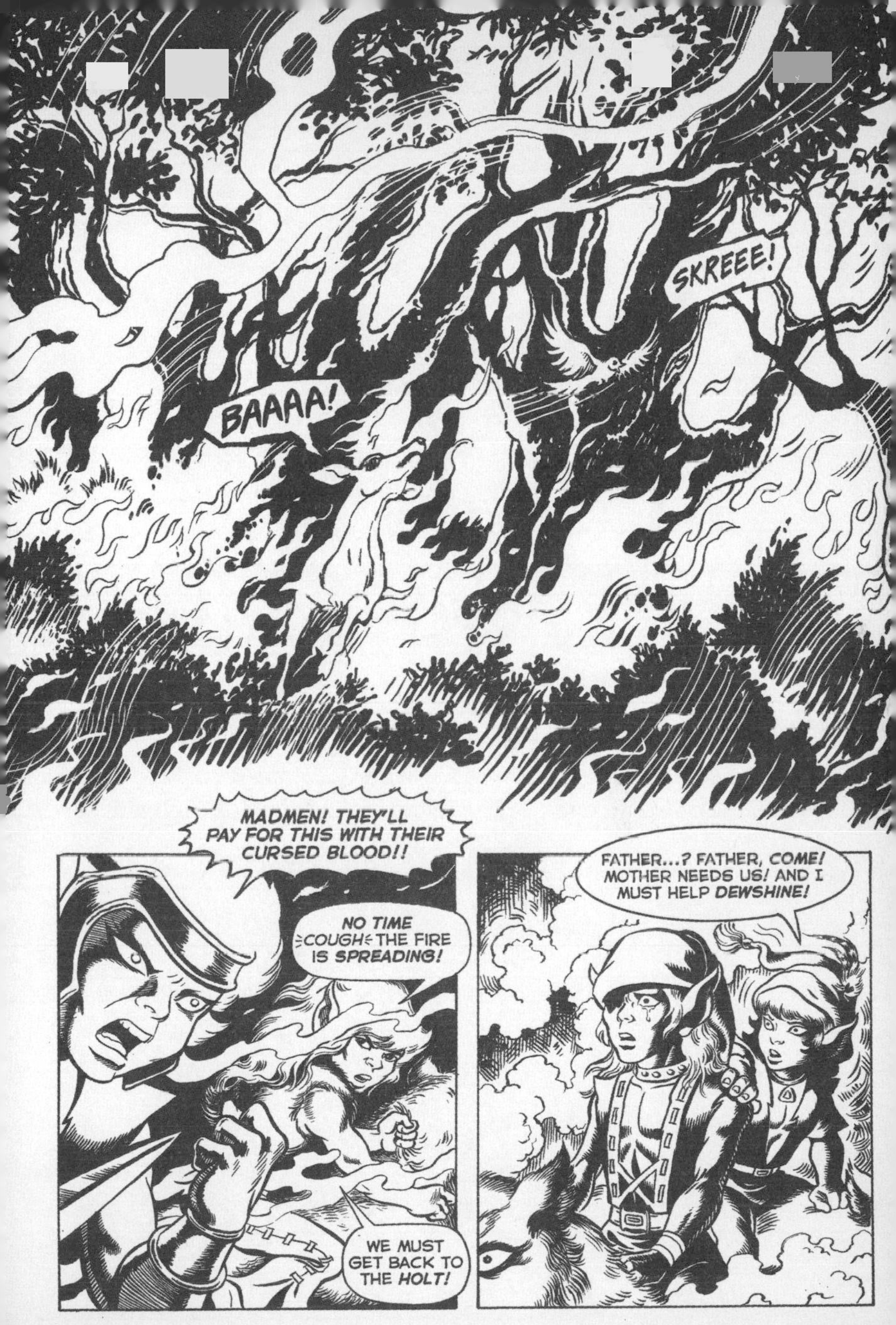
BAAAA!
SKREEE!
MADMEN! THEY'LL PAY FOR THIS WITH THEIR CURSED BLOOD!!
NO TIME =COUGH= THE FIRE IS SPREADING!
WE MUST GET BACK TO THE HOLT!
FATHER...? FATHER, COME! MOTHER NEEDS US! AND I MUST HELP DEWSHINE!

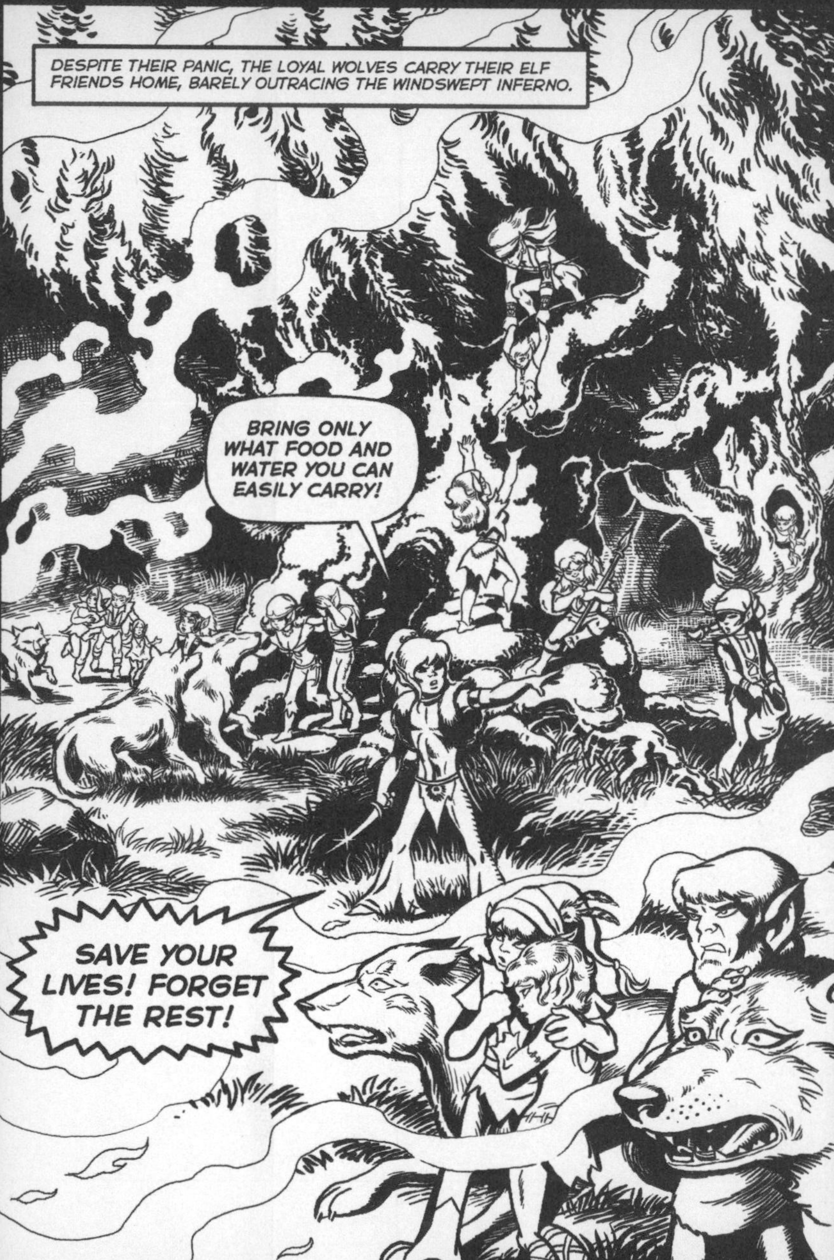
DESPITE THEIR PANIC, THE LOYAL WOLVES CARRY THEIR ELF FRIENDS HOME, BARELY OUTRACING THE WINDSWEPT INFERNO.
BRING ONLY WHAT FOOD AND WATER YOU CAN EASILY CARRY!
SAVE YOUR LIVES! FORGET THE REST!

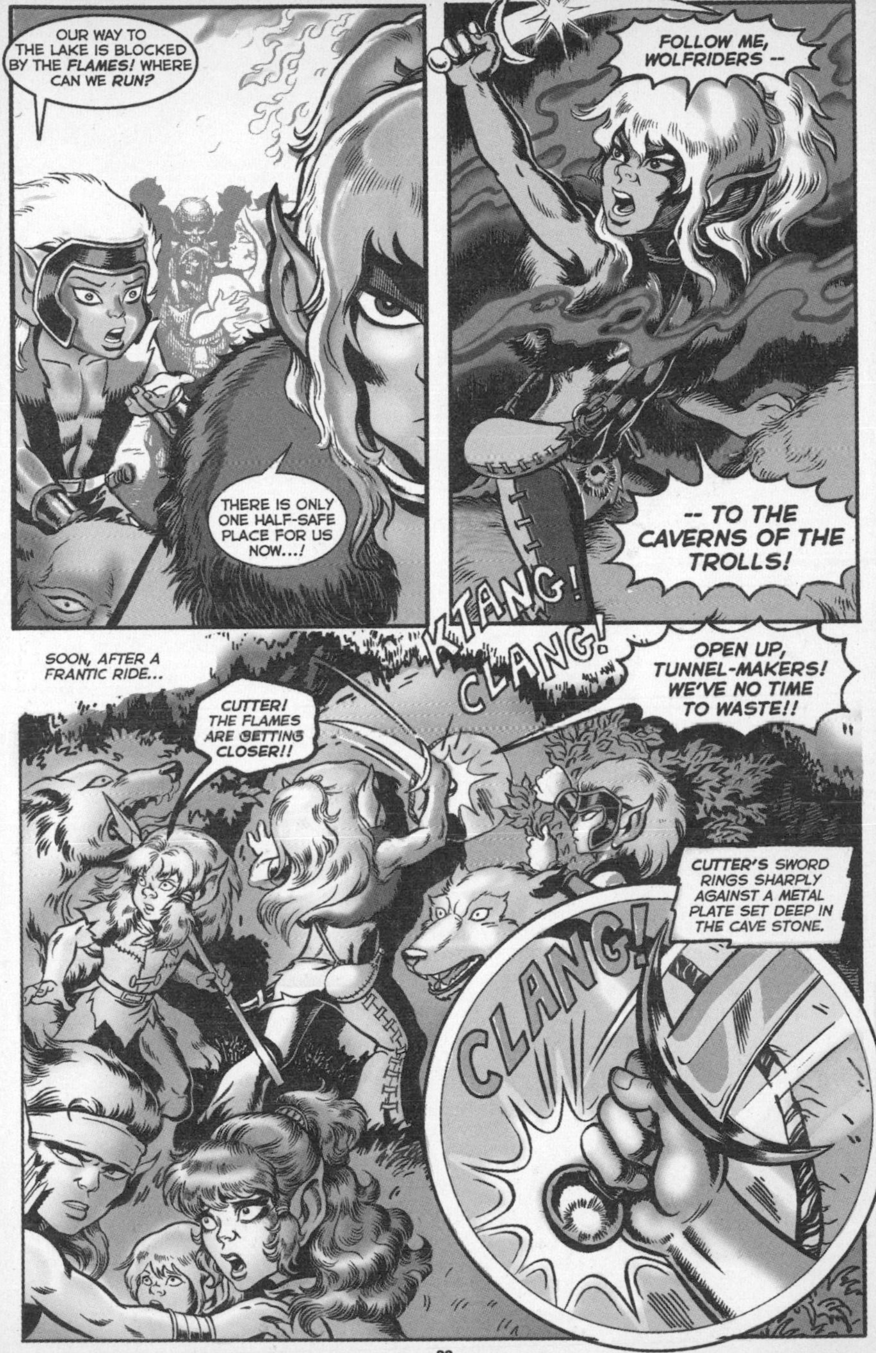

OUR WAY TO THE LAKE IS BLOCKED BY THE *FLAMES!* WHERE CAN WE *RUN?*
THERE IS ONLY ONE HALF-SAFE PLACE FOR US NOW...!
FOLLOW ME, WOLFRIDERS --
-- TO THE CAVERNS OF THE TROLLS!
SOON, AFTER A FRANTIC RIDE...
KTANG!
CLANG!
OPEN UP, TUNNEL-MAKERS! WE'VE NO TIME TO WASTE!!
CUTTER! THE FLAMES ARE GETTING CLOSER!!
CUTTER'S SWORD RINGS SHARPLY AGAINST A METAL PLATE SET DEEP IN THE CAVE STONE.
CLANG!

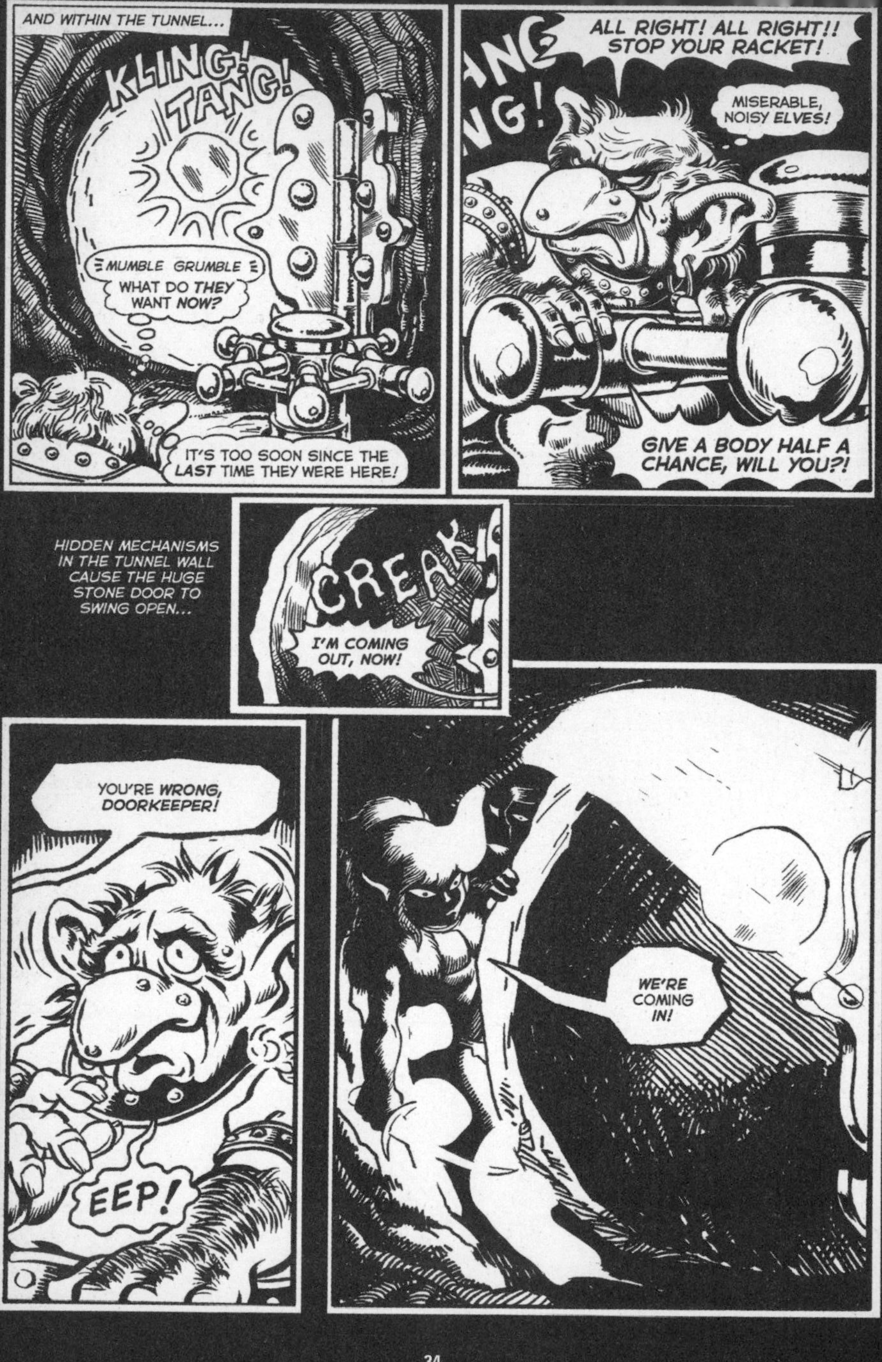
AND WITHIN THE TUNNEL...
KLING! TANG!
MUMBLE GRUMBLE
WHAT DO THEY WANT NOW?
IT'S TOO SOON SINCE THE LAST TIME THEY WERE HERE!
ALL RIGHT! ALL RIGHT!! STOP YOUR RACKET!
MISERABLE, NOISY ELVES!
GIVE A BODY HALF A CHANCE, WILL YOU?!
HIDDEN MECHANISMS IN THE TUNNEL WALL CAUSE THE HUGE STONE DOOR TO SWING OPEN...
CREAK
I'M COMING OUT, NOW!
YOU'RE WRONG, DOORKEEPER!
EEP!
WE'RE COMING IN!

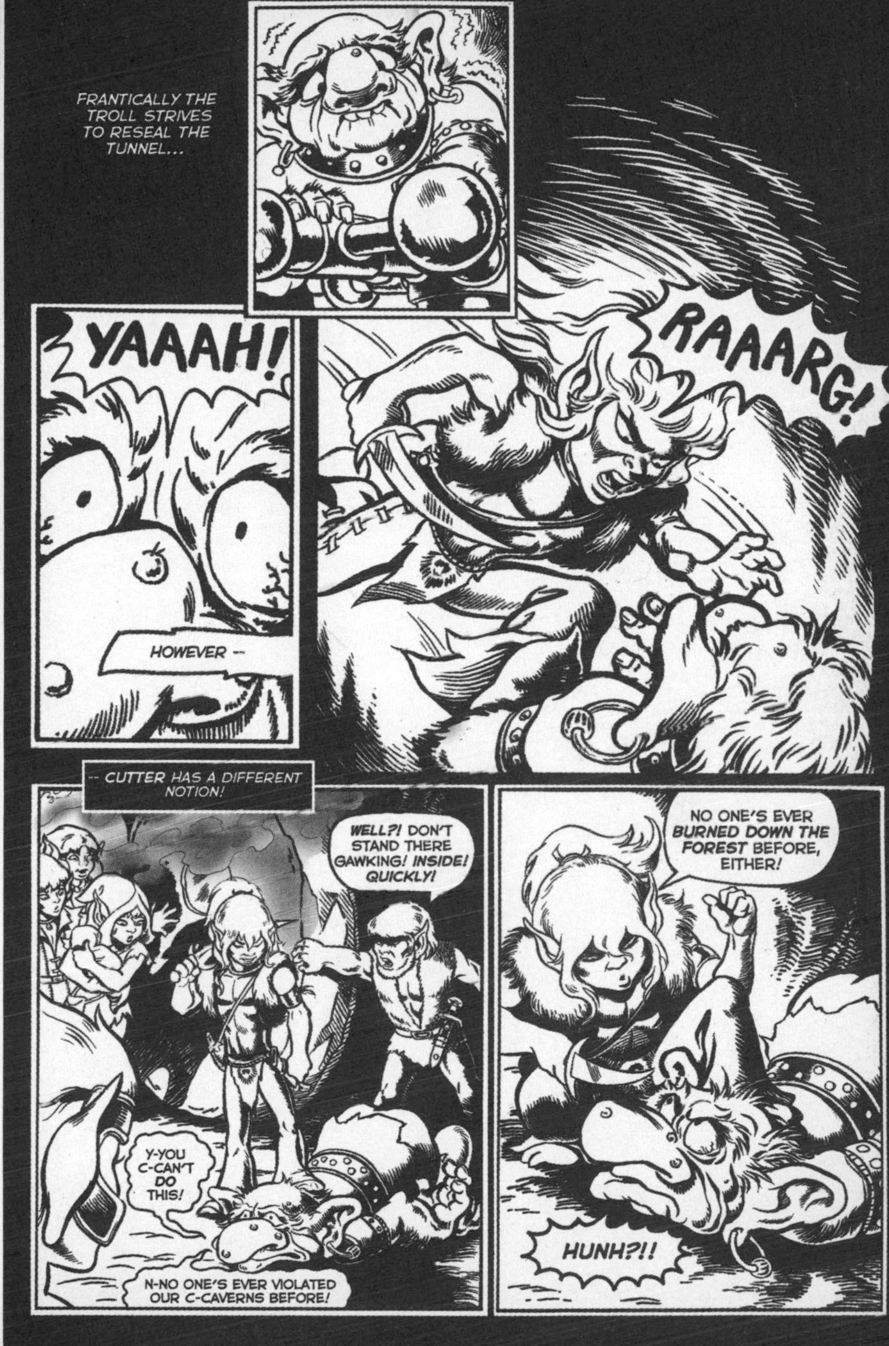
FRANTICALLY THE TROLL STRIVES TO RESEAL THE TUNNEL...
YAAAH!
HOWEVER --
RAAARG!
-- CUTTER HAS A DIFFERENT NOTION!
WELL?! DON'T STAND THERE GAWKING! INSIDE! QUICKLY!
Y-YOU C-CAN'T DO THIS!
N-NO ONE'S EVER VIOLATED OUR C-CAVERNS BEFORE!
NO ONE'S EVER BURNED DOWN THE FOREST BEFORE, EITHER!
HUNH?!!

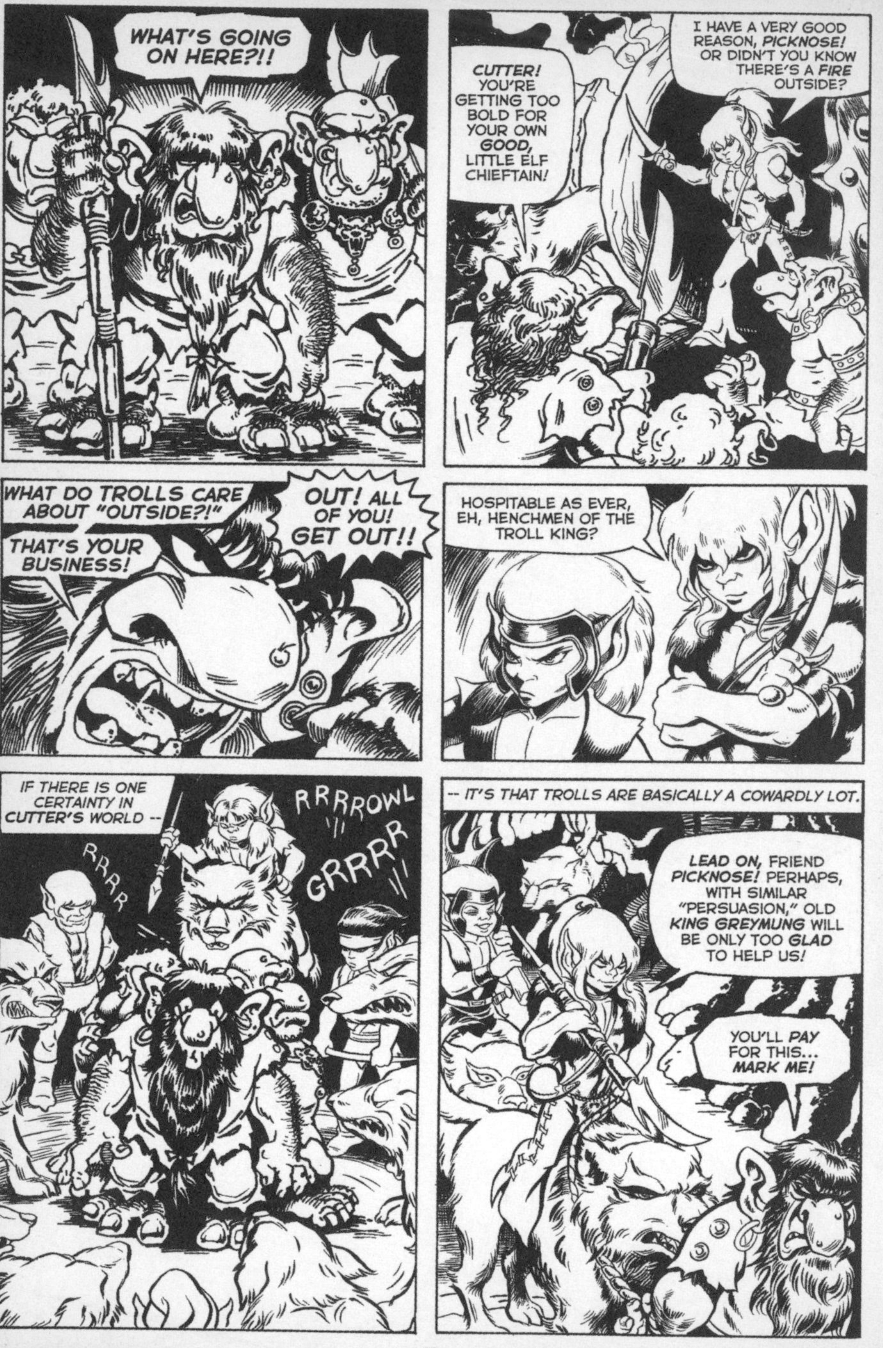
WHAT'S GOING ON HERE?!!
CUTTER! YOU'RE GETTING TOO BOLD FOR YOUR OWN GOOD, LITTLE ELF CHIEFTAIN!
I HAVE A VERY GOOD REASON, PICKNOSE! OR DIDN'T YOU KNOW THERE'S A FIRE OUTSIDE?
WHAT DO TROLLS CARE ABOUT "OUTSIDE?!"
THAT'S YOUR BUSINESS!
OUT! ALL OF YOU! GET OUT!!
HOSPITABLE AS EVER, EH, HENCHMEN OF THE TROLL KING?
IF THERE IS ONE CERTAINTY IN CUTTER'S WORLD --
RRRROWL
RRRR
GRRRR
-- IT'S THAT TROLLS ARE BASICALLY A COWARDLY LOT.
LEAD ON, FRIEND PICKNOSE! PERHAPS, WITH SIMILAR "PERSUASION," OLD KING GREYMUNG WILL BE ONLY TOO GLAD TO HELP US!
YOU'LL PAY FOR THIS... MARK ME!

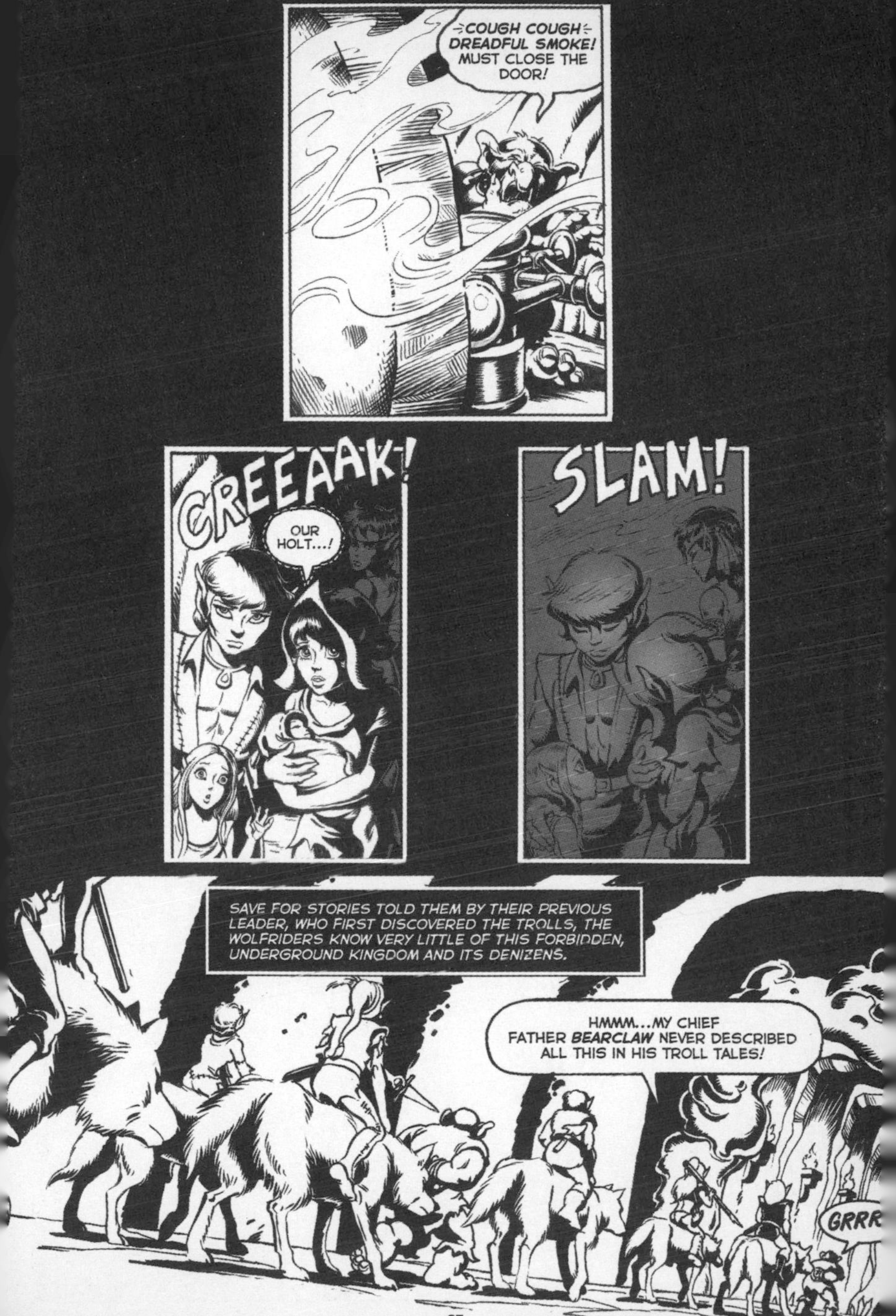

-COUGH COUGH- DREADFUL SMOKE! MUST CLOSE THE DOOR!
CREEAAK!
OUR HOLT...!
SLAM!
SAVE FOR STORIES TOLD THEM BY THEIR PREVIOUS LEADER, WHO FIRST DISCOVERED THE TROLLS, THE WOLFRIDERS KNOW VERY LITTLE OF THIS FORBIDDEN, UNDERGROUND KINGDOM AND ITS DENIZENS.
HMMM...MY CHIEF FATHER BEARCLAW NEVER DESCRIBED ALL THIS IN HIS TROLL TALES!
GRRR

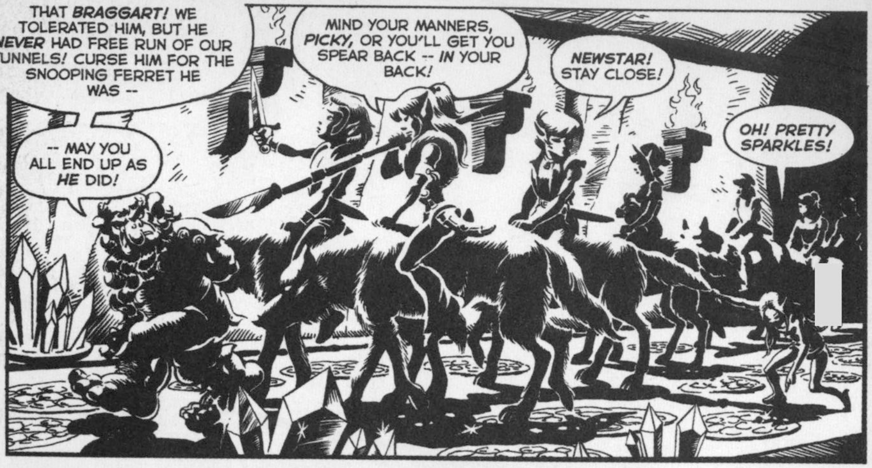
THAT BRAGGART! WE TOLERATED HIM, BUT HE NEVER HAD FREE RUN OF OUR TUNNELS! CURSE HIM FOR THE SNOOPING FERRET HE WAS --
-- MAY YOU ALL END UP AS HE DID!
MIND YOUR MANNERS, PICKY, OR YOU'LL GET YOU SPEAR BACK -- IN YOUR BACK!
NEWSTAR! STAY CLOSE!
OH! PRETTY SPARKLES!

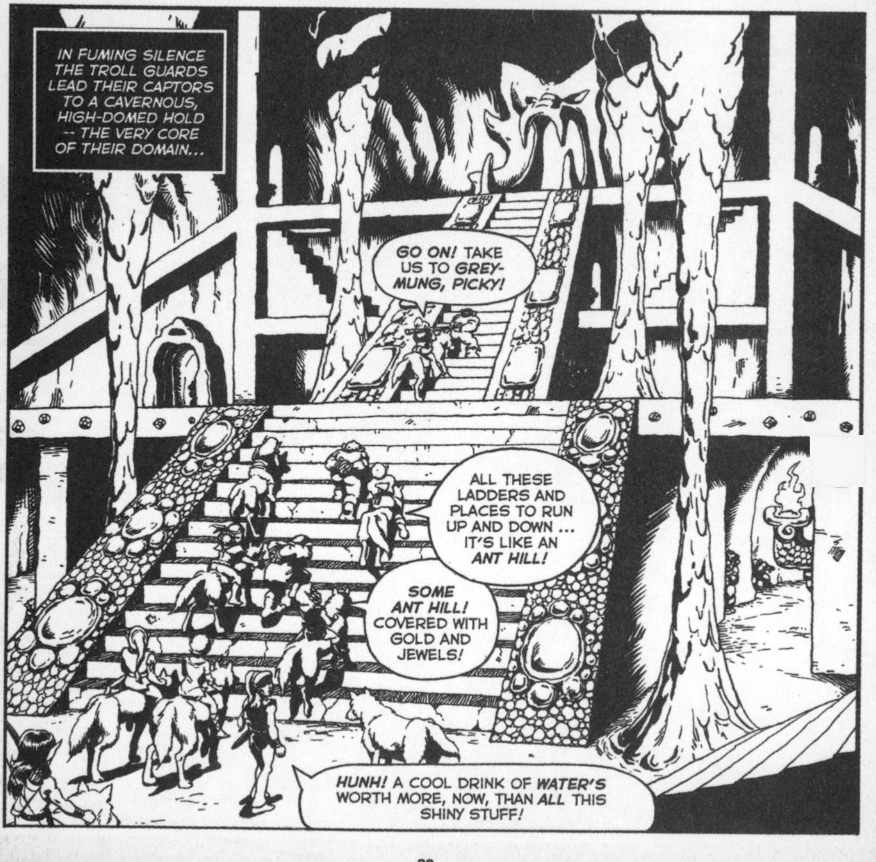
IN FUMING SILENCE THE TROLL GUARDS LEAD THEIR CAPTORS TO A CAVERNOUS, HIGH-DOMED HOLD -- THE VERY CORE OF THEIR DOMAIN...
GO ON! TAKE US TO GREY-MUNG, PICKY!
ALL THESE LADDERS AND PLACES TO RUN UP AND DOWN ... IT'S LIKE AN ANT HILL!
SOME ANT HILL! COVERED WITH GOLD AND JEWELS!
HUNH! A COOL DRINK OF WATER'S WORTH MORE, NOW, THAN ALL THIS SHINY STUFF!

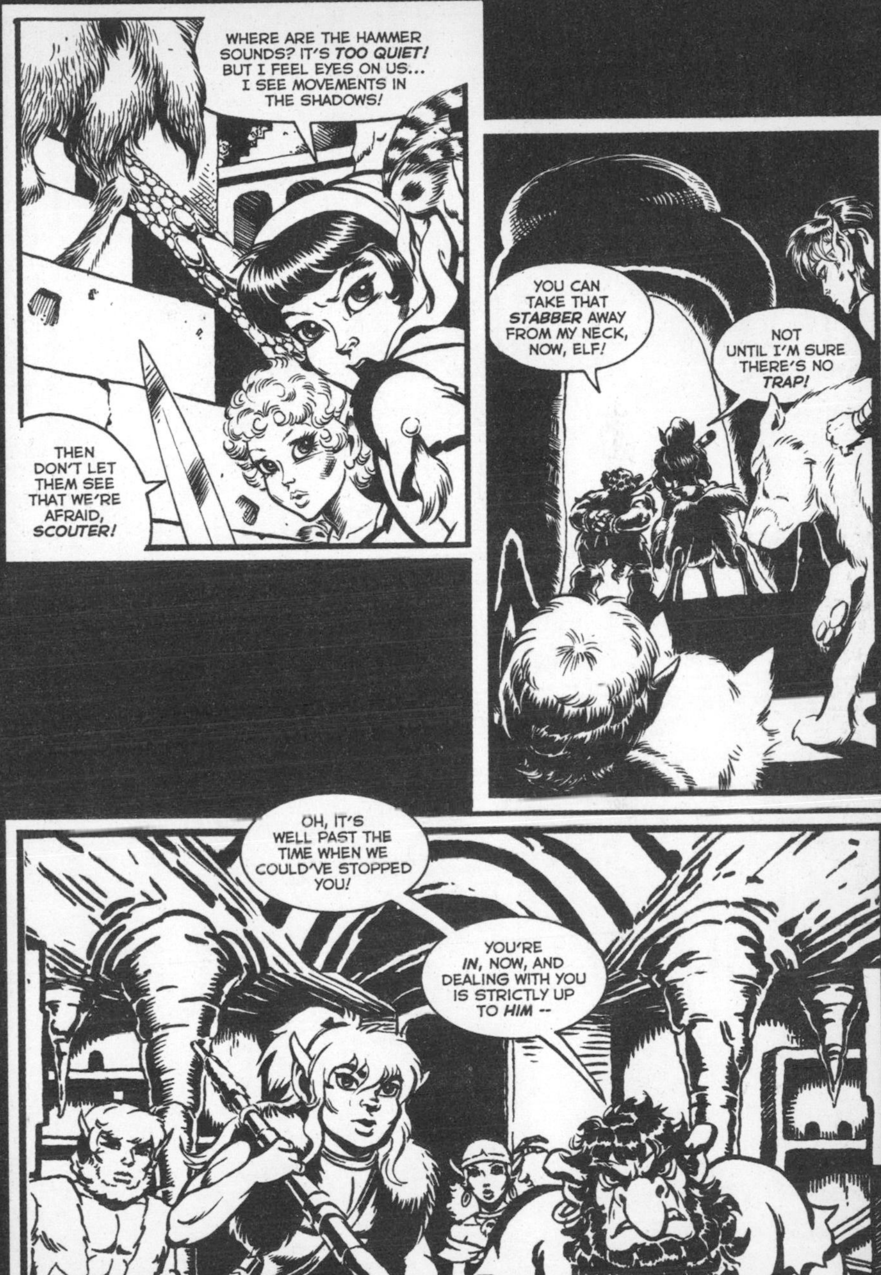
WHERE ARE THE HAMMER SOUNDS? IT'S TOO QUIET! BUT I FEEL EYES ON US... I SEE MOVEMENTS IN THE SHADOWS!
THEN DON'T LET THEM SEE THAT WE'RE AFRAID, SCOUTER!
YOU CAN TAKE THAT STABBER AWAY FROM MY NECK, NOW, ELF!
NOT UNTIL I'M SURE THERE'S NO TRAP!
OH, IT'S WELL PAST THE TIME WHEN WE COULD'VE STOPPED YOU!
YOU'RE IN, NOW, AND DEALING WITH YOU IS STRICTLY UP TO HIM --

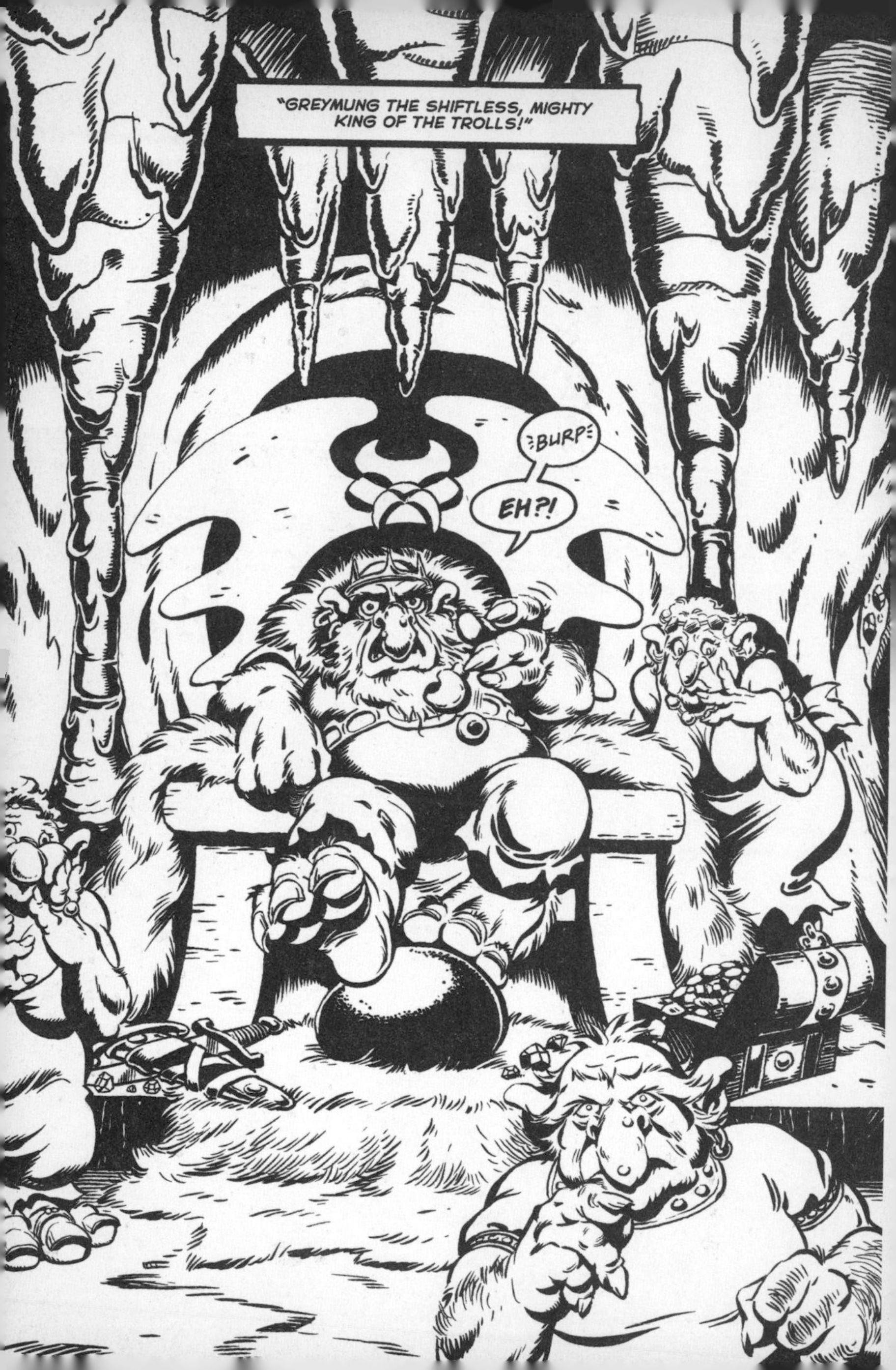
"GREYMUNG THE SHIFTLESS, MIGHTY KING OF THE TROLLS!"
BURP
EH?!

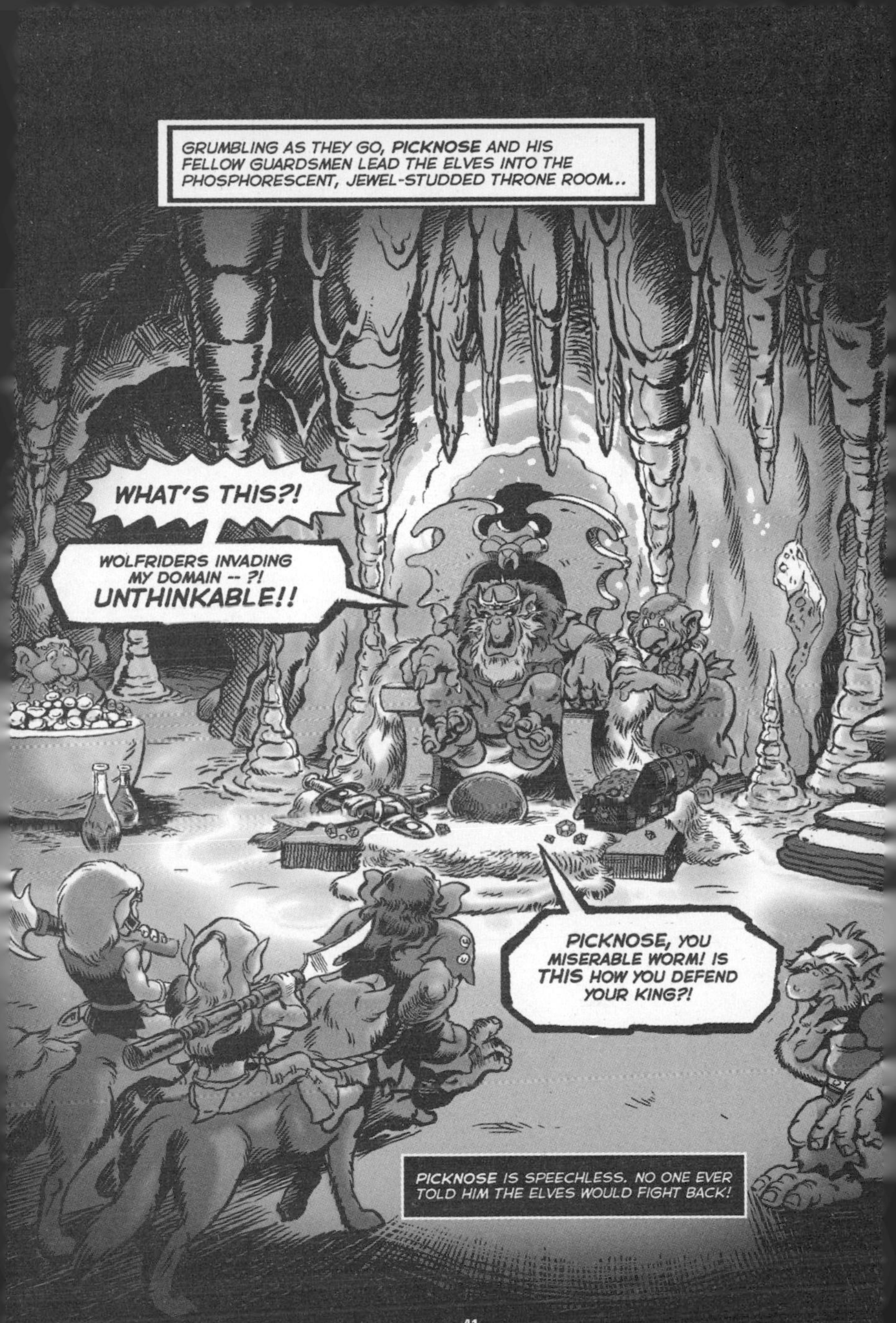
GRUMBLING AS THEY GO, PICKNOSE AND HIS FELLOW GUARDSMEN LEAD THE ELVES INTO THE PHOSPHORESCENT, JEWEL-STUDDED THRONE ROOM...
WHAT'S THIS?!
WOLFRIDERS INVADING MY DOMAIN -- ?! UNTHINKABLE!!
PICKNOSE, YOU MISERABLE WORM! IS THIS HOW YOU DEFEND YOUR KING?!
PICKNOSE IS SPEECHLESS. NO ONE EVER TOLD HIM THE ELVES WOULD FIGHT BACK!

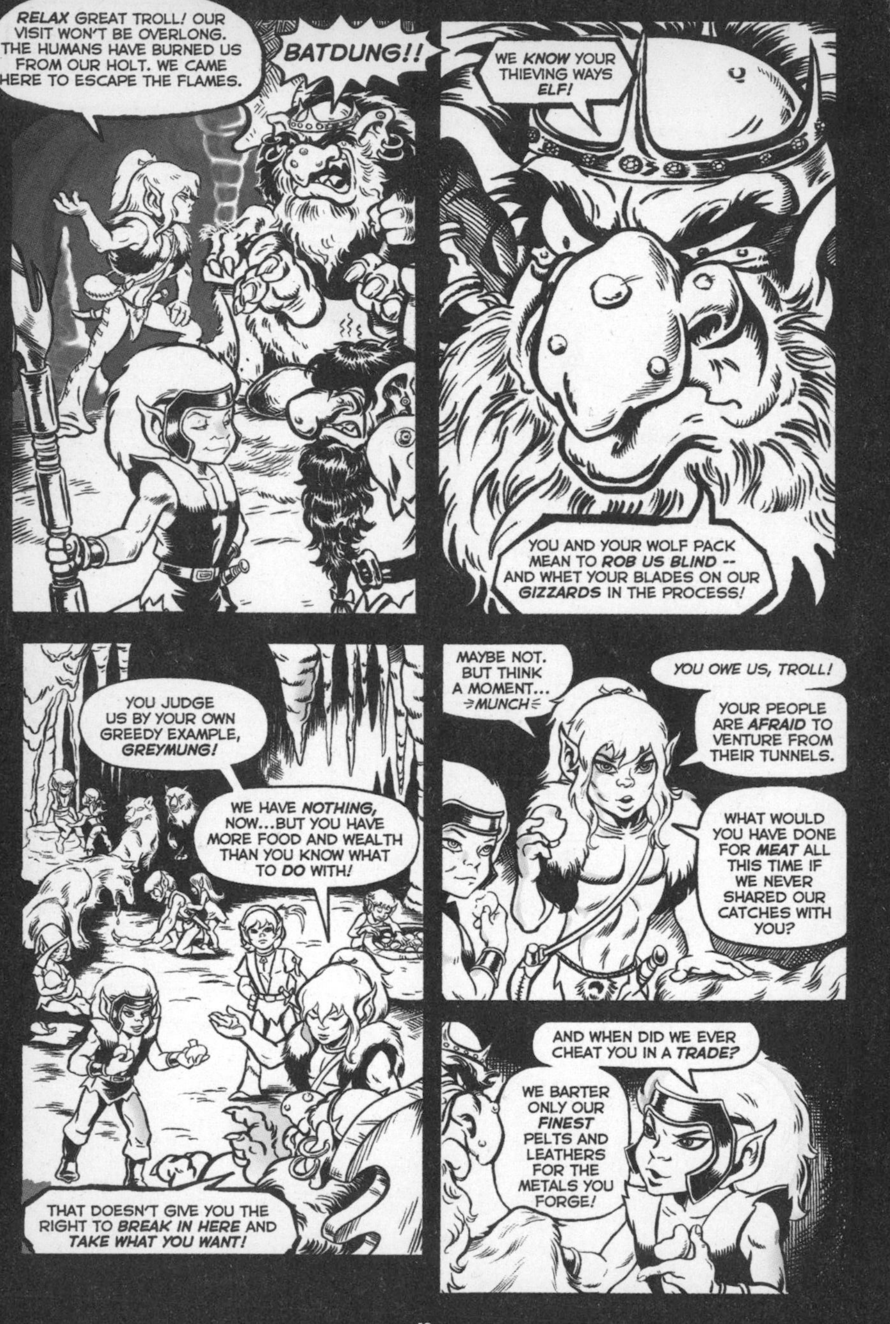
RELAX GREAT TROLL! OUR VISIT WON'T BE OVERLONG. THE HUMANS HAVE BURNED US FROM OUR HOLT. WE CAME HERE TO ESCAPE THE FLAMES.
BATDUNG!!
WE KNOW YOUR THIEVING WAYS ELF!
YOU AND YOUR WOLF PACK MEAN TO ROB US BLIND -- AND WHET YOUR BLADES ON OUR GIZZARDS IN THE PROCESS!
YOU JUDGE US BY YOUR OWN GREEDY EXAMPLE, GREYMUNG!
WE HAVE NOTHING, NOW...BUT YOU HAVE MORE FOOD AND WEALTH THAN YOU KNOW WHAT TO DO WITH!
THAT DOESN'T GIVE YOU THE RIGHT TO BREAK IN HERE AND TAKE WHAT YOU WANT!
MAYBE NOT. BUT THINK A MOMENT... MUNCH
YOU OWE US, TROLL!
YOUR PEOPLE ARE AFRAID TO VENTURE FROM THEIR TUNNELS.
WHAT WOULD YOU HAVE DONE FOR MEAT ALL THIS TIME IF WE NEVER SHARED OUR CATCHES WITH YOU?
AND WHEN DID WE EVER CHEAT YOU IN A TRADE?
WE BARTER ONLY OUR FINEST PELTS AND LEATHERS FOR THE METALS YOU FORGE!

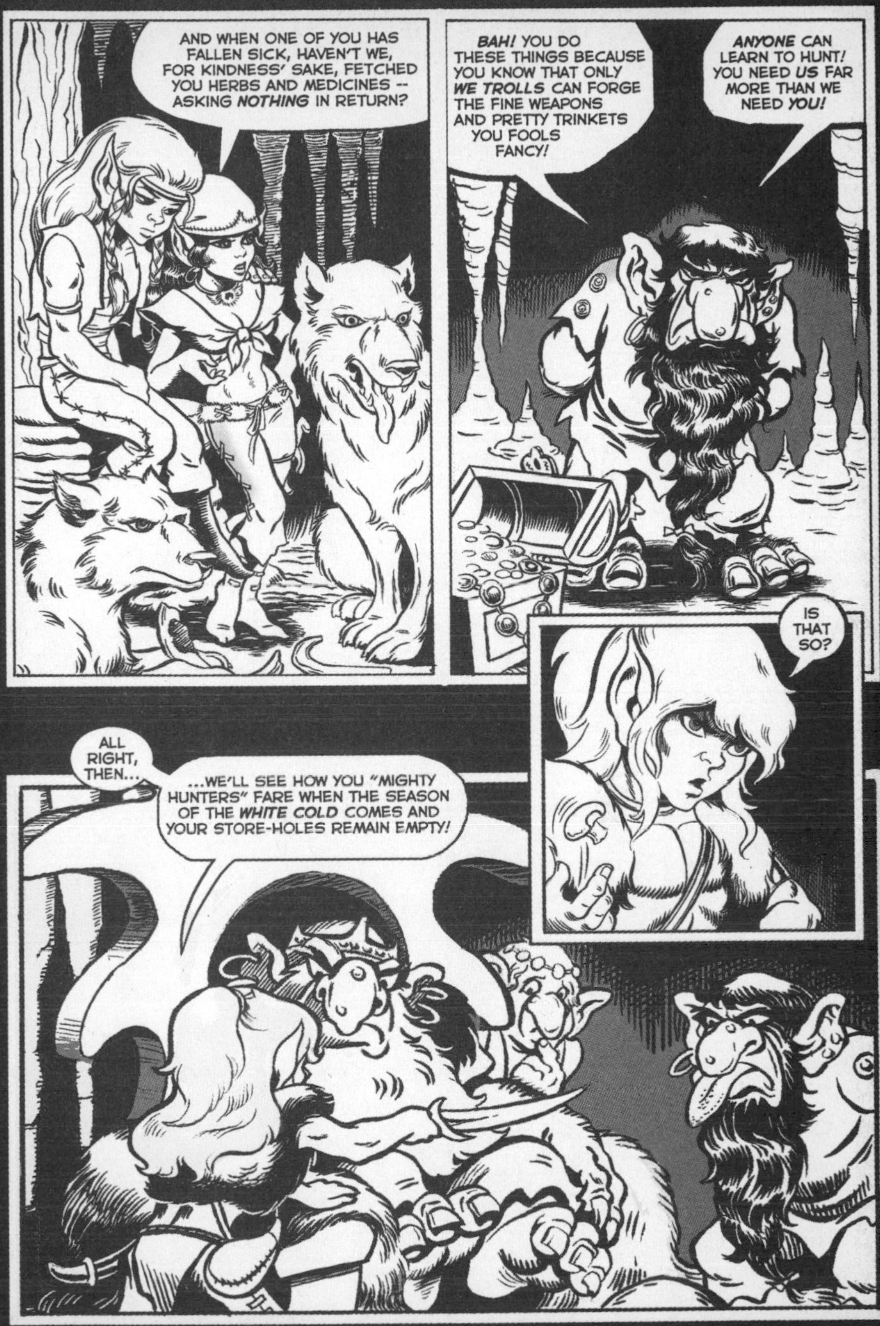
AND WHEN ONE OF YOU HAS FALLEN SICK, HAVEN'T WE, FOR KINDNESS' SAKE, FETCHED YOU HERBS AND MEDICINES -- ASKING NOTHING IN RETURN?
BAH! YOU DO THESE THINGS BECAUSE YOU KNOW THAT ONLY WE TROLLS CAN FORGE THE FINE WEAPONS AND PRETTY TRINKETS YOU FOOLS FANCY!
ANYONE CAN LEARN TO HUNT! YOU NEED US FAR MORE THAN WE NEED YOU!
IS THAT SO?
ALL RIGHT, THEN...
...WE'LL SEE HOW YOU "MIGHTY HUNTERS" FARE WHEN THE SEASON OF THE WHITE COLD COMES AND YOUR STORE-HOLES REMAIN EMPTY!

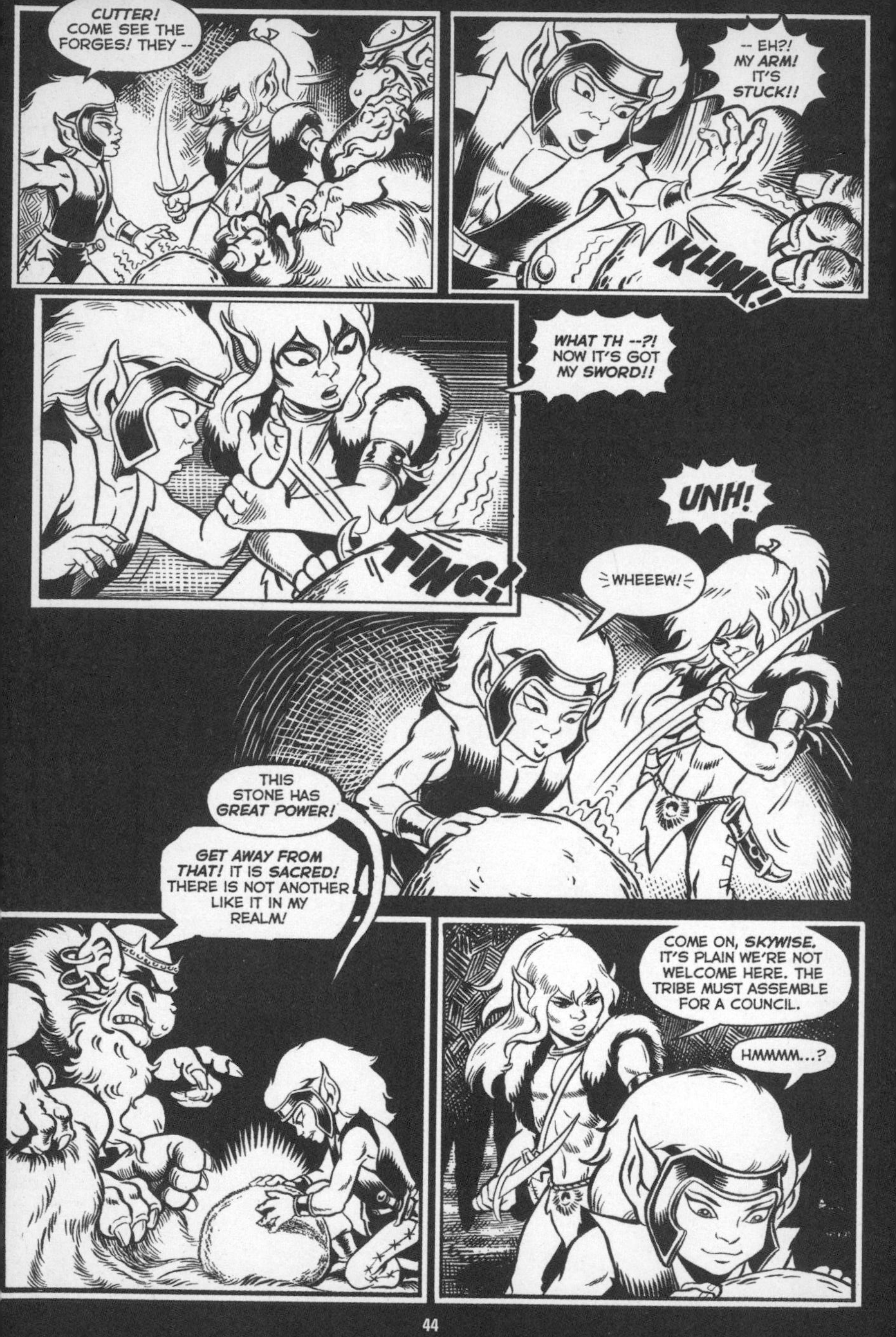
CUTTER! COME SEE THE FORGES! THEY --
-- EH?! MY ARM! IT'S STUCK!!
KLUNK!
WHAT TH --?! NOW IT'S GOT MY SWORD!!
TING!
UNH!
WHEEEW!
THIS STONE HAS GREAT POWER!
GET AWAY FROM THAT! IT IS SACRED! THERE IS NOT ANOTHER LIKE IT IN MY REALM!
COME ON, SKYWISE. IT'S PLAIN WE'RE NOT WELCOME HERE. THE TRIBE MUST ASSEMBLE FOR A COUNCIL.
HMMMM...?

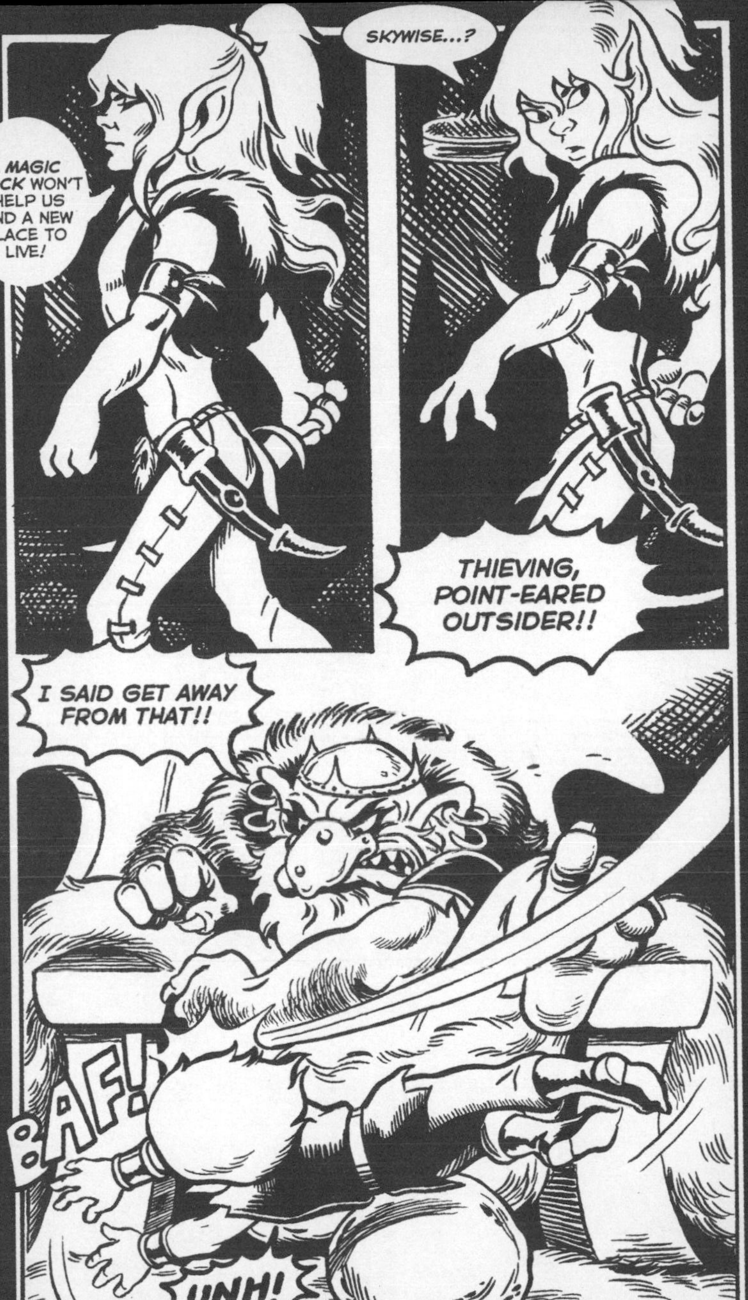
A MAGIC ROCK WON'T HELP US FIND A NEW PLACE TO LIVE!
SKYWISE...?
THIEVING, POINT-EARED OUTSIDER!!
I SAID GET AWAY FROM THAT!!
BAF!
UNH!

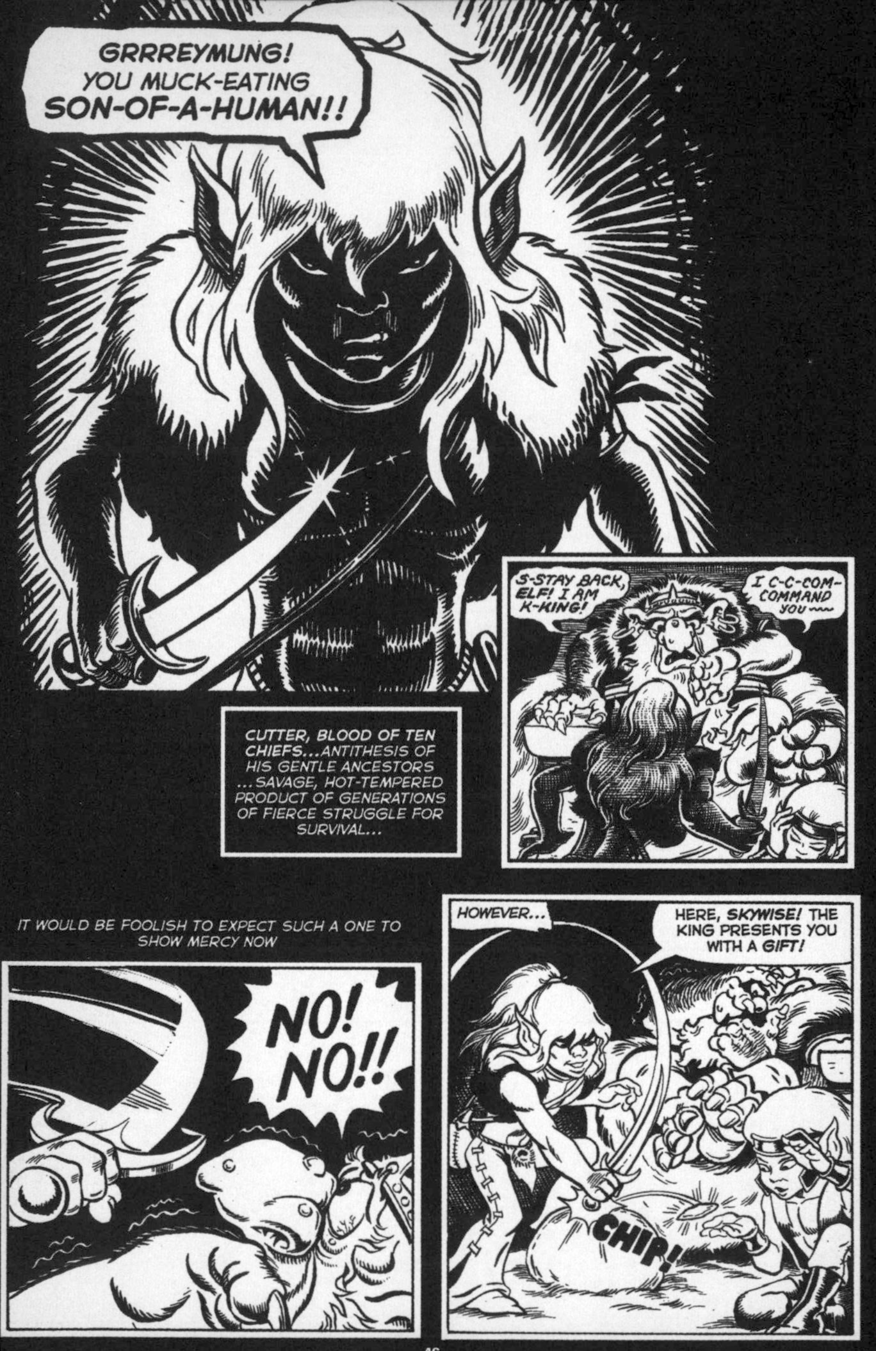
GRRREYMUNG! YOU MUCK-EATING SON-OF-A-HUMAN!!
S-STAY BACK, ELF! I AM K-KING!
I C-C-COM-COMMAND YOU~~
CUTTER, BLOOD OF TEN CHIEFS...ANTITHESIS OF HIS GENTLE ANCESTORS ...SAVAGE, HOT-TEMPERED PRODUCT OF GENERATIONS OF FIERCE STRUGGLE FOR SURVIVAL...
IT WOULD BE FOOLISH TO EXPECT SUCH A ONE TO SHOW MERCY NOW
NO! NO!!
HOWEVER...
HERE, SKYWISE! THE KING PRESENTS YOU WITH A GIFT!
CHIP!

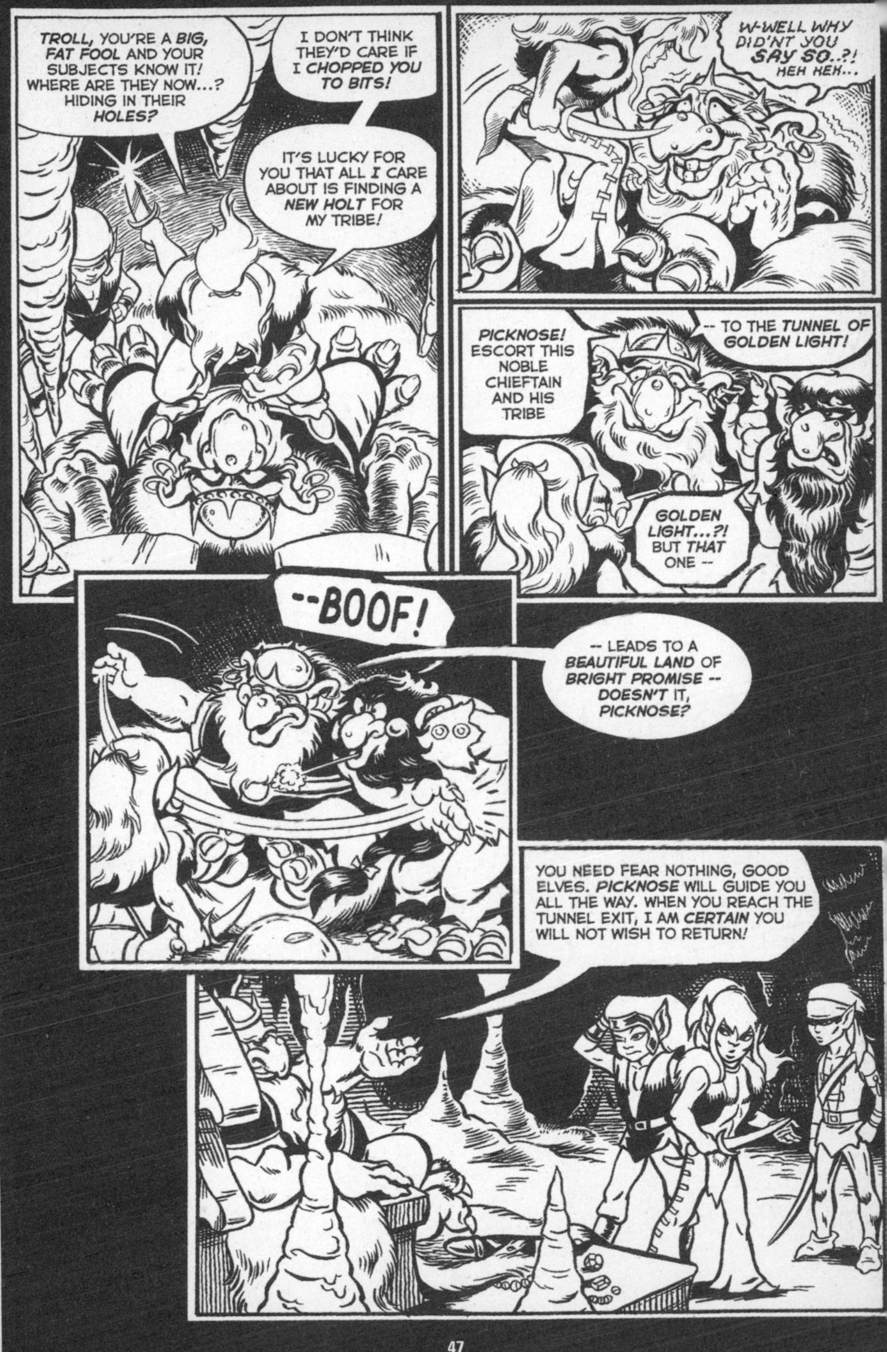
TROLL, YOU'RE A BIG, FAT FOOL AND YOUR SUBJECTS KNOW IT! WHERE ARE THEY NOW...? HIDING IN THEIR HOLES?
I DON'T THINK THEY'D CARE IF I CHOPPED YOU TO BITS!
IT'S LUCKY FOR YOU THAT ALL I CARE ABOUT IS FINDING A NEW HOLT FOR MY TRIBE!
W-WELL WHY DIDN'T YOU SAY SO..?! HEH HEH...
PICKNOSE! ESCORT THIS NOBLE CHIEFTAIN AND HIS TRIBE
-- TO THE TUNNEL OF GOLDEN LIGHT!
GOLDEN LIGHT...?! BUT THAT ONE --
--BOOF!
-- LEADS TO A BEAUTIFUL LAND OF BRIGHT PROMISE -- DOESN'T IT, PICKNOSE?
YOU NEED FEAR NOTHING, GOOD ELVES. PICKNOSE WILL GUIDE YOU ALL THE WAY. WHEN YOU REACH THE TUNNEL EXIT, I AM CERTAIN YOU WILL NOT WISH TO RETURN!

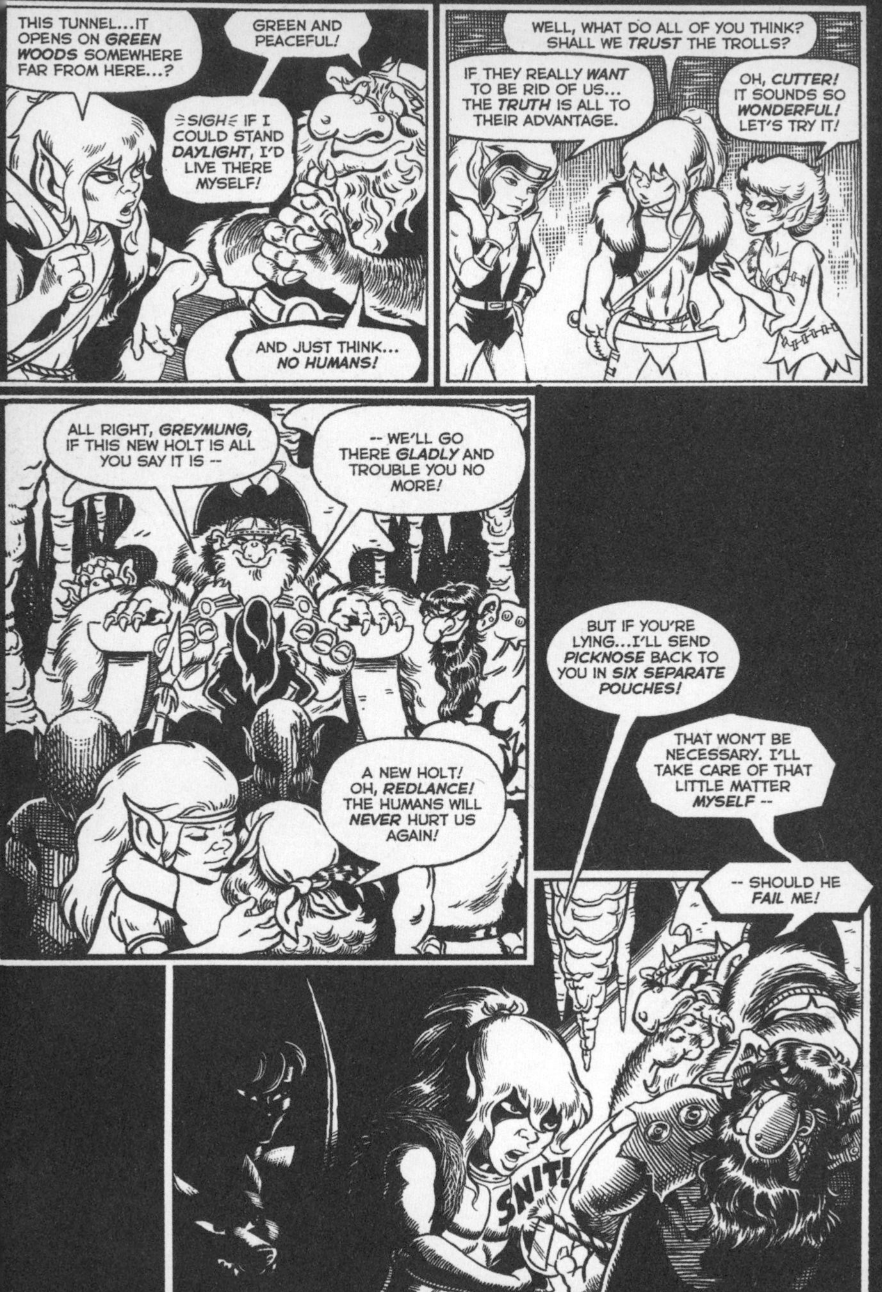
THIS TUNNEL...IT OPENS ON GREEN WOODS SOMEWHERE FAR FROM HERE...?
GREEN AND PEACEFUL!
≶SIGH≶ IF I COULD STAND DAYLIGHT, I'D LIVE THERE MYSELF!
AND JUST THINK... NO HUMANS!
WELL, WHAT DO ALL OF YOU THINK? SHALL WE TRUST THE TROLLS?
IF THEY REALLY WANT TO BE RID OF US... THE TRUTH IS ALL TO THEIR ADVANTAGE.
OH, CUTTER! IT SOUNDS SO WONDERFUL! LET'S TRY IT!
ALL RIGHT, GREYMUNG, IF THIS NEW HOLT IS ALL YOU SAY IT IS --
-- WE'LL GO THERE GLADLY AND TROUBLE YOU NO MORE!
A NEW HOLT! OH, REDLANCE! THE HUMANS WILL NEVER HURT US AGAIN!
BUT IF YOU'RE LYING...I'LL SEND PICKNOSE BACK TO YOU IN SIX SEPARATE POUCHES!
THAT WON'T BE NECESSARY. I'LL TAKE CARE OF THAT LITTLE MATTER MYSELF --
-- SHOULD HE FAIL ME!
SNIT!

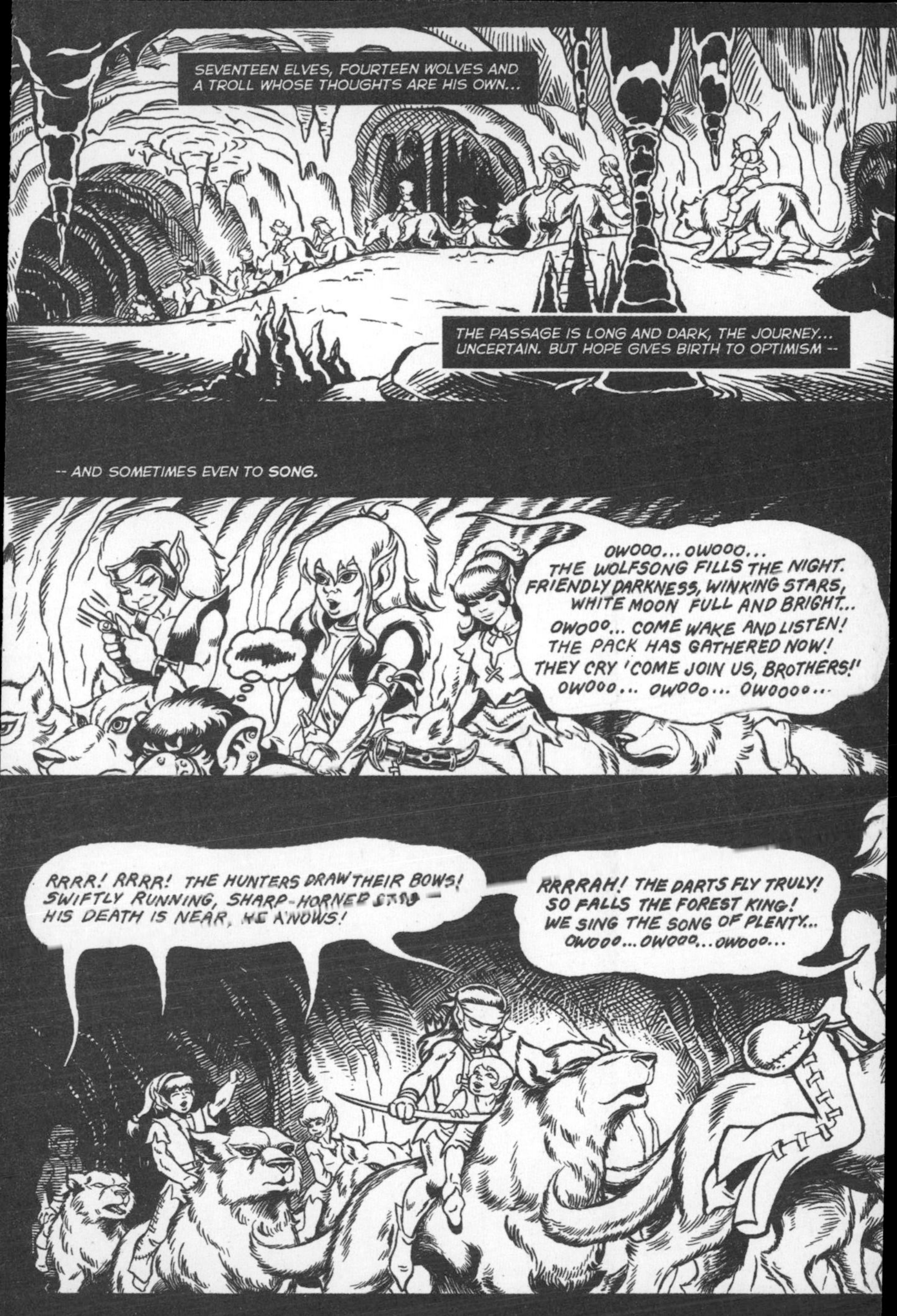
SEVENTEEN ELVES, FOURTEEN WOLVES AND A TROLL WHOSE THOUGHTS ARE HIS OWN...
THE PASSAGE IS LONG AND DARK, THE JOURNEY... UNCERTAIN. BUT HOPE GIVES BIRTH TO OPTIMISM --
-- AND SOMETIMES EVEN TO SONG.
OWOOO... OWOOO... THE WOLFSONG FILLS THE NIGHT. FRIENDLY DARKNESS, WINKING STARS, WHITE MOON FULL AND BRIGHT... OWOOO... COME WAKE AND LISTEN! THE PACK HAS GATHERED NOW! THEY CRY 'COME JOIN US, BROTHERS!' OWOOO... OWOOO... OWOOOO...
RRRR! RRRR! THE HUNTERS DRAW THEIR BOWS! SWIFTLY RUNNING, SHARP-HORNED STAG — HIS DEATH IS NEAR, HE KNOWS!
RRRRAH! THE DARTS FLY TRULY! SO FALLS THE FOREST KING! WE SING THE SONG OF PLENTY... OWOOO... OWOOO... OWOOO...

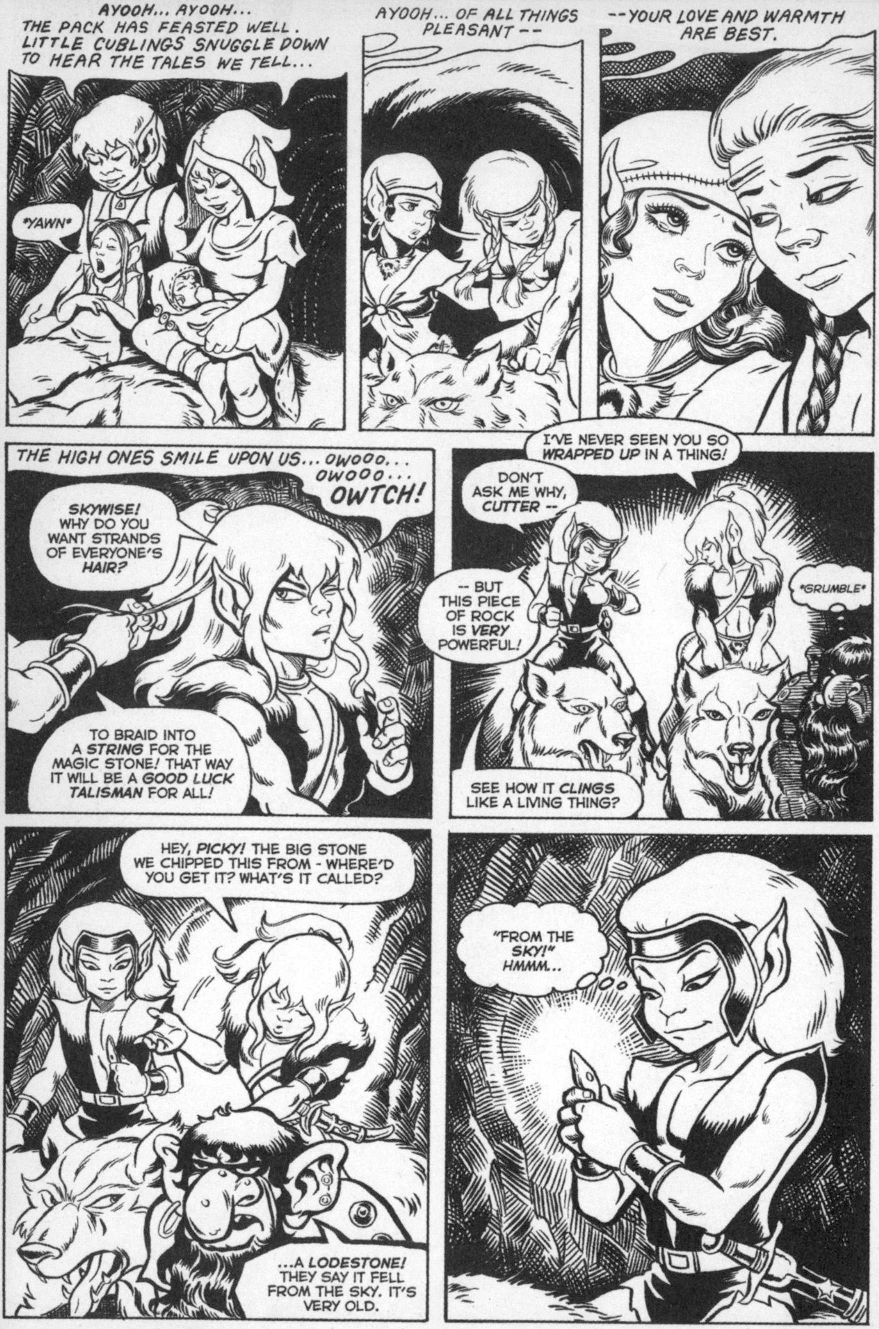
AYOOH... AYOOH... THE PACK HAS FEASTED WELL. LITTLE CUBLINGS SNUGGLE DOWN TO HEAR THE TALES WE TELL...
YAWN
AYOOH... OF ALL THINGS PLEASANT --
--YOUR LOVE AND WARMTH ARE BEST.
THE HIGH ONES SMILE UPON US... OWOOO... OWOOO... OWTCH!
SKYWISE! WHY DO YOU WANT STRANDS OF EVERYONE'S HAIR?
TO BRAID INTO A STRING FOR THE MAGIC STONE! THAT WAY IT WILL BE A GOOD LUCK TALISMAN FOR ALL!
I'VE NEVER SEEN YOU SO WRAPPED UP IN A THING!
DON'T ASK ME WHY, CUTTER --
-- BUT THIS PIECE OF ROCK IS VERY POWERFUL!
GRUMBLE
SEE HOW IT CLINGS LIKE A LIVING THING?
HEY, PICKY! THE BIG STONE WE CHIPPED THIS FROM - WHERE'D YOU GET IT? WHAT'S IT CALLED?
...A LODESTONE! THEY SAY IT FELL FROM THE SKY. IT'S VERY OLD.
"FROM THE SKY!" HMMM...

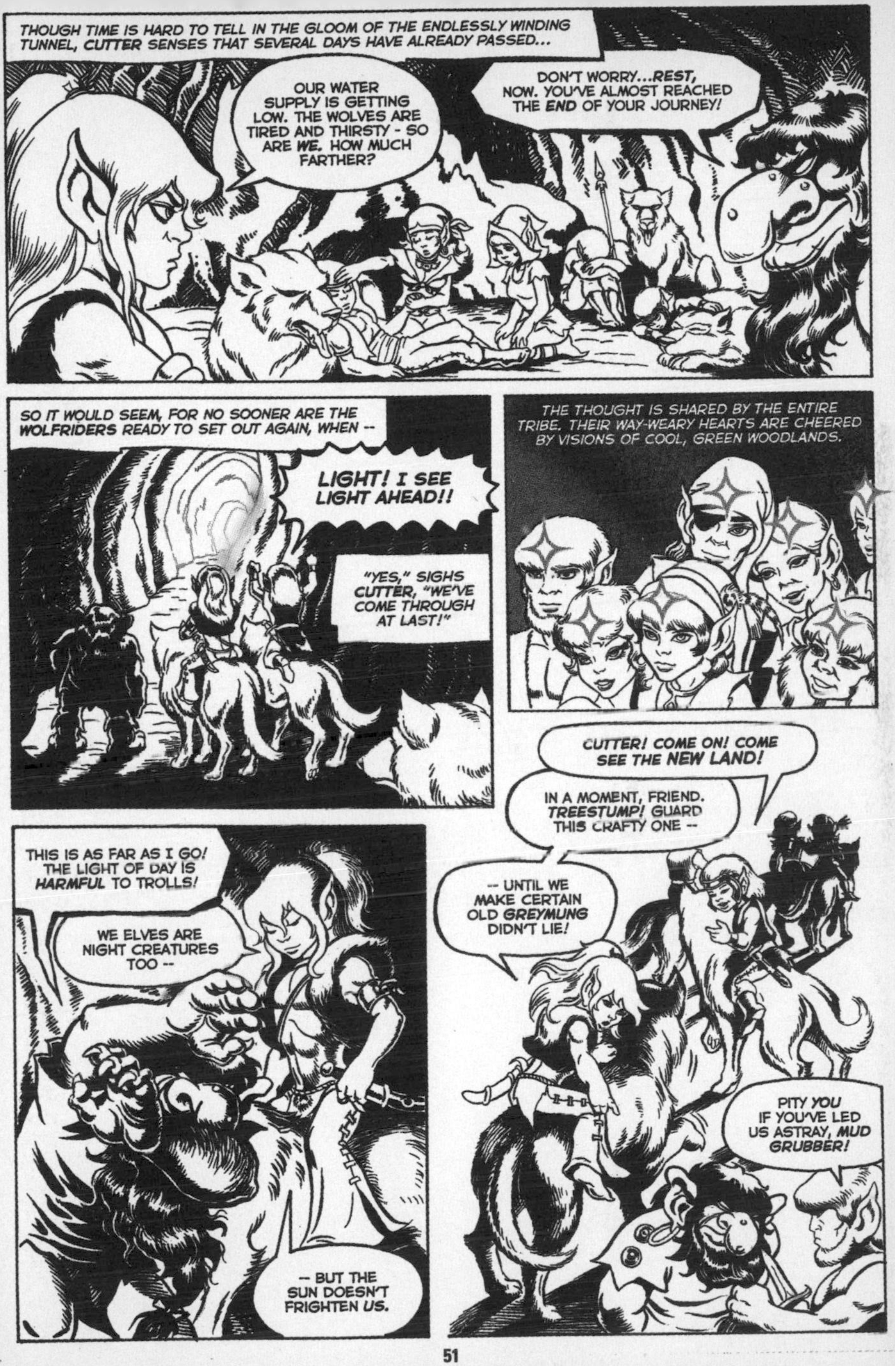
THOUGH TIME IS HARD TO TELL IN THE GLOOM OF THE ENDLESSLY WINDING TUNNEL, CUTTER SENSES THAT SEVERAL DAYS HAVE ALREADY PASSED...
OUR WATER SUPPLY IS GETTING LOW. THE WOLVES ARE TIRED AND THIRSTY - SO ARE WE. HOW MUCH FARTHER?
DON'T WORRY...REST, NOW. YOU'VE ALMOST REACHED THE END OF YOUR JOURNEY!
SO IT WOULD SEEM, FOR NO SOONER ARE THE WOLFRIDERS READY TO SET OUT AGAIN, WHEN --
LIGHT! I SEE LIGHT AHEAD!!
"YES," SIGHS CUTTER, "WE'VE COME THROUGH AT LAST!"
THE THOUGHT IS SHARED BY THE ENTIRE TRIBE. THEIR WAY-WEARY HEARTS ARE CHEERED BY VISIONS OF COOL, GREEN WOODLANDS.
THIS IS AS FAR AS I GO! THE LIGHT OF DAY IS HARMFUL TO TROLLS!
WE ELVES ARE NIGHT CREATURES TOO --
-- BUT THE SUN DOESN'T FRIGHTEN US.
CUTTER! COME ON! COME SEE THE NEW LAND!
IN A MOMENT, FRIEND. TREESTUMP! GUARD THIS CRAFTY ONE --
-- UNTIL WE MAKE CERTAIN OLD GREYMUNG DIDN'T LIE!
PITY YOU IF YOU'VE LED US ASTRAY, MUD GRUBBER!

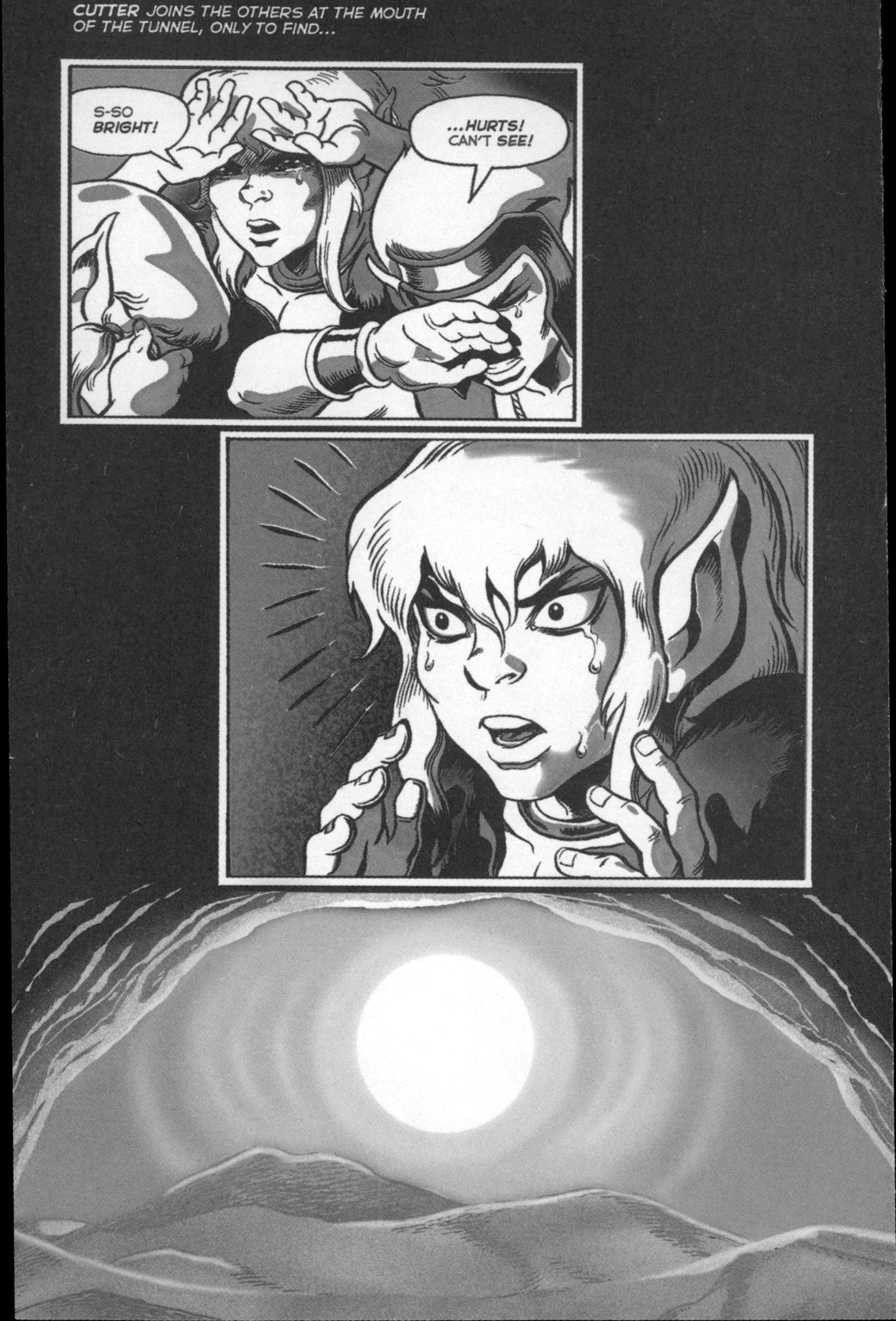
CUTTER JOINS THE OTHERS AT THE MOUTH OF THE TUNNEL, ONLY TO FIND...
S-SO BRIGHT!
...HURTS! CAN'T SEE!

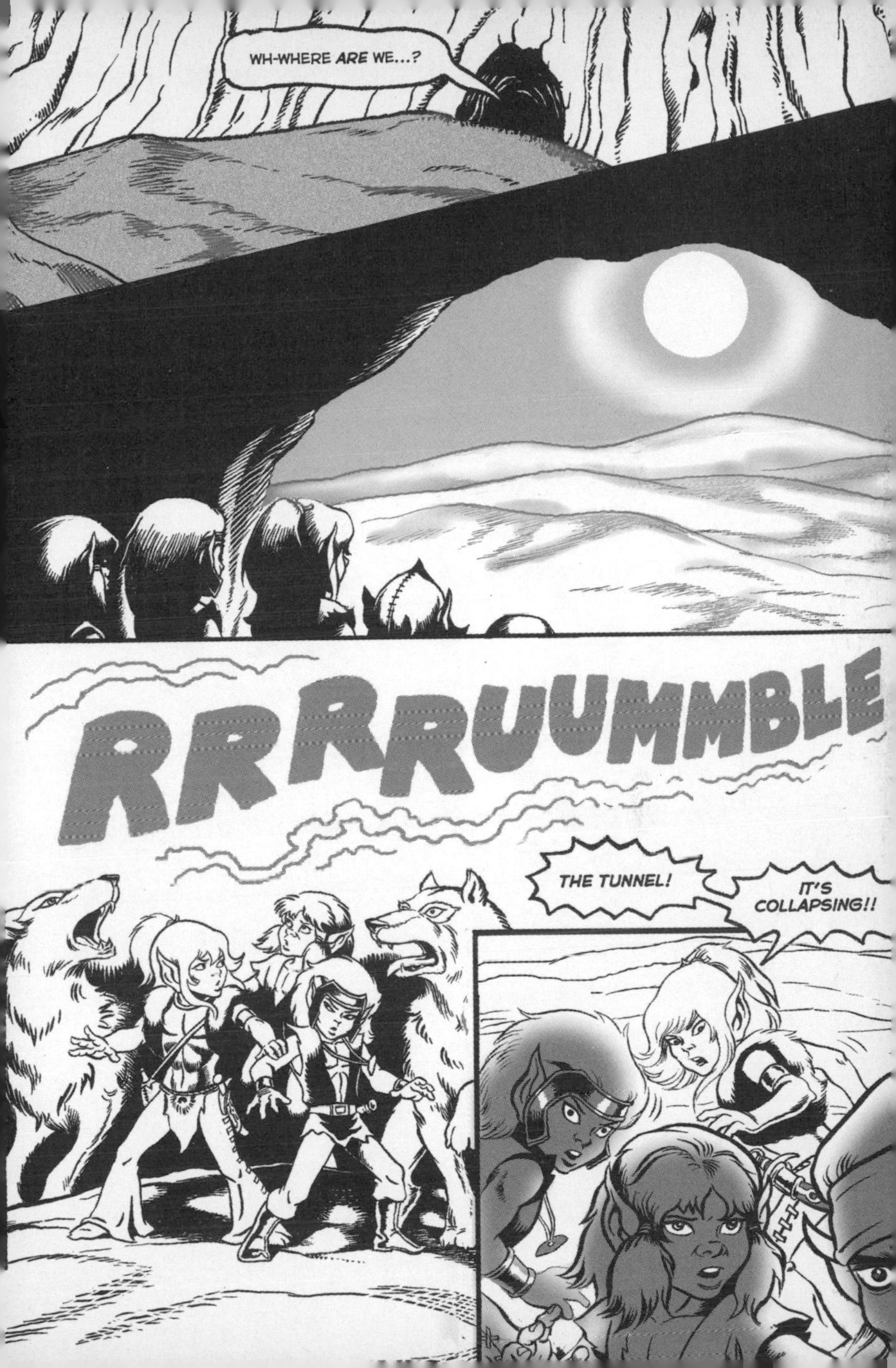
WH-WHERE ARE WE...?
RRRRUUMMBLE
THE TUNNEL!
IT'S COLLAPSING!!

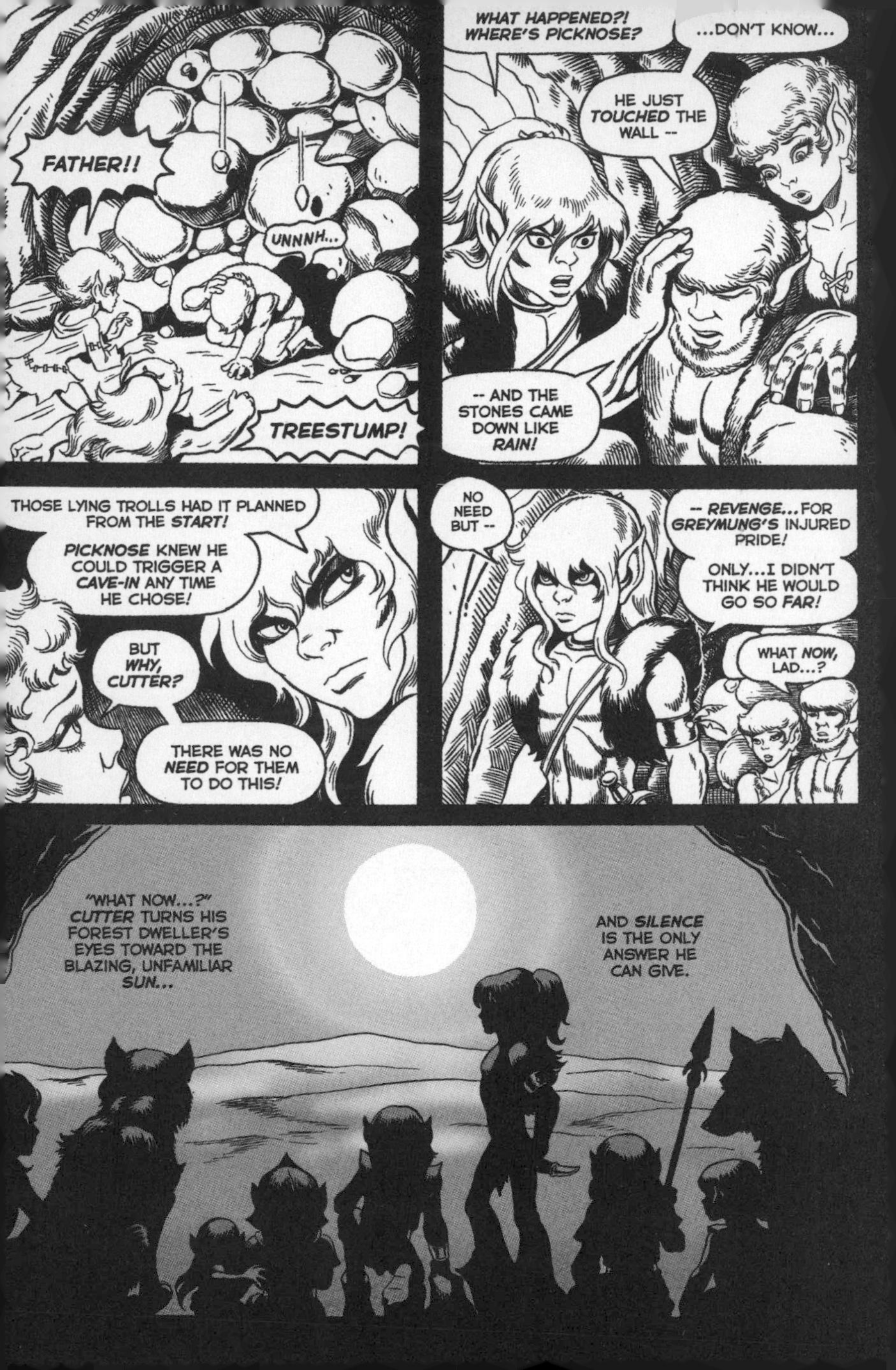
FATHER!!
UNNNH...
TREESTUMP!
WHAT HAPPENED?! WHERE'S PICKNOSE?
...DON'T KNOW...
HE JUST TOUCHED THE WALL --
-- AND THE STONES CAME DOWN LIKE RAIN!
THOSE LYING TROLLS HAD IT PLANNED FROM THE START!
PICKNOSE KNEW HE COULD TRIGGER A CAVE-IN ANY TIME HE CHOSE!
BUT WHY, CUTTER?
THERE WAS NO NEED FOR THEM TO DO THIS!
NO NEED BUT --
-- REVENGE... FOR GREYMUNG'S INJURED PRIDE!
ONLY... I DIDN'T THINK HE WOULD GO SO FAR!
WHAT NOW, LAD...?
"WHAT NOW...?" CUTTER TURNS HIS FOREST DWELLER'S EYES TOWARD THE BLAZING, UNFAMILIAR SUN...
AND SILENCE IS THE ONLY ANSWER HE CAN GIVE.

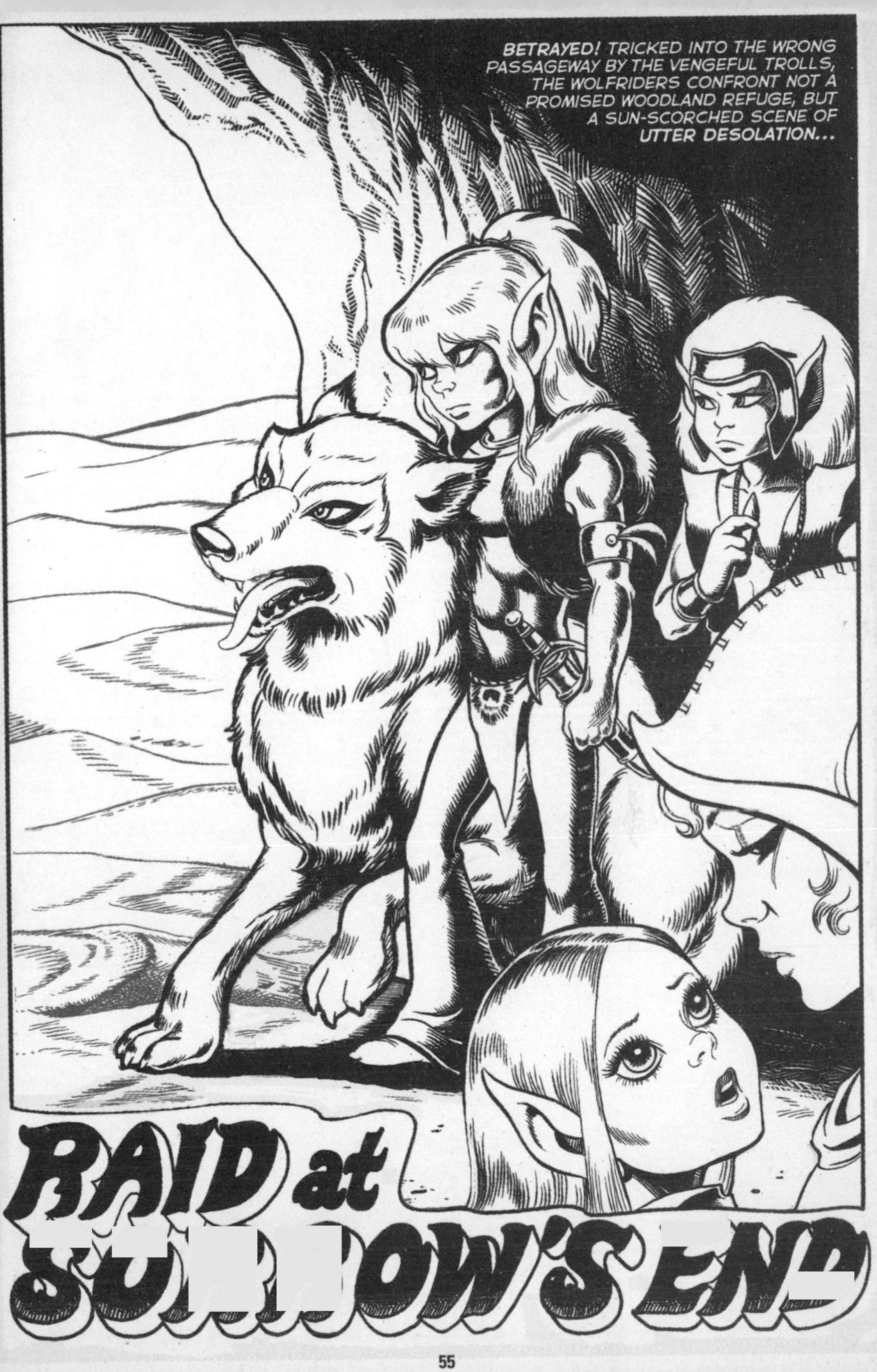
BETRAYED! TRICKED INTO THE WRONG PASSAGEWAY BY THE VENGEFUL TROLLS, THE WOLFRIDERS CONFRONT NOT A PROMISED WOODLAND REFUGE, BUT A SUN-SCORCHED SCENE OF UTTER DESOLATION...
RAID at

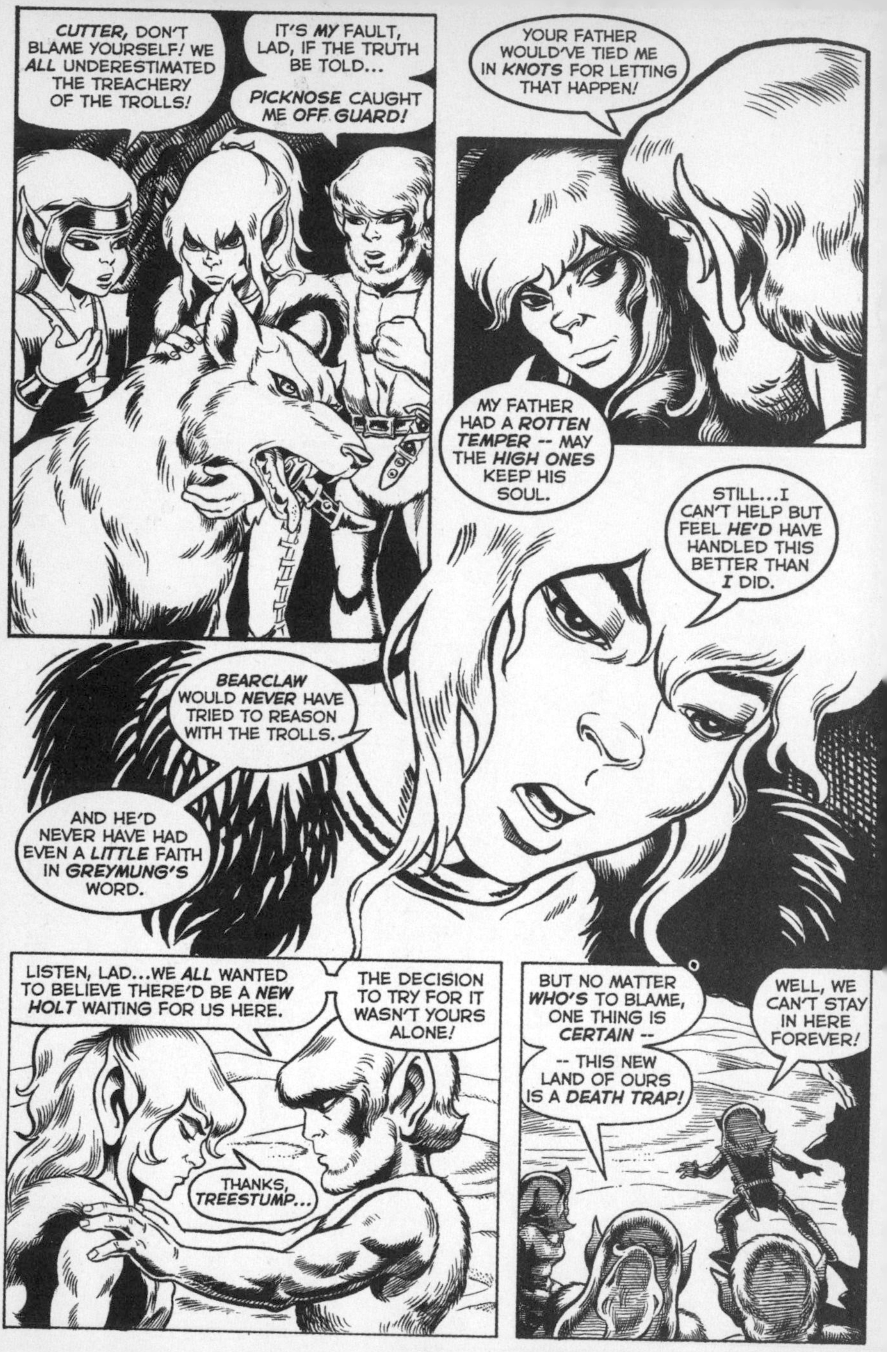

CUTTER, DON'T BLAME YOURSELF! WE ALL UNDERESTIMATED THE TREACHERY OF THE TROLLS!
IT'S MY FAULT, LAD, IF THE TRUTH BE TOLD...
PICKNOSE CAUGHT ME OFF GUARD!
YOUR FATHER WOULD'VE TIED ME IN KNOTS FOR LETTING THAT HAPPEN!
MY FATHER HAD A ROTTEN TEMPER -- MAY THE HIGH ONES KEEP HIS SOUL.
STILL...I CAN'T HELP BUT FEEL HE'D HAVE HANDLED THIS BETTER THAN I DID.
BEARCLAW WOULD NEVER HAVE TRIED TO REASON WITH THE TROLLS.
AND HE'D NEVER HAVE HAD EVEN A LITTLE FAITH IN GREYMUNG'S WORD.
LISTEN, LAD...WE ALL WANTED TO BELIEVE THERE'D BE A NEW HOLT WAITING FOR US HERE.
THE DECISION TO TRY FOR IT WASN'T YOURS ALONE!
THANKS, TREESTUMP...
BUT NO MATTER WHO'S TO BLAME, ONE THING IS CERTAIN --
-- THIS NEW LAND OF OURS IS A DEATH TRAP!
WELL, WE CAN'T STAY IN HERE FOREVER!

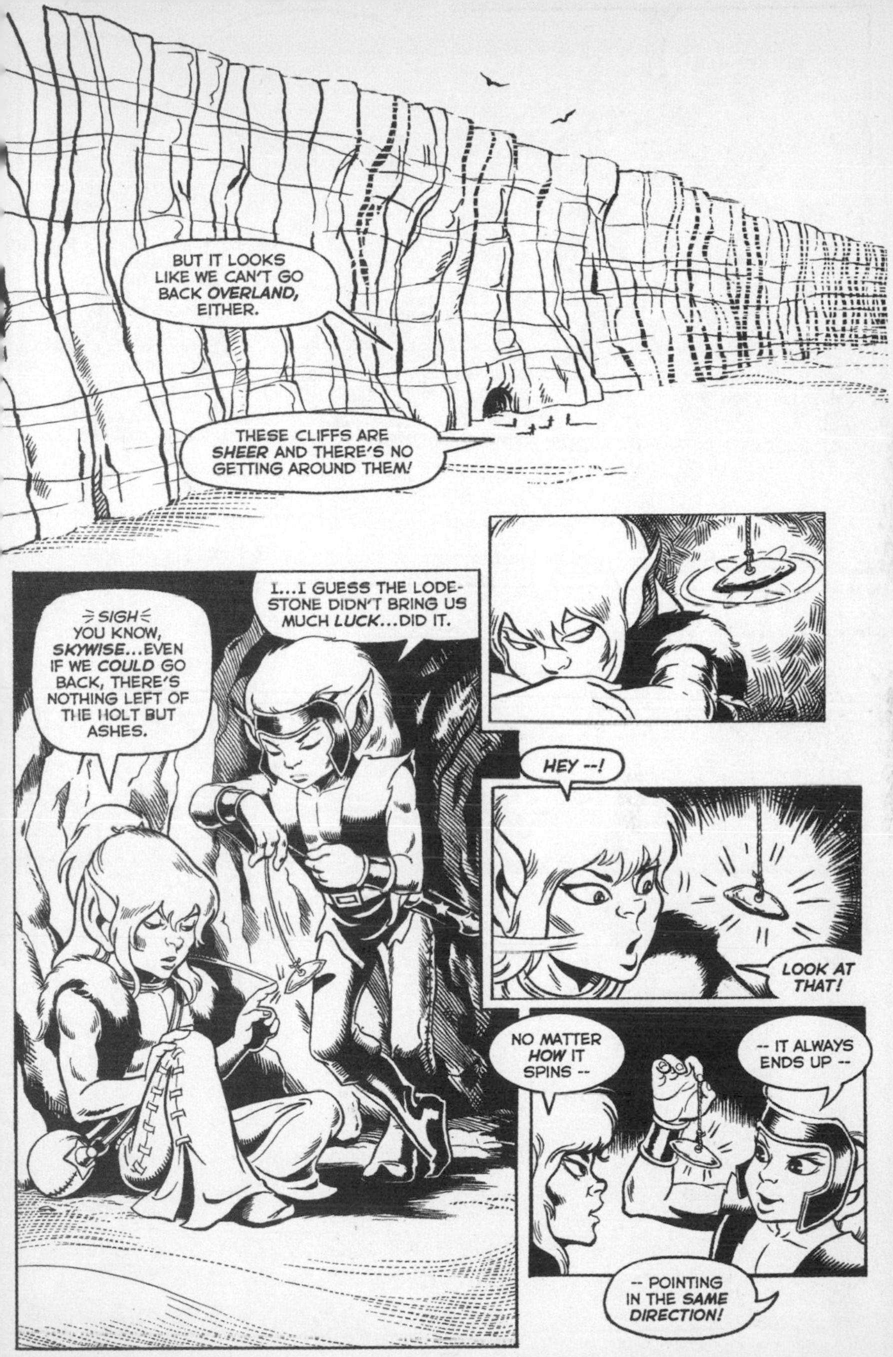
BUT IT LOOKS LIKE WE CAN'T GO BACK OVERLAND, EITHER.
THESE CLIFFS ARE SHEER AND THERE'S NO GETTING AROUND THEM!
SIGH YOU KNOW, SKYWISE...EVEN IF WE COULD GO BACK, THERE'S NOTHING LEFT OF THE HOLT BUT ASHES.
I...I GUESS THE LODE-STONE DIDN'T BRING US MUCH LUCK...DID IT.
HEY --!
LOOK AT THAT!
NO MATTER HOW IT SPINS --
-- IT ALWAYS ENDS UP --
-- POINTING IN THE SAME DIRECTION!

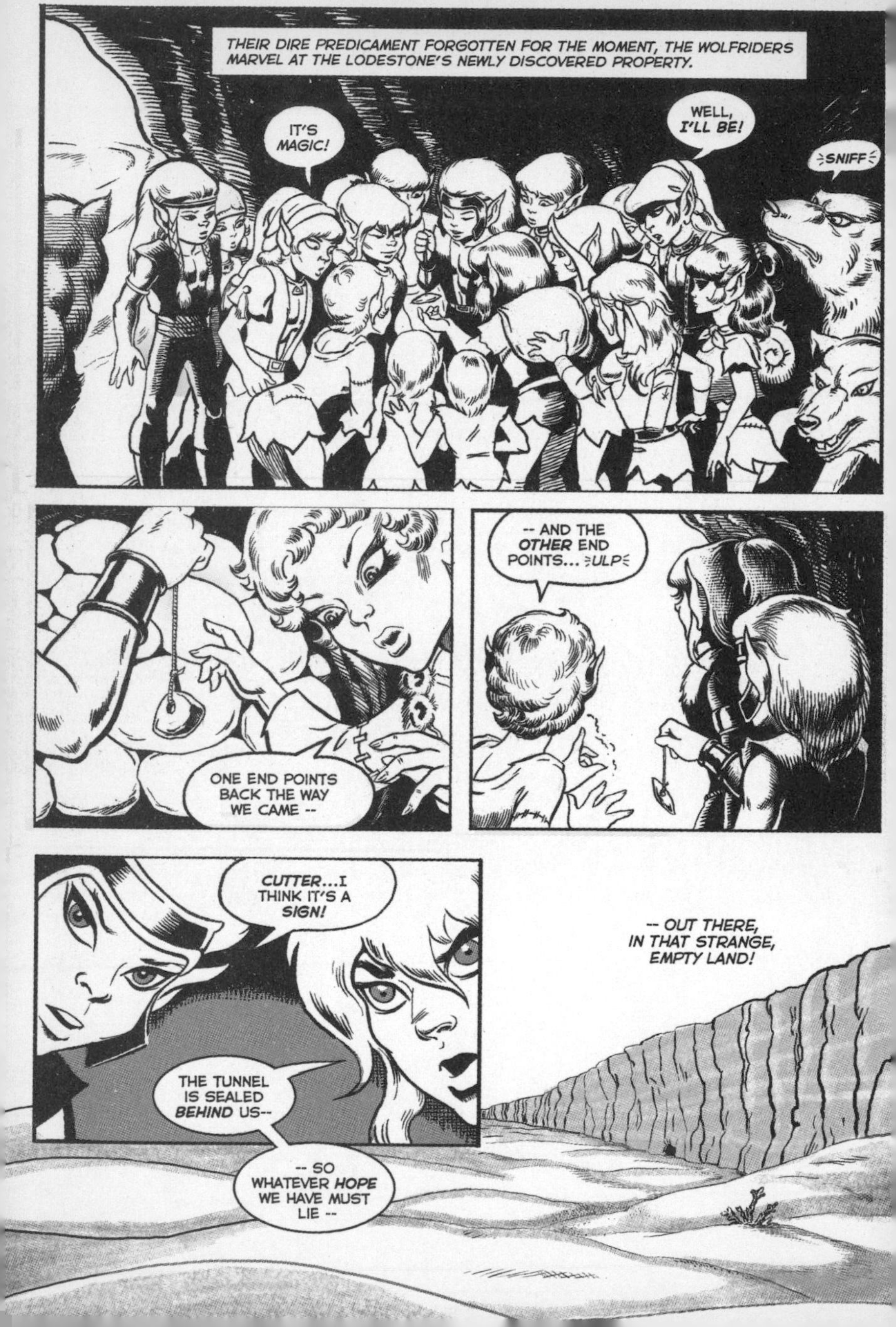
THEIR DIRE PREDICAMENT FORGOTTEN FOR THE MOMENT, THE WOLFRIDERS MARVEL AT THE LODESTONE'S NEWLY DISCOVERED PROPERTY.
IT'S MAGIC!
WELL, I'LL BE!
SNIFF
ONE END POINTS BACK THE WAY WE CAME --
-- AND THE OTHER END POINTS... ULP
CUTTER...I THINK IT'S A SIGN!
THE TUNNEL IS SEALED BEHIND US--
-- SO WHATEVER HOPE WE HAVE MUST LIE --
-- OUT THERE, IN THAT STRANGE, EMPTY LAND!

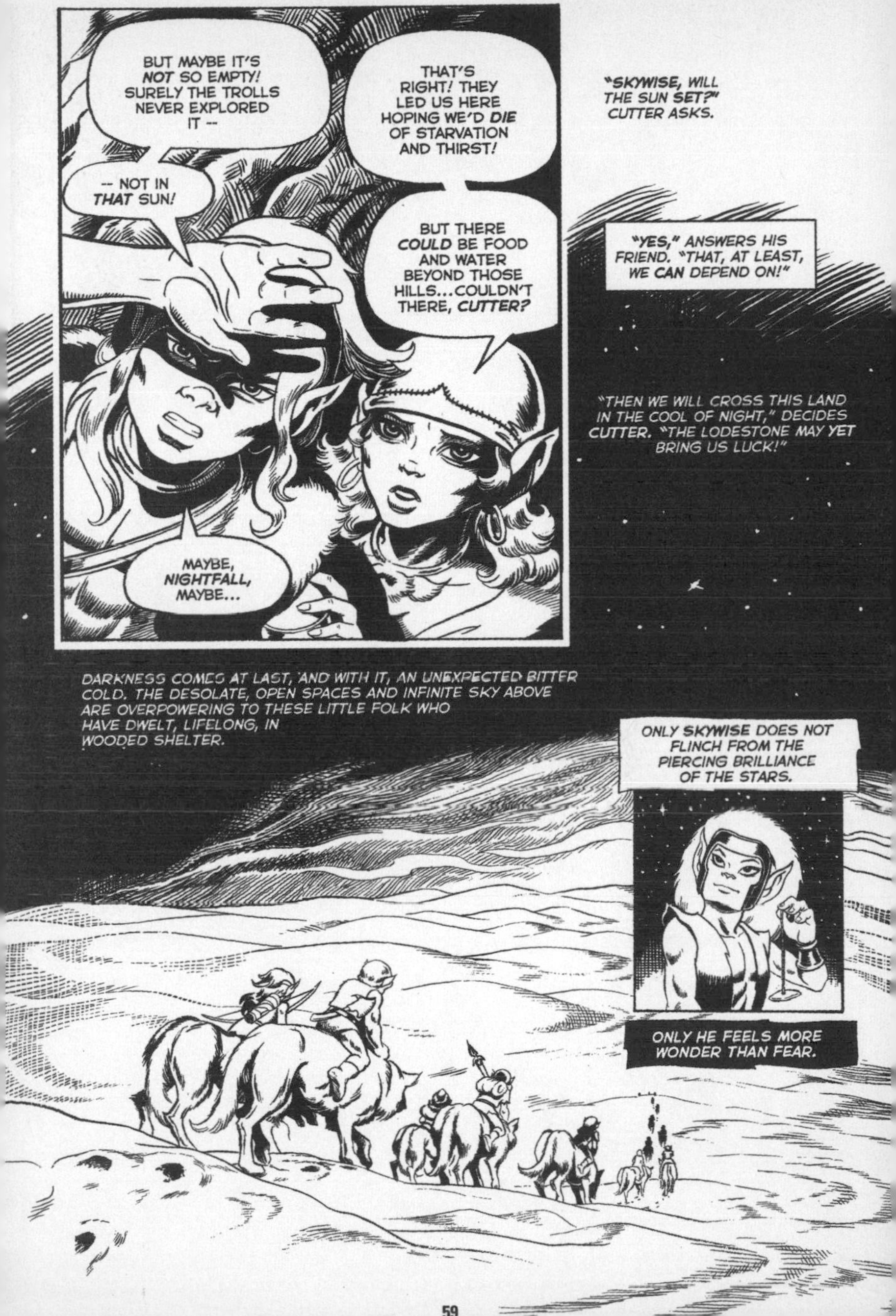

BUT MAYBE IT'S NOT SO EMPTY! SURELY THE TROLLS NEVER EXPLORED IT --
-- NOT IN THAT SUN!
THAT'S RIGHT! THEY LED US HERE HOPING WE'D DIE OF STARVATION AND THIRST!
BUT THERE COULD BE FOOD AND WATER BEYOND THOSE HILLS...COULDN'T THERE, CUTTER?
MAYBE, NIGHTFALL, MAYBE...
"SKYWISE, WILL THE SUN SET?" CUTTER ASKS.
"YES," ANSWERS HIS FRIEND. "THAT, AT LEAST, WE CAN DEPEND ON!"
"THEN WE WILL CROSS THIS LAND IN THE COOL OF NIGHT," DECIDES CUTTER. "THE LODESTONE MAY YET BRING US LUCK!"
DARKNESS COMES AT LAST, AND WITH IT, AN UNEXPECTED BITTER COLD. THE DESOLATE, OPEN SPACES AND INFINITE SKY ABOVE ARE OVERPOWERING TO THESE LITTLE FOLK WHO HAVE DWELT, LIFELONG, IN WOODED SHELTER.
ONLY SKYWISE DOES NOT FLINCH FROM THE PIERCING BRILLIANCE OF THE STARS.
ONLY HE FEELS MORE WONDER THAN FEAR.

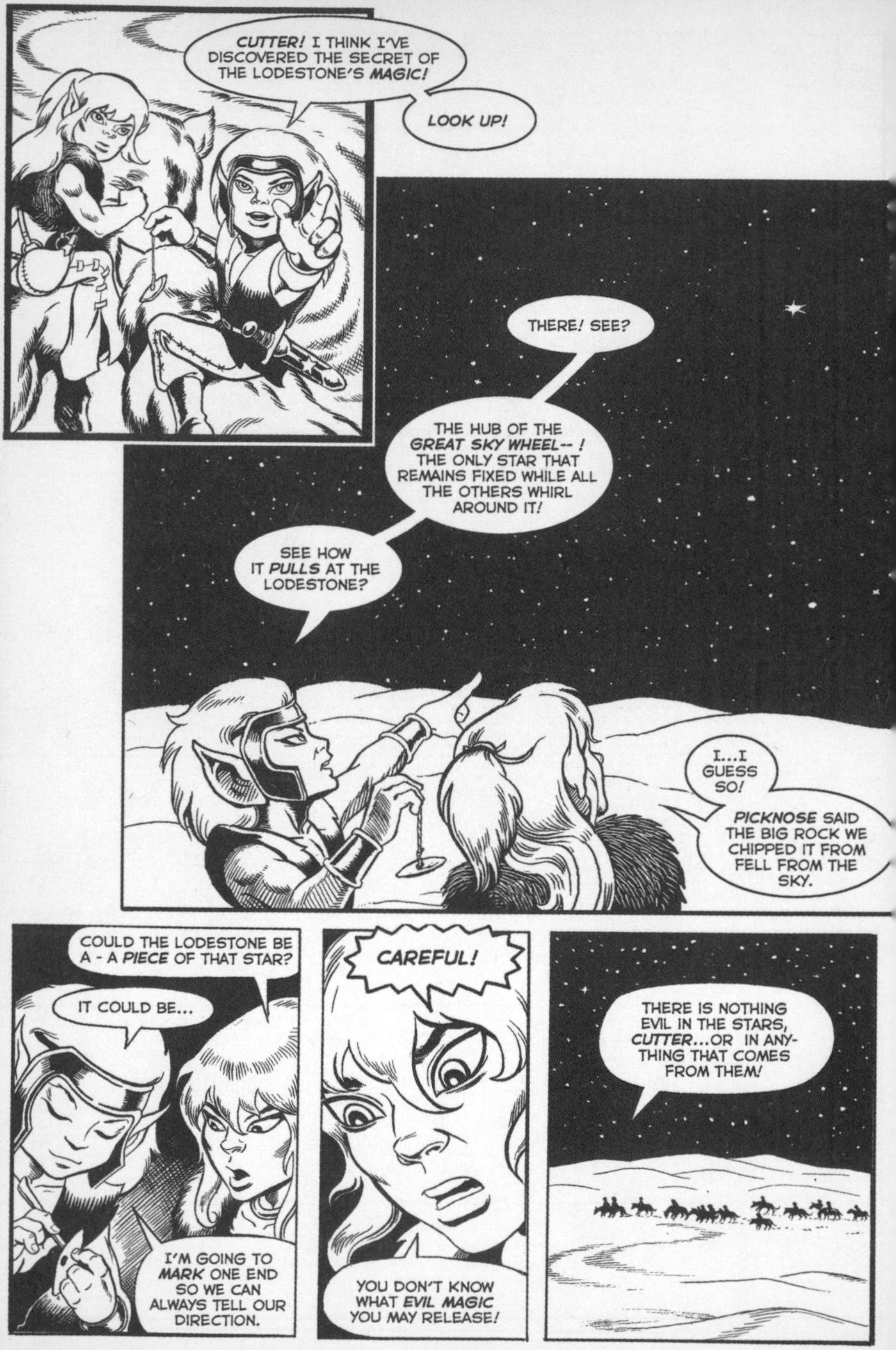
CUTTER! I THINK I'VE DISCOVERED THE SECRET OF THE LODESTONE'S MAGIC!
LOOK UP!
THERE! SEE?
THE HUB OF THE GREAT SKY WHEEL-- ! THE ONLY STAR THAT REMAINS FIXED WHILE ALL THE OTHERS WHIRL AROUND IT!
SEE HOW IT PULLS AT THE LODESTONE?
I...I GUESS SO!
PICKNOSE SAID THE BIG ROCK WE CHIPPED IT FROM FELL FROM THE SKY.
COULD THE LODESTONE BE A - A PIECE OF THAT STAR?
IT COULD BE...
I'M GOING TO MARK ONE END SO WE CAN ALWAYS TELL OUR DIRECTION.
CAREFUL!
YOU DON'T KNOW WHAT EVIL MAGIC YOU MAY RELEASE!
THERE IS NOTHING EVIL IN THE STARS, CUTTER...OR IN ANY-THING THAT COMES FROM THEM!

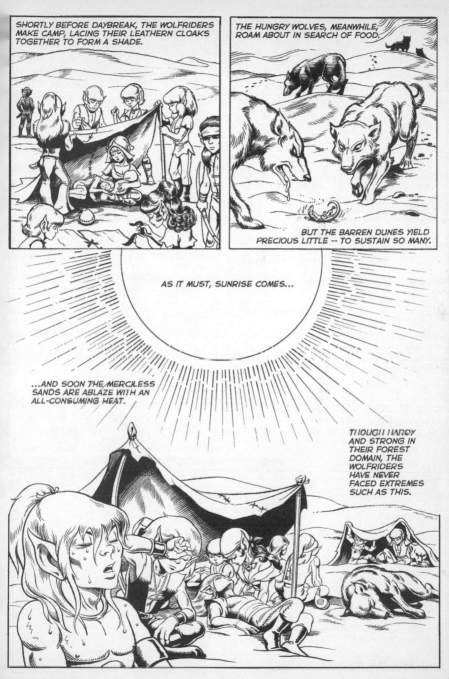

SHORTLY BEFORE DAYBREAK, THE WOLFRIDERS MAKE CAMP, LACING THEIR LEATHERN CLOAKS TOGETHER TO FORM A SHADE.

THE HUNGRY WOLVES, MEANWHILE, ROAM ABOUT IN SEARCH OF FOOD.

BUT THE BARREN DUNES YIELD PRECIOUS LITTLE -- TO SUSTAIN SO MANY.

AS IT MUST, SUNRISE COMES...

...AND SOON THE MERCILESS SANDS ARE ABLAZE WITH AN ALL-CONSUMING HEAT.

THOUGH HARDY AND STRONG IN THEIR FOREST DOMAIN, THE WOLFRIDERS HAVE NEVER FACED EXTREMES SUCH AS THIS.

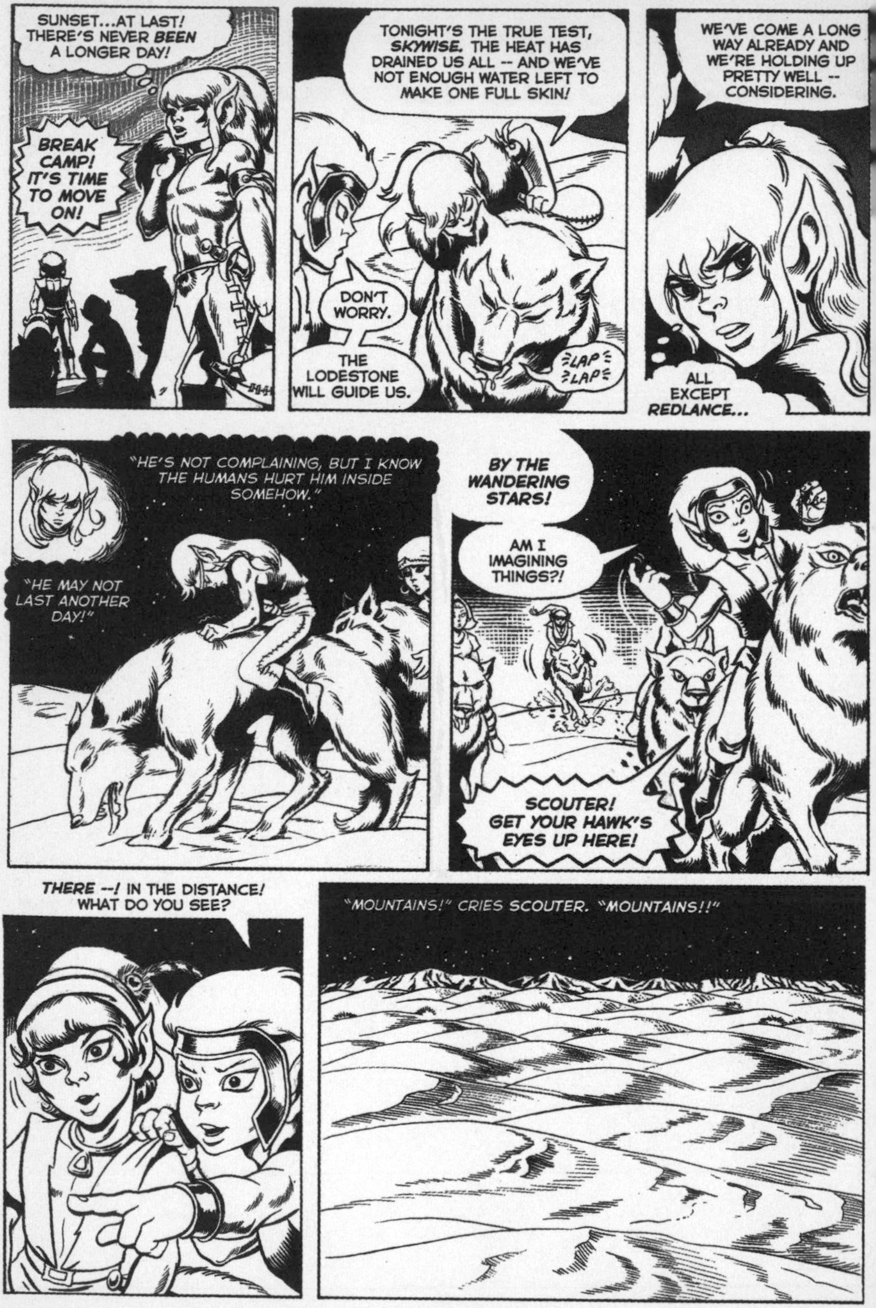
SUNSET...AT LAST! THERE'S NEVER BEEN A LONGER DAY!
BREAK CAMP! IT'S TIME TO MOVE ON!
TONIGHT'S THE TRUE TEST, SKYWISE. THE HEAT HAS DRAINED US ALL -- AND WE'VE NOT ENOUGH WATER LEFT TO MAKE ONE FULL SKIN!
DON'T WORRY.
THE LODESTONE WILL GUIDE US.
LAP LAP
WE'VE COME A LONG WAY ALREADY AND WE'RE HOLDING UP PRETTY WELL -- CONSIDERING.
ALL EXCEPT REDLANCE...
"HE'S NOT COMPLAINING, BUT I KNOW THE HUMANS HURT HIM INSIDE SOMEHOW."
"HE MAY NOT LAST ANOTHER DAY!"
BY THE WANDERING STARS!
AM I IMAGINING THINGS?!
SCOUTER! GET YOUR HAWK'S EYES UP HERE!
THERE --! IN THE DISTANCE! WHAT DO YOU SEE?
"MOUNTAINS!" CRIES SCOUTER. "MOUNTAINS!!"

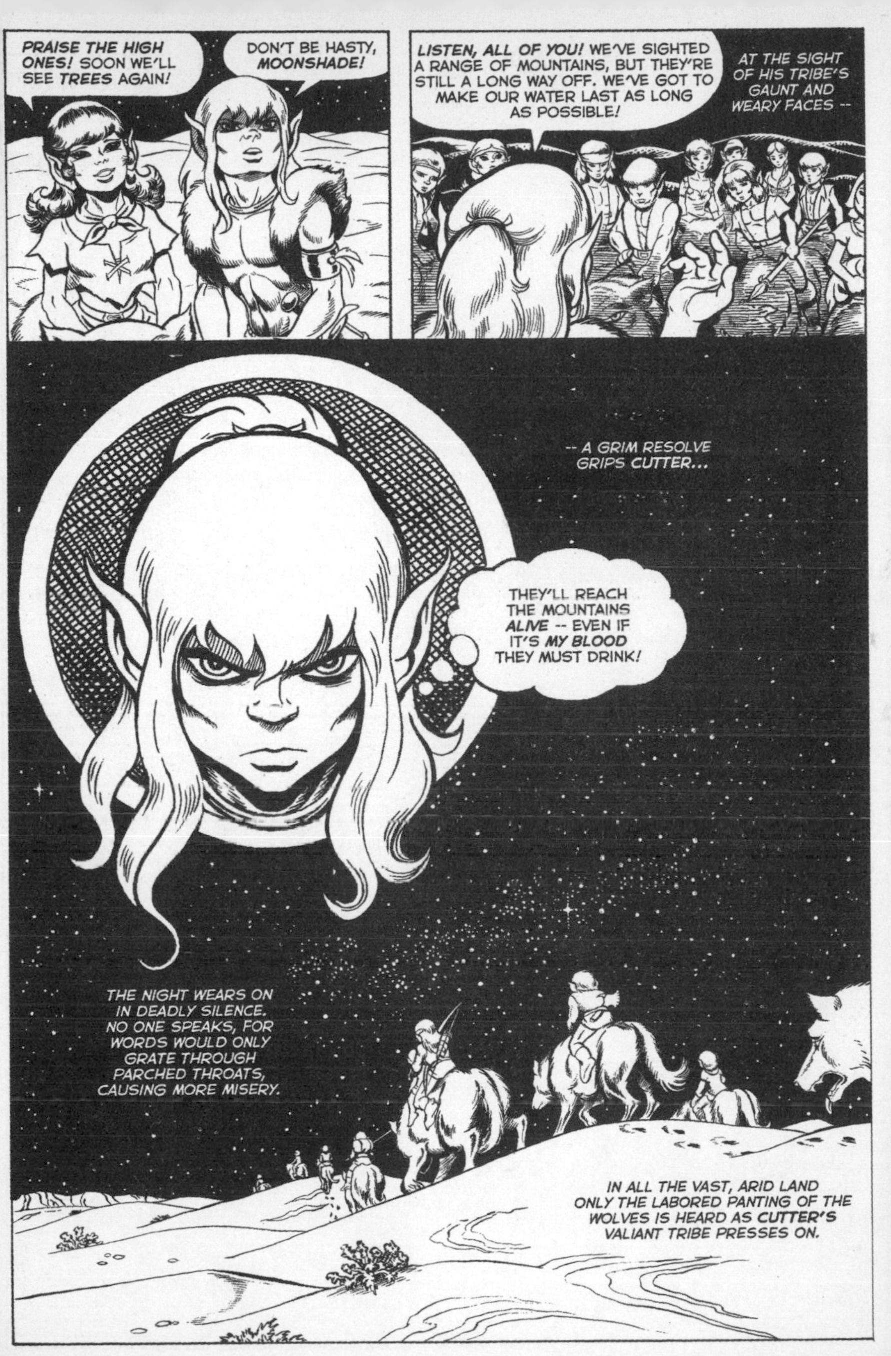
PRAISE THE HIGH ONES! SOON WE'LL SEE TREES AGAIN!
DON'T BE HASTY, MOONSHADE!
LISTEN, ALL OF YOU! WE'VE SIGHTED A RANGE OF MOUNTAINS, BUT THEY'RE STILL A LONG WAY OFF. WE'VE GOT TO MAKE OUR WATER LAST AS LONG AS POSSIBLE!
AT THE SIGHT OF HIS TRIBE'S GAUNT AND WEARY FACES --
-- A GRIM RESOLVE GRIPS CUTTER...
THEY'LL REACH THE MOUNTAINS ALIVE -- EVEN IF IT'S MY BLOOD THEY MUST DRINK!
THE NIGHT WEARS ON IN DEADLY SILENCE. NO ONE SPEAKS, FOR WORDS WOULD ONLY GRATE THROUGH PARCHED THROATS, CAUSING MORE MISERY.
IN ALL THE VAST, ARID LAND ONLY THE LABORED PANTING OF THE WOLVES IS HEARD AS CUTTER'S VALIANT TRIBE PRESSES ON.

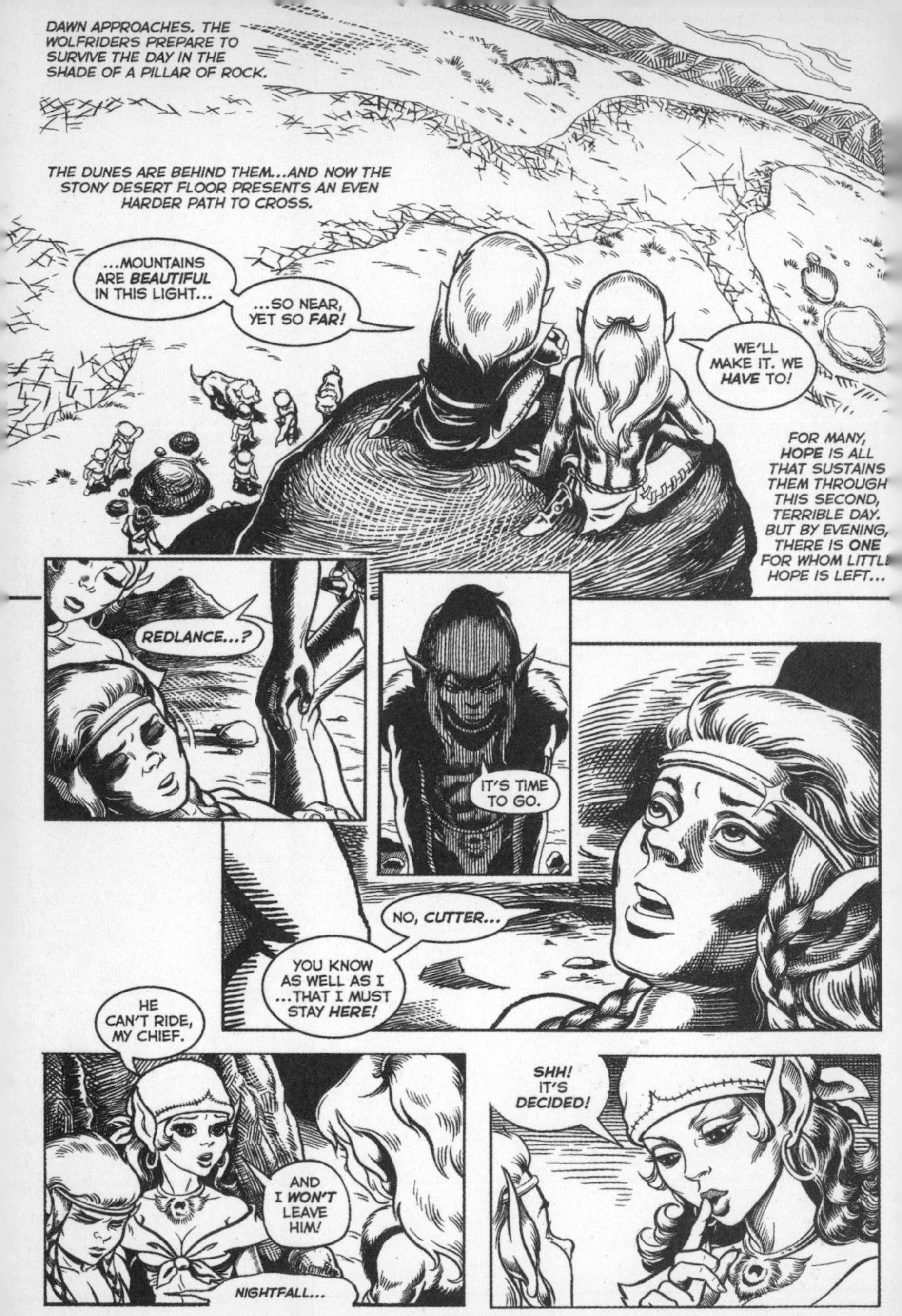
DAWN APPROACHES. THE WOLFRIDERS PREPARE TO SURVIVE THE DAY IN THE SHADE OF A PILLAR OF ROCK.
THE DUNES ARE BEHIND THEM...AND NOW THE STONY DESERT FLOOR PRESENTS AN EVEN HARDER PATH TO CROSS.
...MOUNTAINS ARE BEAUTIFUL IN THIS LIGHT...
...SO NEAR, YET SO FAR!
WE'LL MAKE IT. WE HAVE TO!
FOR MANY, HOPE IS ALL THAT SUSTAINS THEM THROUGH THIS SECOND, TERRIBLE DAY. BUT BY EVENING, THERE IS ONE FOR WHOM LITTLE HOPE IS LEFT...
REDLANCE...?
IT'S TIME TO GO.
NO, CUTTER...
YOU KNOW AS WELL AS I ...THAT I MUST STAY HERE!
HE CAN'T RIDE, MY CHIEF.
AND I WON'T LEAVE HIM!
NIGHTFALL...
SHH! IT'S DECIDED!

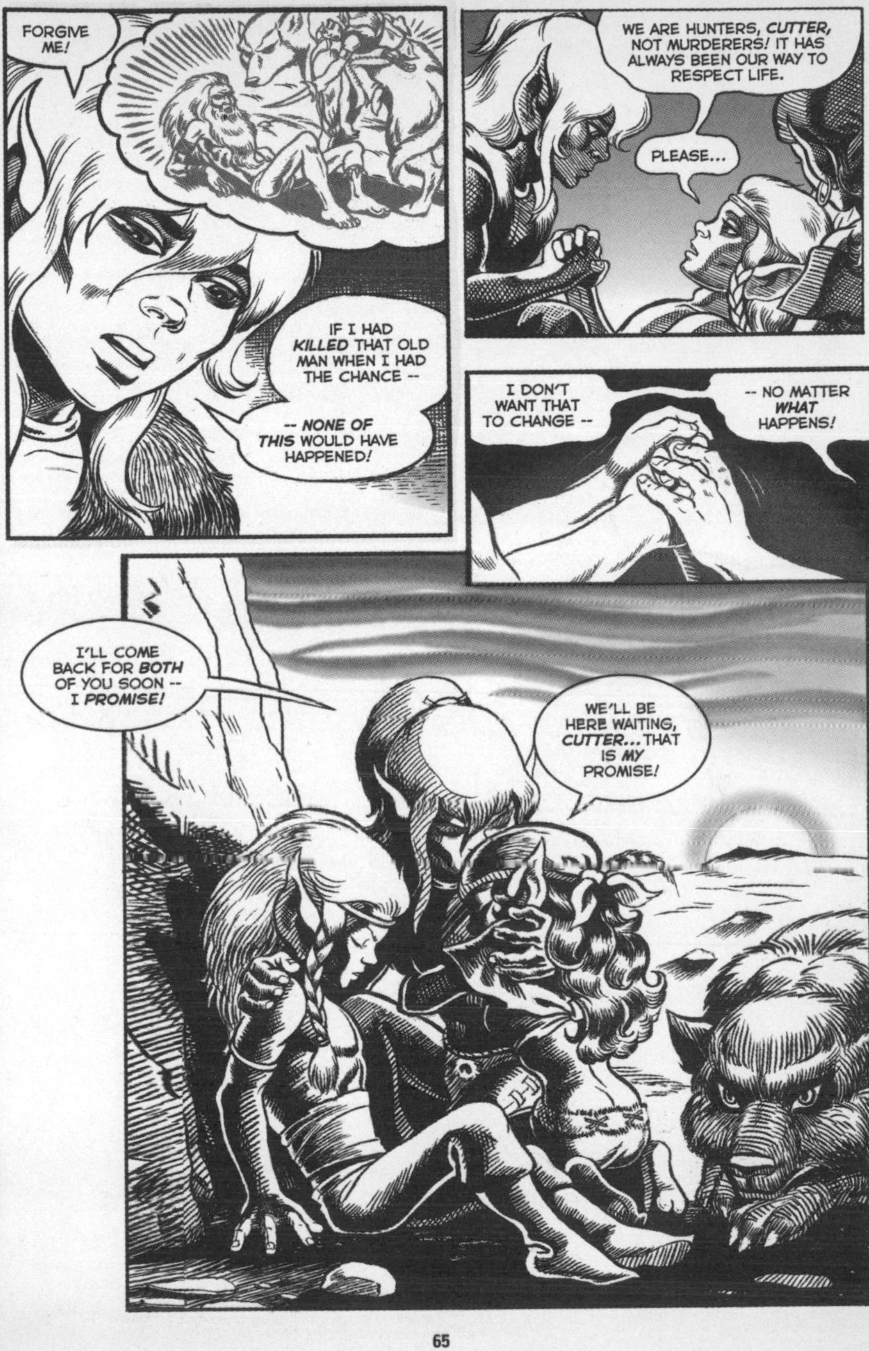
FORGIVE ME!
IF I HAD KILLED THAT OLD MAN WHEN I HAD THE CHANCE --
-- NONE OF THIS WOULD HAVE HAPPENED!
WE ARE HUNTERS, CUTTER, NOT MURDERERS! IT HAS ALWAYS BEEN OUR WAY TO RESPECT LIFE.
PLEASE...
I DON'T WANT THAT TO CHANGE --
-- NO MATTER WHAT HAPPENS!
I'LL COME BACK FOR BOTH OF YOU SOON -- I PROMISE!
WE'LL BE HERE WAITING, CUTTER... THAT IS MY PROMISE!

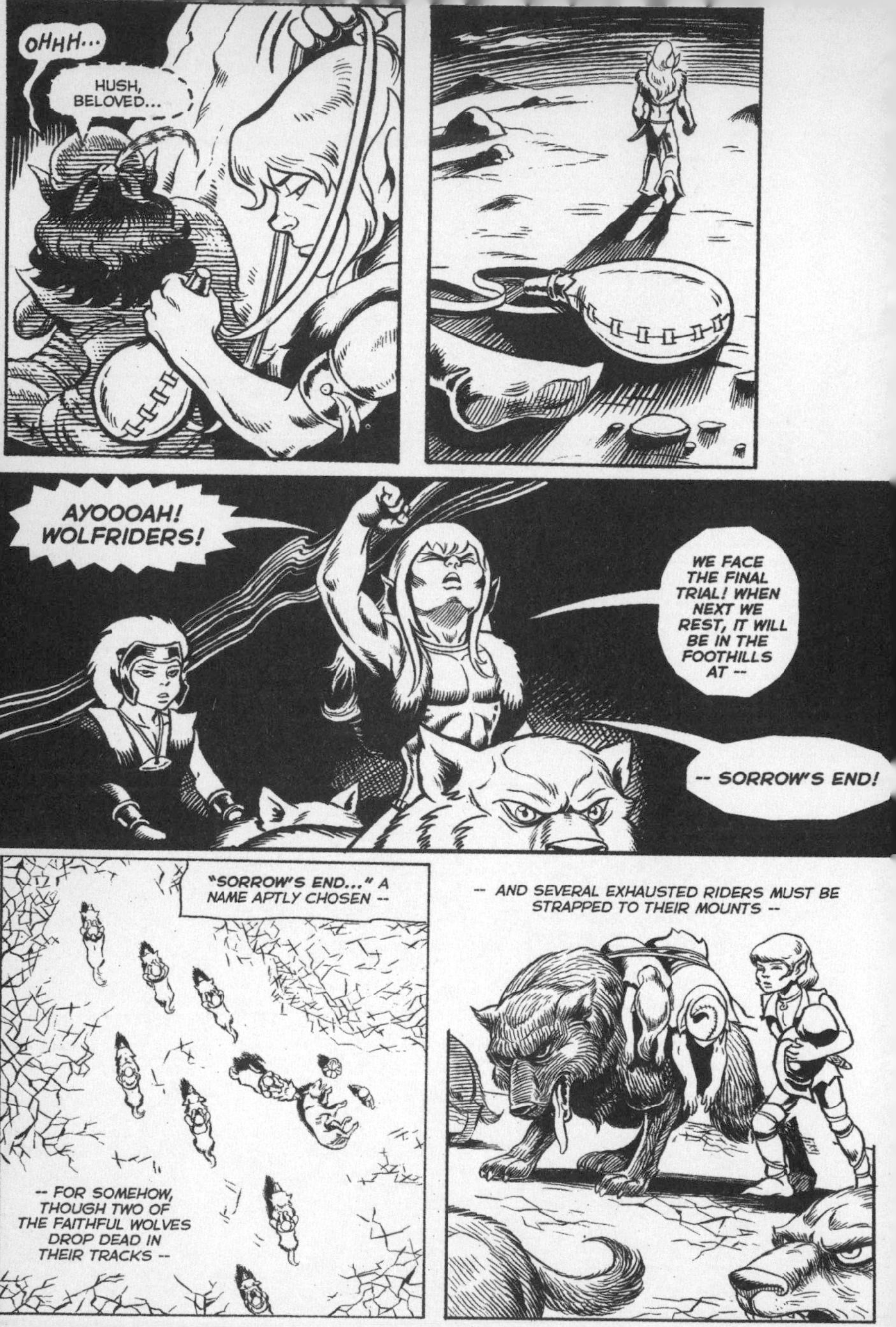
OHHH...
HUSH, BELOVED...
AYOOOAH! WOLFRIDERS!
WE FACE THE FINAL TRIAL! WHEN NEXT WE REST, IT WILL BE IN THE FOOTHILLS AT --
-- SORROW'S END!
"SORROW'S END..." A NAME APTLY CHOSEN --
-- FOR SOMEHOW, THOUGH TWO OF THE FAITHFUL WOLVES DROP DEAD IN THEIR TRACKS --
-- AND SEVERAL EXHAUSTED RIDERS MUST BE STRAPPED TO THEIR MOUNTS --

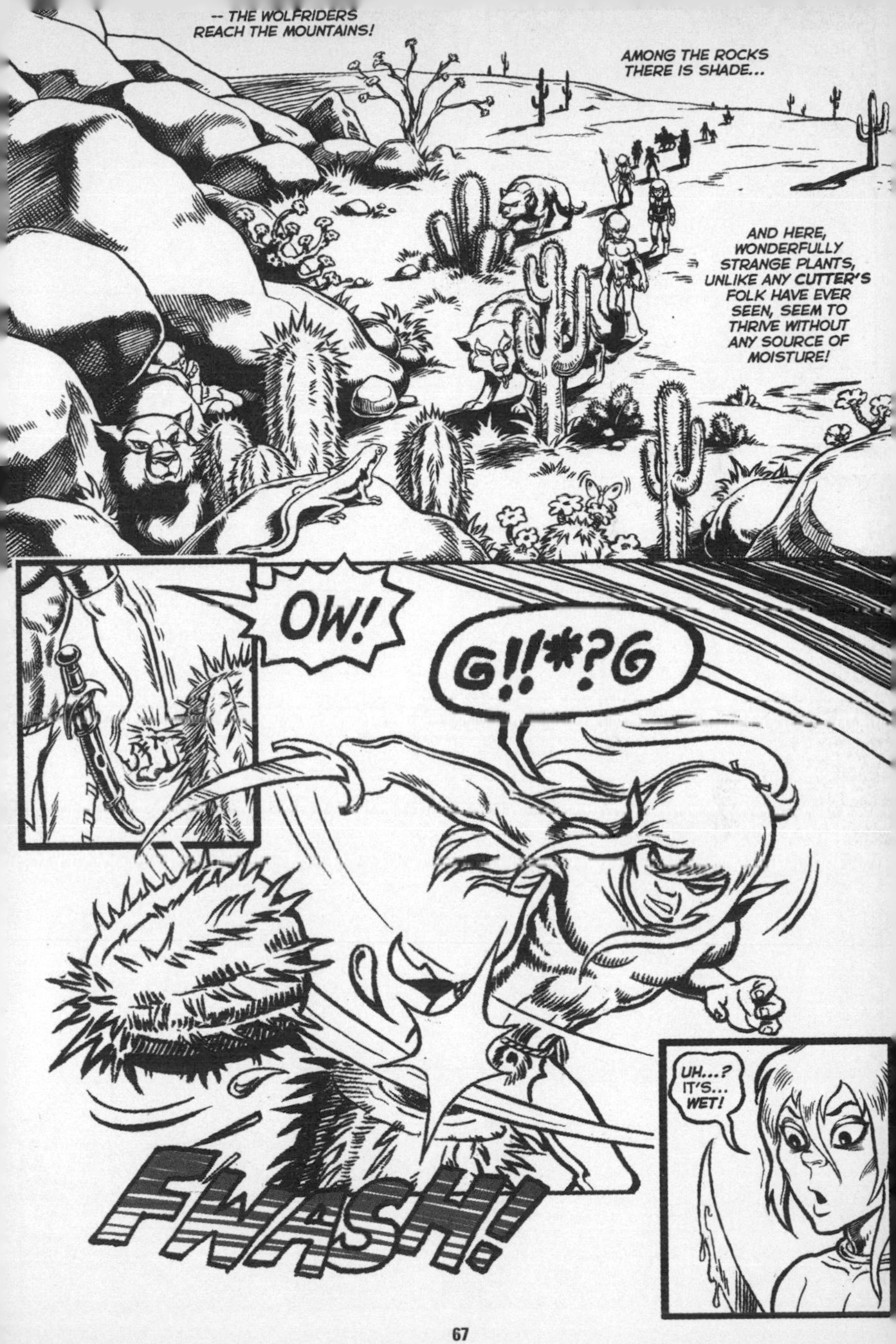

-- THE WOLFRIDERS REACH THE MOUNTAINS!
AMONG THE ROCKS THERE IS SHADE...
AND HERE, WONDERFULLY STRANGE PLANTS, UNLIKE ANY CUTTER'S FOLK HAVE EVER SEEN, SEEM TO THRIVE WITHOUT ANY SOURCE OF MOISTURE!
OW!
G!!*?G
FWASH!
UH...? IT'S... WET!

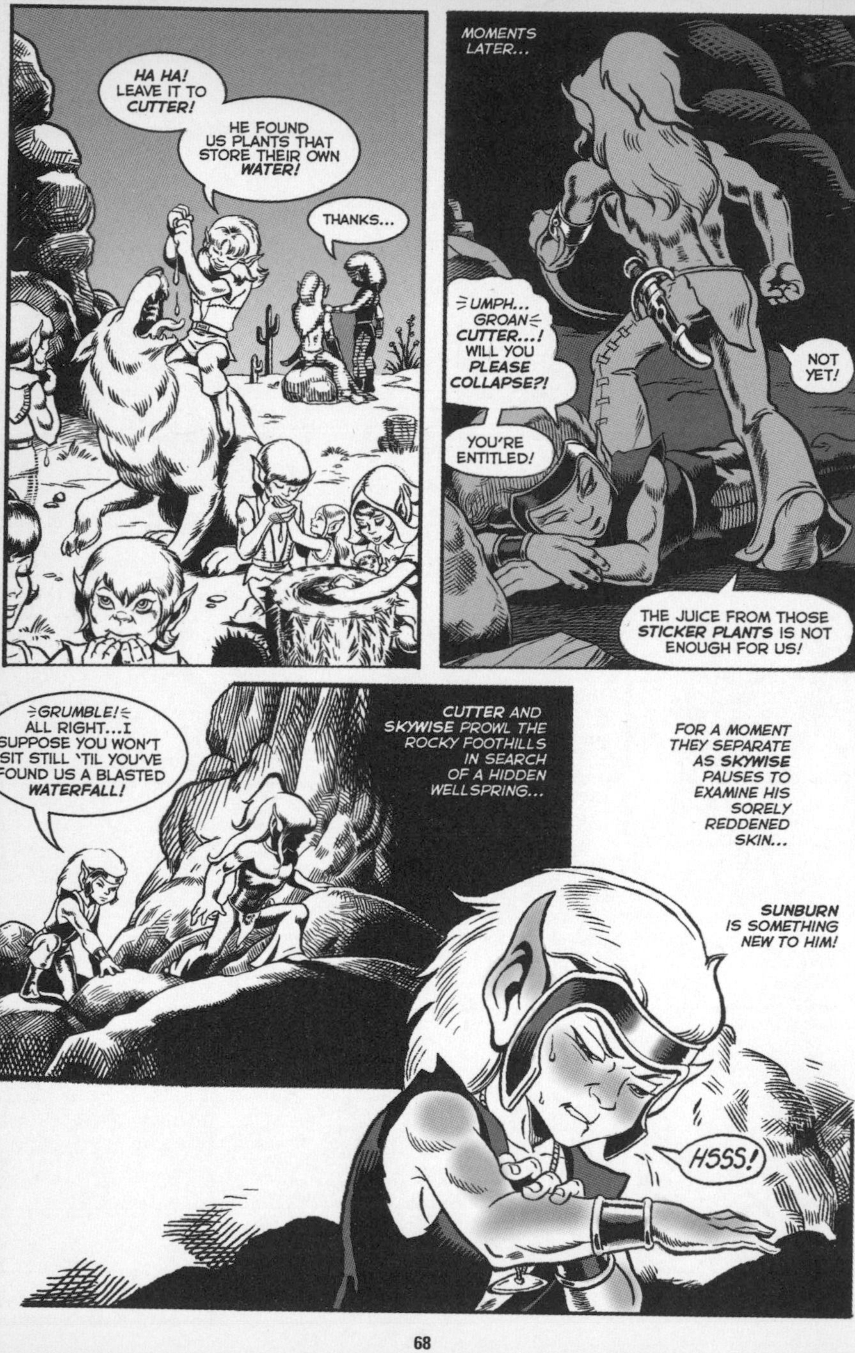
HA HA! LEAVE IT TO CUTTER!
HE FOUND US PLANTS THAT STORE THEIR OWN WATER!
THANKS...
MOMENTS LATER...
UMPH... GROAN CUTTER...! WILL YOU PLEASE COLLAPSE?!
NOT YET!
YOU'RE ENTITLED!
THE JUICE FROM THOSE STICKER PLANTS IS NOT ENOUGH FOR US!
GRUMBLE! ALL RIGHT...I SUPPOSE YOU WON'T SIT STILL 'TIL YOU'VE FOUND US A BLASTED WATERFALL!
CUTTER AND SKYWISE PROWL THE ROCKY FOOTHILLS IN SEARCH OF A HIDDEN WELLSPRING...
FOR A MOMENT THEY SEPARATE AS SKYWISE PAUSES TO EXAMINE HIS SORELY REDDENED SKIN...
SUNBURN IS SOMETHING NEW TO HIM!
HSSS!

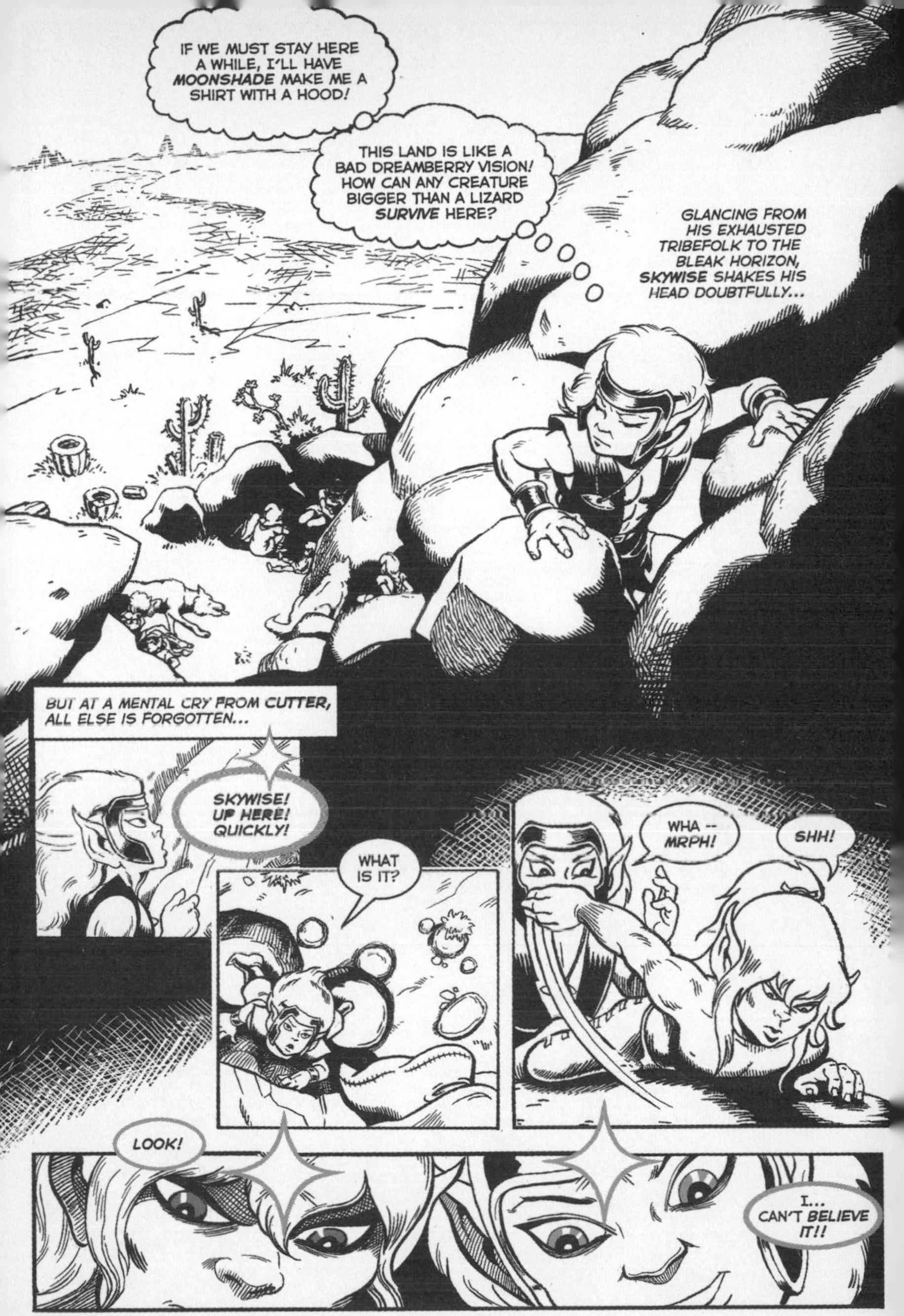

IF WE MUST STAY HERE A WHILE, I'LL HAVE MOONSHADE MAKE ME A SHIRT WITH A HOOD!
THIS LAND IS LIKE A BAD DREAMBERRY VISION! HOW CAN ANY CREATURE BIGGER THAN A LIZARD SURVIVE HERE?
GLANCING FROM HIS EXHAUSTED TRIBEFOLK TO THE BLEAK HORIZON, SKYWISE SHAKES HIS HEAD DOUBTFULLY...
BUT AT A MENTAL CRY FROM CUTTER, ALL ELSE IS FORGOTTEN...
SKYWISE! UP HERE! QUICKLY!
WHAT IS IT?
WHA -- MRPH!
SHH!
LOOK!
I... CAN'T BELIEVE IT!!

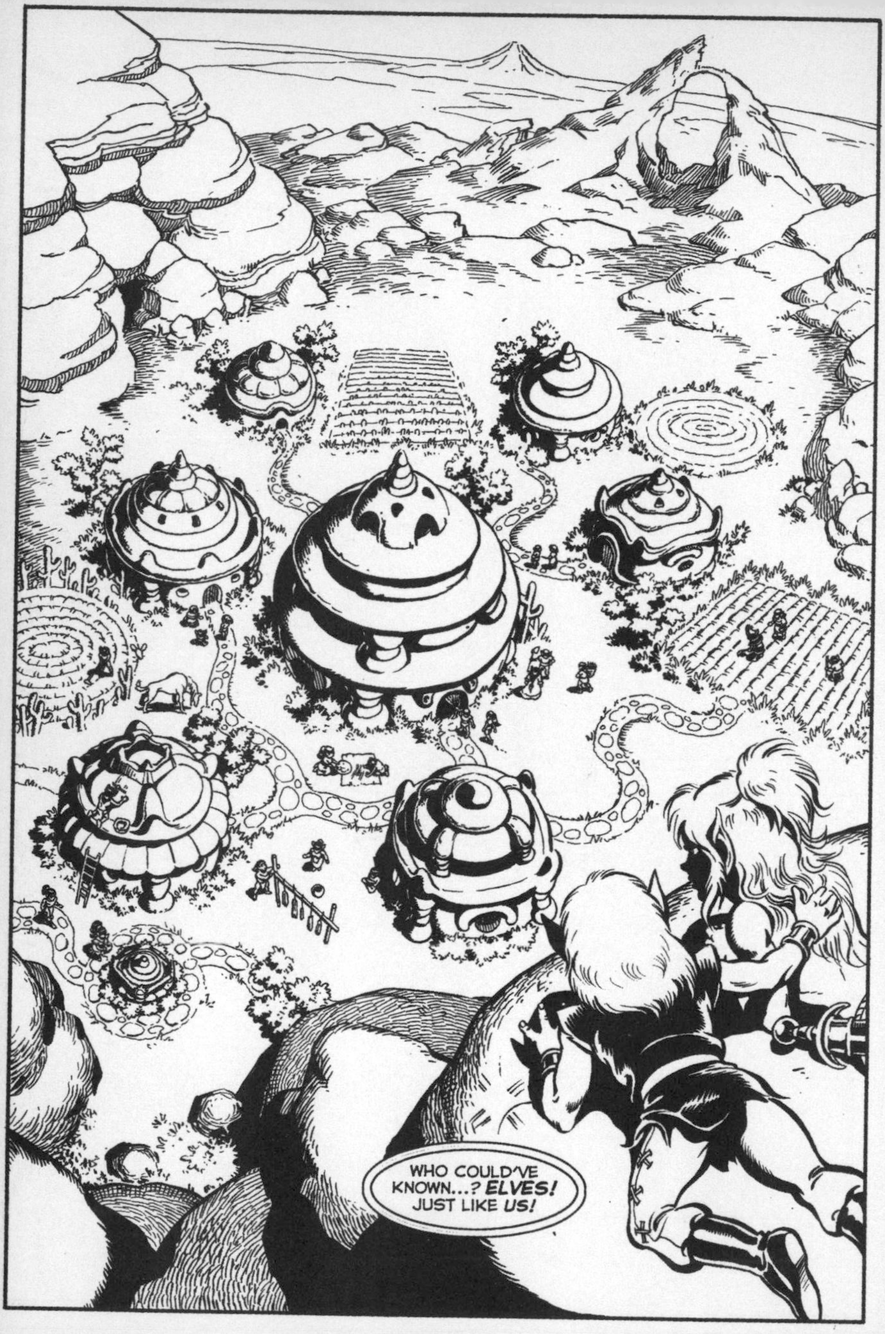
WHO COULD'VE KNOWN...? ELVES! JUST LIKE US!

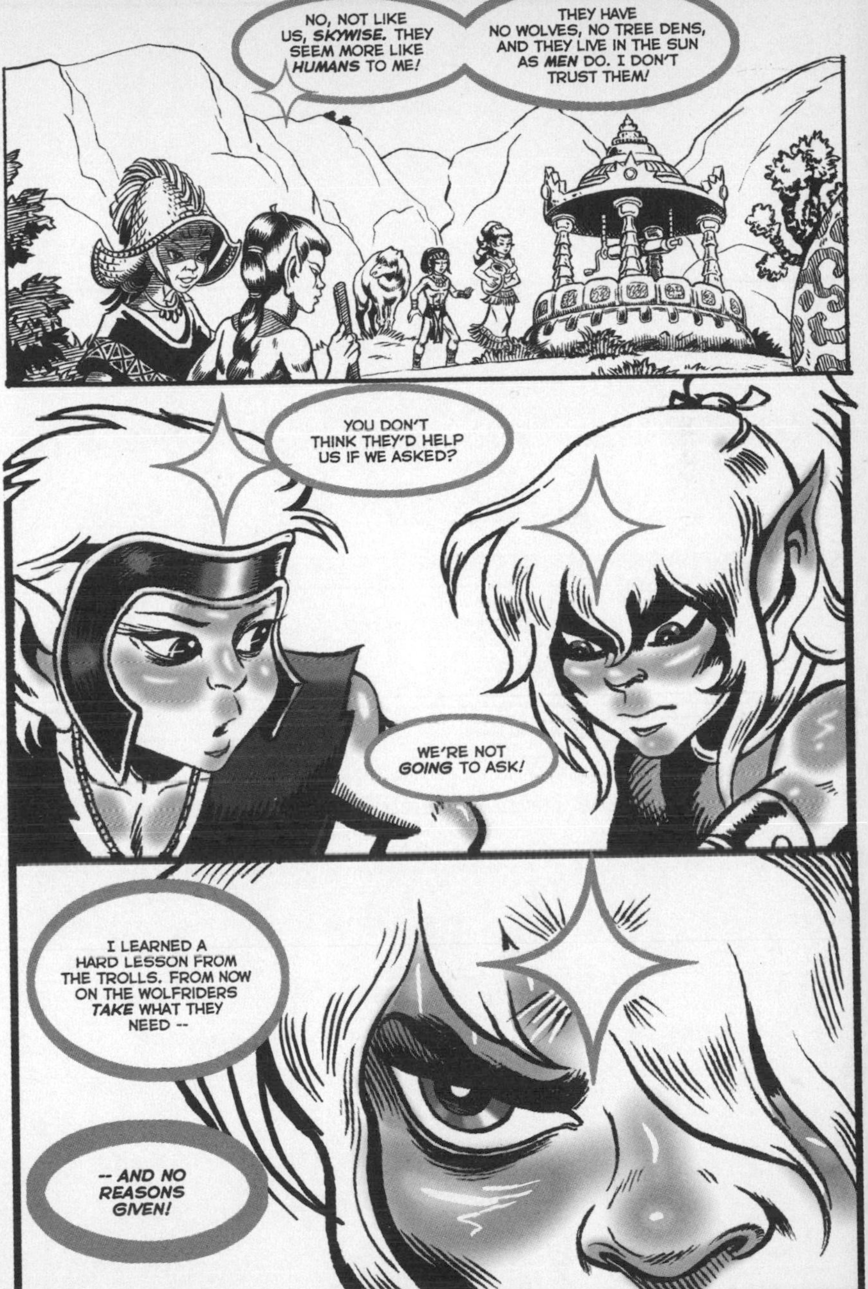
NO, NOT LIKE US, SKYWISE. THEY SEEM MORE LIKE HUMANS TO ME!
THEY HAVE NO WOLVES, NO TREE DENS, AND THEY LIVE IN THE SUN AS MEN DO. I DON'T TRUST THEM!
YOU DON'T THINK THEY'D HELP US IF WE ASKED?
WE'RE NOT GOING TO ASK!
I LEARNED A HARD LESSON FROM THE TROLLS. FROM NOW ON THE WOLFRIDERS TAKE WHAT THEY NEED --
-- AND NO REASONS GIVEN!

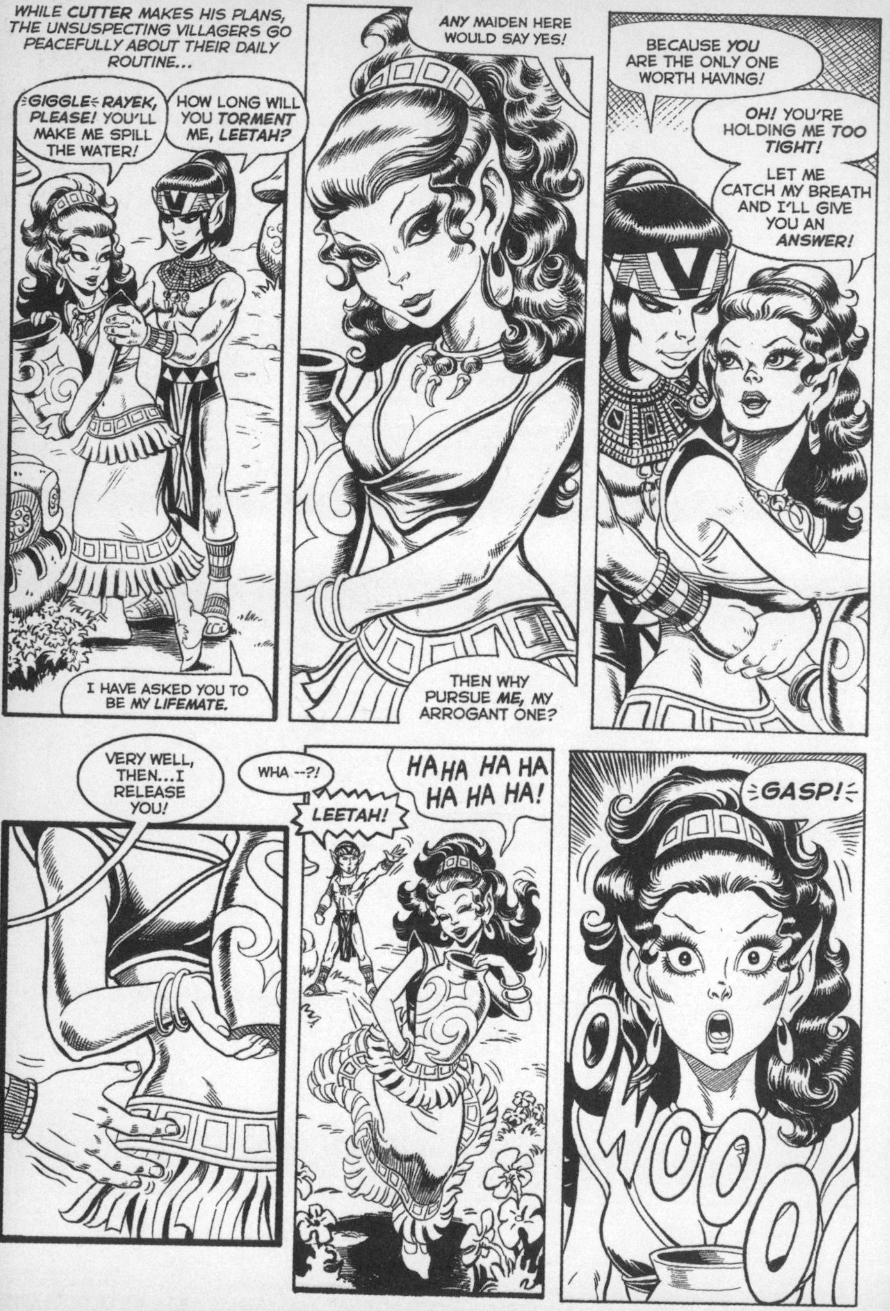
WHILE CUTTER MAKES HIS PLANS, THE UNSUSPECTING VILLAGERS GO PEACEFULLY ABOUT THEIR DAILY ROUTINE...
GIGGLE RAYEK, PLEASE! YOU'LL MAKE ME SPILL THE WATER!
HOW LONG WILL YOU TORMENT ME, LEETAH?
I HAVE ASKED YOU TO BE MY LIFEMATE.
ANY MAIDEN HERE WOULD SAY YES!
THEN WHY PURSUE ME, MY ARROGANT ONE?
BECAUSE YOU ARE THE ONLY ONE WORTH HAVING!
OH! YOU'RE HOLDING ME TOO TIGHT!
LET ME CATCH MY BREATH AND I'LL GIVE YOU AN ANSWER!
VERY WELL, THEN...I RELEASE YOU!
WHA --?!
LEETAH!
HA HA HA HA HA HA HA!
GASP!
WOOOO

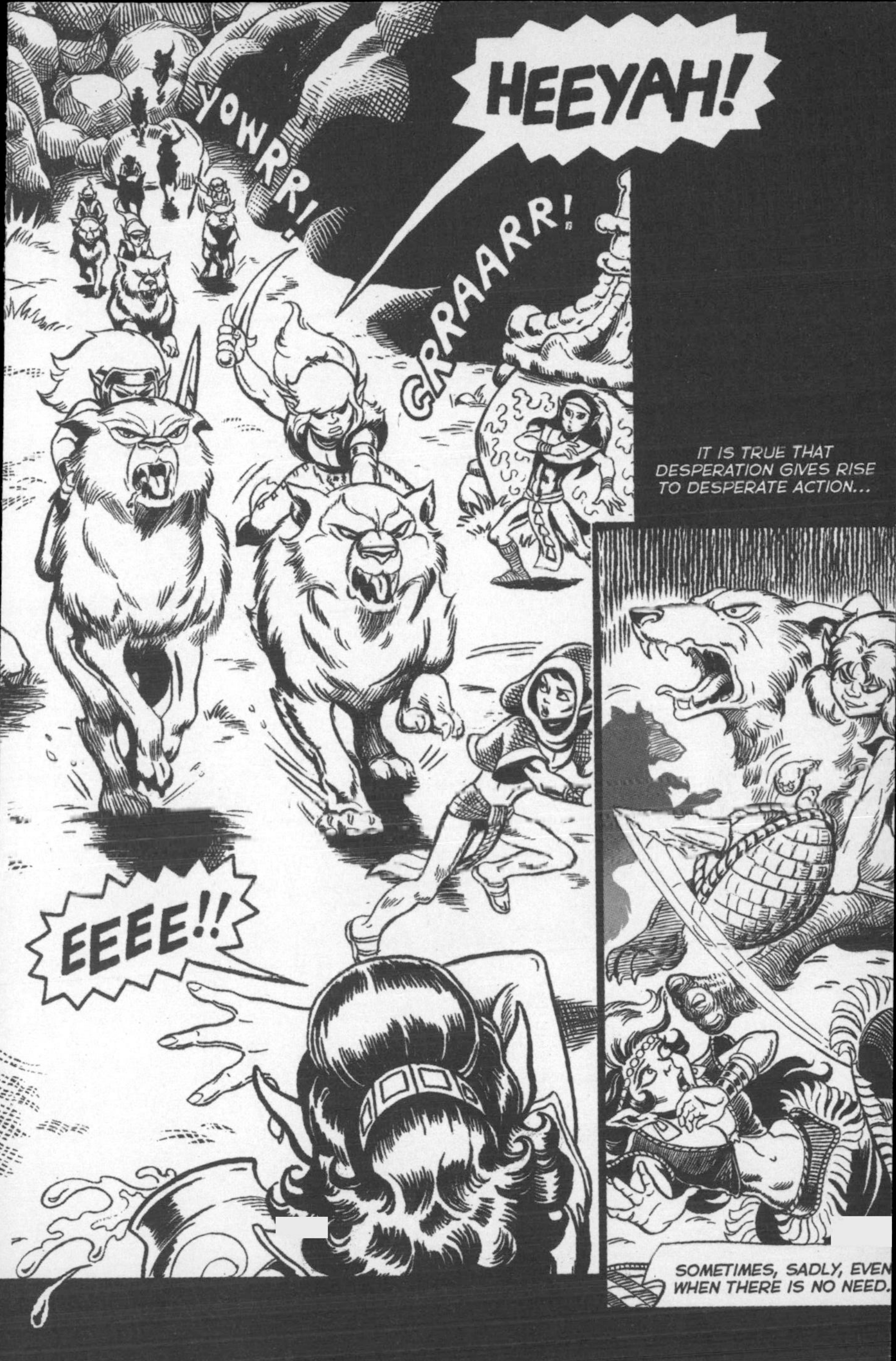
YOWRRR!
HEEYAH!
GRRAARR!
IT IS TRUE THAT DESPERATION GIVES RISE TO DESPERATE ACTION...
EEEE!!
SOMETIMES, SADLY, EVEN WHEN THERE IS NO NEED.

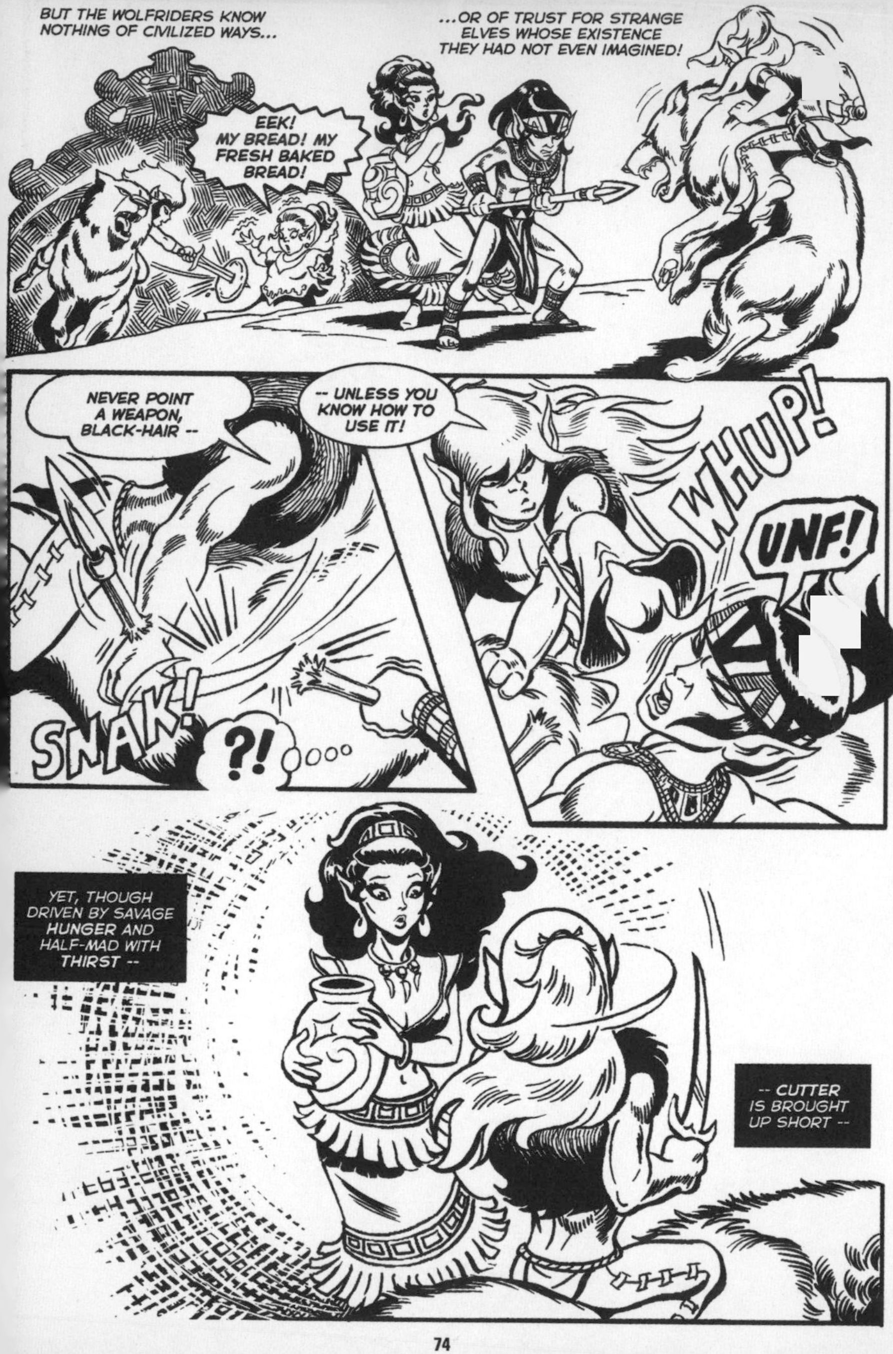

BUT THE WOLFRIDERS KNOW NOTHING OF CIVILIZED WAYS...
...OR OF TRUST FOR STRANGE ELVES WHOSE EXISTENCE THEY HAD NOT EVEN IMAGINED!
EEK! MY BREAD! MY FRESH BAKED BREAD!
NEVER POINT A WEAPON, BLACK-HAIR --
-- UNLESS YOU KNOW HOW TO USE IT!
SNAK!
?!
WHUP!
UNF!
YET, THOUGH DRIVEN BY SAVAGE HUNGER AND HALF-MAD WITH THIRST --
-- CUTTER IS BROUGHT UP SHORT --

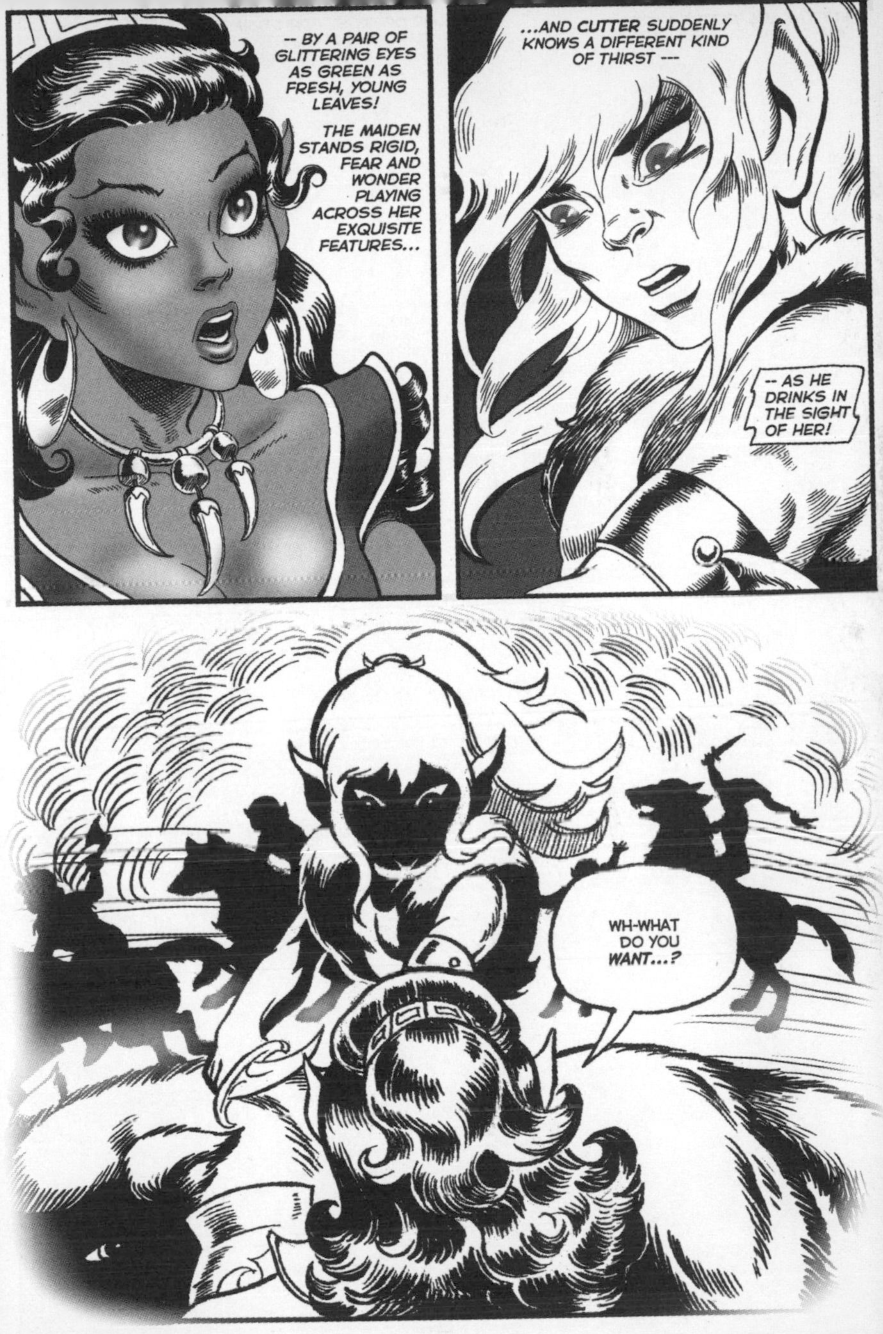
-- BY A PAIR OF GLITTERING EYES AS GREEN AS FRESH, YOUNG LEAVES!
THE MAIDEN STANDS RIGID, FEAR AND WONDER PLAYING ACROSS HER EXQUISITE FEATURES...
...AND CUTTER SUDDENLY KNOWS A DIFFERENT KIND OF THIRST ---
-- AS HE DRINKS IN THE SIGHT OF HER!
WH-WHAT DO YOU WANT...?

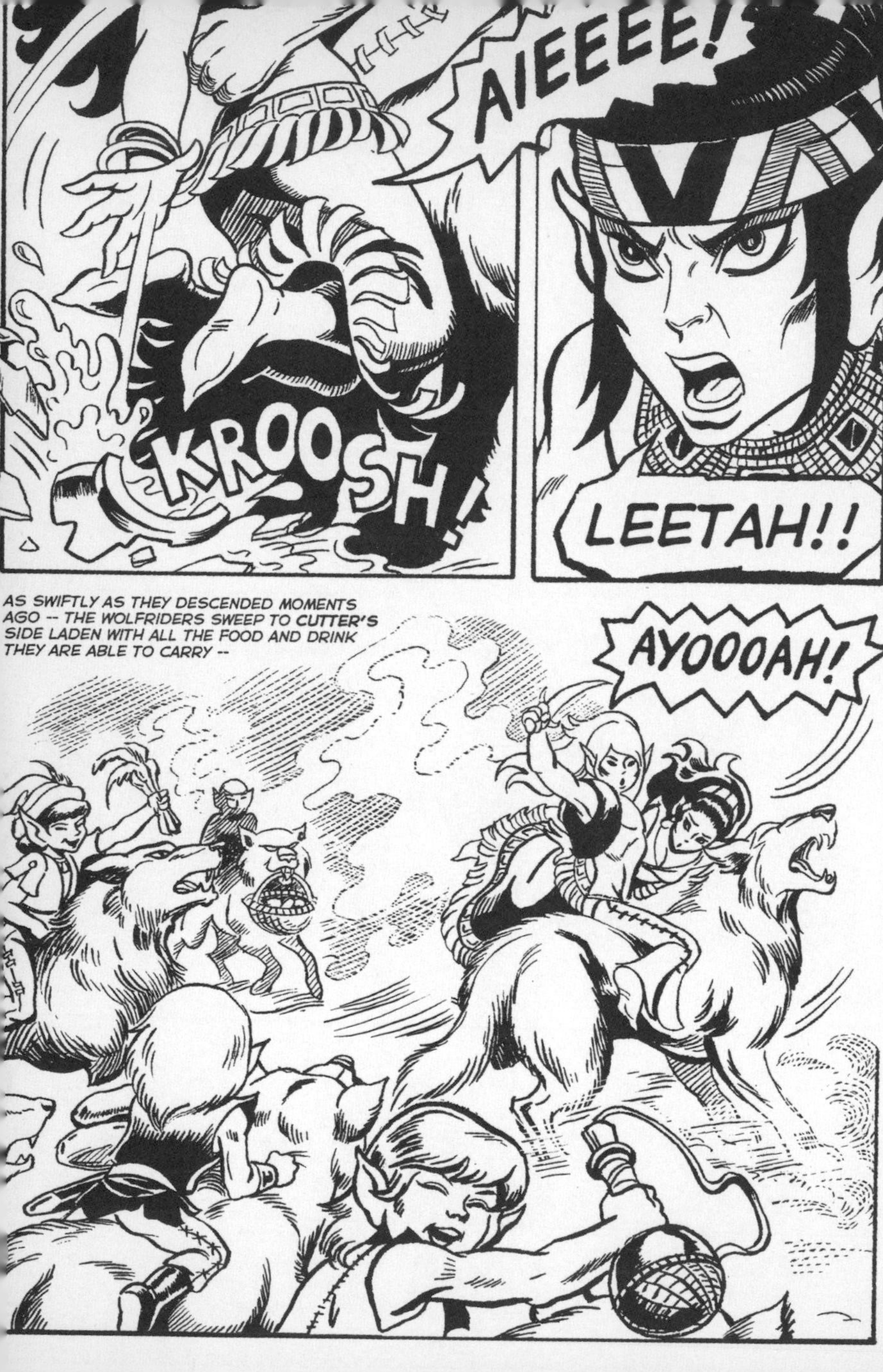
AIEEEEE!
KROOSH!
LEETAH!!
AS SWIFTLY AS THEY DESCENDED MOMENTS AGO -- THE WOLFRIDERS SWEEP TO CUTTER'S SIDE LADEN WITH ALL THE FOOD AND DRINK THEY ARE ABLE TO CARRY --
AYOOOAH!

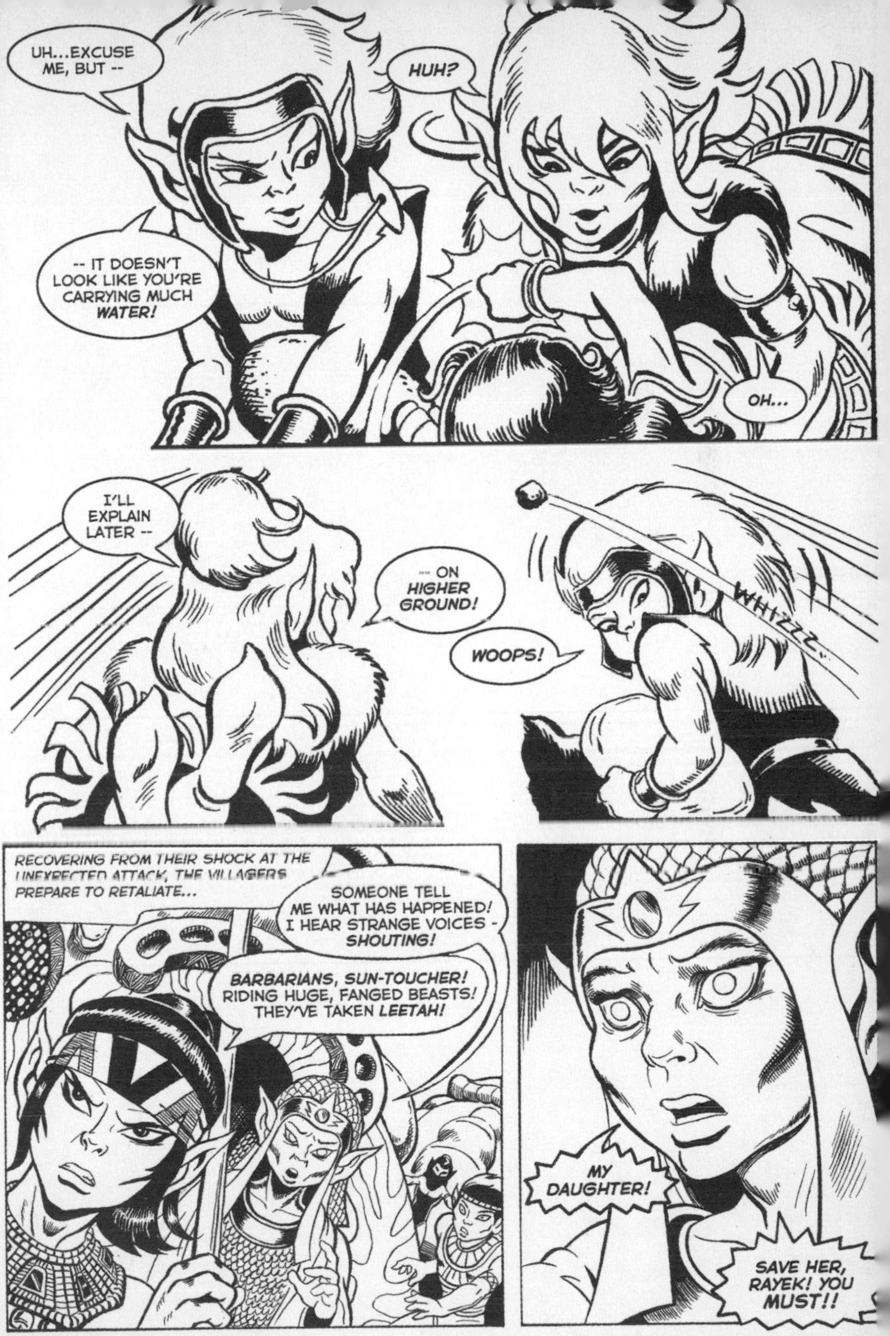
UH...EXCUSE ME, BUT --
HUH?
-- IT DOESN'T LOOK LIKE YOU'RE CARRYING MUCH *WATER!*
OH...
I'LL EXPLAIN LATER --
-- ON *HIGHER GROUND!*
WHIZZZ
WOOPS!
RECOVERING FROM THEIR SHOCK AT THE UNEXPECTED ATTACK, THE VILLAGERS PREPARE TO RETALIATE...
SOMEONE TELL ME WHAT HAS HAPPENED! I HEAR STRANGE VOICES - *SHOUTING!*
BARBARIANS, SUN-TOUCHER! RIDING HUGE, FANGED BEASTS! THEY'VE TAKEN *LEETAH!*
MY DAUGHTER!
SAVE HER, RAYEK! YOU MUST!!

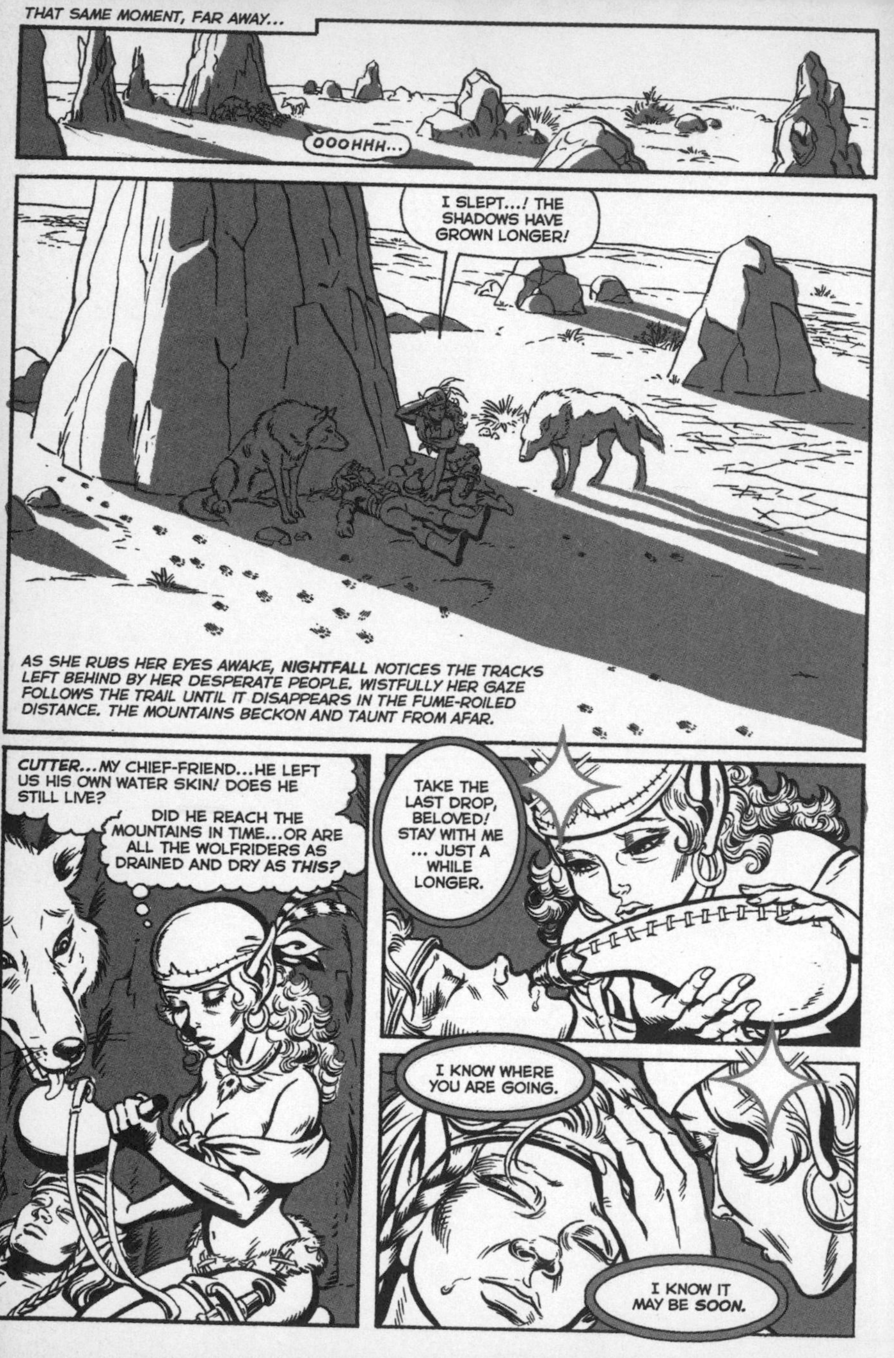
THAT SAME MOMENT, FAR AWAY...
OOOHHH...
I SLEPT...! THE SHADOWS HAVE GROWN LONGER!
AS SHE RUBS HER EYES AWAKE, NIGHTFALL NOTICES THE TRACKS LEFT BEHIND BY HER DESPERATE PEOPLE. WISTFULLY HER GAZE FOLLOWS THE TRAIL UNTIL IT DISAPPEARS IN THE FUME-ROILED DISTANCE. THE MOUNTAINS BECKON AND TAUNT FROM AFAR.
CUTTER...MY CHIEF-FRIEND...HE LEFT US HIS OWN WATER SKIN! DOES HE STILL LIVE?
DID HE REACH THE MOUNTAINS IN TIME...OR ARE ALL THE WOLFRIDERS AS DRAINED AND DRY AS THIS?
TAKE THE LAST DROP, BELOVED! STAY WITH ME ... JUST A WHILE LONGER.
I KNOW WHERE YOU ARE GOING.
I KNOW IT MAY BE SOON.

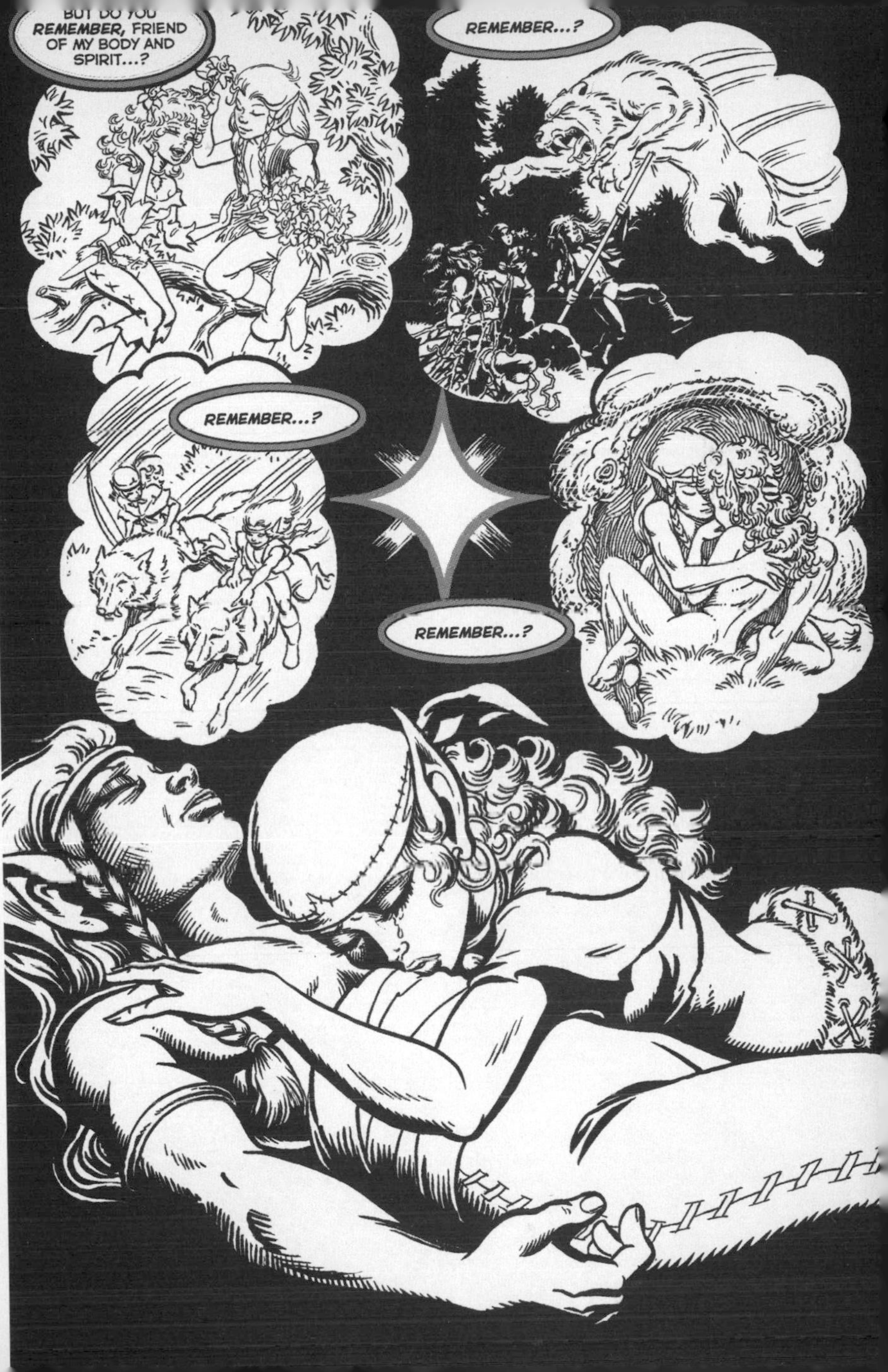
BUT DO YOU REMEMBER, FRIEND OF MY BODY AND SPIRIT...?
REMEMBER...?
REMEMBER...?
REMEMBER...?

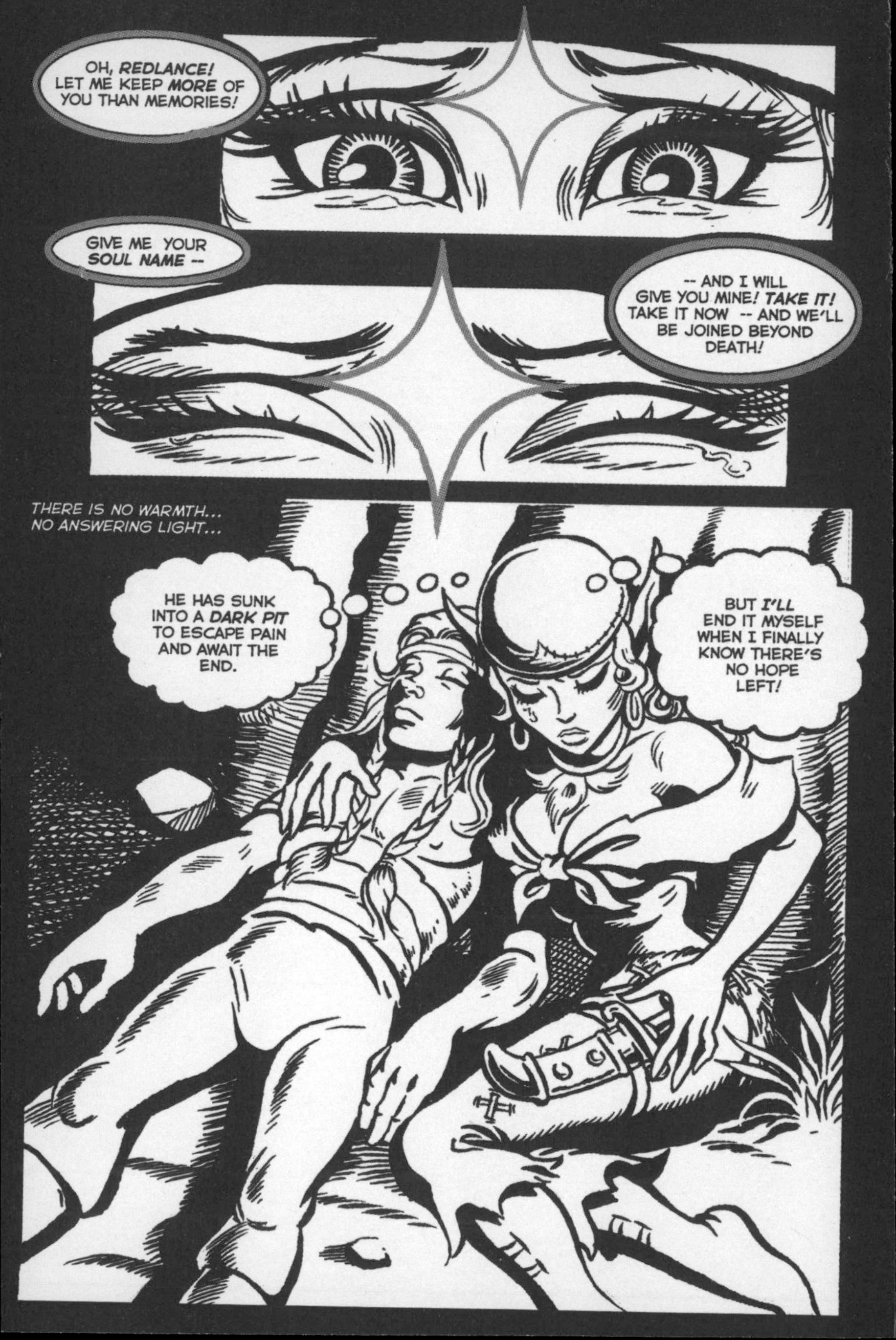
OH, REDLANCE! LET ME KEEP MORE OF YOU THAN MEMORIES!
GIVE ME YOUR SOUL NAME --
-- AND I WILL GIVE YOU MINE! TAKE IT! TAKE IT NOW -- AND WE'LL BE JOINED BEYOND DEATH!
THERE IS NO WARMTH... NO ANSWERING LIGHT...
HE HAS SUNK INTO A DARK PIT TO ESCAPE PAIN AND AWAIT THE END.
BUT I'LL END IT MYSELF WHEN I FINALLY KNOW THERE'S NO HOPE LEFT!

ANGRY VILLAGERS SWARM INTO THE HIGH HILLS WHERE THE WOLFRIDERS HAVE TAKEN REFUGE...

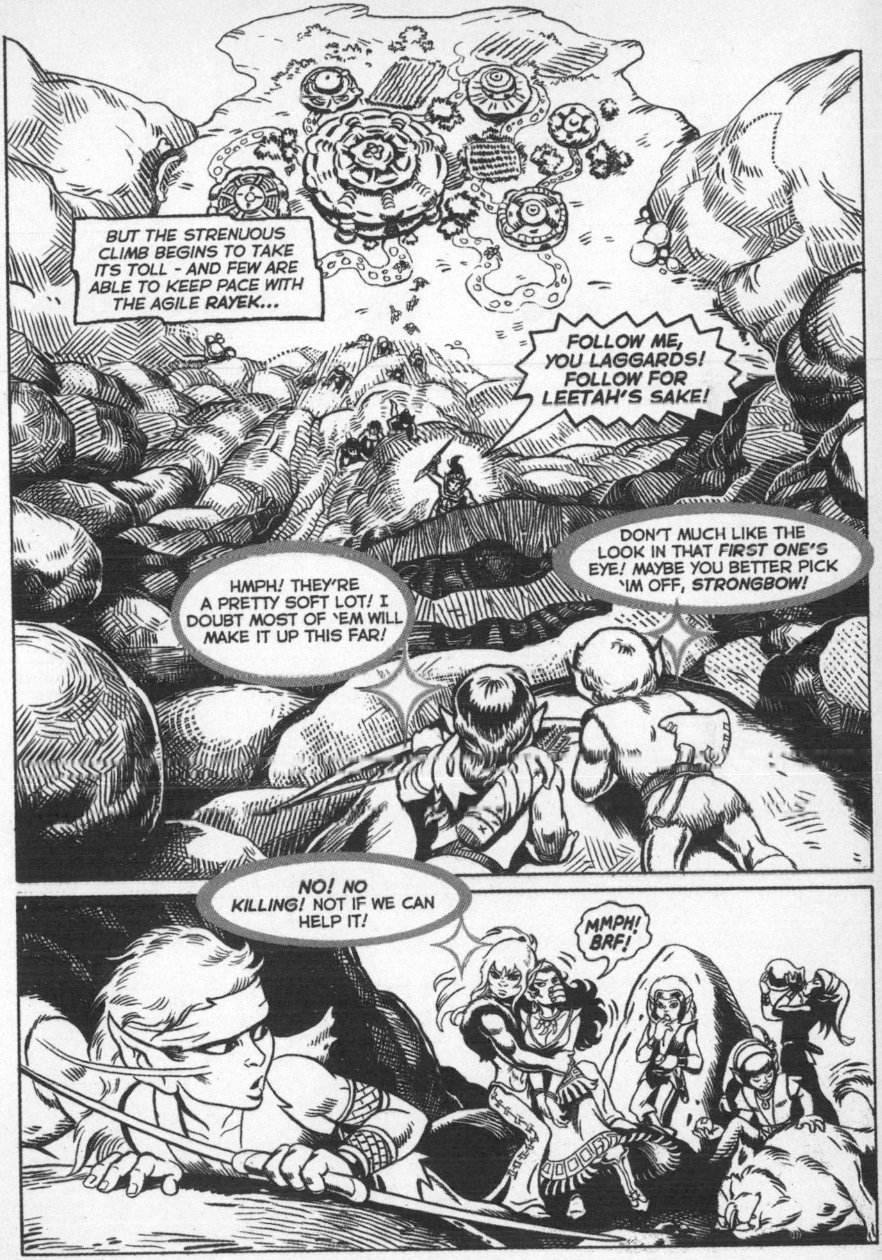
BUT THE STRENUOUS CLIMB BEGINS TO TAKE ITS TOLL - AND FEW ARE ABLE TO KEEP PACE WITH THE AGILE RAYEK...
FOLLOW ME, YOU LAGGARDS! FOLLOW FOR LEETAH'S SAKE!
HMPH! THEY'RE A PRETTY SOFT LOT! I DOUBT MOST OF 'EM WILL MAKE IT UP THIS FAR!
DON'T MUCH LIKE THE LOOK IN THAT FIRST ONE'S EYE! MAYBE YOU BETTER PICK 'IM OFF, STRONGBOW!
NO! NO KILLING! NOT IF WE CAN HELP IT!
MMPH! BRF!

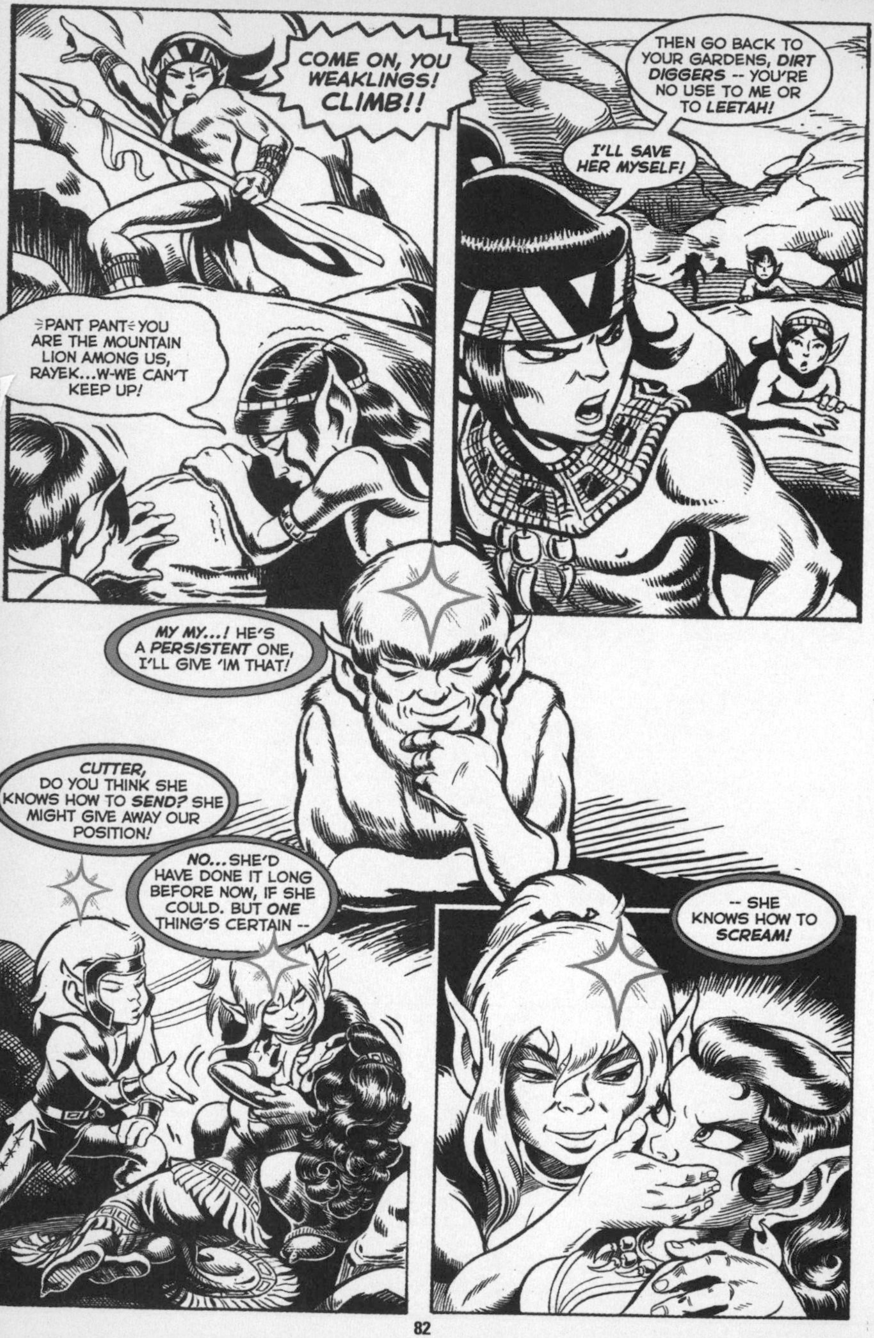
COME ON, YOU WEAKLINGS! CLIMB!!
THEN GO BACK TO YOUR GARDENS, DIRT DIGGERS -- YOU'RE NO USE TO ME OR TO LEETAH!
I'LL SAVE HER MYSELF!
=PANT PANT= YOU ARE THE MOUNTAIN LION AMONG US, RAYEK...W-WE CAN'T KEEP UP!
MY MY...! HE'S A PERSISTENT ONE, I'LL GIVE 'IM THAT!
CUTTER, DO YOU THINK SHE KNOWS HOW TO SEND? SHE MIGHT GIVE AWAY OUR POSITION!
NO...SHE'D HAVE DONE IT LONG BEFORE NOW, IF SHE COULD. BUT ONE THING'S CERTAIN --
-- SHE KNOWS HOW TO SCREAM!

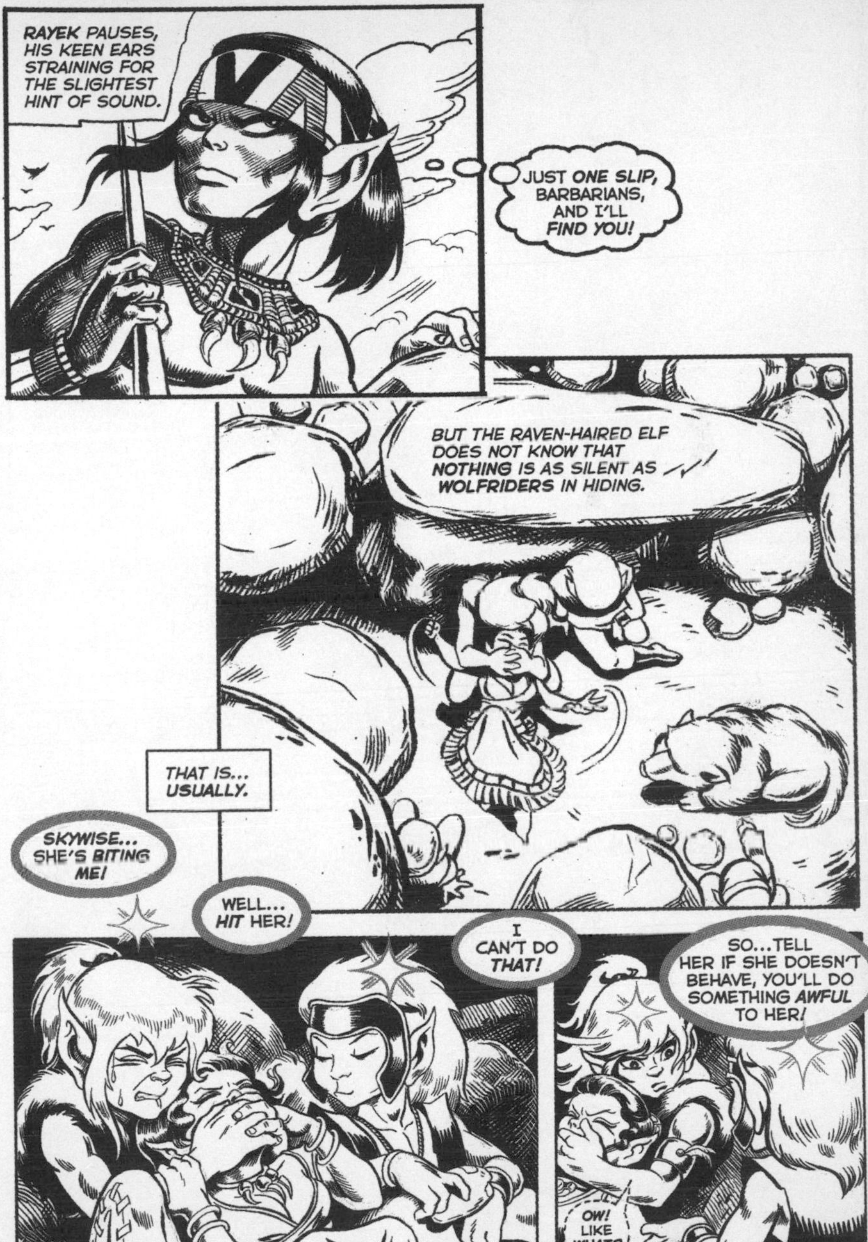

RAYEK PAUSES, HIS KEEN EARS STRAINING FOR THE SLIGHTEST HINT OF SOUND.
JUST ONE SLIP, BARBARIANS, AND I'LL FIND YOU!
BUT THE RAVEN-HAIRED ELF DOES NOT KNOW THAT NOTHING IS AS SILENT AS WOLFRIDERS IN HIDING.
THAT IS... USUALLY.
SKYWISE... SHE'S BITING ME!
WELL... HIT HER!
I CAN'T DO THAT!
SO...TELL HER IF SHE DOESN'T BEHAVE, YOU'LL DO SOMETHING AWFUL TO HER!
OW! LIKE WHAT?

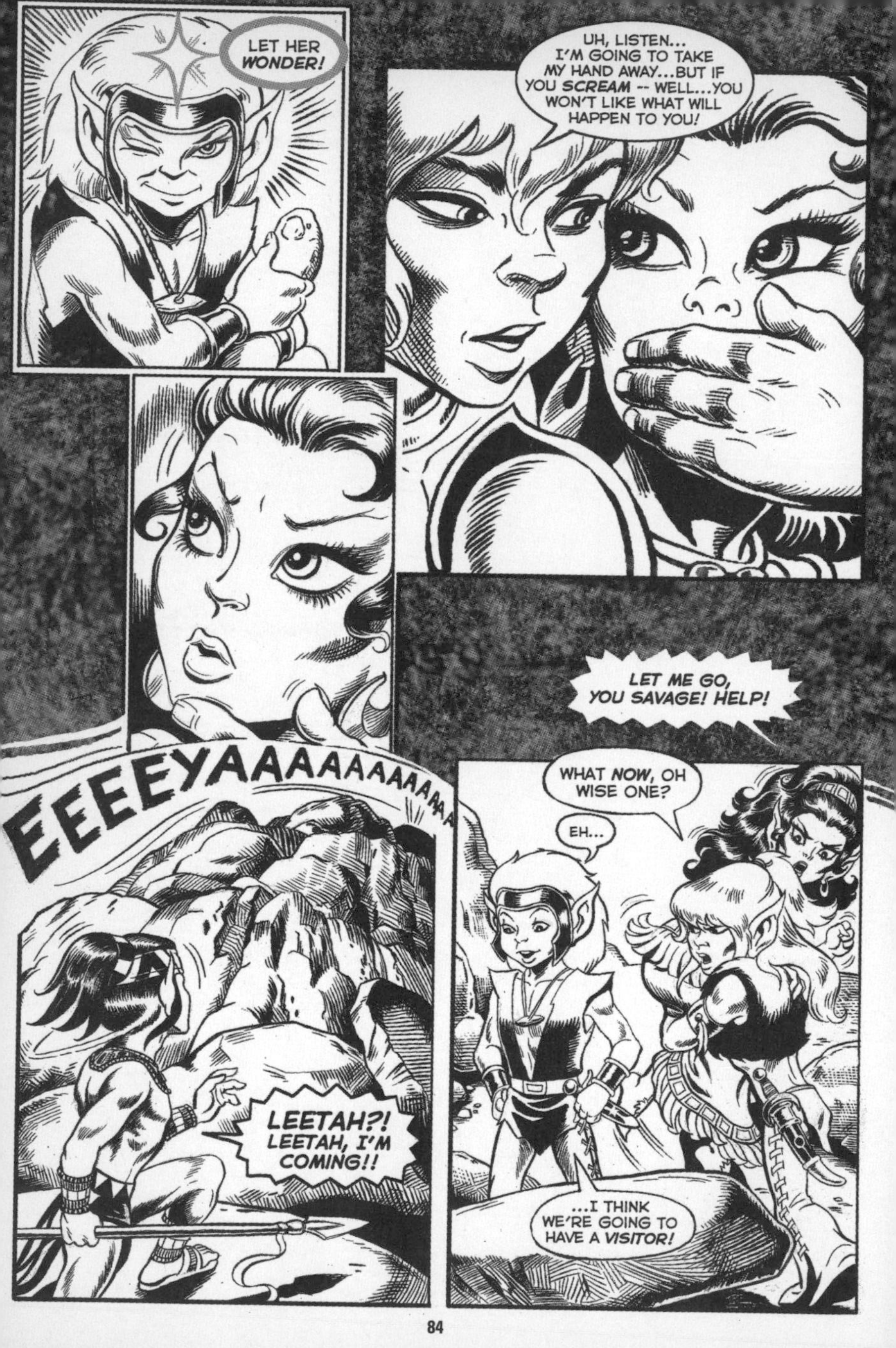
LET HER WONDER!
UH, LISTEN... I'M GOING TO TAKE MY HAND AWAY...BUT IF YOU SCREAM -- WELL...YOU WON'T LIKE WHAT WILL HAPPEN TO YOU!
LET ME GO, YOU SAVAGE! HELP!
EEEEYAAAAAAAAAAAA
LEETAH?! LEETAH, I'M COMING!!
WHAT NOW, OH WISE ONE?
EH...
...I THINK WE'RE GOING TO HAVE A VISITOR!

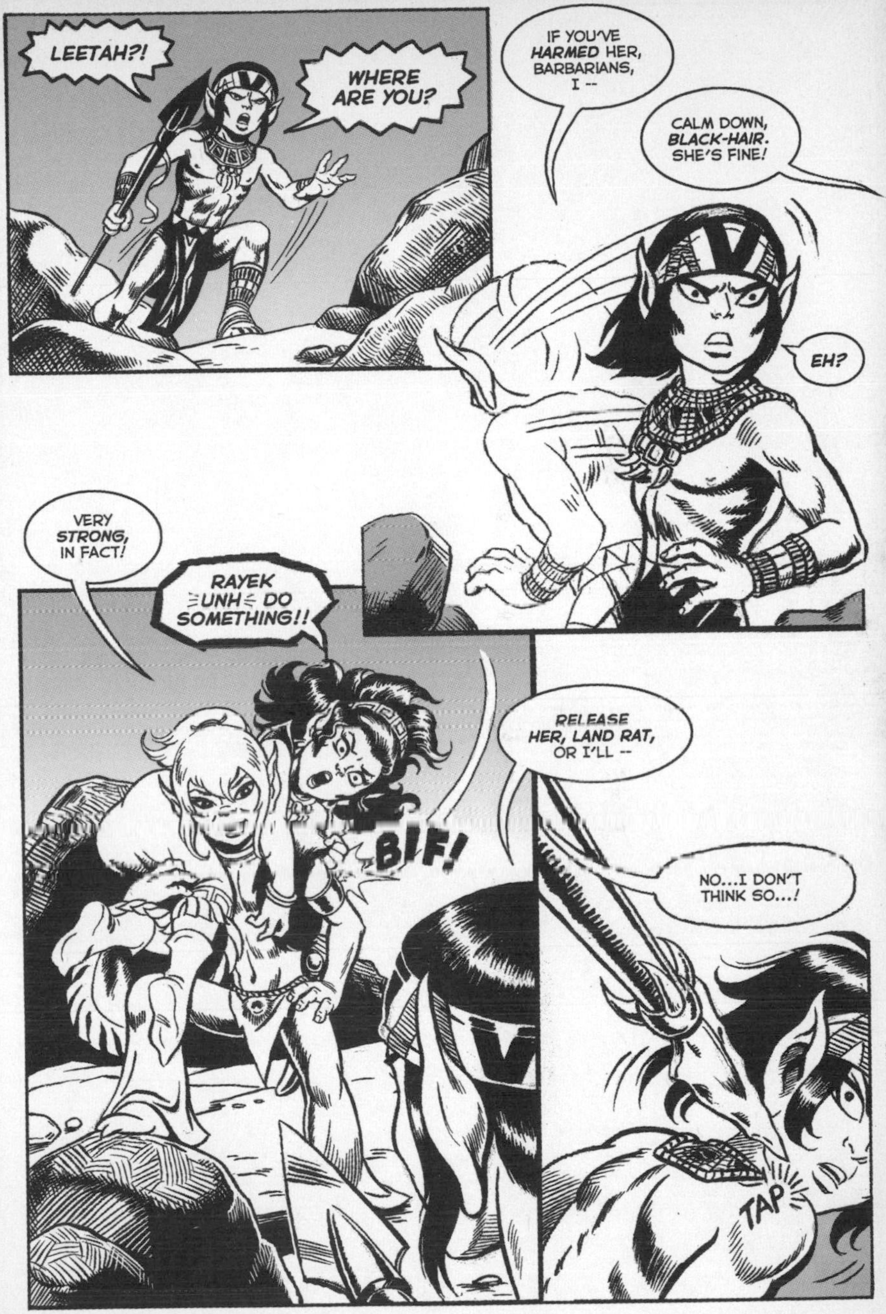
LEETAH?!
WHERE ARE YOU?
IF YOU'VE HARMED HER, BARBARIANS, I --
CALM DOWN, BLACK-HAIR. SHE'S FINE!
EH?
VERY STRONG, IN FACT!
RAYEK UNH DO SOMETHING!!
BIF!
RELEASE HER, LAND RAT, OR I'LL --
NO...I DON'T THINK SO...!
TAP

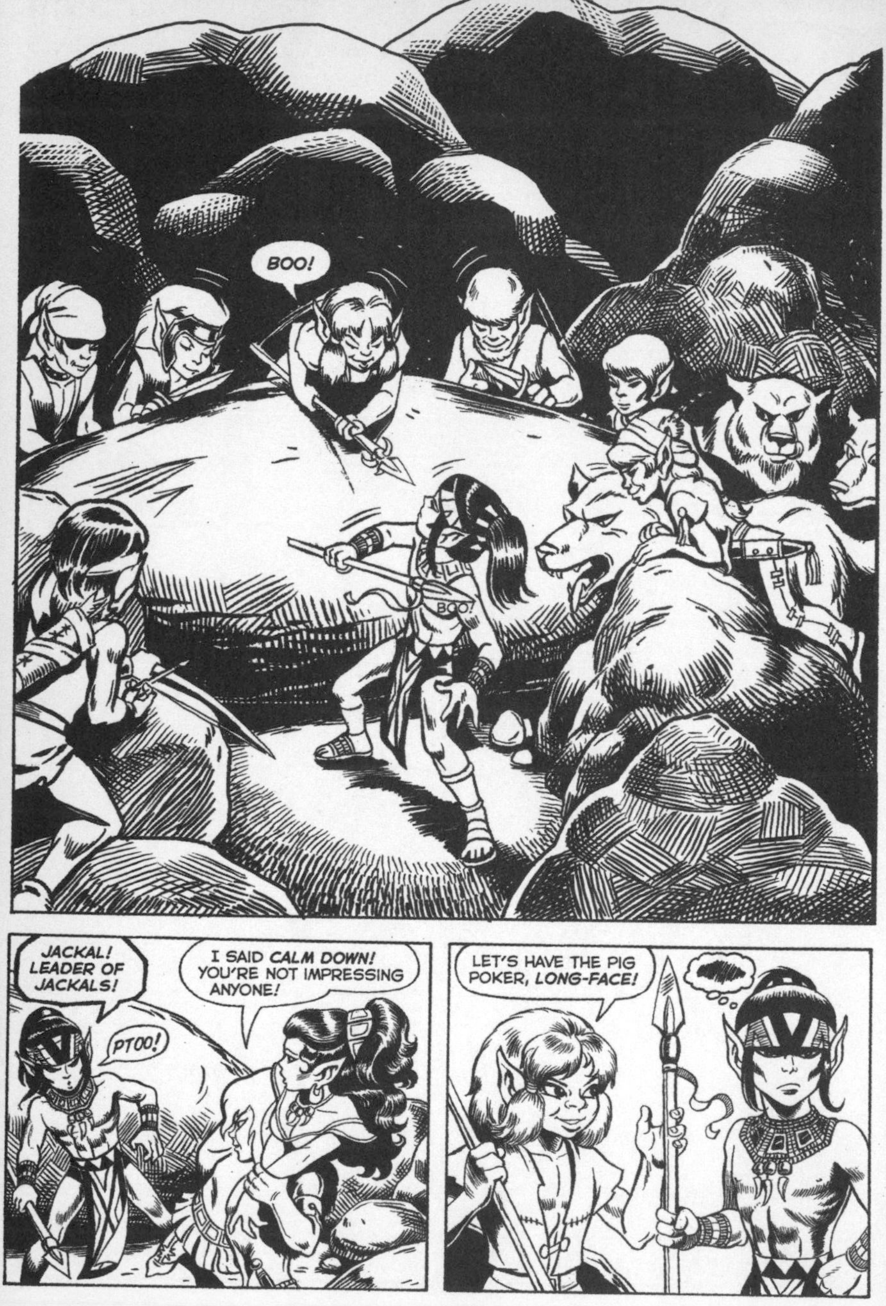
BOO!
BOO!
JACKAL! LEADER OF JACKALS!
PTOO!
I SAID CALM DOWN! YOU'RE NOT IMPRESSING ANYONE!
LET'S HAVE THE PIG POKER, LONG-FACE!

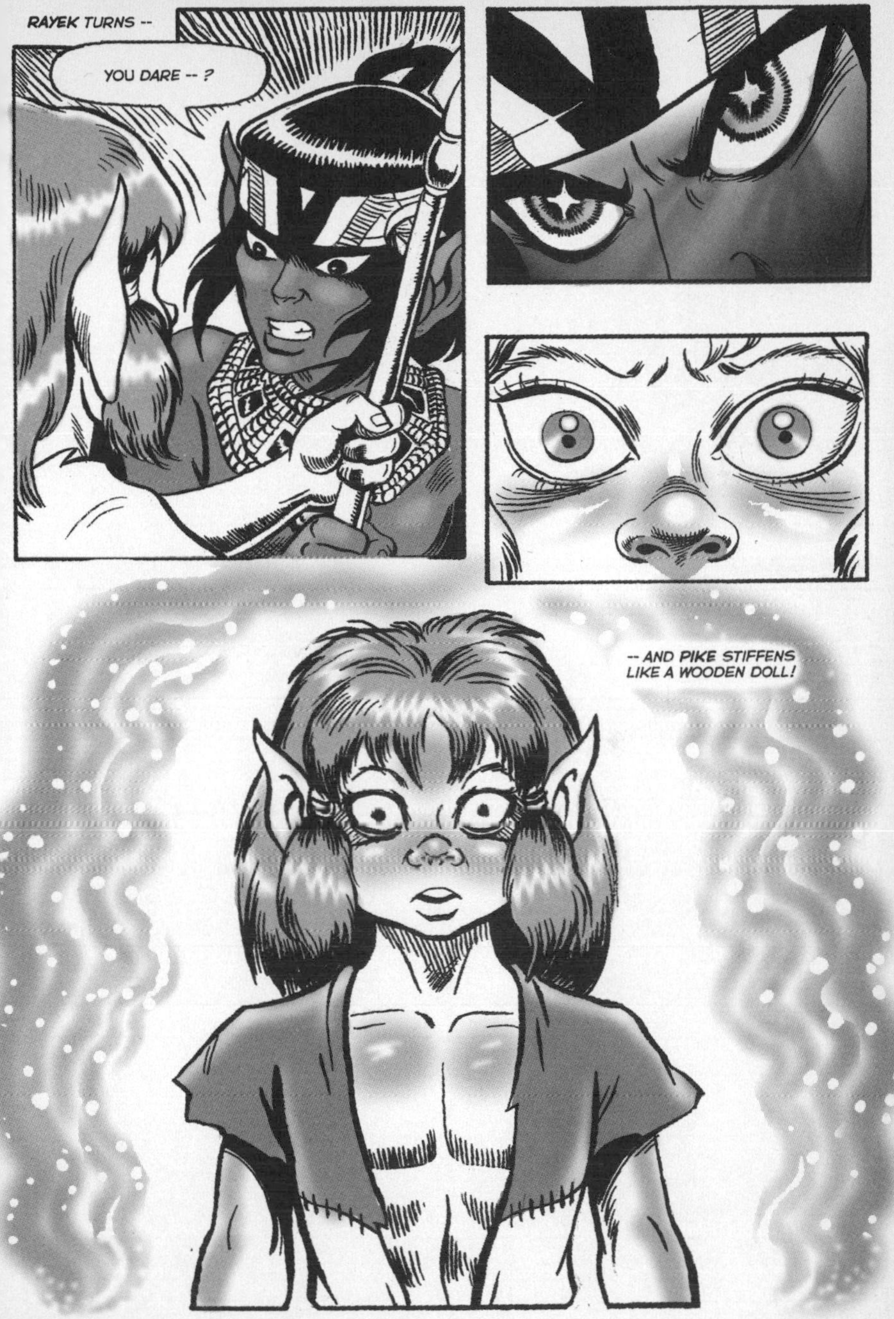
RAYEK TURNS --
YOU DARE -- ?
-- AND PIKE STIFFENS LIKE A WOODEN DOLL!

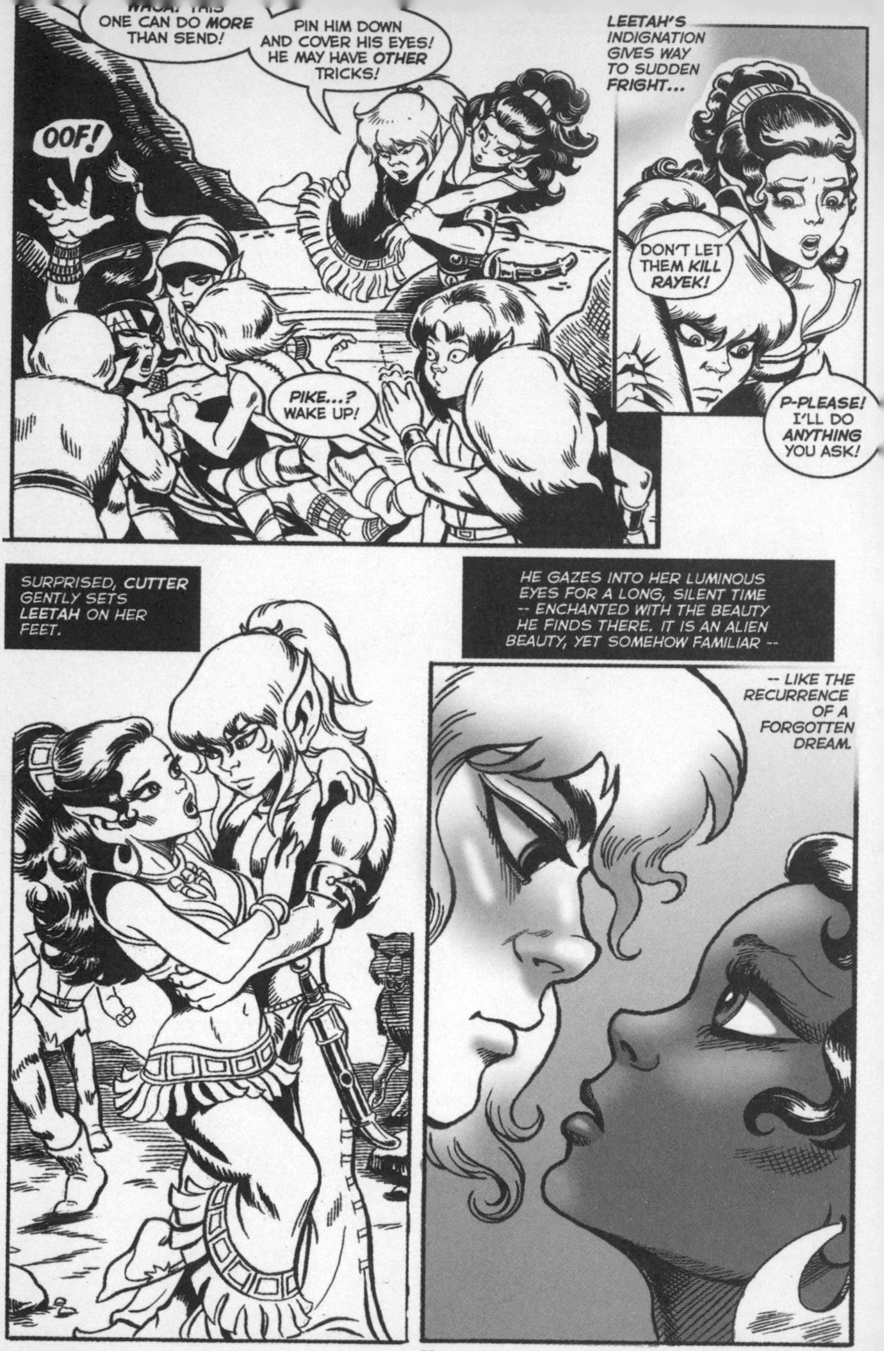

WHOA! THIS ONE CAN DO MORE THAN SEND!
PIN HIM DOWN AND COVER HIS EYES! HE MAY HAVE OTHER TRICKS!
OOF!
PIKE...? WAKE UP!
LEETAH'S INDIGNATION GIVES WAY TO SUDDEN FRIGHT...
DON'T LET THEM KILL RAYEK!
P-PLEASE! I'LL DO ANYTHING YOU ASK!
SURPRISED, CUTTER GENTLY SETS LEETAH ON HER FEET.
HE GAZES INTO HER LUMINOUS EYES FOR A LONG, SILENT TIME -- ENCHANTED WITH THE BEAUTY HE FINDS THERE. IT IS AN ALIEN BEAUTY, YET SOMEHOW FAMILIAR --
-- LIKE THE RECURRENCE OF A FORGOTTEN DREAM.

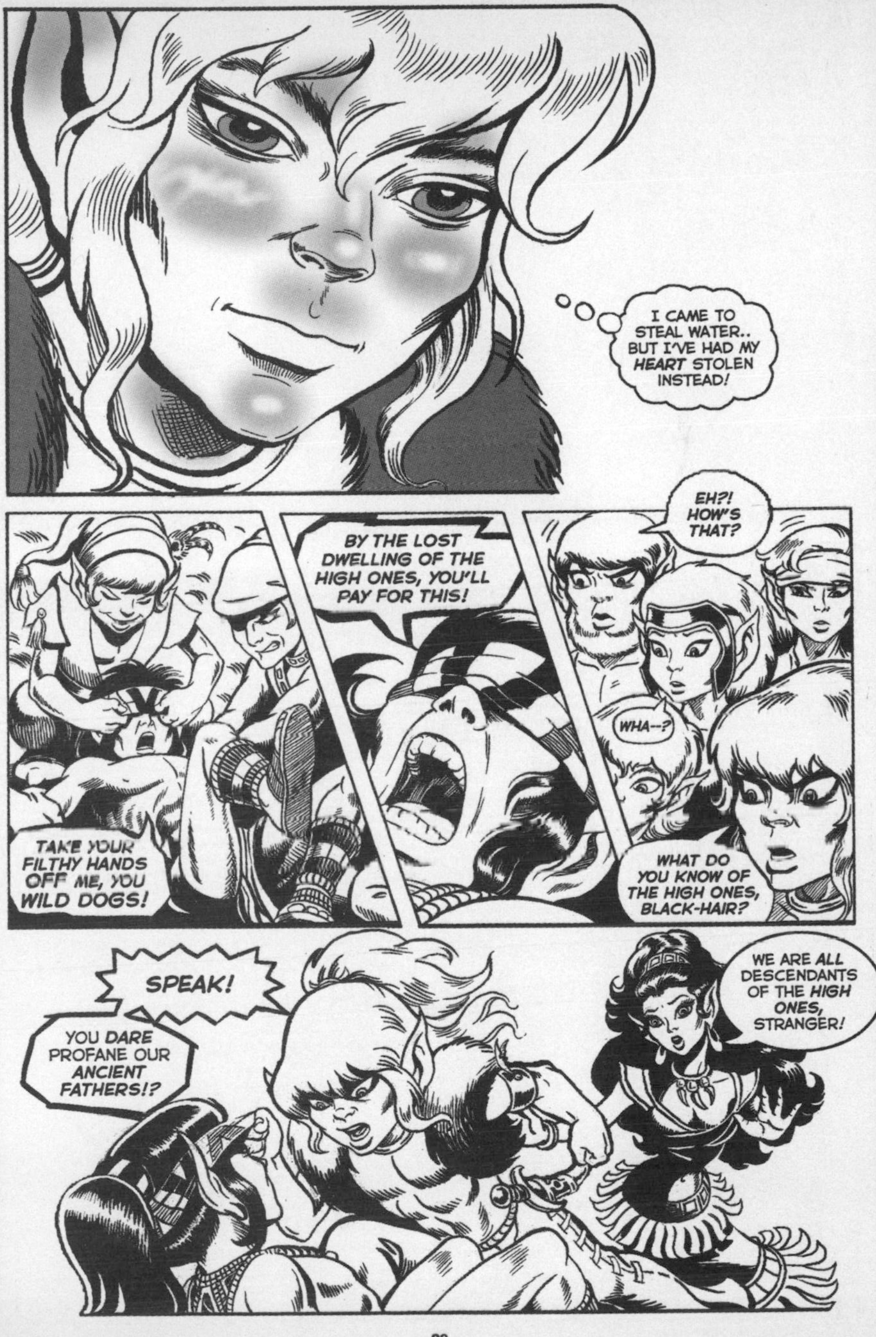
I CAME TO STEAL WATER.. BUT I'VE HAD MY HEART STOLEN INSTEAD!
TAKE YOUR FILTHY HANDS OFF ME, YOU WILD DOGS!
BY THE LOST DWELLING OF THE HIGH ONES, YOU'LL PAY FOR THIS!
EH?! HOW'S THAT?
WHA--?
WHAT DO YOU KNOW OF THE HIGH ONES, BLACK-HAIR?
SPEAK!
YOU DARE PROFANE OUR ANCIENT FATHERS!?
WE ARE ALL DESCENDANTS OF THE HIGH ONES, STRANGER!

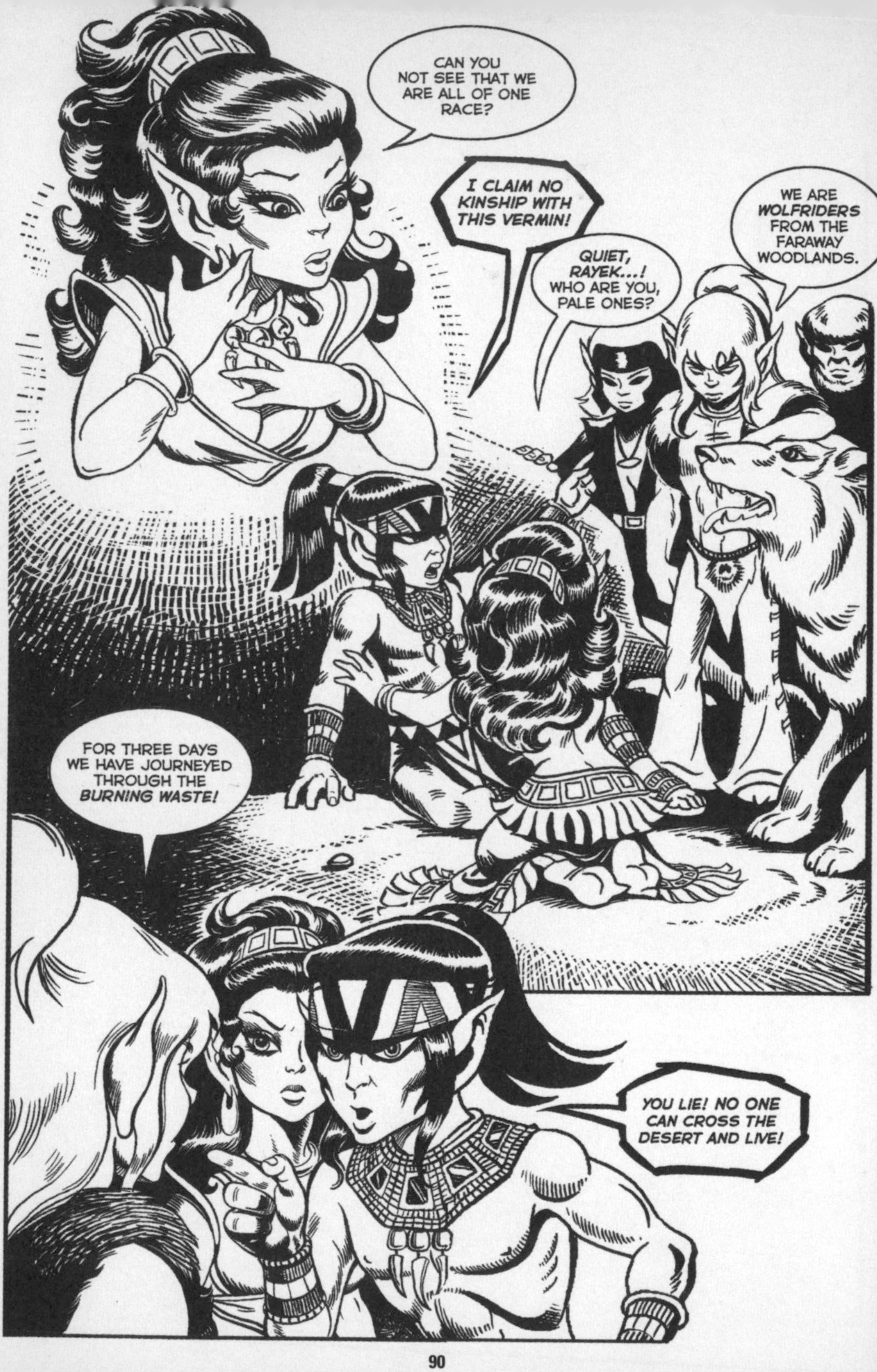
CAN YOU NOT SEE THAT WE ARE ALL OF ONE RACE?
I CLAIM NO KINSHIP WITH THIS VERMIN!
QUIET, RAYEK...! WHO ARE YOU, PALE ONES?
WE ARE WOLFRIDERS FROM THE FARAWAY WOODLANDS.
FOR THREE DAYS WE HAVE JOURNEYED THROUGH THE BURNING WASTE!
YOU LIE! NO ONE CAN CROSS THE DESERT AND LIVE!

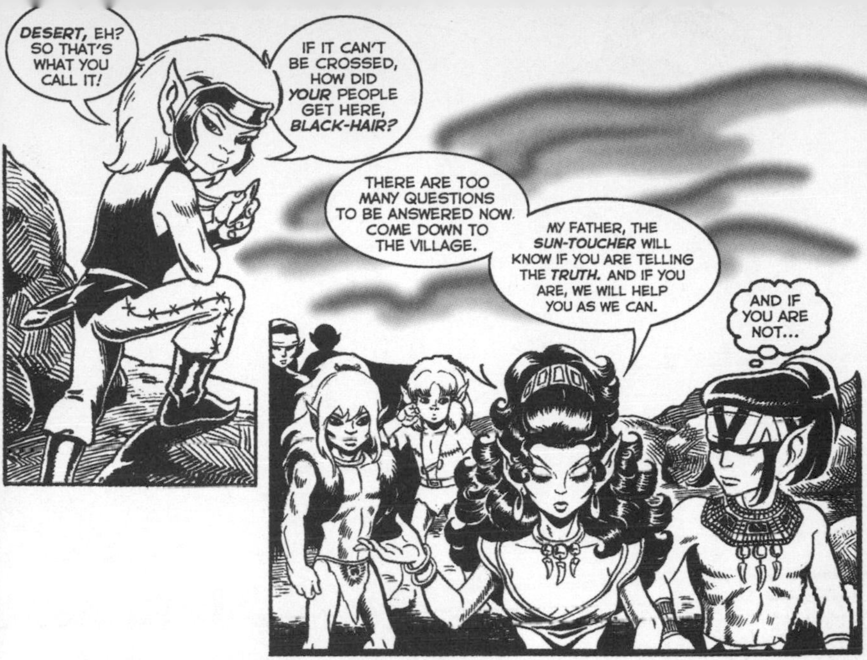
DESERT, EH? SO THAT'S WHAT YOU CALL IT!
IF IT CAN'T BE CROSSED, HOW DID YOUR PEOPLE GET HERE, BLACK-HAIR?
THERE ARE TOO MANY QUESTIONS TO BE ANSWERED NOW. COME DOWN TO THE VILLAGE.
MY FATHER, THE SUN-TOUCHER WILL KNOW IF YOU ARE TELLING THE TRUTH. AND IF YOU ARE, WE WILL HELP YOU AS WE CAN.
AND IF YOU ARE NOT...

FROM THEIR HIDING PLACE ON THE OTHER SIDE OF THE HILL, ***MOONSHADE, RAINSONG, CLEARBROOK, DEWSHINE*** AND THE CHILDREN ARE BROUGHT INTO THE STRANGE, ELFIN VILLAGE. SURROUNDED BY CURIOUS ONLOOKERS, THE SULLEN, WARY WOLFRIDERS ASSEMBLE BEFORE A GENTLE YET COMMANDING FIGURE...

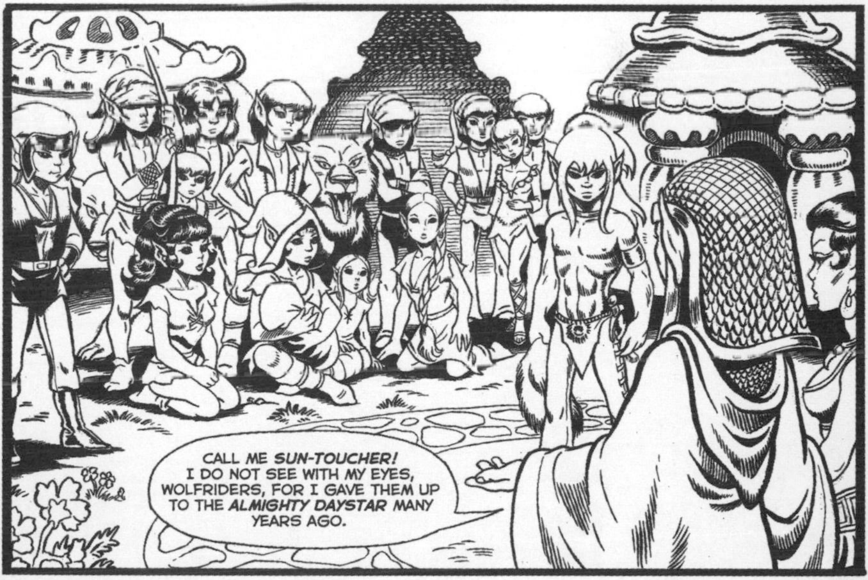
CALL ME SUN-TOUCHER! I DO NOT SEE WITH MY EYES, WOLFRIDERS, FOR I GAVE THEM UP TO THE ALMIGHTY DAYSTAR MANY YEARS AGO.

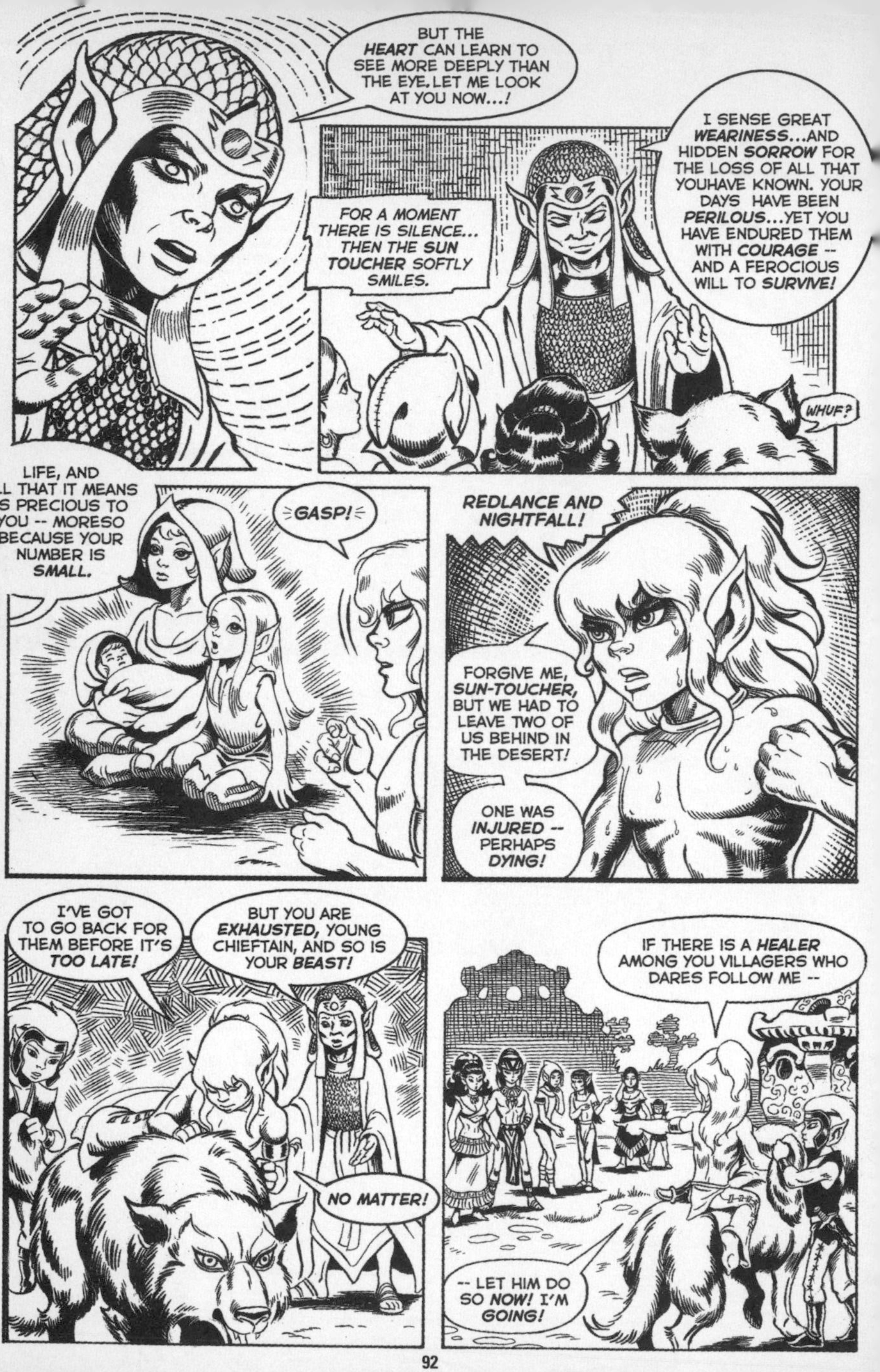

BUT THE HEART CAN LEARN TO SEE MORE DEEPLY THAN THE EYE. LET ME LOOK AT YOU NOW...!
FOR A MOMENT THERE IS SILENCE... THEN THE SUN TOUCHER SOFTLY SMILES.
I SENSE GREAT WEARINESS...AND HIDDEN SORROW FOR THE LOSS OF ALL THAT YOUHAVE KNOWN. YOUR DAYS HAVE BEEN PERILOUS...YET YOU HAVE ENDURED THEM WITH COURAGE -- AND A FEROCIOUS WILL TO SURVIVE!
WHUF?
LIFE, AND ALL THAT IT MEANS IS PRECIOUS TO YOU -- MORESO BECAUSE YOUR NUMBER IS SMALL.
GASP!
REDLANCE AND NIGHTFALL!
FORGIVE ME, SUN-TOUCHER, BUT WE HAD TO LEAVE TWO OF US BEHIND IN THE DESERT!
ONE WAS INJURED -- PERHAPS DYING!
I'VE GOT TO GO BACK FOR THEM BEFORE IT'S TOO LATE!
BUT YOU ARE EXHAUSTED, YOUNG CHIEFTAIN, AND SO IS YOUR BEAST!
NO MATTER!
IF THERE IS A HEALER AMONG YOU VILLAGERS WHO DARES FOLLOW ME --
-- LET HIM DO SO NOW! I'M GOING!

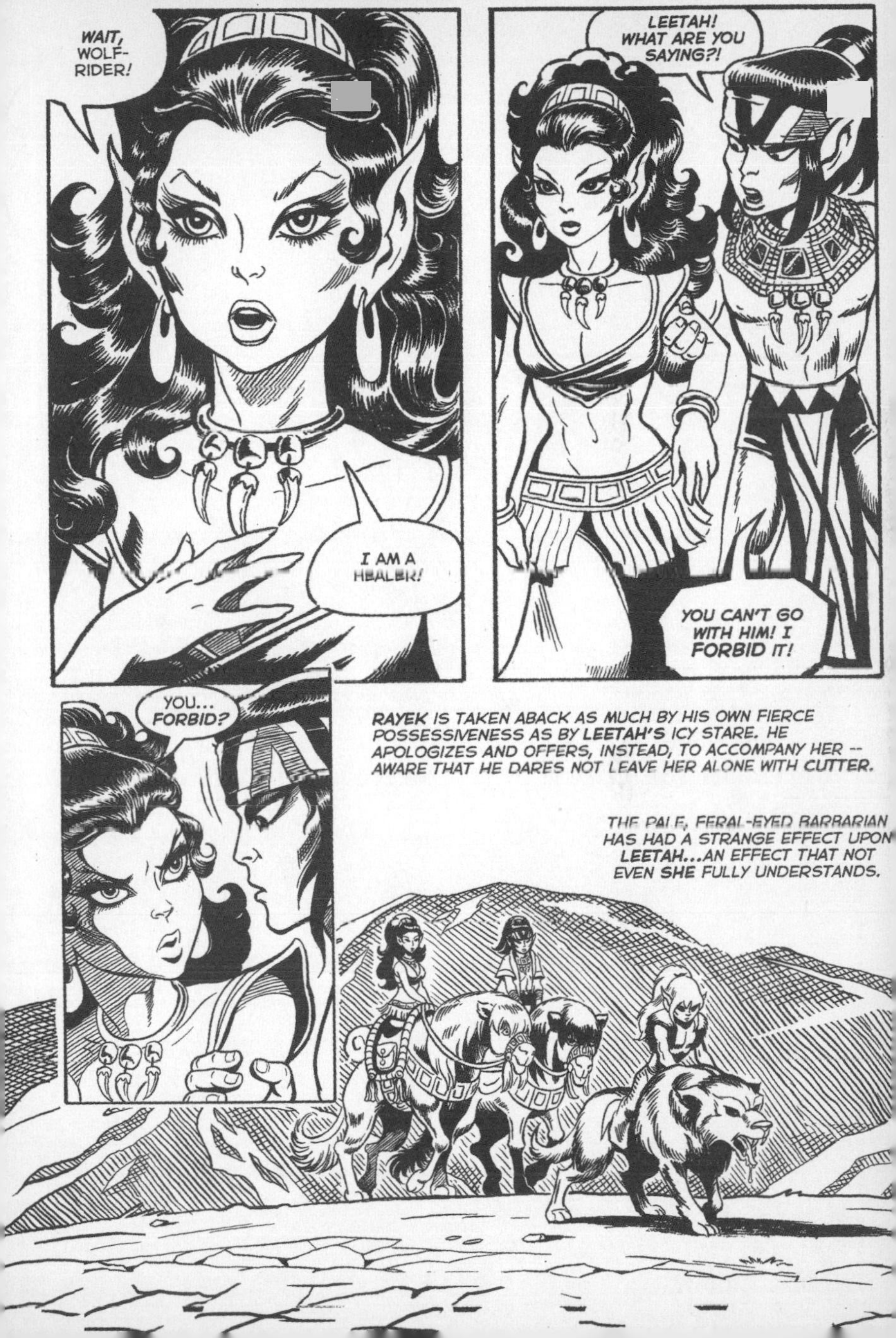
WAIT, WOLF-RIDER!
I AM A HEALER!
LEETAH! WHAT ARE YOU SAYING?!
YOU CAN'T GO WITH HIM! I FORBID IT!
YOU... FORBID?
RAYEK IS TAKEN ABACK AS MUCH BY HIS OWN FIERCE POSSESSIVENESS AS BY LEETAH'S ICY STARE. HE APOLOGIZES AND OFFERS, INSTEAD, TO ACCOMPANY HER -- AWARE THAT HE DARES NOT LEAVE HER ALONE WITH CUTTER.
THE PALE, FERAL-EYED BARBARIAN HAS HAD A STRANGE EFFECT UPON LEETAH...AN EFFECT THAT NOT EVEN SHE FULLY UNDERSTANDS.

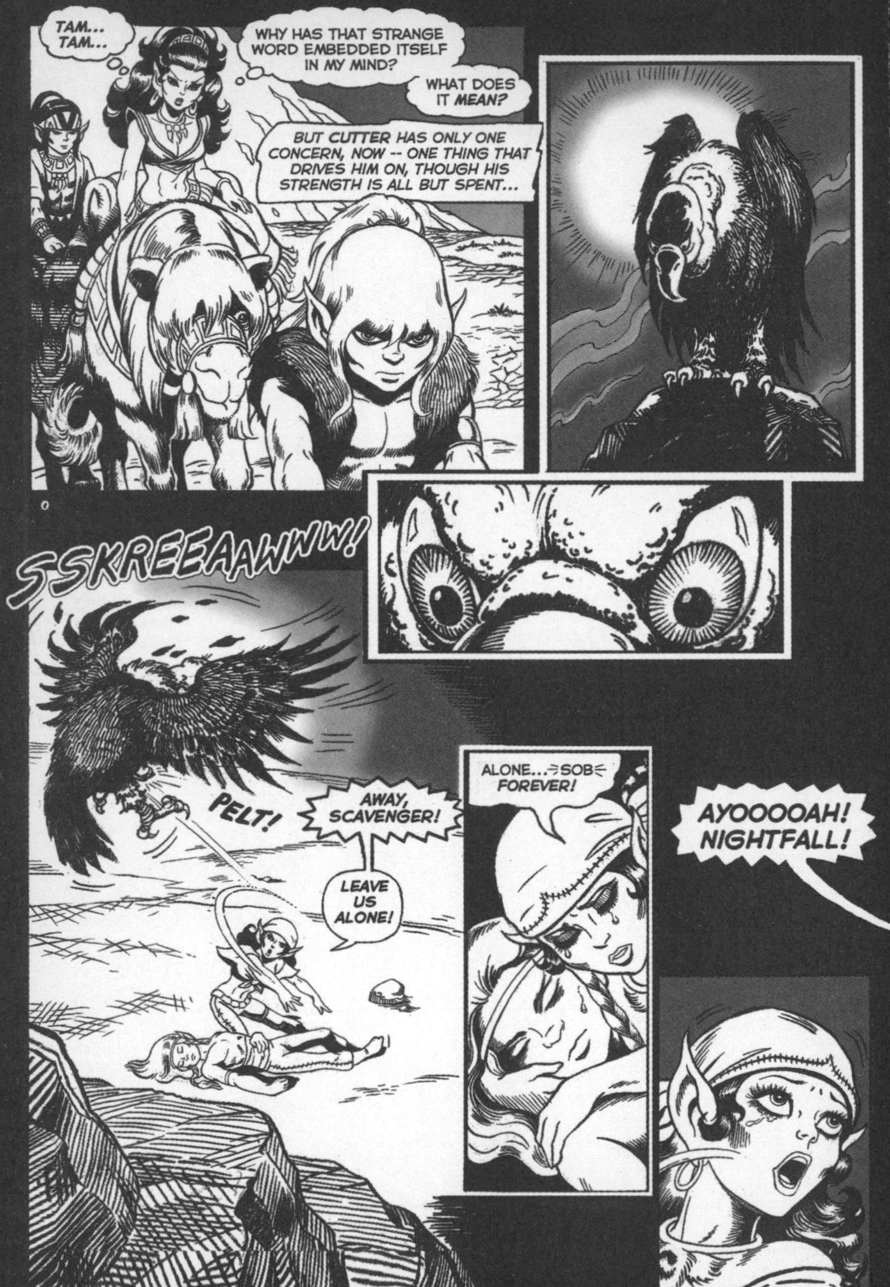
TAM... TAM...
WHY HAS THAT STRANGE WORD EMBEDDED ITSELF IN MY MIND?
WHAT DOES IT MEAN?
BUT CUTTER HAS ONLY ONE CONCERN, NOW -- ONE THING THAT DRIVES HIM ON, THOUGH HIS STRENGTH IS ALL BUT SPENT...
SSKREEAAWWW!
PELT!
AWAY, SCAVENGER!
LEAVE US ALONE!
ALONE... ⇒SOB⇐ FOREVER!
AYOOOOAH! NIGHTFALL!

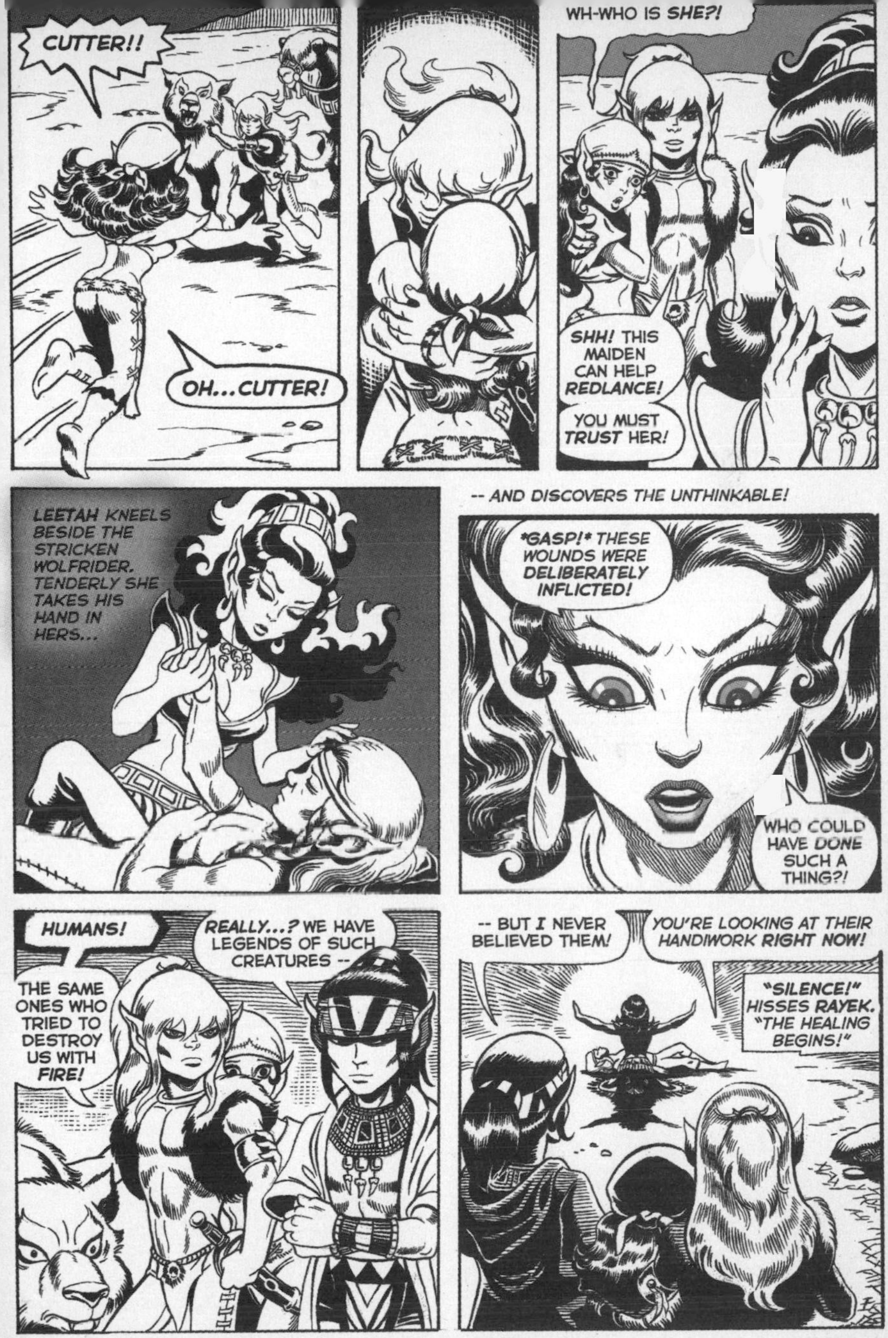
CUTTER!!
OH...CUTTER!
WH-WHO IS SHE?!
SHH! THIS MAIDEN CAN HELP REDLANCE!
YOU MUST TRUST HER!
LEETAH KNEELS BESIDE THE STRICKEN WOLFRIDER. TENDERLY SHE TAKES HIS HAND IN HERS...
-- AND DISCOVERS THE UNTHINKABLE!
GASP! THESE WOUNDS WERE DELIBERATELY INFLICTED!
WHO COULD HAVE DONE SUCH A THING?!
HUMANS!
THE SAME ONES WHO TRIED TO DESTROY US WITH FIRE!
REALLY...? WE HAVE LEGENDS OF SUCH CREATURES --
-- BUT I NEVER BELIEVED THEM!
YOU'RE LOOKING AT THEIR HANDIWORK RIGHT NOW!
"SILENCE!" HISSES RAYEK. "THE HEALING BEGINS!"

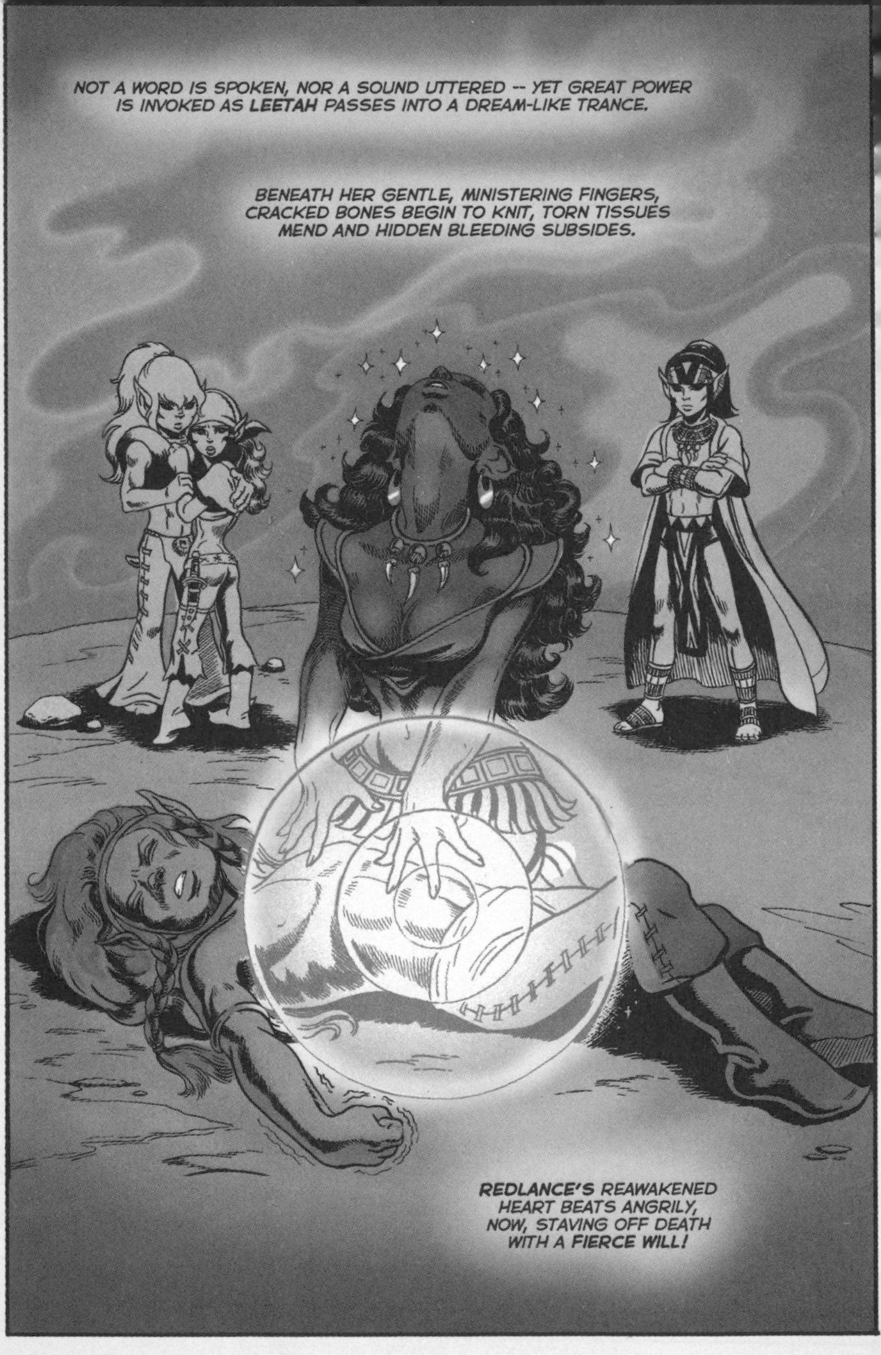
NOT A WORD IS SPOKEN, NOR A SOUND UTTERED -- YET GREAT POWER IS INVOKED AS LEETAH PASSES INTO A DREAM-LIKE TRANCE.
BENEATH HER GENTLE, MINISTERING FINGERS, CRACKED BONES BEGIN TO KNIT, TORN TISSUES MEND AND HIDDEN BLEEDING SUBSIDES.
REDLANCE'S REAWAKENED HEART BEATS ANGRILY, NOW, STAVING OFF DEATH WITH A FIERCE WILL!

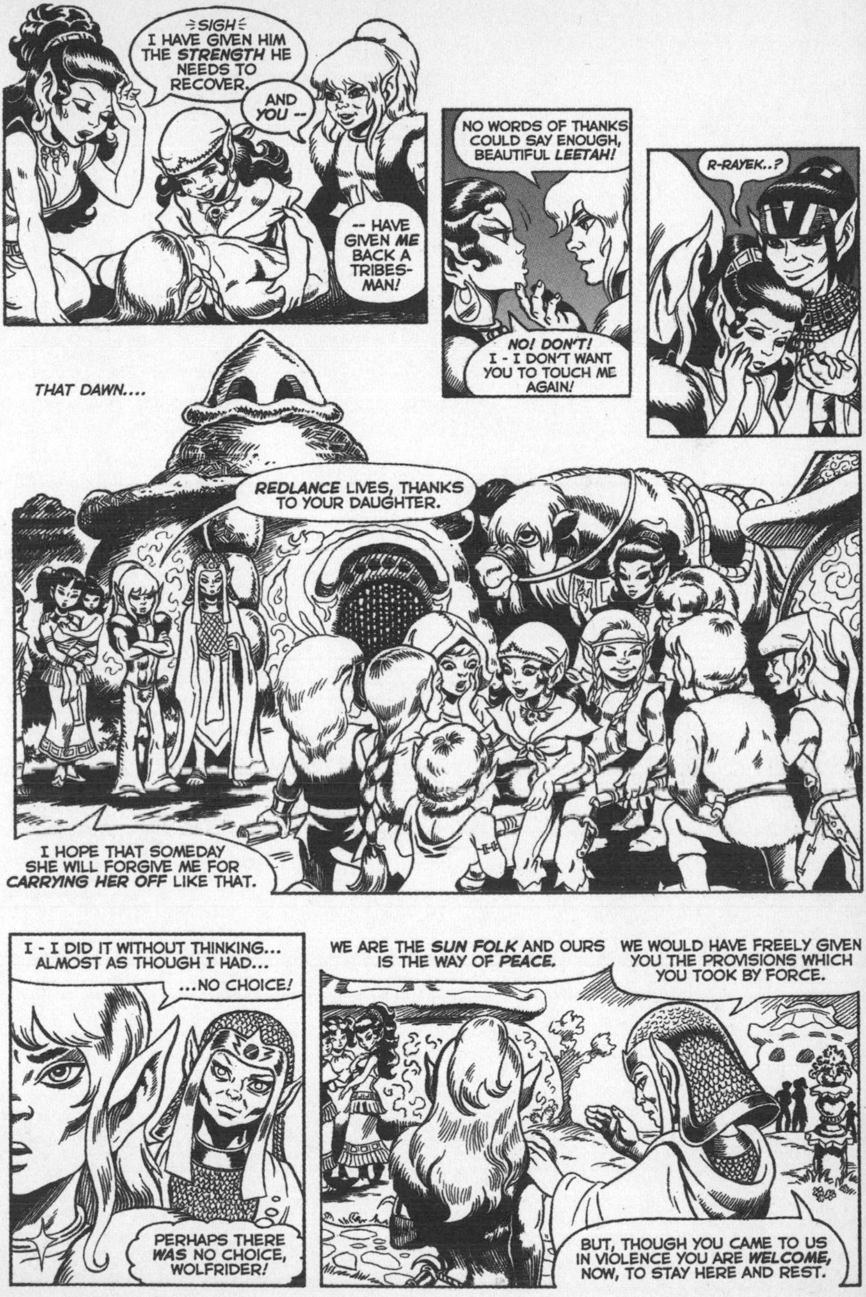

=SIGH= I HAVE GIVEN HIM THE STRENGTH HE NEEDS TO RECOVER.
AND YOU --
-- HAVE GIVEN ME BACK A TRIBES-MAN!
NO WORDS OF THANKS COULD SAY ENOUGH, BEAUTIFUL LEETAH!
NO! DON'T! I - I DON'T WANT YOU TO TOUCH ME AGAIN!
R-RAYEK..?
THAT DAWN....
REDLANCE LIVES, THANKS TO YOUR DAUGHTER.
I HOPE THAT SOMEDAY SHE WILL FORGIVE ME FOR CARRYING HER OFF LIKE THAT.
I - I DID IT WITHOUT THINKING... ALMOST AS THOUGH I HAD...
...NO CHOICE!
PERHAPS THERE WAS NO CHOICE, WOLFRIDER!
WE ARE THE SUN FOLK AND OURS IS THE WAY OF PEACE.
WE WOULD HAVE FREELY GIVEN YOU THE PROVISIONS WHICH YOU TOOK BY FORCE.
BUT, THOUGH YOU CAME TO US IN VIOLENCE YOU ARE WELCOME, NOW, TO STAY HERE AND REST.

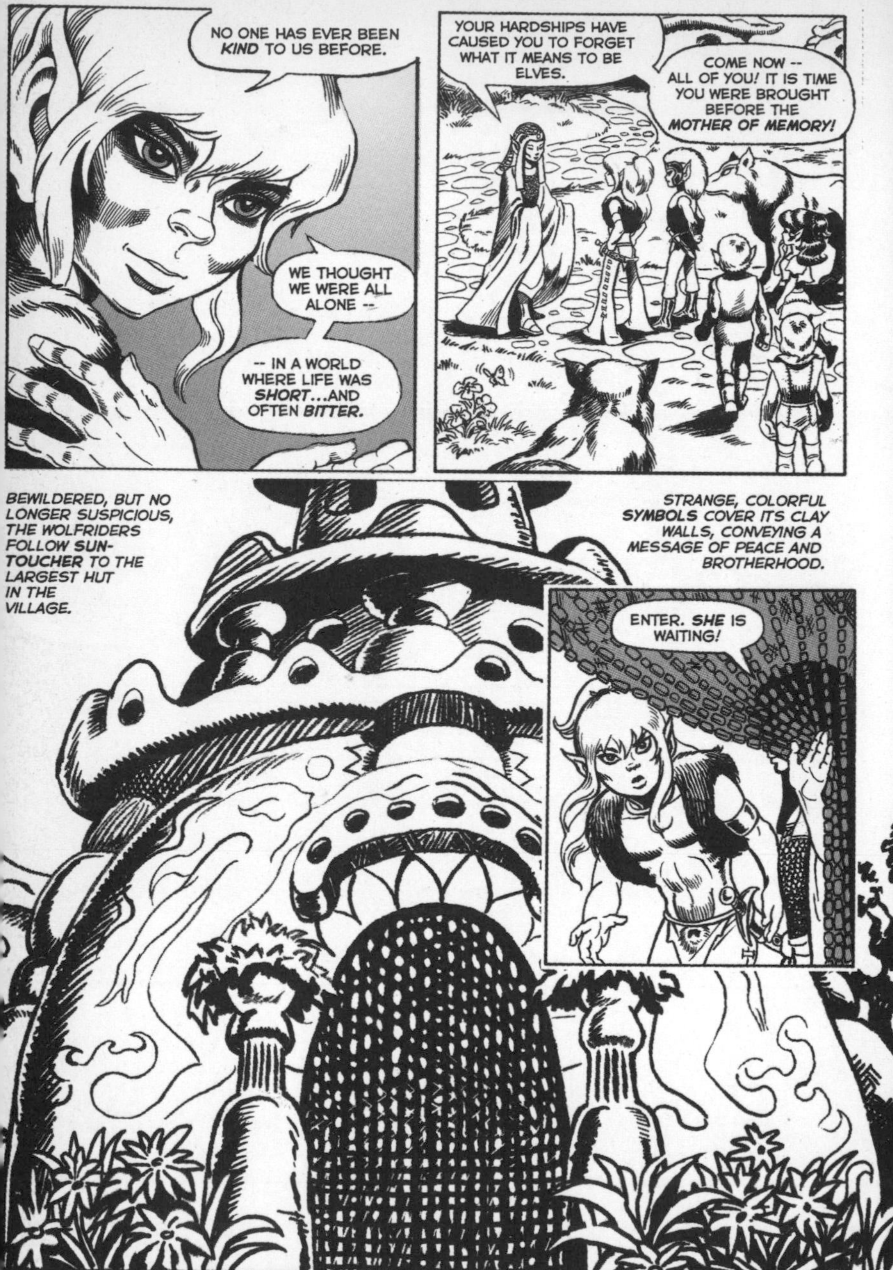

NO ONE HAS EVER BEEN *KIND* TO US BEFORE.
WE THOUGHT WE WERE ALL ALONE --
-- IN A WORLD WHERE LIFE WAS *SHORT*...AND OFTEN *BITTER.*
YOUR HARDSHIPS HAVE CAUSED YOU TO FORGET WHAT IT MEANS TO BE ELVES.
COME NOW -- ALL OF YOU! IT IS TIME YOU WERE BROUGHT BEFORE THE ***MOTHER OF MEMORY!***
BEWILDERED, BUT NO LONGER SUSPICIOUS, THE WOLFRIDERS FOLLOW ***SUN-TOUCHER*** *TO THE LARGEST HUT IN THE VILLAGE.*
STRANGE, COLORFUL ***SYMBOLS*** *COVER ITS CLAY WALLS, CONVEYING A MESSAGE OF PEACE AND BROTHERHOOD.*
ENTER. ***SHE*** IS WAITING!

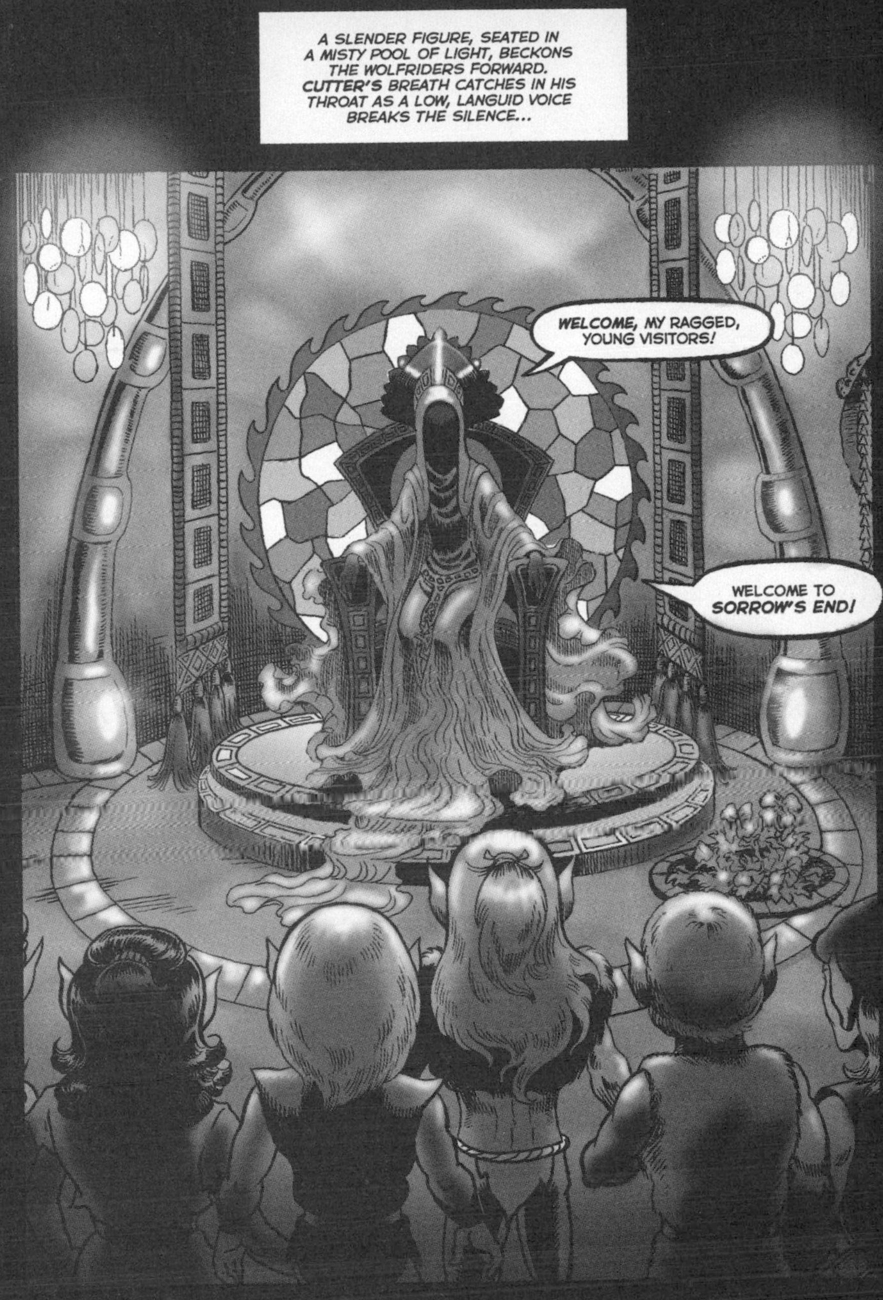

A SLENDER FIGURE, SEATED IN A MISTY POOL OF LIGHT, BECKONS THE WOLFRIDERS FORWARD. CUTTER'S BREATH CATCHES IN HIS THROAT AS A LOW, LANGUID VOICE BREAKS THE SILENCE...
WELCOME, MY RAGGED, YOUNG VISITORS!
WELCOME TO SORROW'S END!

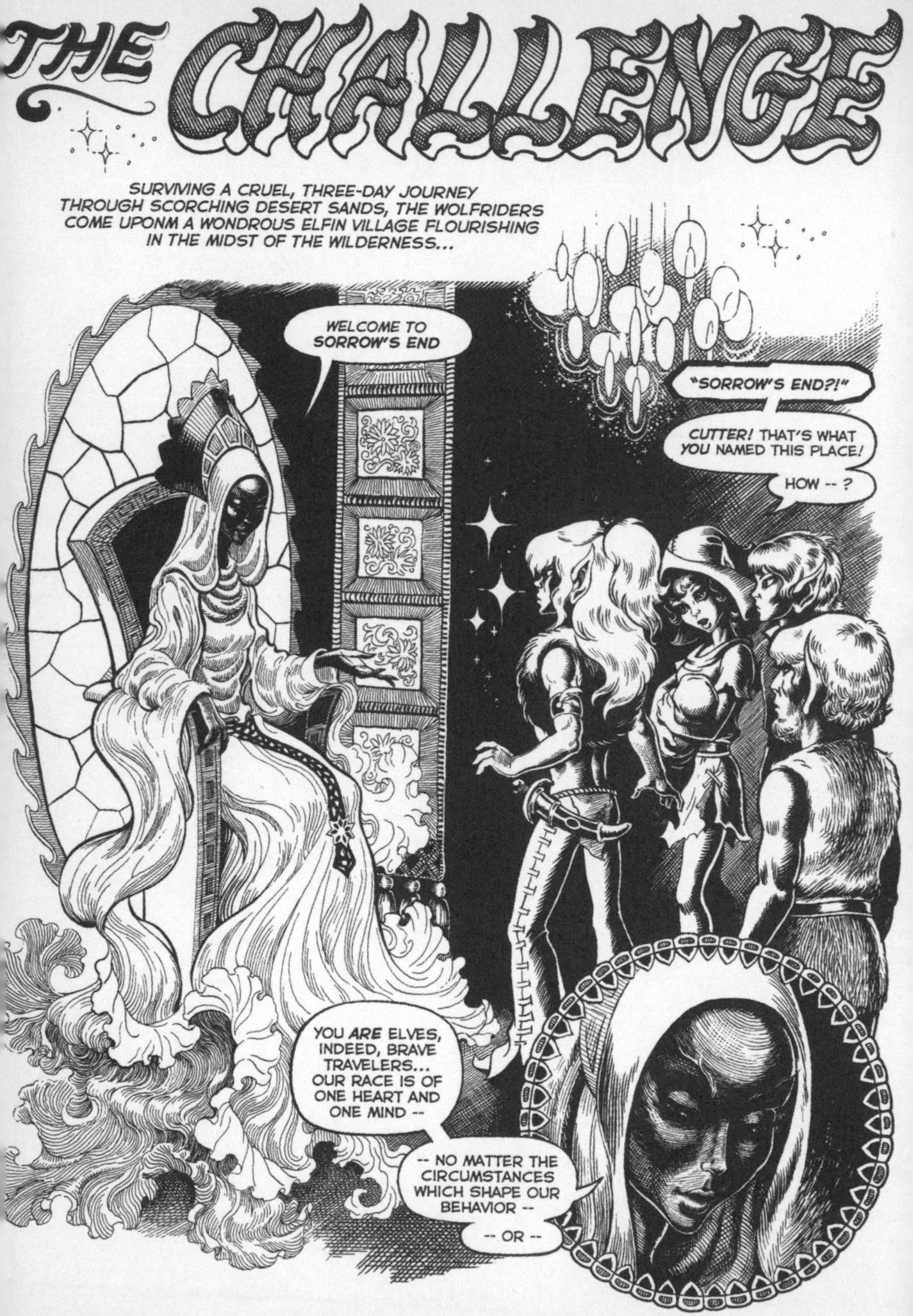
THE CHALLENGE
SURVIVING A CRUEL, THREE-DAY JOURNEY THROUGH SCORCHING DESERT SANDS, THE WOLFRIDERS COME UPONM A WONDROUS ELFIN VILLAGE FLOURISHING IN THE MIDST OF THE WILDERNESS...
WELCOME TO SORROW'S END
"SORROW'S END?!"
CUTTER! THAT'S WHAT YOU NAMED THIS PLACE!
HOW -- ?
YOU ARE ELVES, INDEED, BRAVE TRAVELERS... OUR RACE IS OF ONE HEART AND ONE MIND --
-- NO MATTER THE CIRCUMSTANCES WHICH SHAPE OUR BEHAVIOR --
-- OR --

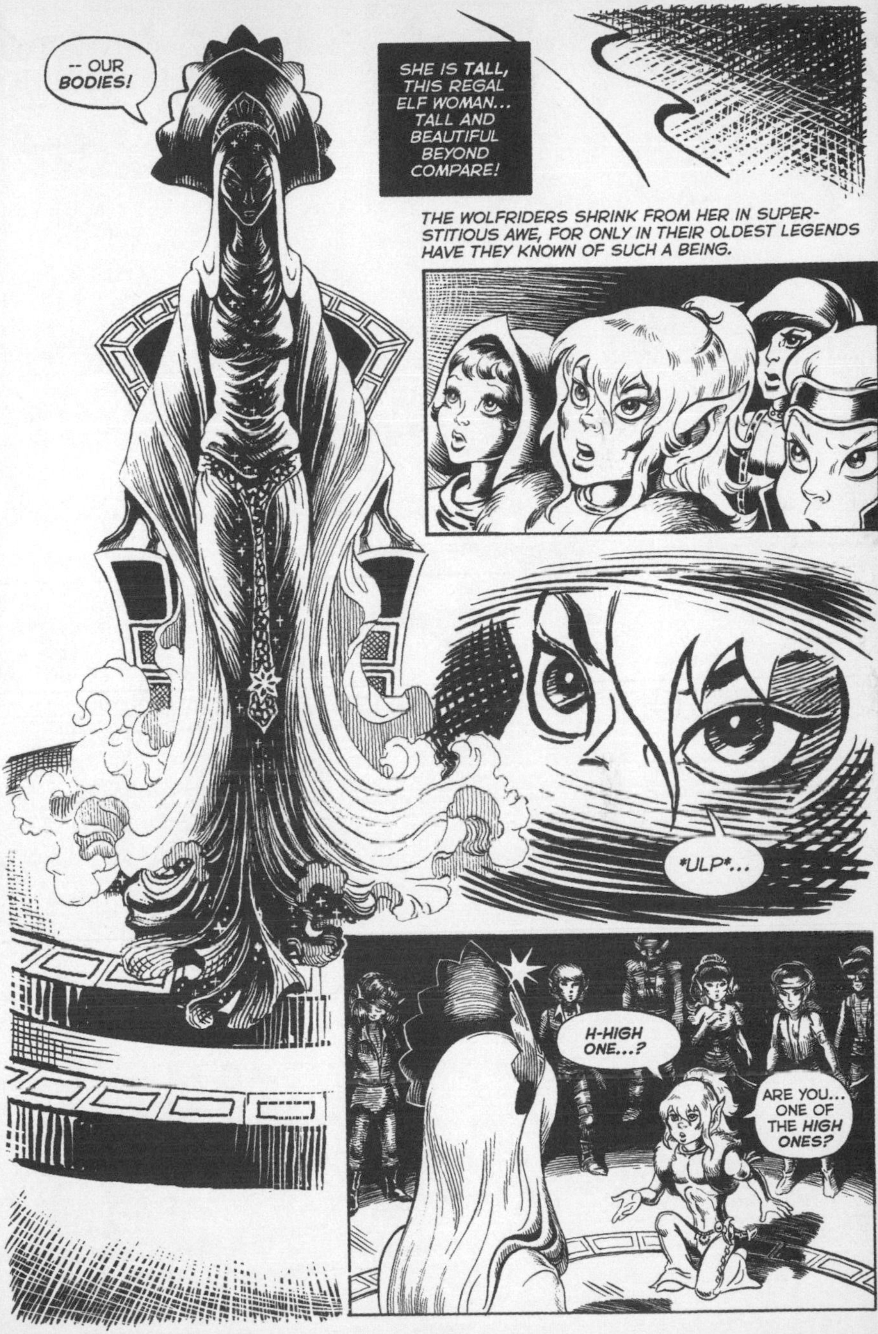
-- OUR BODIES!
SHE IS TALL, THIS REGAL ELF WOMAN... TALL AND BEAUTIFUL BEYOND COMPARE!
THE WOLFRIDERS SHRINK FROM HER IN SUPERSTITIOUS AWE, FOR ONLY IN THEIR OLDEST LEGENDS HAVE THEY KNOWN OF SUCH A BEING.
ULP...
H-HIGH ONE...?
ARE YOU... ONE OF THE HIGH ONES?

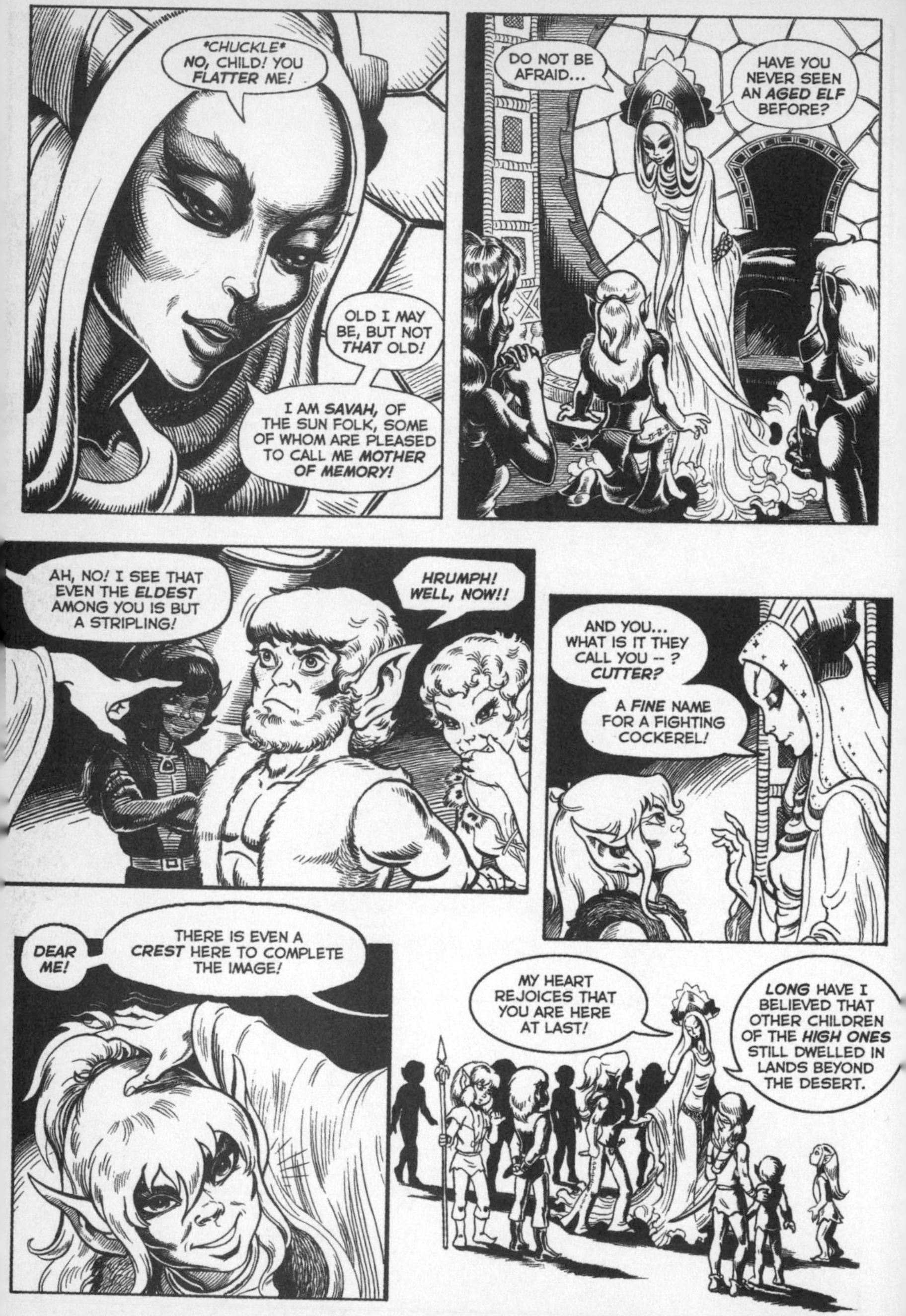
CHUCKLE NO, CHILD! YOU FLATTER ME!
OLD I MAY BE, BUT NOT THAT OLD!
I AM SAVAH, OF THE SUN FOLK, SOME OF WHOM ARE PLEASED TO CALL ME MOTHER OF MEMORY!
DO NOT BE AFRAID...
HAVE YOU NEVER SEEN AN AGED ELF BEFORE?
AH, NO! I SEE THAT EVEN THE ELDEST AMONG YOU IS BUT A STRIPLING!
HRUMPH! WELL, NOW!!
AND YOU... WHAT IS IT THEY CALL YOU -- ? CUTTER?
A FINE NAME FOR A FIGHTING COCKEREL!
DEAR ME!
THERE IS EVEN A CREST HERE TO COMPLETE THE IMAGE!
MY HEART REJOICES THAT YOU ARE HERE AT LAST!
LONG HAVE I BELIEVED THAT OTHER CHILDREN OF THE HIGH ONES STILL DWELLED IN LANDS BEYOND THE DESERT.

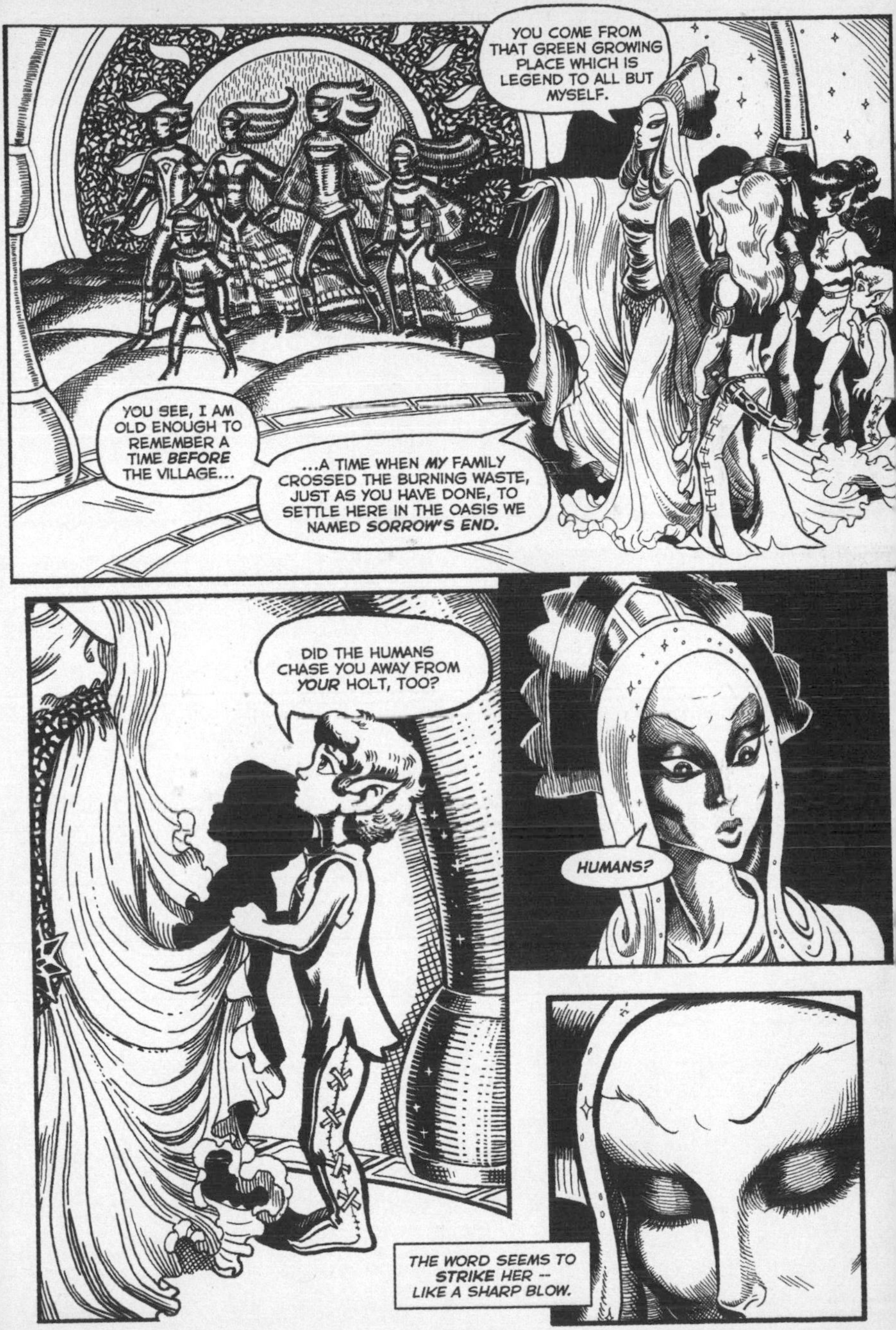
YOU COME FROM THAT GREEN GROWING PLACE WHICH IS LEGEND TO ALL BUT MYSELF.
YOU SEE, I AM OLD ENOUGH TO REMEMBER A TIME *BEFORE* THE VILLAGE...
...A TIME WHEN *MY* FAMILY CROSSED THE BURNING WASTE, JUST AS YOU HAVE DONE, TO SETTLE HERE IN THE OASIS WE NAMED *SORROW'S END.*
DID THE HUMANS CHASE YOU AWAY FROM *YOUR* HOLT, TOO?
HUMANS?
THE WORD SEEMS TO STRIKE HER -- LIKE A SHARP BLOW.

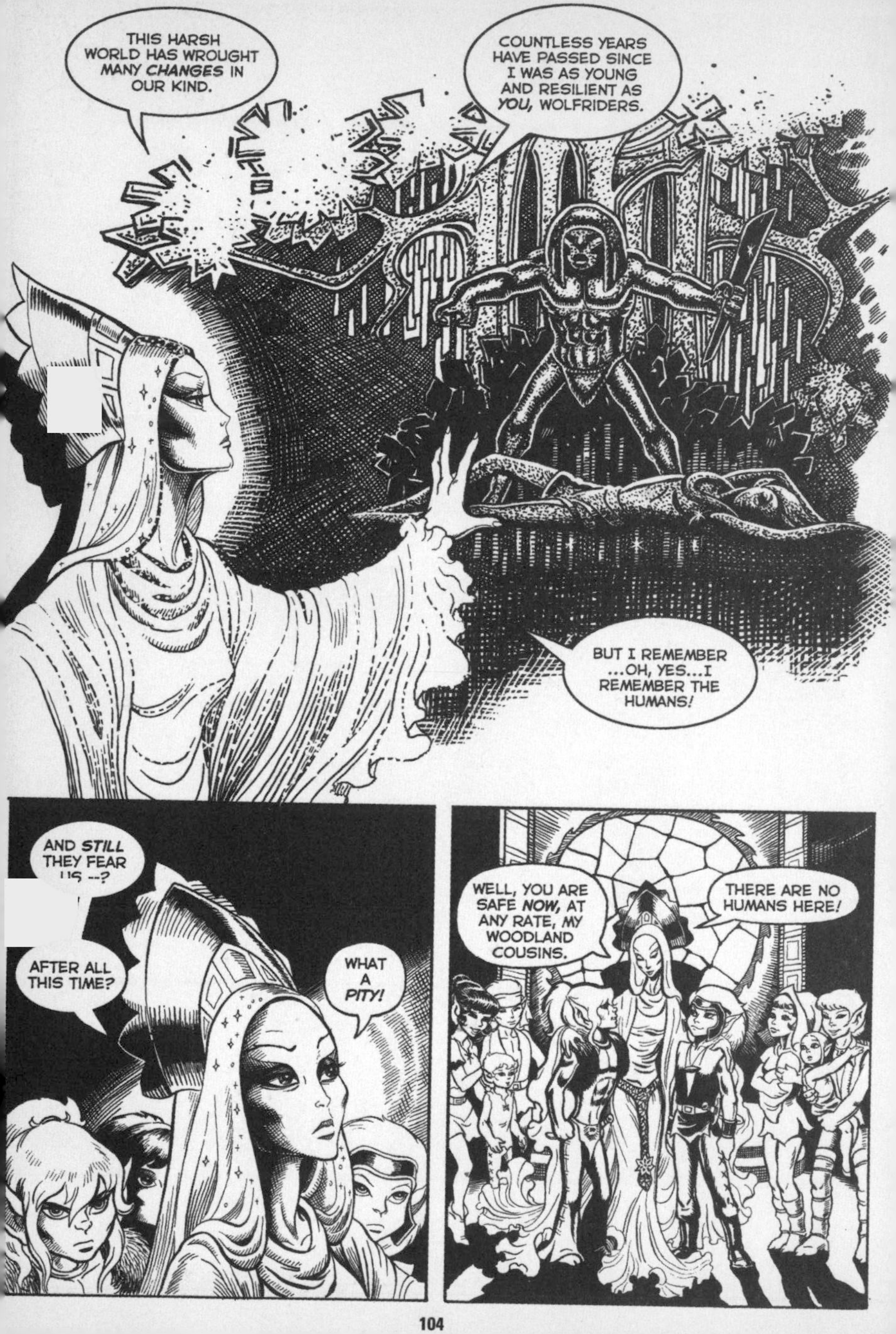
THIS HARSH WORLD HAS WROUGHT MANY CHANGES IN OUR KIND.
COUNTLESS YEARS HAVE PASSED SINCE I WAS AS YOUNG AND RESILIENT AS YOU, WOLFRIDERS.
BUT I REMEMBER ...OH, YES...I REMEMBER THE HUMANS!
AND STILL THEY FEAR US --?
AFTER ALL THIS TIME?
WHAT A PITY!
WELL, YOU ARE SAFE NOW, AT ANY RATE, MY WOODLAND COUSINS.
THERE ARE NO HUMANS HERE!

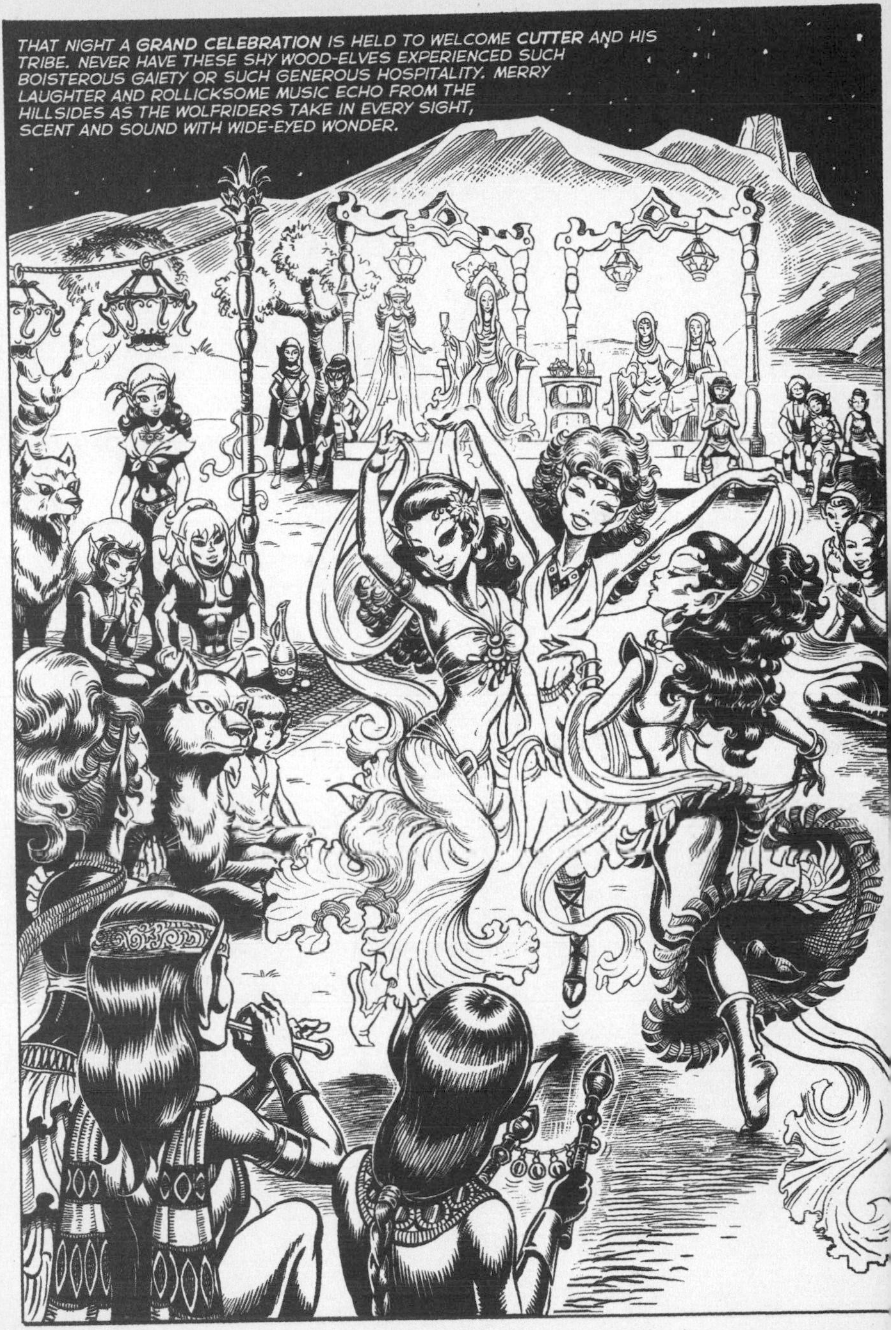
THAT NIGHT A **GRAND CELEBRATION** IS HELD TO WELCOME **CUTTER** AND HIS TRIBE. NEVER HAVE THESE SHY WOOD-ELVES EXPERIENCED SUCH BOISTEROUS GAIETY OR SUCH GENEROUS HOSPITALITY. MERRY LAUGHTER AND ROLLICKSOME MUSIC ECHO FROM THE HILLSIDES AS THE WOLFRIDERS TAKE IN EVERY SIGHT, SCENT AND SOUND WITH WIDE-EYED WONDER.

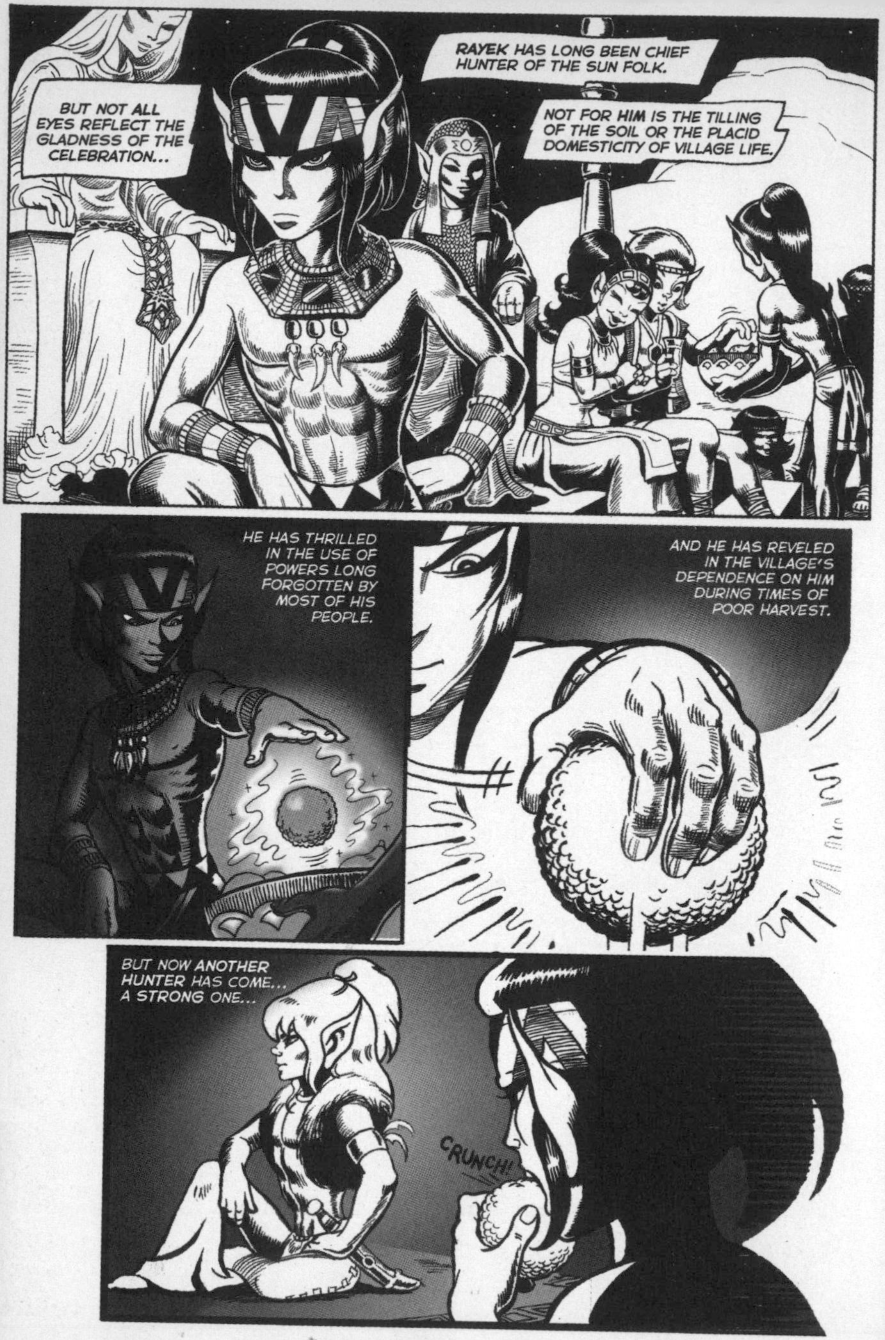
BUT NOT ALL EYES REFLECT THE GLADNESS OF THE CELEBRATION...
RAYEK HAS LONG BEEN CHIEF HUNTER OF THE SUN FOLK.
NOT FOR HIM IS THE TILLING OF THE SOIL OR THE PLACID DOMESTICITY OF VILLAGE LIFE.
HE HAS THRILLED IN THE USE OF POWERS LONG FORGOTTEN BY MOST OF HIS PEOPLE.
AND HE HAS REVELED IN THE VILLAGE'S DEPENDENCE ON HIM DURING TIMES OF POOR HARVEST.
BUT NOW ANOTHER HUNTER HAS COME... A STRONG ONE...
CRUNCH!

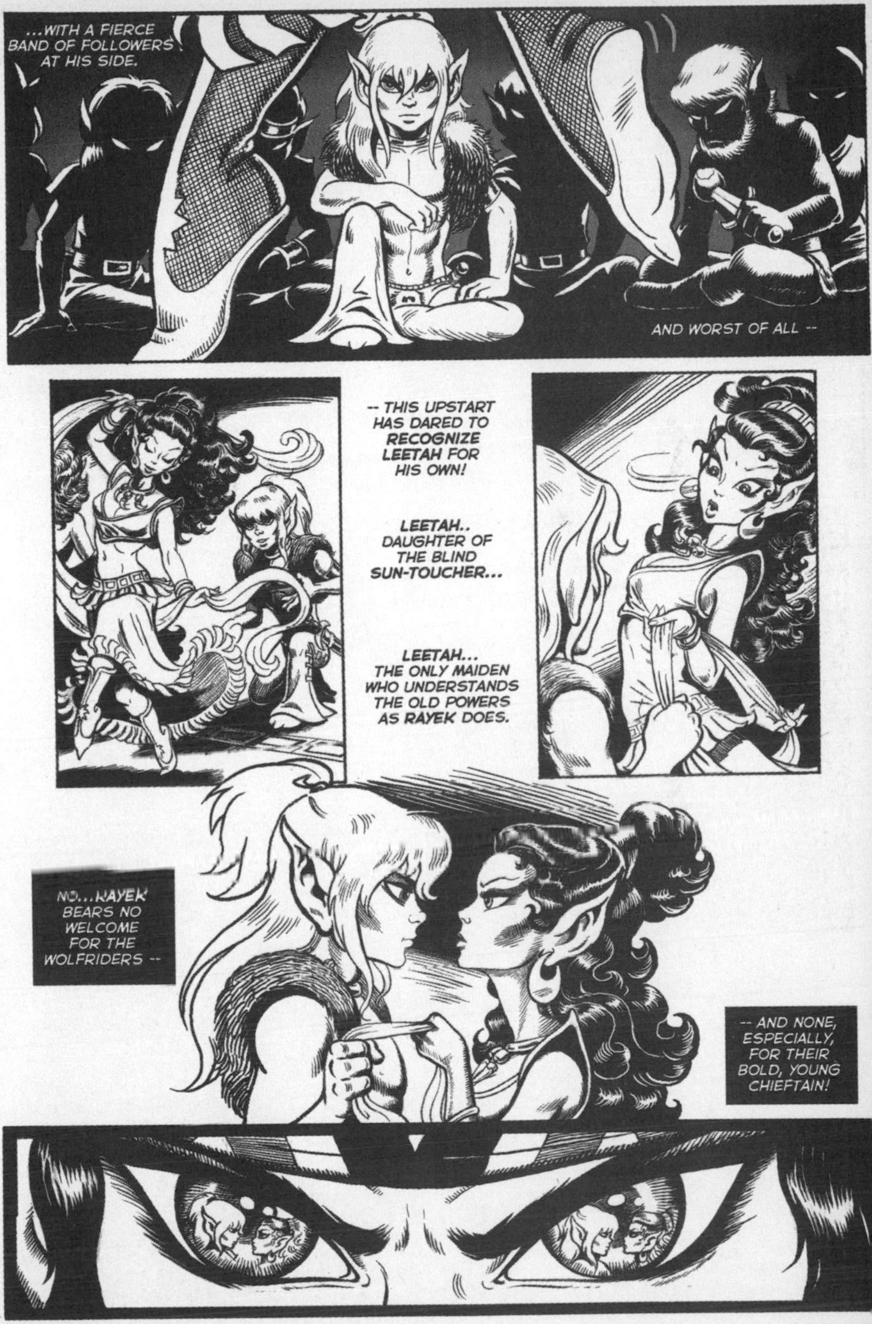
...WITH A FIERCE BAND OF FOLLOWERS AT HIS SIDE.
AND WORST OF ALL --
-- THIS UPSTART HAS DARED TO RECOGNIZE LEETAH FOR HIS OWN!
LEETAH.. DAUGHTER OF THE BLIND SUN-TOUCHER...
LEETAH... THE ONLY MAIDEN WHO UNDERSTANDS THE OLD POWERS AS RAYEK DOES.
NO... RAYEK BEARS NO WELCOME FOR THE WOLFRIDERS --
-- AND NONE, ESPECIALLY, FOR THEIR BOLD, YOUNG CHIEFTAIN!

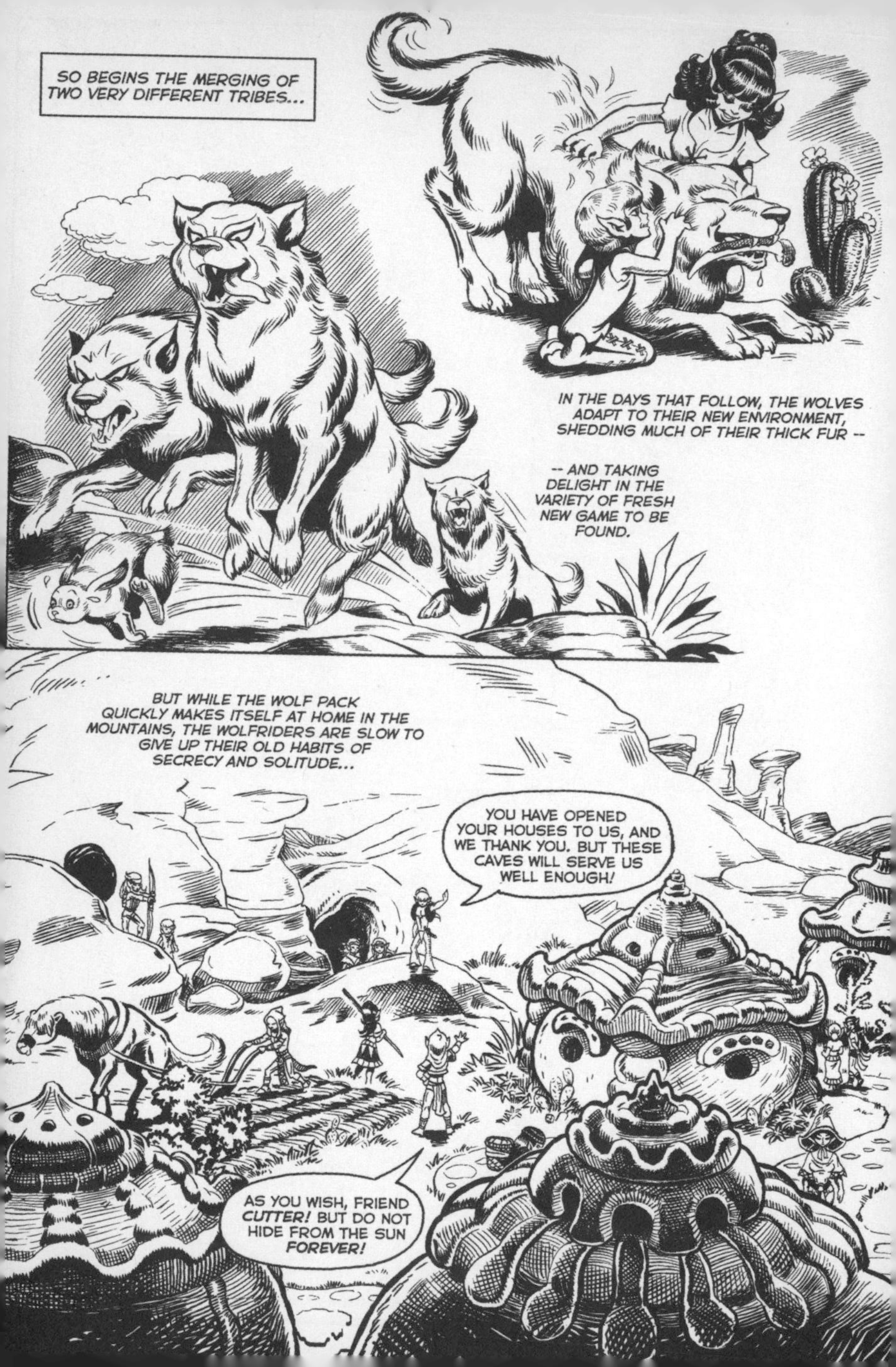
SO BEGINS THE MERGING OF TWO VERY DIFFERENT TRIBES...
IN THE DAYS THAT FOLLOW, THE WOLVES ADAPT TO THEIR NEW ENVIRONMENT, SHEDDING MUCH OF THEIR THICK FUR --
-- AND TAKING DELIGHT IN THE VARIETY OF FRESH NEW GAME TO BE FOUND.
BUT WHILE THE WOLF PACK QUICKLY MAKES ITSELF AT HOME IN THE MOUNTAINS, THE WOLFRIDERS ARE SLOW TO GIVE UP THEIR OLD HABITS OF SECRECY AND SOLITUDE...
YOU HAVE OPENED YOUR HOUSES TO US, AND WE THANK YOU. BUT THESE CAVES WILL SERVE US WELL ENOUGH!
AS YOU WISH, FRIEND CUTTER! BUT DO NOT HIDE FROM THE SUN FOREVER!

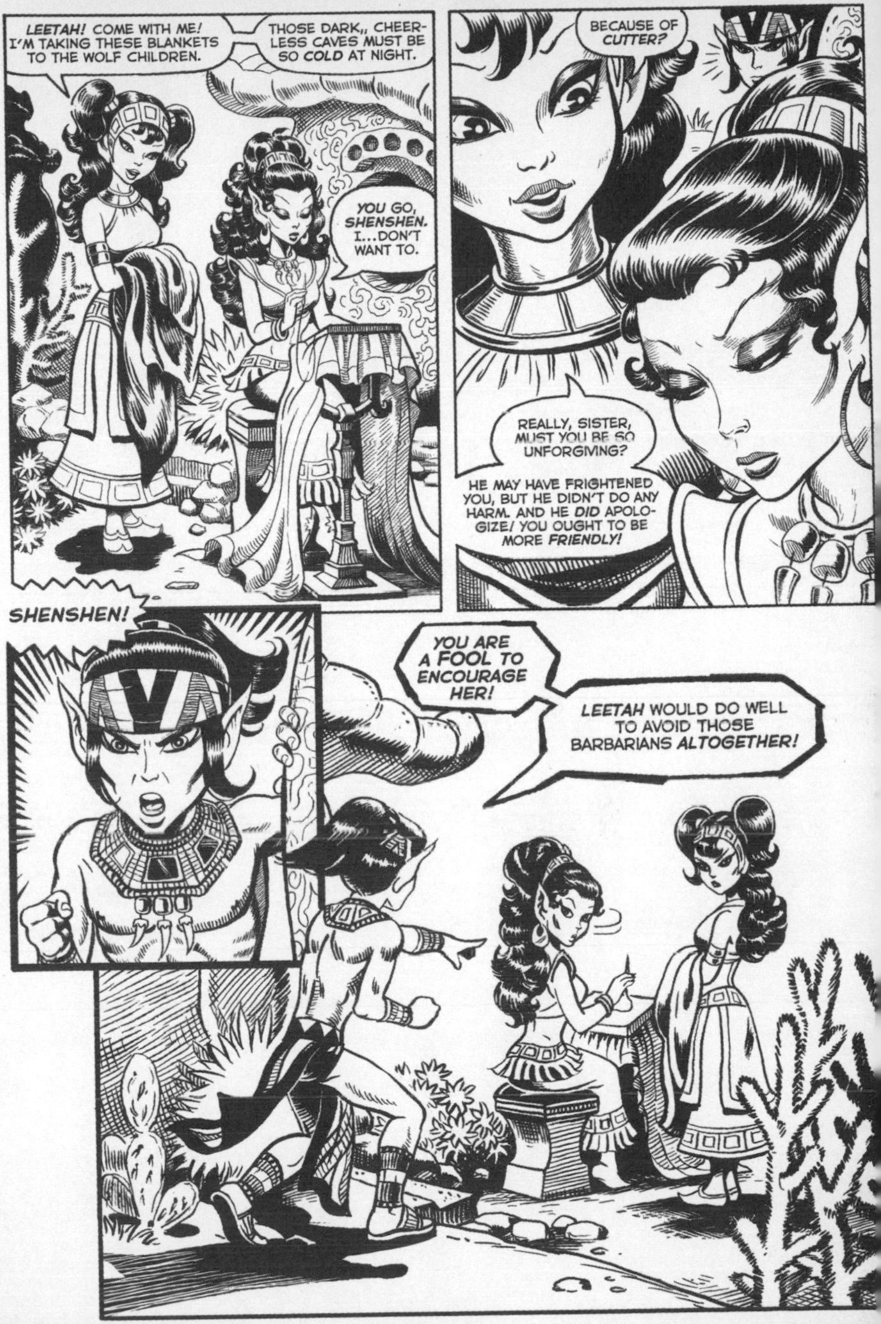

LEETAH! COME WITH ME! I'M TAKING THESE BLANKETS TO THE WOLF CHILDREN.
THOSE DARK,, CHEERLESS CAVES MUST BE SO COLD AT NIGHT.
YOU GO, SHENSHEN. I...DON'T WANT TO.
BECAUSE OF CUTTER?
REALLY, SISTER, MUST YOU BE SO UNFORGIVING?
HE MAY HAVE FRIGHTENED YOU, BUT HE DIDN'T DO ANY HARM. AND HE DID APOLOGIZE! YOU OUGHT TO BE MORE FRIENDLY!
SHENSHEN!
YOU ARE A FOOL TO ENCOURAGE HER!
LEETAH WOULD DO WELL TO AVOID THOSE BARBARIANS ALTOGETHER!

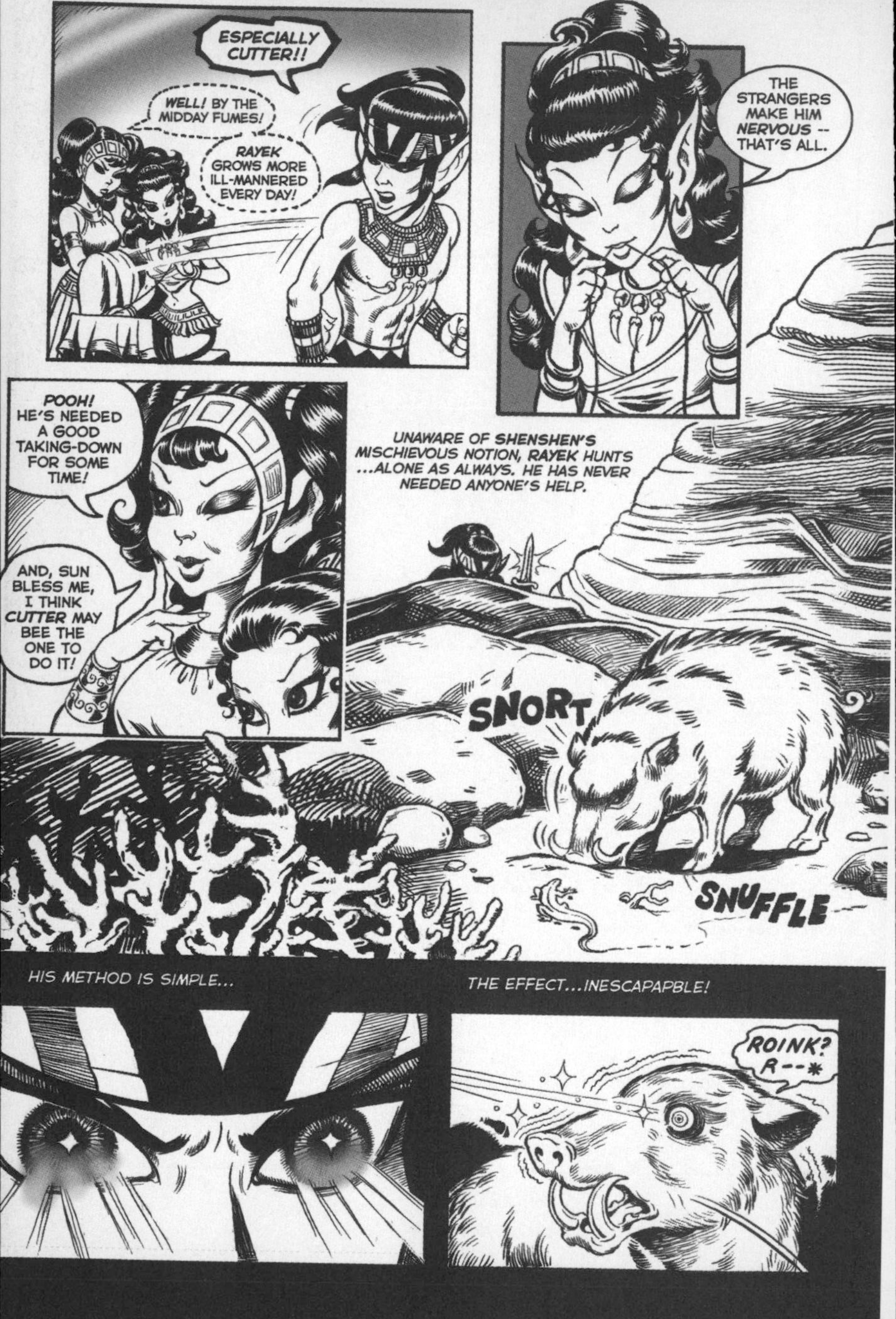
ESPECIALLY CUTTER!!
WELL! BY THE MIDDAY FUMES!
RAYEK GROWS MORE ILL-MANNERED EVERY DAY!
THE STRANGERS MAKE HIM NERVOUS -- THAT'S ALL.
POOH! HE'S NEEDED A GOOD TAKING-DOWN FOR SOME TIME!
AND, SUN BLESS ME, I THINK CUTTER MAY BEE THE ONE TO DO IT!
UNAWARE OF SHENSHEN'S MISCHIEVOUS NOTION, RAYEK HUNTS ...ALONE AS ALWAYS. HE HAS NEVER NEEDED ANYONE'S HELP.
SNORT
SNUFFLE
HIS METHOD IS SIMPLE...
THE EFFECT...INESCAPAPBLE!
ROINK? R--*

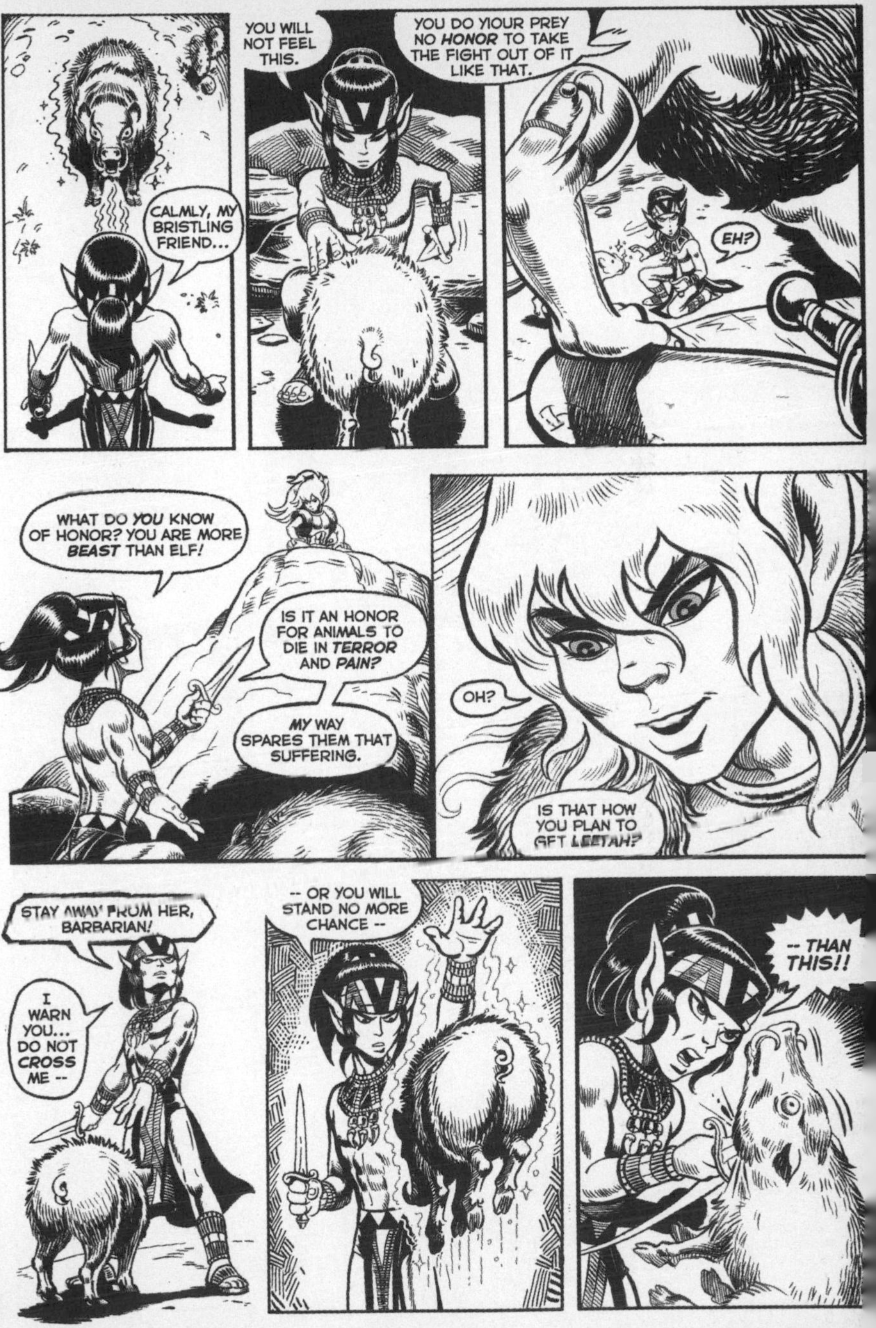
CALMLY, MY BRISTLING FRIEND...
YOU WILL NOT FEEL THIS.
YOU DO YIOUR PREY NO HONOR TO TAKE THE FIGHT OUT OF IT LIKE THAT.
EH?
WHAT DO YOU KNOW OF HONOR? YOU ARE MORE BEAST THAN ELF!
IS IT AN HONOR FOR ANIMALS TO DIE IN TERROR AND PAIN?
MY WAY SPARES THEM THAT SUFFERING.
OH?
IS THAT HOW YOU PLAN TO GET LEETAH?
STAY AWAY FROM HER, BARBARIAN!
I WARN YOU... DO NOT CROSS ME --
-- OR YOU WILL STAND NO MORE CHANCE --
-- THAN THIS!!

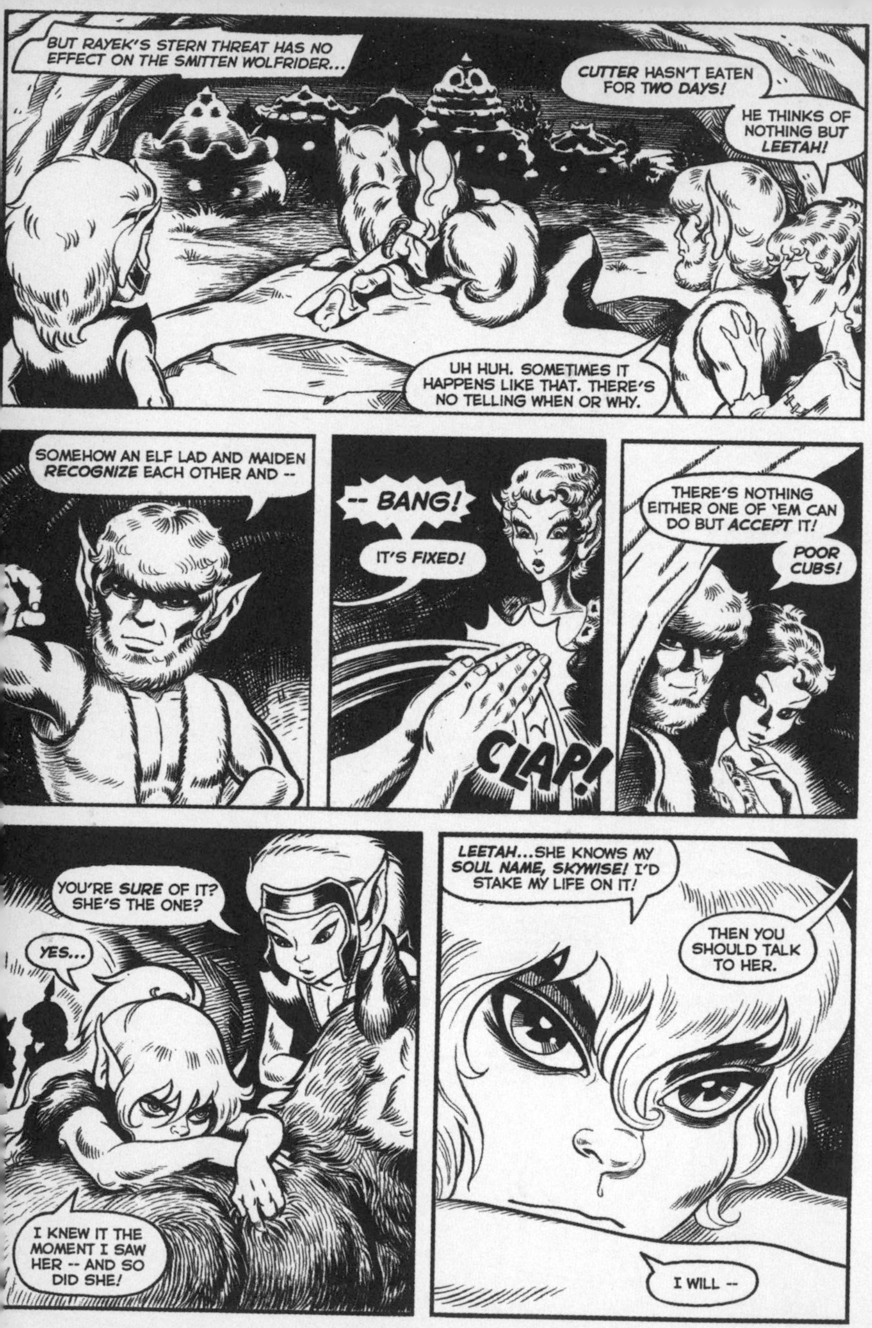
BUT RAYEK'S STERN THREAT HAS NO EFFECT ON THE SMITTEN WOLFRIDER...
CUTTER HASN'T EATEN FOR TWO DAYS!
HE THINKS OF NOTHING BUT LEETAH!
UH HUH. SOMETIMES IT HAPPENS LIKE THAT. THERE'S NO TELLING WHEN OR WHY.
SOMEHOW AN ELF LAD AND MAIDEN RECOGNIZE EACH OTHER AND --
-- BANG!
IT'S FIXED!
CLAP!
THERE'S NOTHING EITHER ONE OF 'EM CAN DO BUT ACCEPT IT!
POOR CUBS!
YOU'RE SURE OF IT? SHE'S THE ONE?
YES...
I KNEW IT THE MOMENT I SAW HER -- AND SO DID SHE!
LEETAH...SHE KNOWS MY SOUL NAME, SKYWISE! I'D STAKE MY LIFE ON IT!
THEN YOU SHOULD TALK TO HER.
I WILL --

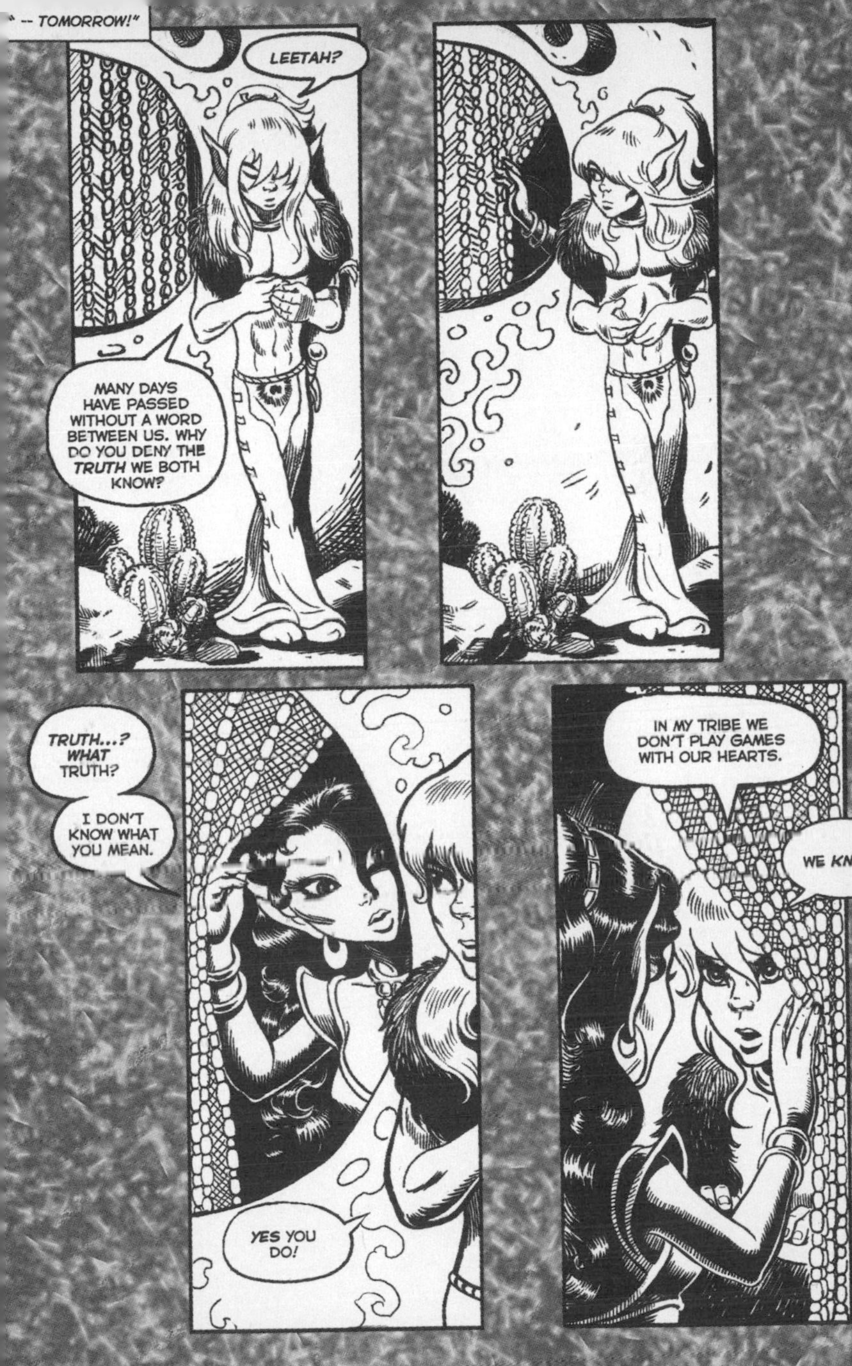
" -- TOMORROW!"
LEETAH?
MANY DAYS HAVE PASSED WITHOUT A WORD BETWEEN US. WHY DO YOU DENY THE TRUTH WE BOTH KNOW?
TRUTH...? WHAT TRUTH?
I DON'T KNOW WHAT YOU MEAN.
YES YOU DO!
IN MY TRIBE WE DON'T PLAY GAMES WITH OUR HEARTS.
WE KNOW!

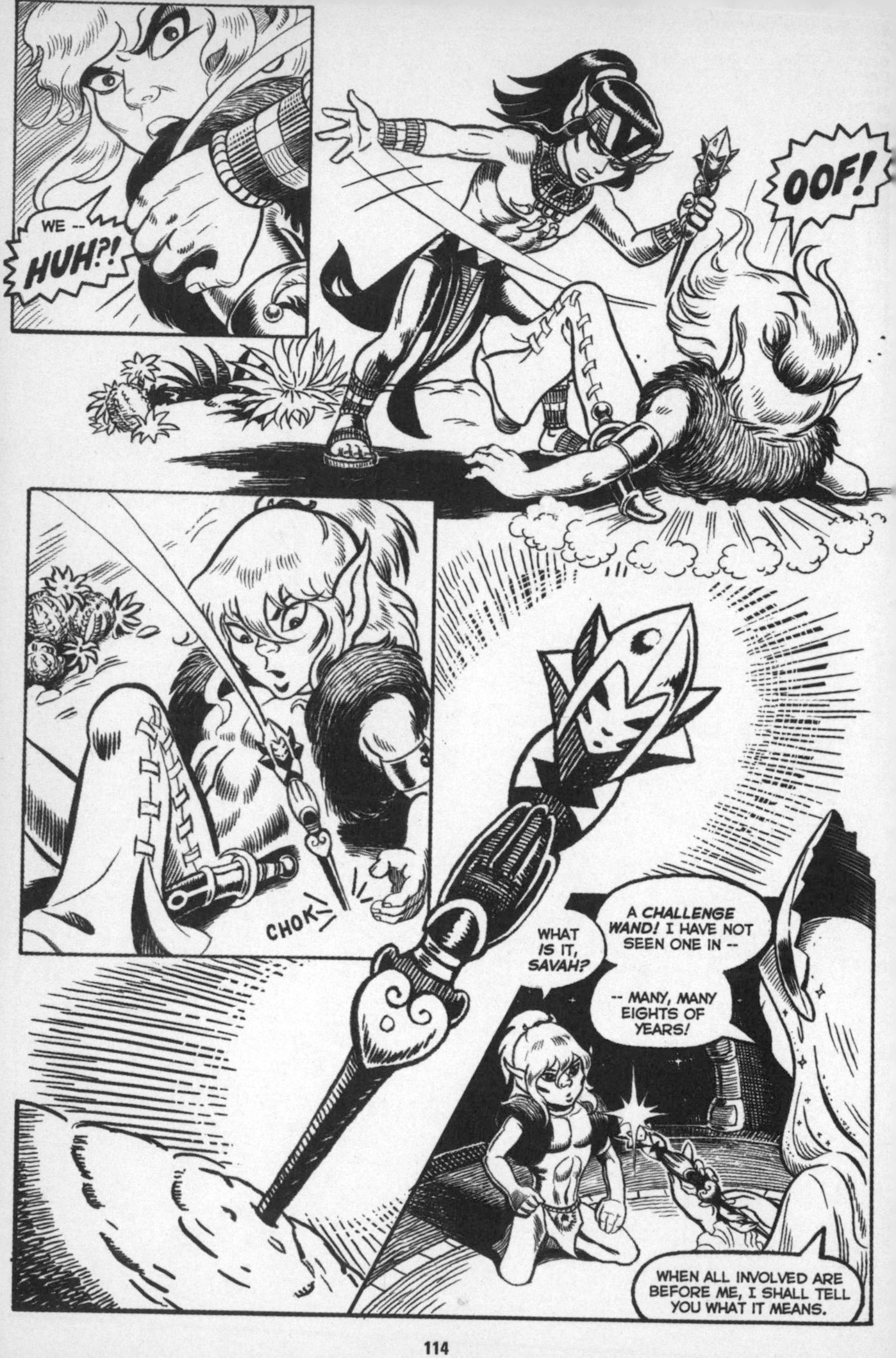

WE --
HUH?!
OOF!
CHOK
WHAT IS IT, SAVAH?
A CHALLENGE WAND! I HAVE NOT SEEN ONE IN --
-- MANY, MANY EIGHTS OF YEARS!
WHEN ALL INVOLVED ARE BEFORE ME, I SHALL TELL YOU WHAT IT MEANS.

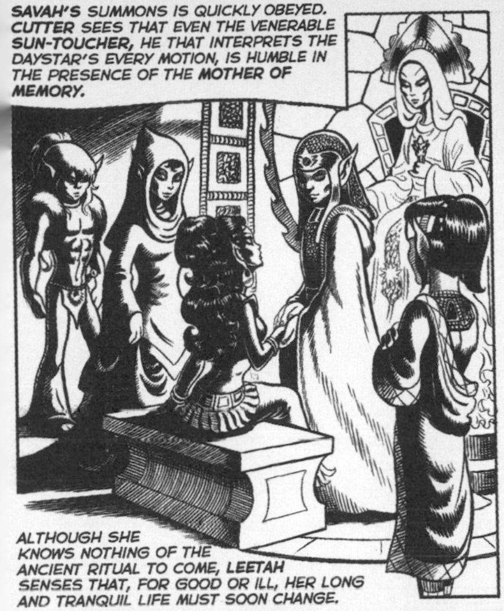
SAVAH'S SUMMONS IS QUICKLY OBEYED. CUTTER SEES THAT EVEN THE VENERABLE SUN-TOUCHER, HE THAT INTERPRETS THE DAYSTAR'S EVERY MOTION, IS HUMBLE IN THE PRESENCE OF THE MOTHER OF MEMORY.
ALTHOUGH SHE KNOWS NOTHING OF THE ANCIENT RITUAL TO COME, LEETAH SENSES THAT, FOR GOOD OR ILL, HER LONG AND TRANQUIL LIFE MUST SOON CHANGE.

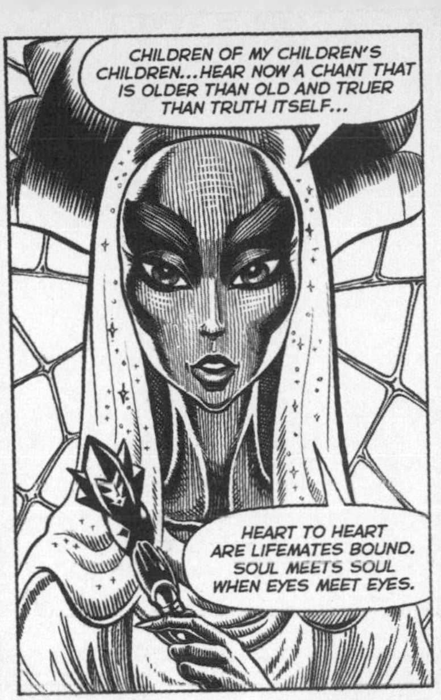
CHILDREN OF MY CHILDREN'S CHILDREN...HEAR NOW A CHANT THAT IS OLDER THAN OLD AND TRUER THAN TRUTH ITSELF...
HEART TO HEART ARE LIFEMATES BOUND. SOUL MEETS SOUL WHEN EYES MEET EYES.

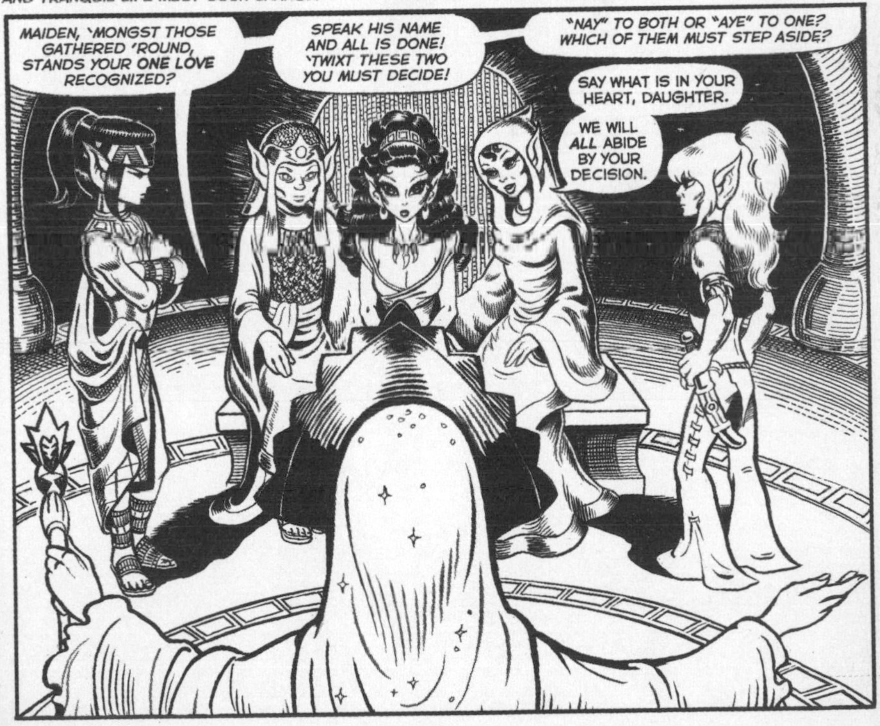
MAIDEN, 'MONGST THOSE GATHERED 'ROUND, STANDS YOUR ONE LOVE RECOGNIZED?
SPEAK HIS NAME AND ALL IS DONE! 'TWIXT THESE TWO YOU MUST DECIDE!
"NAY" TO BOTH OR "AYE" TO ONE? WHICH OF THEM MUST STEP ASIDE?
SAY WHAT IS IN YOUR HEART, DAUGHTER.
WE WILL ALL ABIDE BY YOUR DECISION.

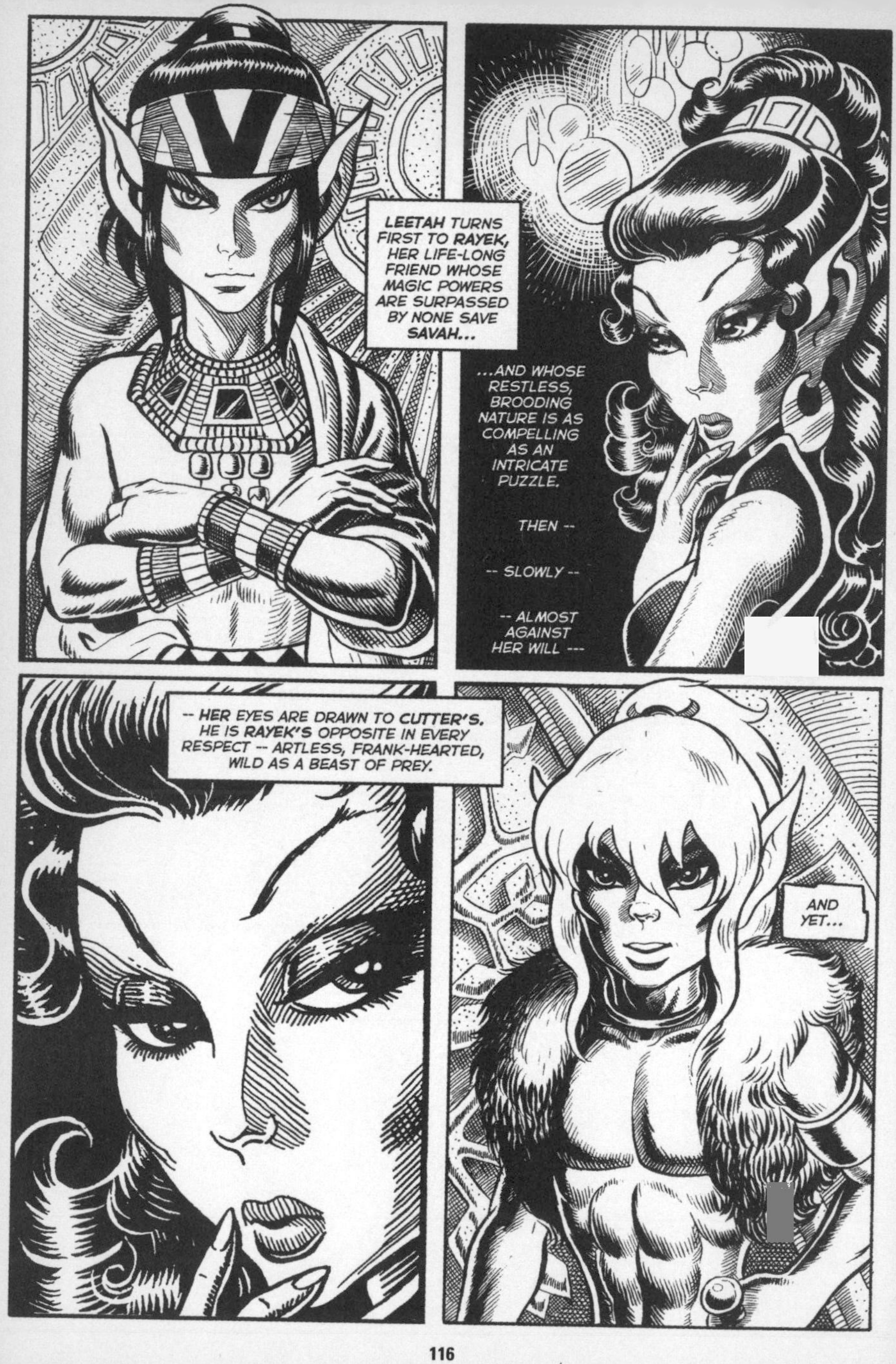

LEETAH TURNS FIRST TO RAYEK, HER LIFE-LONG FRIEND WHOSE MAGIC POWERS ARE SURPASSED BY NONE SAVE SAVAH...
...AND WHOSE RESTLESS, BROODING NATURE IS AS COMPELLING AS AN INTRICATE PUZZLE.
THEN --
-- SLOWLY --
-- ALMOST AGAINST HER WILL ---
-- HER EYES ARE DRAWN TO CUTTER'S. HE IS RAYEK'S OPPOSITE IN EVERY RESPECT -- ARTLESS, FRANK-HEARTED, WILD AS A BEAST OF PREY.
AND YET...

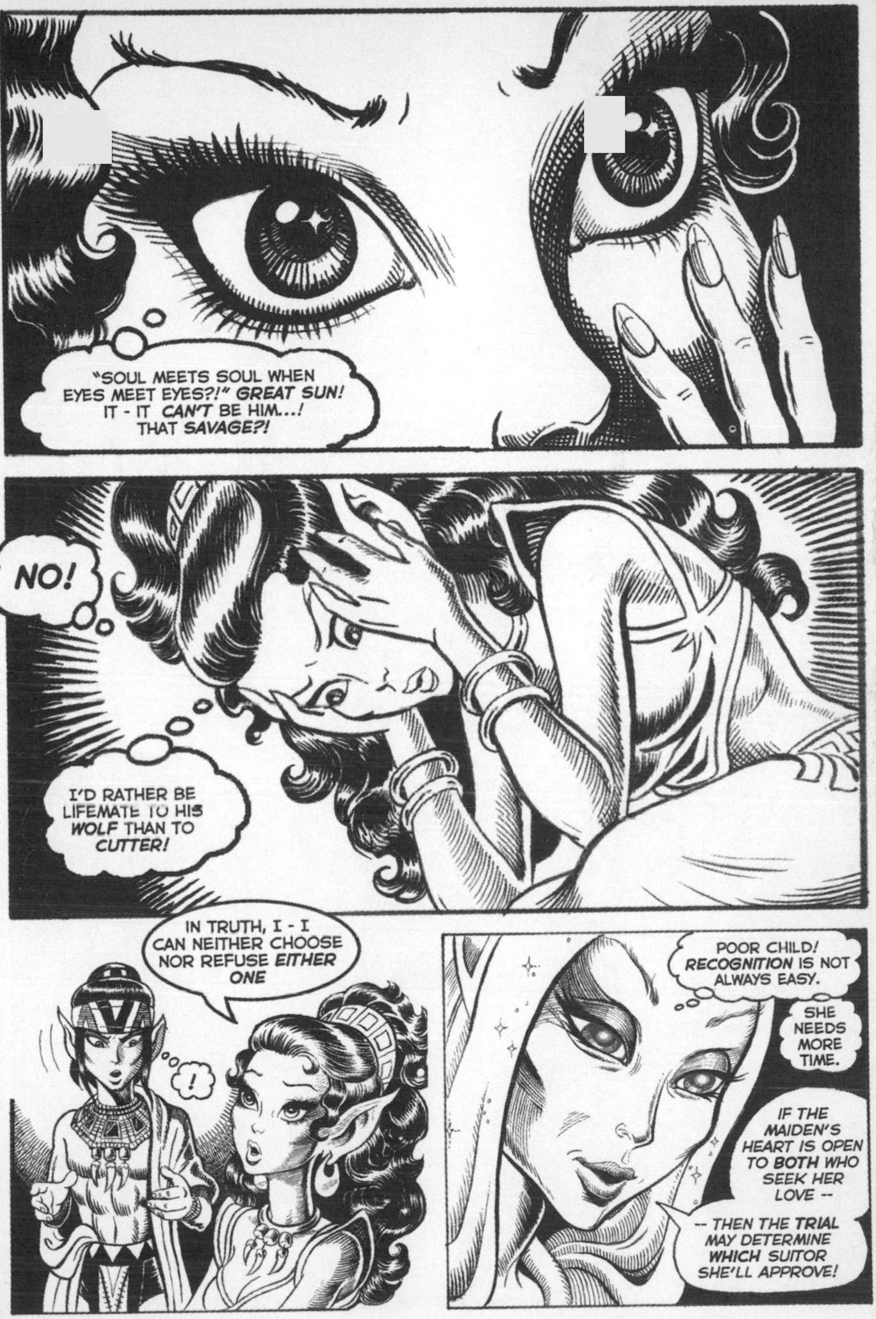
"SOUL MEETS SOUL WHEN EYES MEET EYES?!" GREAT SUN! IT - IT CAN'T BE HIM...! THAT SAVAGE?!
NO!
I'D RATHER BE LIFEMATE TO HIS WOLF THAN TO CUTTER!
IN TRUTH, I - I CAN NEITHER CHOOSE NOR REFUSE EITHER ONE
!
POOR CHILD! RECOGNITION IS NOT ALWAYS EASY.
SHE NEEDS MORE TIME.
IF THE MAIDEN'S HEART IS OPEN TO BOTH WHO SEEK HER LOVE --
-- THEN THE TRIAL MAY DETERMINE WHICH SUITOR SHE'LL APPROVE!

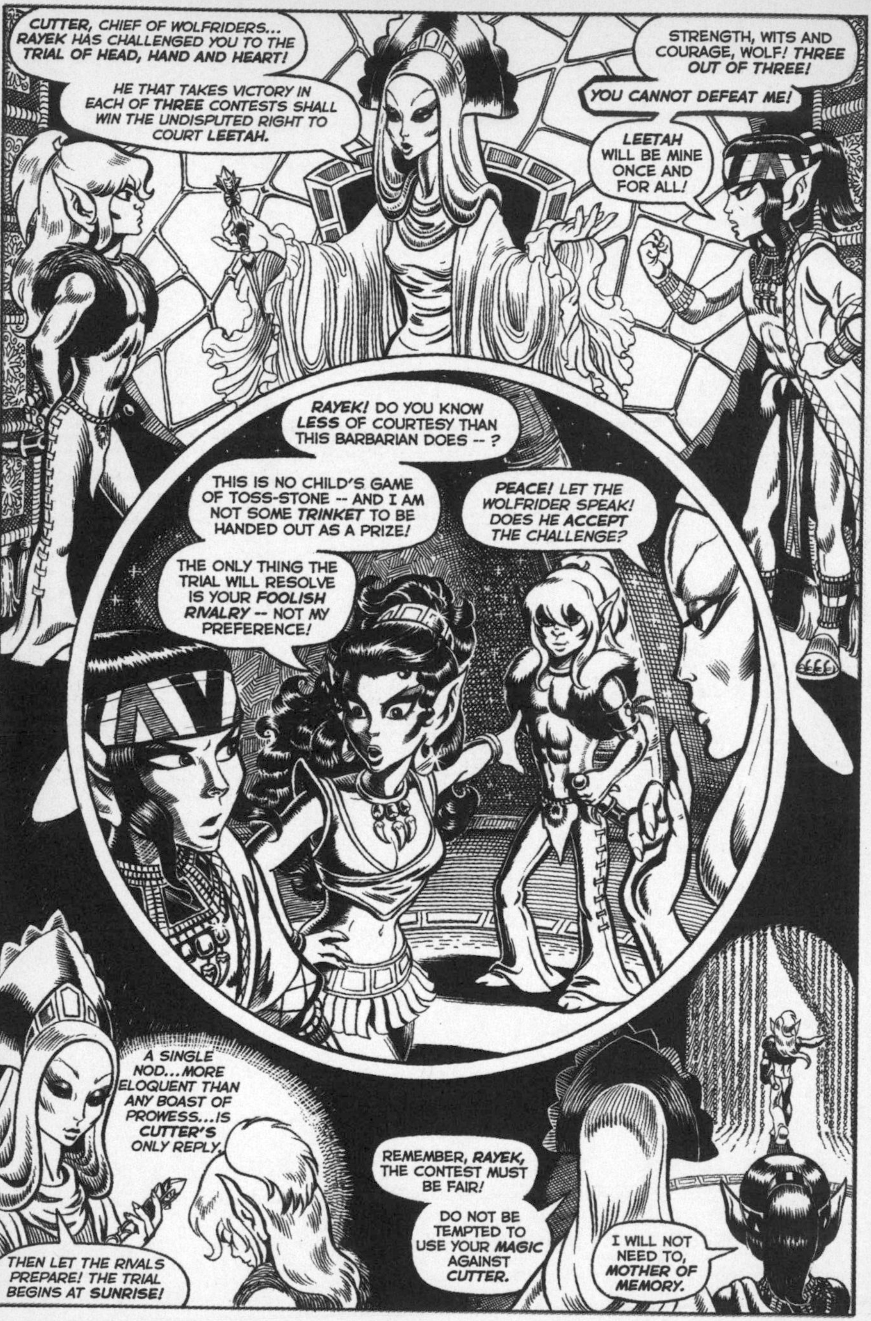
CUTTER, CHIEF OF WOLFRIDERS... RAYEK HAS CHALLENGED YOU TO THE TRIAL OF HEAD, HAND AND HEART!
HE THAT TAKES VICTORY IN EACH OF THREE CONTESTS SHALL WIN THE UNDISPUTED RIGHT TO COURT LEETAH.
STRENGTH, WITS AND COURAGE, WOLF! THREE OUT OF THREE!
YOU CANNOT DEFEAT ME!
LEETAH WILL BE MINE ONCE AND FOR ALL!
RAYEK! DO YOU KNOW LESS OF COURTESY THAN THIS BARBARIAN DOES -- ?
THIS IS NO CHILD'S GAME OF TOSS-STONE -- AND I AM NOT SOME TRINKET TO BE HANDED OUT AS A PRIZE!
THE ONLY THING THE TRIAL WILL RESOLVE IS YOUR FOOLISH RIVALRY -- NOT MY PREFERENCE!
PEACE! LET THE WOLFRIDER SPEAK! DOES HE ACCEPT THE CHALLENGE?
A SINGLE NOD...MORE ELOQUENT THAN ANY BOAST OF PROWESS...IS CUTTER'S ONLY REPLY.
THEN LET THE RIVALS PREPARE! THE TRIAL BEGINS AT SUNRISE!
REMEMBER, RAYEK, THE CONTEST MUST BE FAIR!
DO NOT BE TEMPTED TO USE YOUR MAGIC AGAINST CUTTER.
I WILL NOT NEED TO, MOTHER OF MEMORY.

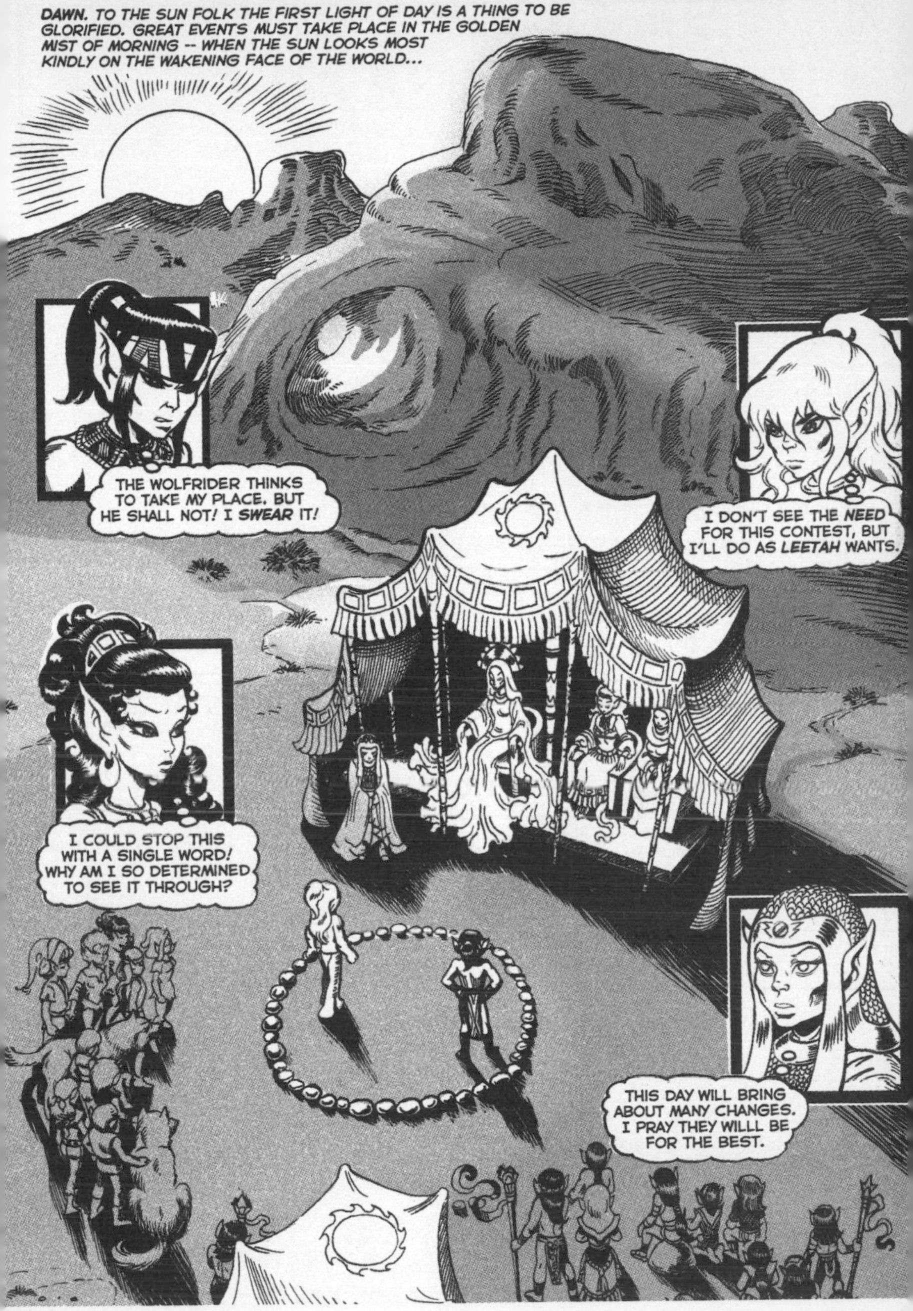
DAWN. TO THE SUN FOLK THE FIRST LIGHT OF DAY IS A THING TO BE GLORIFIED. GREAT EVENTS MUST TAKE PLACE IN THE GOLDEN MIST OF MORNING -- WHEN THE SUN LOOKS MOST KINDLY ON THE WAKENING FACE OF THE WORLD...
THE WOLFRIDER THINKS TO TAKE MY PLACE. BUT HE SHALL NOT! I SWEAR IT!
I DON'T SEE THE NEED FOR THIS CONTEST, BUT I'LL DO AS LEETAH WANTS.
I COULD STOP THIS WITH A SINGLE WORD! WHY AM I SO DETERMINED TO SEE IT THROUGH?
THIS DAY WILL BRING ABOUT MANY CHANGES. I PRAY THEY WILLL BE FOR THE BEST.

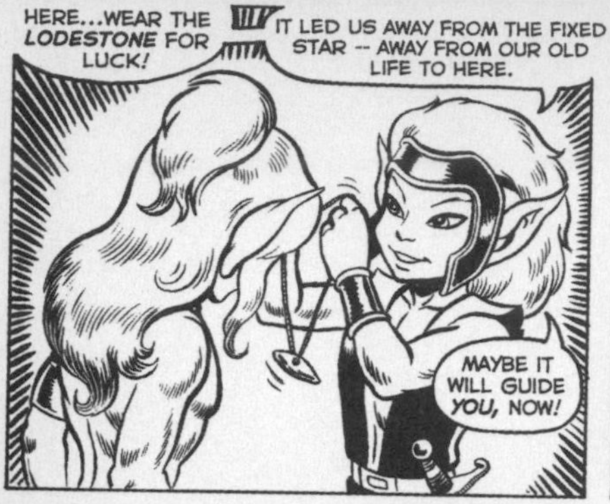
HERE...WEAR THE *LODESTONE* FOR LUCK!
IT LED US AWAY FROM THE FIXED STAR -- AWAY FROM OUR OLD LIFE TO HERE.
MAYBE IT WILL GUIDE *YOU*, NOW!

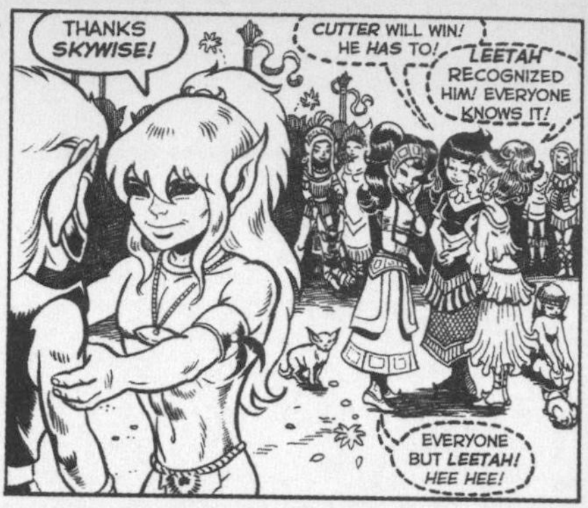
THANKS *SKYWISE!*
CUTTER WILL WIN! HE *HAS* TO!
LEETAH RECOGNIZED HIM! EVERYONE KNOWS IT!
EVERYONE BUT *LEETAH!* HEE HEE!

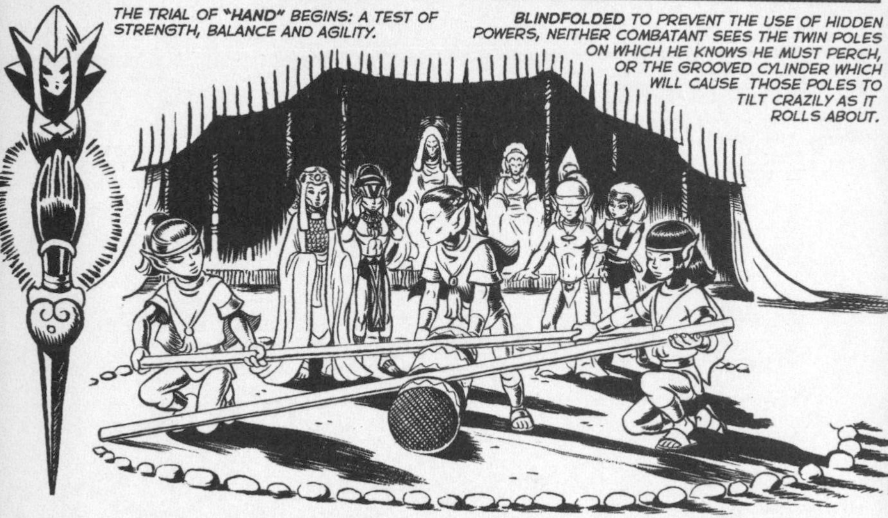
THE TRIAL OF **"HAND"** BEGINS: A TEST OF STRENGTH, BALANCE AND AGILITY.
BLINDFOLDED TO PREVENT THE USE OF HIDDEN POWERS, NEITHER COMBATANT SEES THE TWIN POLES ON WHICH HE KNOWS HE MUST PERCH, OR THE GROOVED CYLINDER WHICH WILL CAUSE THOSE POLES TO TILT CRAZILY AS IT ROLLS ABOUT.

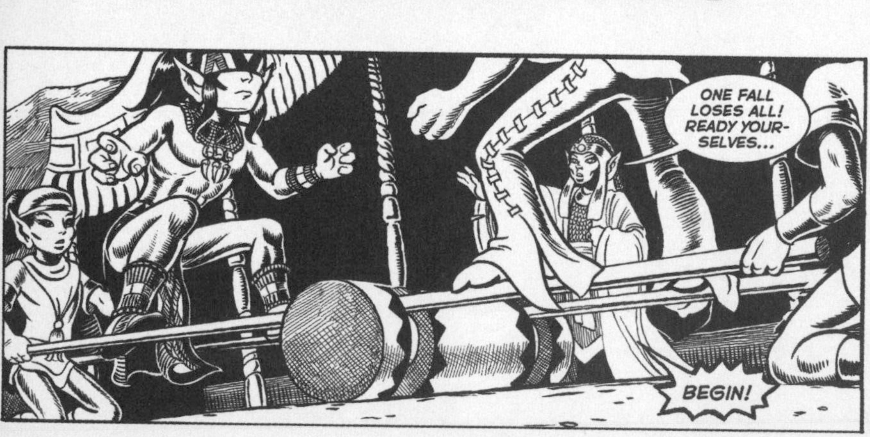
ONE FALL LOSES ALL! READY YOUR-SELVES...
BEGIN!

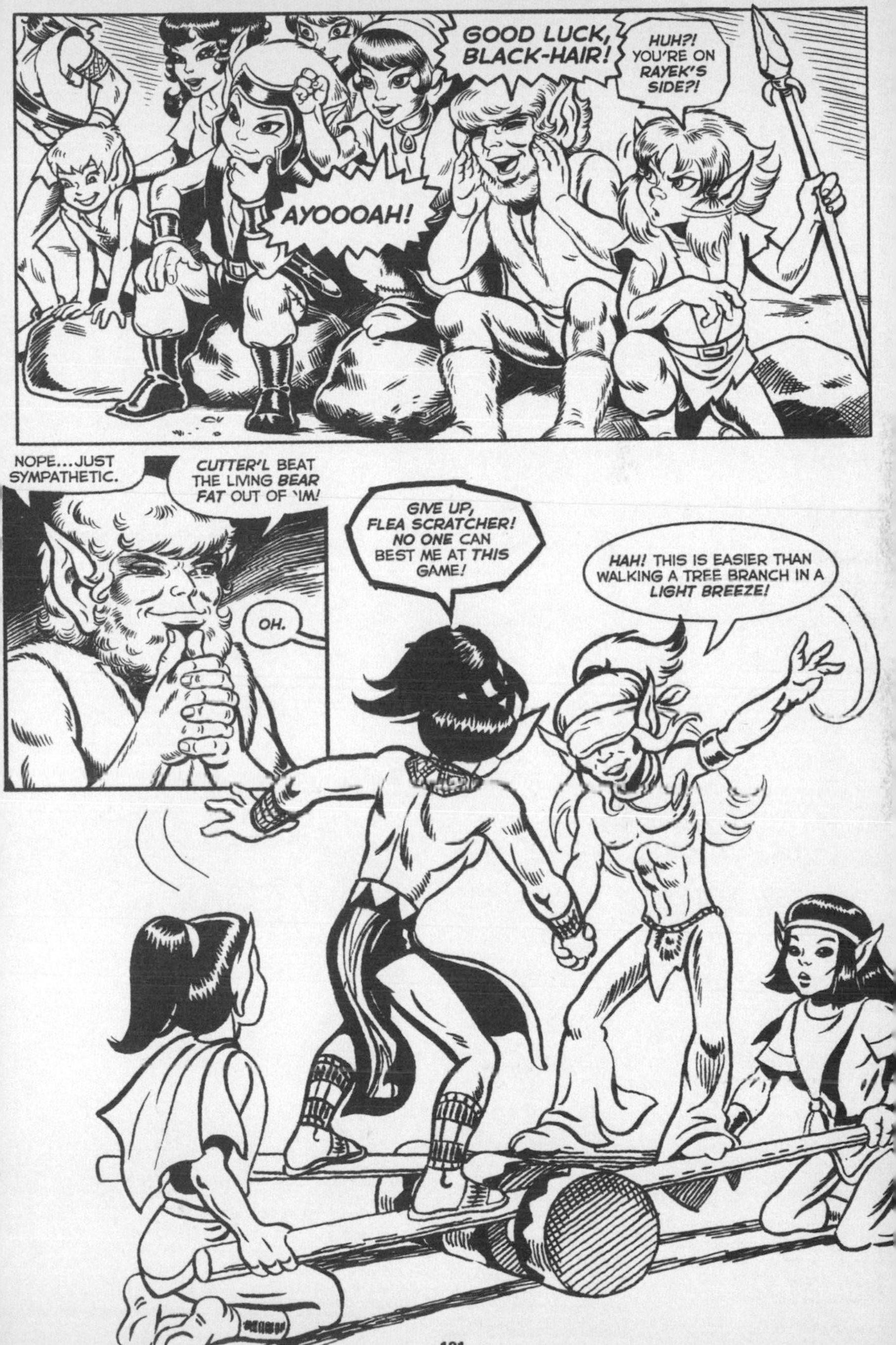
GOOD LUCK, BLACK-HAIR!
HUH?! YOU'RE ON RAYEK'S SIDE?!
AYOOOAH!
NOPE...JUST SYMPATHETIC.
CUTTER'L BEAT THE LIVING BEAR FAT OUT OF 'IM!
OH.
GIVE UP, FLEA SCRATCHER! NO ONE CAN BEST ME AT THIS GAME!
HAH! THIS IS EASIER THAN WALKING A TREE BRANCH IN A LIGHT BREEZE!

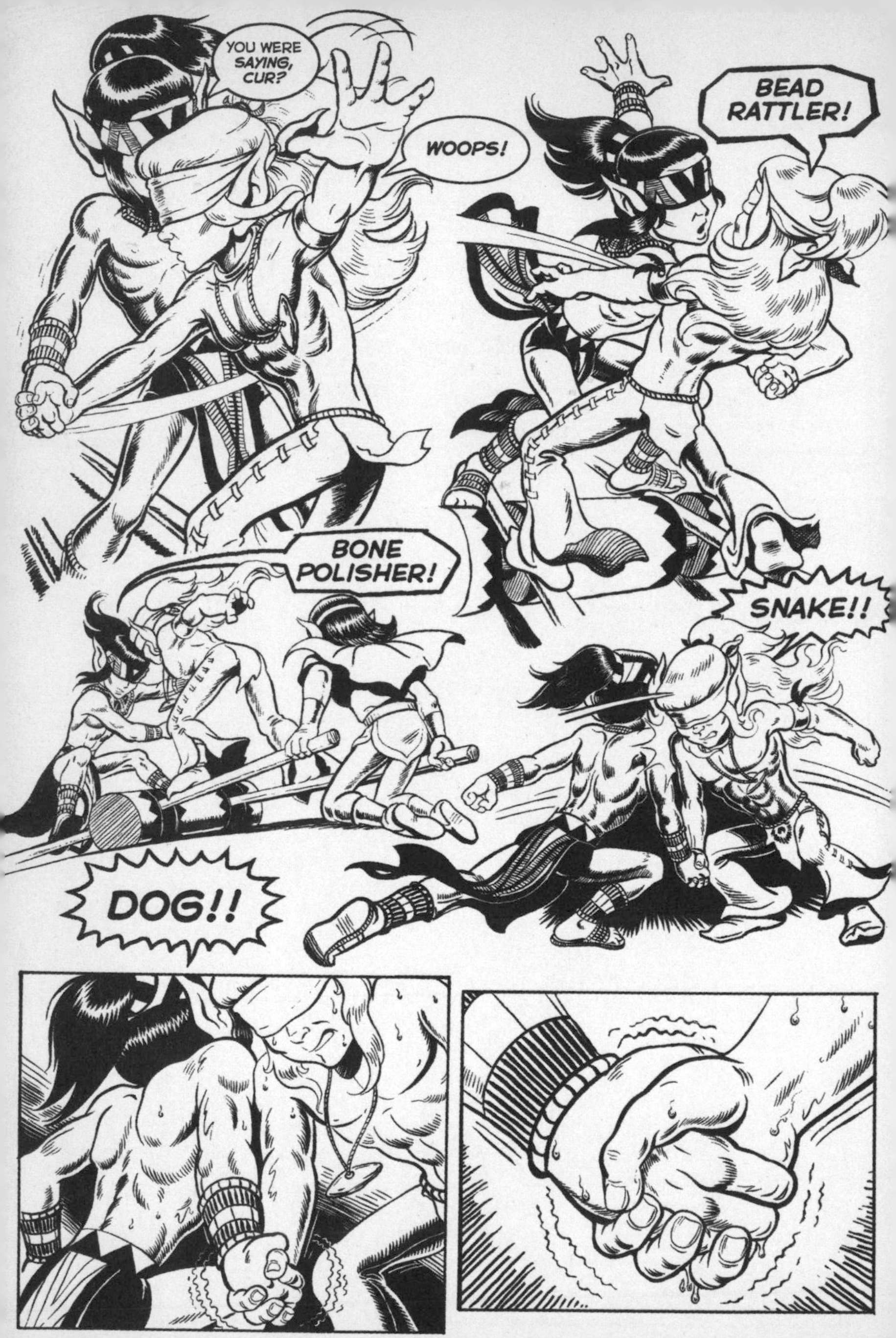
YOU WERE SAYING, CUR?
WOOPS!
BEAD RATTLER!
BONE POLISHER!
SNAKE!!
DOG!!

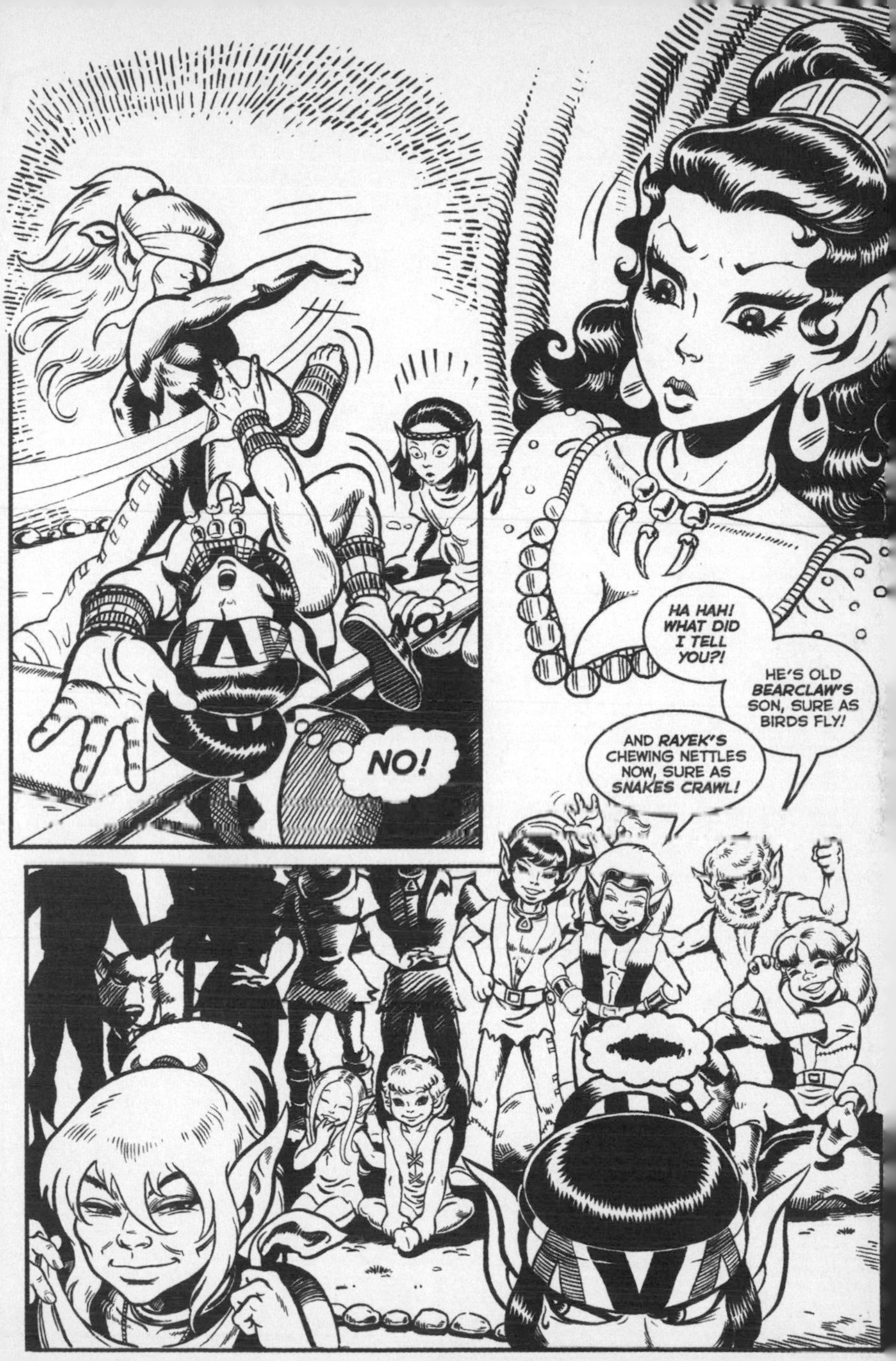
NO!
NO!
HA HAH! WHAT DID I TELL YOU?!
HE'S OLD BEARCLAW'S SON, SURE AS BIRDS FLY!
AND RAYEK'S CHEWING NETTLES NOW, SURE AS SNAKES CRAWL!

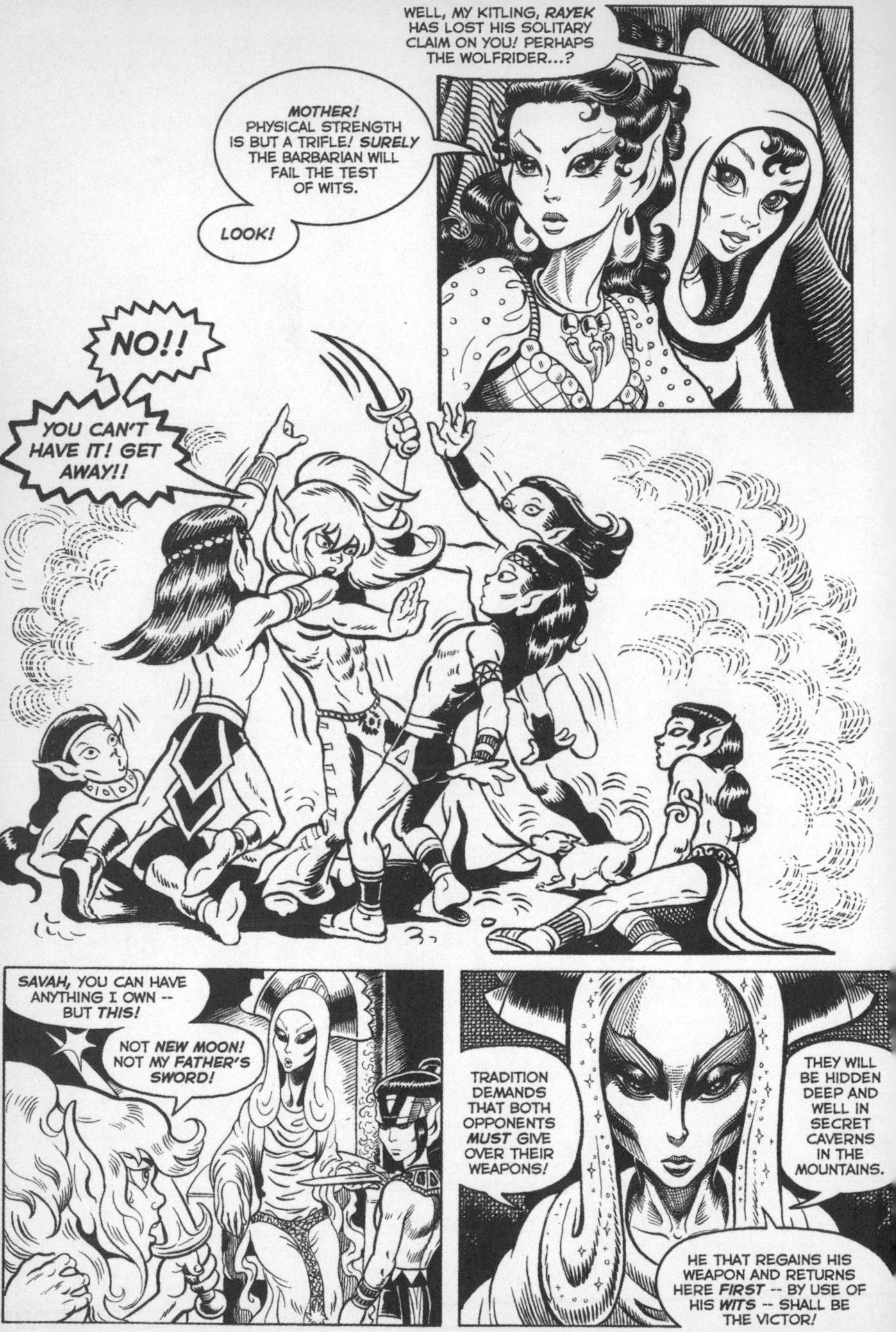
WELL, MY KITLING, RAYEK HAS LOST HIS SOLITARY CLAIM ON YOU! PERHAPS THE WOLFRIDER...?
MOTHER! PHYSICAL STRENGTH IS BUT A TRIFLE! SURELY THE BARBARIAN WILL FAIL THE TEST OF WITS.
LOOK!
NO!!
YOU CAN'T HAVE IT! GET AWAY!!
SAVAH, YOU CAN HAVE ANYTHING I OWN -- BUT THIS!
NOT NEW MOON! NOT MY FATHER'S SWORD!
TRADITION DEMANDS THAT BOTH OPPONENTS MUST GIVE OVER THEIR WEAPONS!
THEY WILL BE HIDDEN DEEP AND WELL IN SECRET CAVERNS IN THE MOUNTAINS.
HE THAT REGAINS HIS WEAPON AND RETURNS HERE FIRST -- BY USE OF HIS WITS -- SHALL BE THE VICTOR!

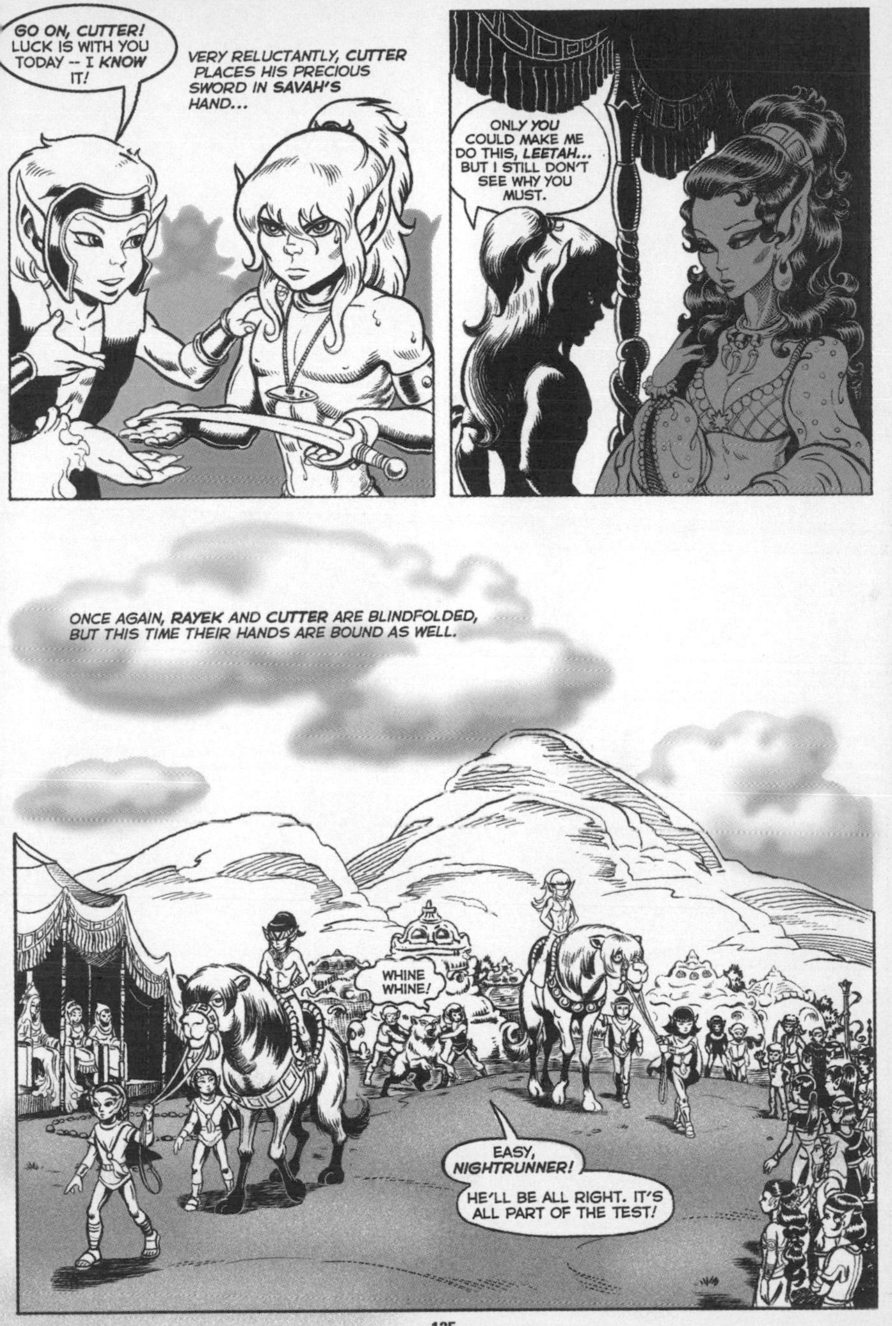
GO ON, CUTTER! LUCK IS WITH YOU TODAY -- I KNOW IT!
VERY RELUCTANTLY, CUTTER PLACES HIS PRECIOUS SWORD IN SAVAH'S HAND...
ONLY YOU COULD MAKE ME DO THIS, LEETAH... BUT I STILL DON'T SEE WHY YOU MUST.
ONCE AGAIN, RAYEK AND CUTTER ARE BLINDFOLDED, BUT THIS TIME THEIR HANDS ARE BOUND AS WELL.
WHINE WHINE!
EASY, NIGHTRUNNER!
HE'LL BE ALL RIGHT. IT'S ALL PART OF THE TEST!

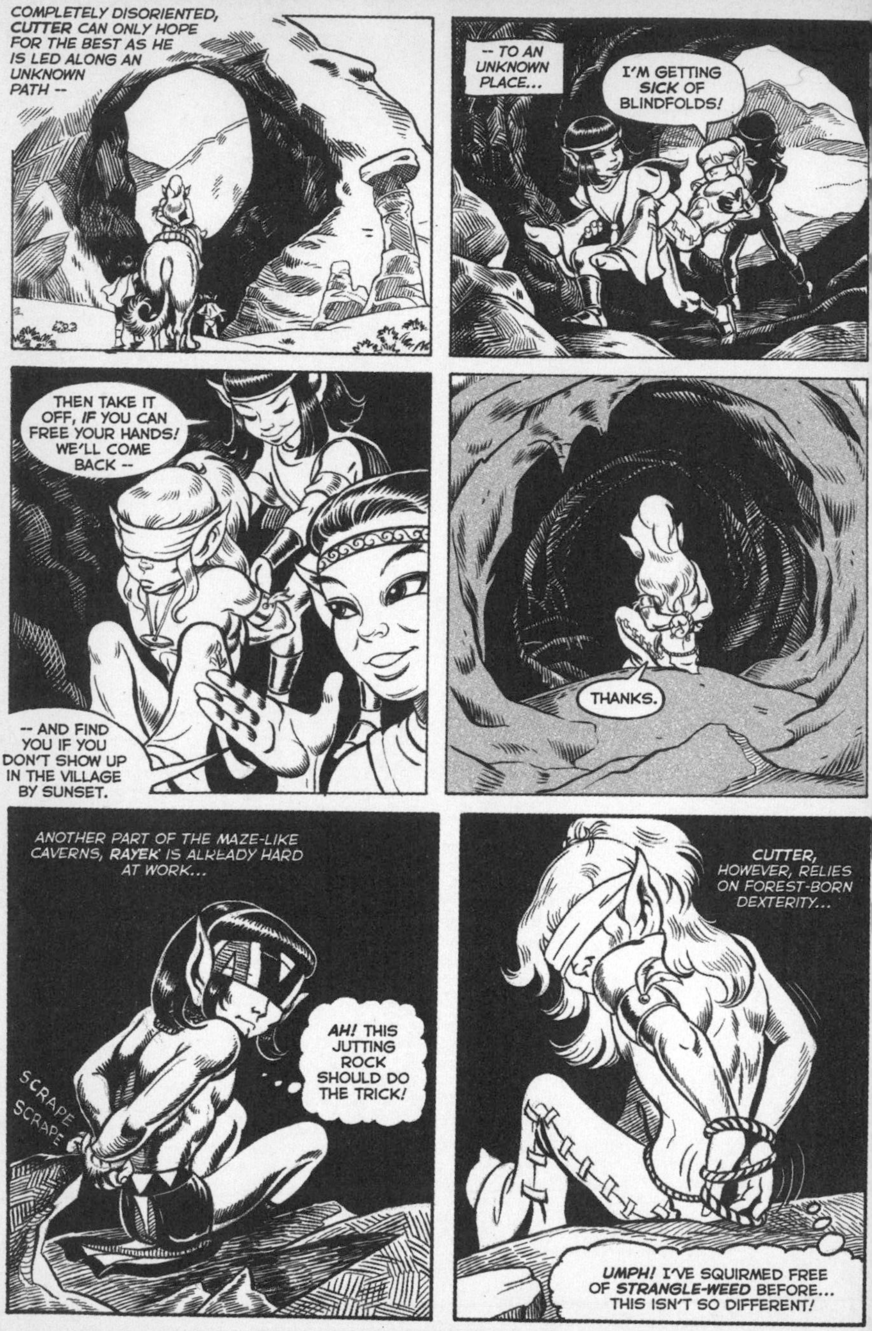
COMPLETELY DISORIENTED, CUTTER CAN ONLY HOPE FOR THE BEST AS HE IS LED ALONG AN UNKNOWN PATH --
-- TO AN UNKNOWN PLACE...
I'M GETTING SICK OF BLINDFOLDS!
THEN TAKE IT OFF, IF YOU CAN FREE YOUR HANDS! WE'LL COME BACK --
-- AND FIND YOU IF YOU DON'T SHOW UP IN THE VILLAGE BY SUNSET.
THANKS.
ANOTHER PART OF THE MAZE-LIKE CAVERNS, RAYEK IS ALREADY HARD AT WORK...
AH! THIS JUTTING ROCK SHOULD DO THE TRICK!
SCRAPE SCRAPE
CUTTER, HOWEVER, RELIES ON FOREST-BORN DEXTERITY...
UMPH! I'VE SQUIRMED FREE OF STRANGLE-WEED BEFORE... THIS ISN'T SO DIFFERENT!

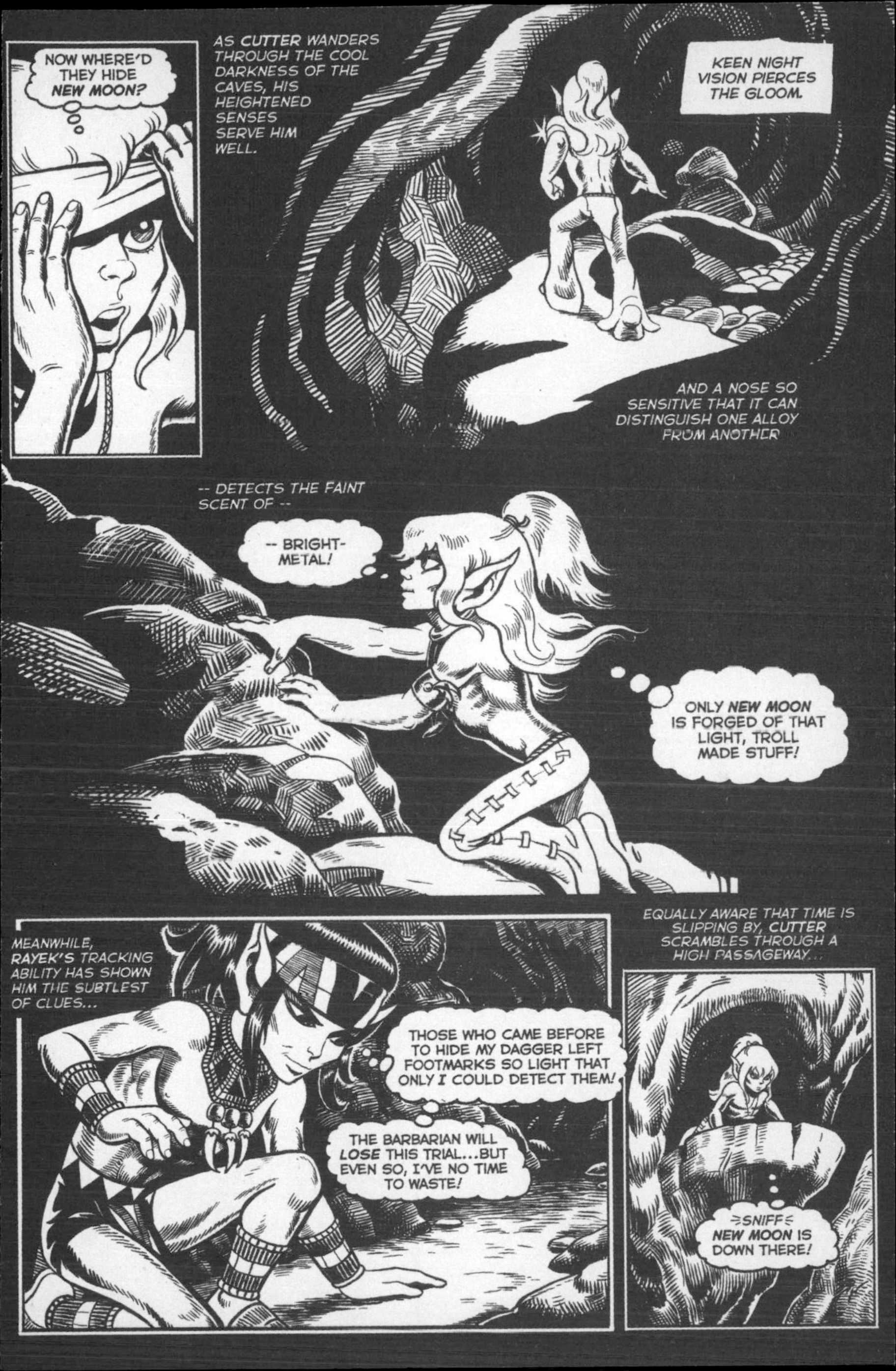
NOW WHERE'D THEY HIDE NEW MOON?
AS CUTTER WANDERS THROUGH THE COOL DARKNESS OF THE CAVES, HIS HEIGHTENED SENSES SERVE HIM WELL.
KEEN NIGHT VISION PIERCES THE GLOOM.
AND A NOSE SO SENSITIVE THAT IT CAN DISTINGUISH ONE ALLOY FROM ANOTHER
-- DETECTS THE FAINT SCENT OF --
-- BRIGHT-METAL!
ONLY NEW MOON IS FORGED OF THAT LIGHT, TROLL MADE STUFF!
MEANWHILE, RAYEK'S TRACKING ABILITY HAS SHOWN HIM THE SUBTLEST OF CLUES...
THOSE WHO CAME BEFORE TO HIDE MY DAGGER LEFT FOOTMARKS SO LIGHT THAT ONLY I COULD DETECT THEM!
THE BARBARIAN WILL LOSE THIS TRIAL...BUT EVEN SO, I'VE NO TIME TO WASTE!
EQUALLY AWARE THAT TIME IS SLIPPING BY, CUTTER SCRAMBLES THROUGH A HIGH PASSAGEWAY...
≡SNIFF≡ NEW MOON IS DOWN THERE!

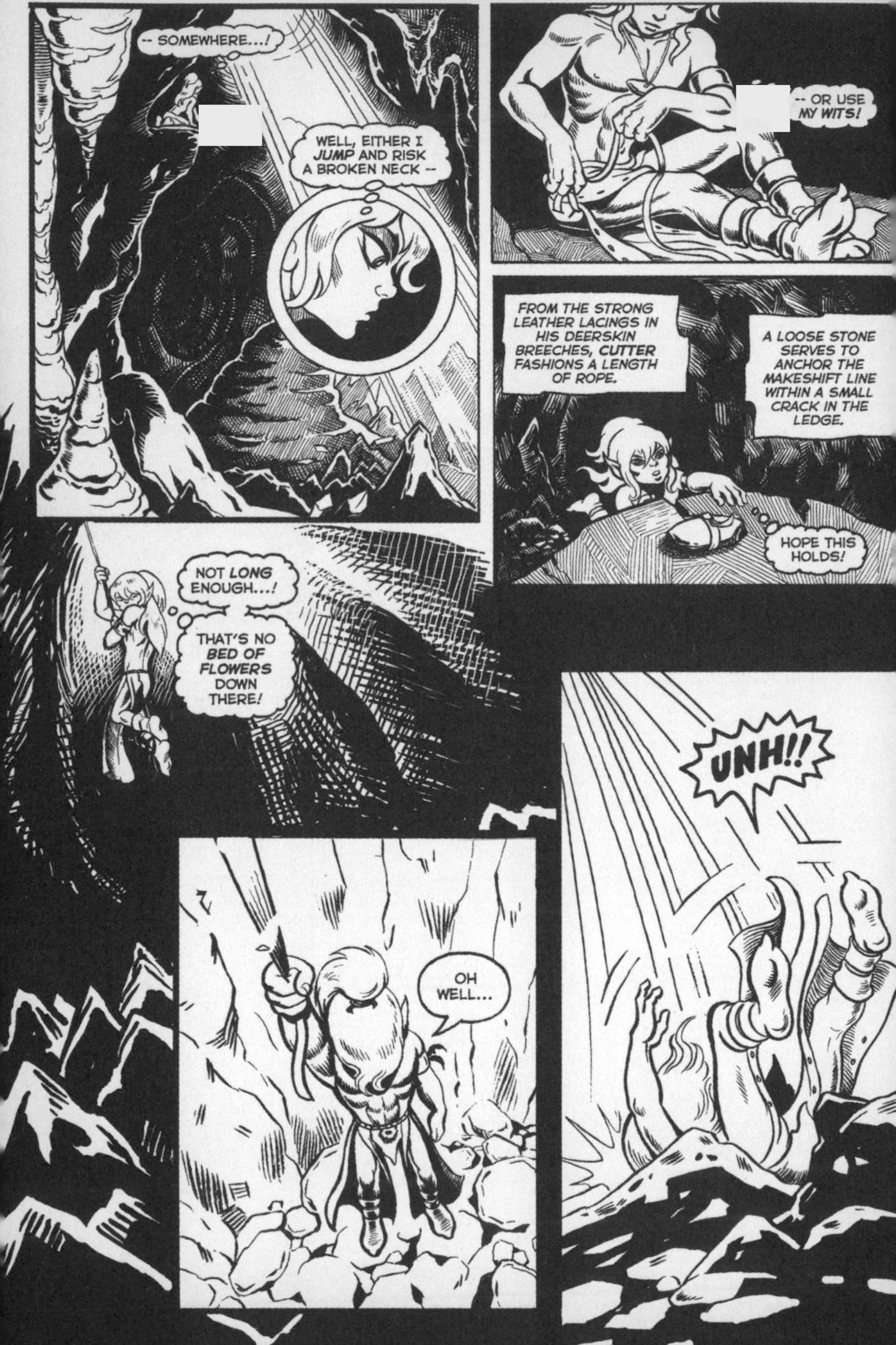
-- SOMEWHERE...!
WELL, EITHER I JUMP AND RISK A BROKEN NECK --
-- OR USE MY WITS!
FROM THE STRONG LEATHER LACINGS IN HIS DEERSKIN BREECHES, CUTTER FASHIONS A LENGTH OF ROPE.
A LOOSE STONE SERVES TO ANCHOR THE MAKESHIFT LINE WITHIN A SMALL CRACK IN THE LEDGE.
HOPE THIS HOLDS!
NOT LONG ENOUGH...!
THAT'S NO BED OF FLOWERS DOWN THERE!
OH WELL...
UNH!!

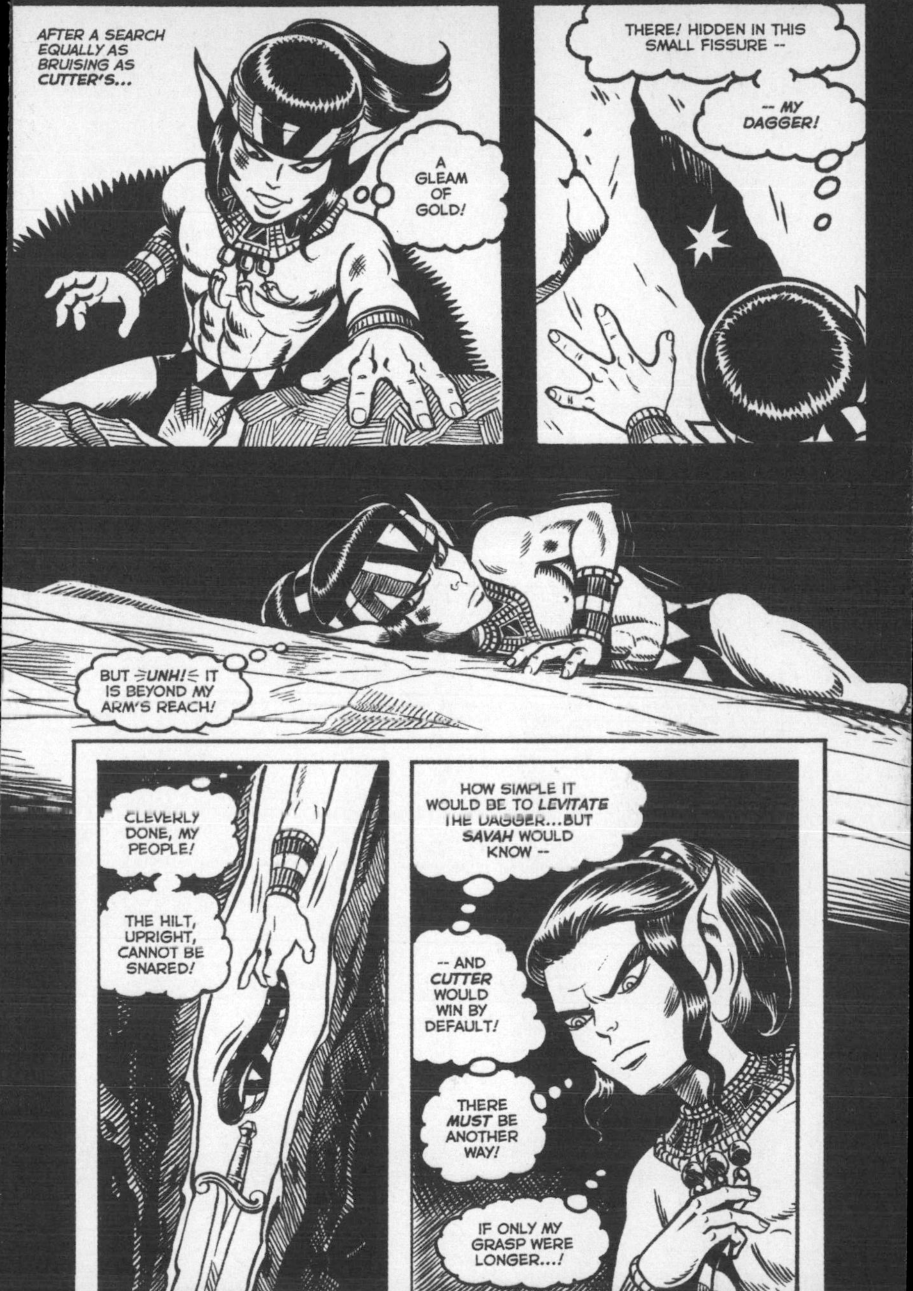
AFTER A SEARCH EQUALLY AS BRUISING AS CUTTER'S...
A GLEAM OF GOLD!
THERE! HIDDEN IN THIS SMALL FISSURE --
-- MY DAGGER!
BUT ≡UNH!≡ IT IS BEYOND MY ARM'S REACH!
CLEVERLY DONE, MY PEOPLE!
THE HILT, UPRIGHT, CANNOT BE SNARED!
HOW SIMPLE IT WOULD BE TO LEVITATE THE DAGGER...BUT SAVAH WOULD KNOW --
-- AND CUTTER WOULD WIN BY DEFAULT!
THERE MUST BE ANOTHER WAY!
IF ONLY MY GRASP WERE LONGER...!

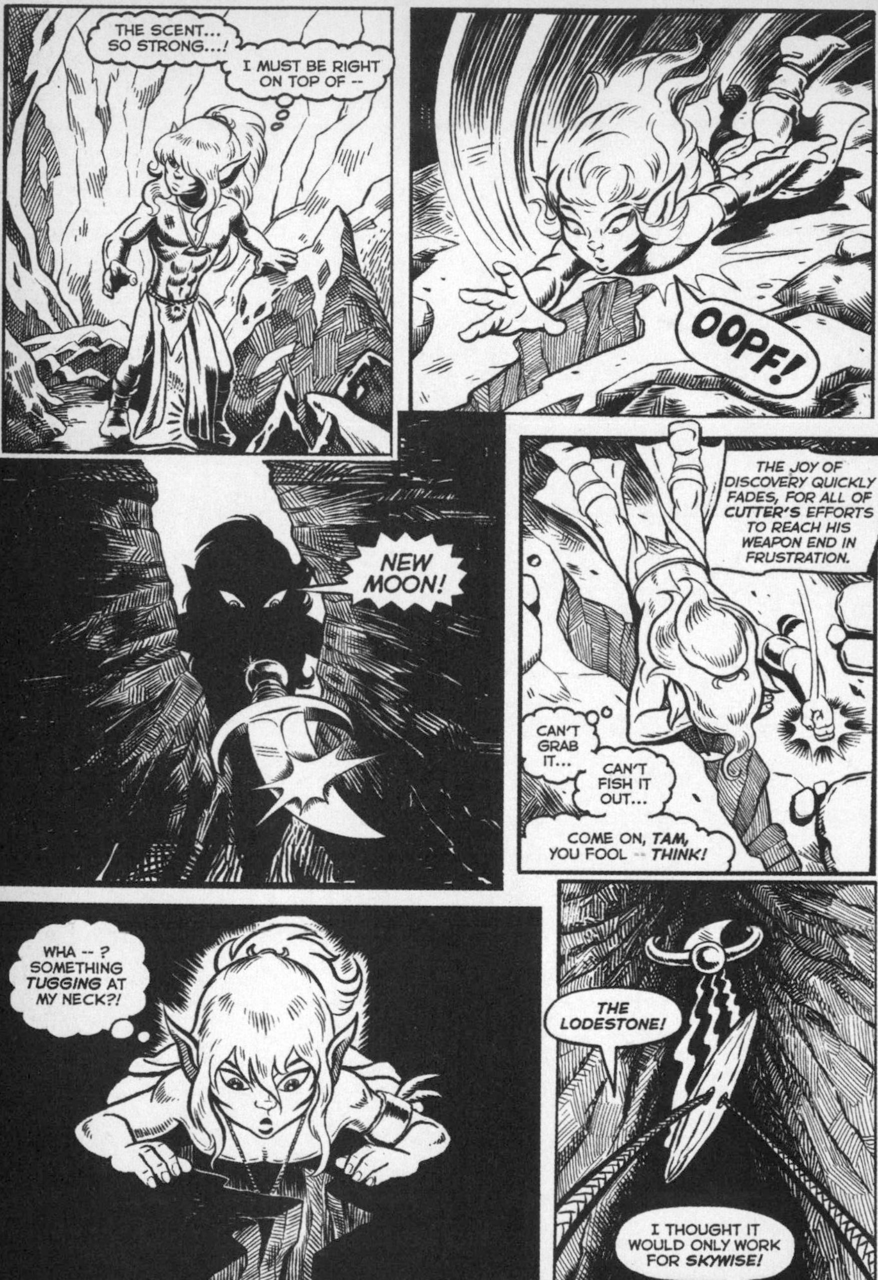
THE SCENT... SO STRONG...!
I MUST BE RIGHT ON TOP OF --
OOPF!
NEW MOON!
THE JOY OF DISCOVERY QUICKLY FADES, FOR ALL OF CUTTER'S EFFORTS TO REACH HIS WEAPON END IN FRUSTRATION.
CAN'T GRAB IT...
CAN'T FISH IT OUT...
COME ON, TAM, YOU FOOL -- THINK!
WHA -- ? SOMETHING TUGGING AT MY NECK?!
THE LODESTONE!
I THOUGHT IT WOULD ONLY WORK FOR SKYWISE!

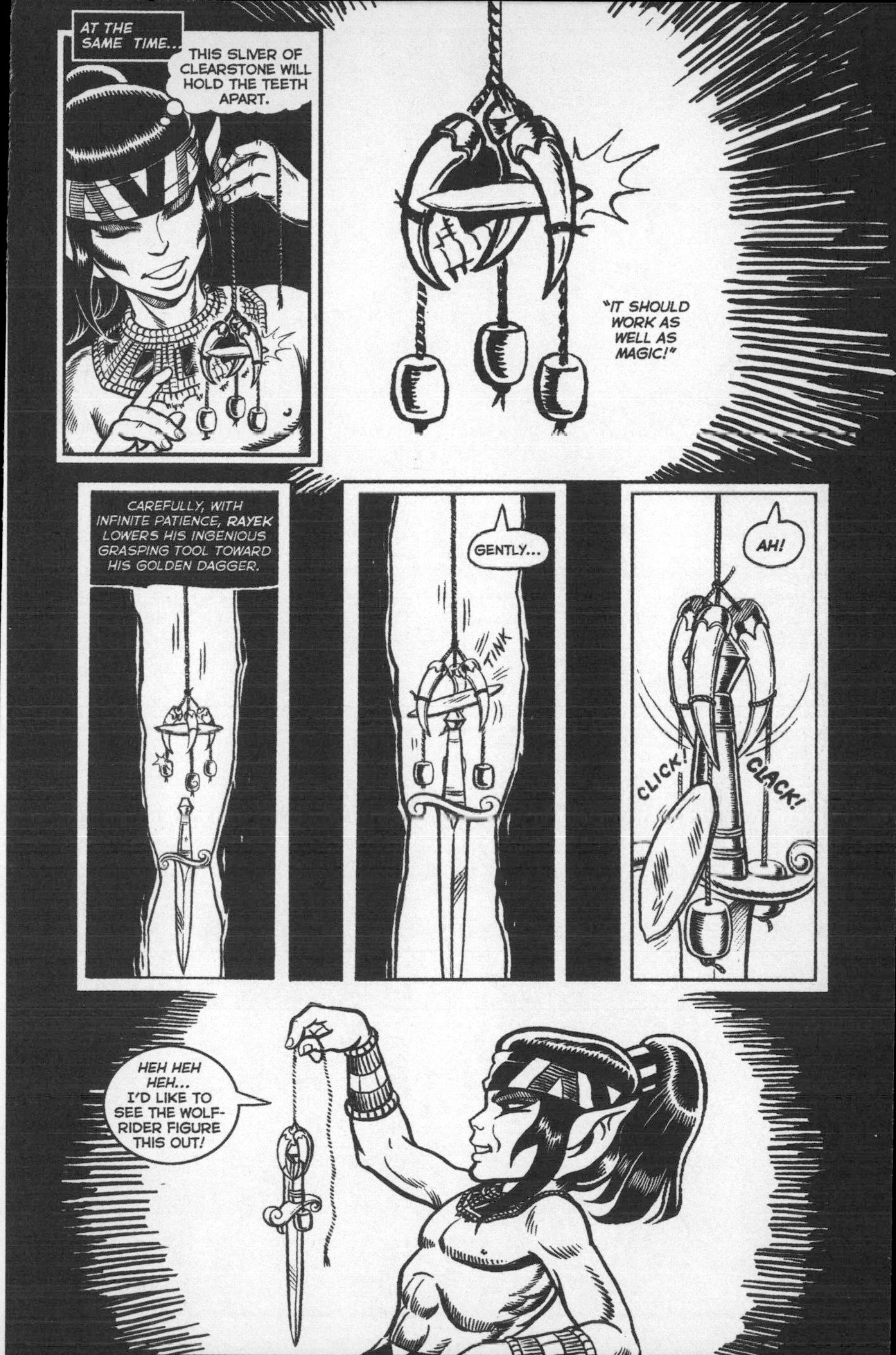
AT THE SAME TIME...
THIS SLIVER OF CLEARSTONE WILL HOLD THE TEETH APART.
"IT SHOULD WORK AS WELL AS MAGIC!"
CAREFULLY, WITH INFINITE PATIENCE, RAYEK LOWERS HIS INGENIOUS GRASPING TOOL TOWARD HIS GOLDEN DAGGER.
GENTLY...
TINK
AH!
CLICK!
CLACK!
HEH HEH HEH... I'D LIKE TO SEE THE WOLF-RIDER FIGURE THIS OUT!

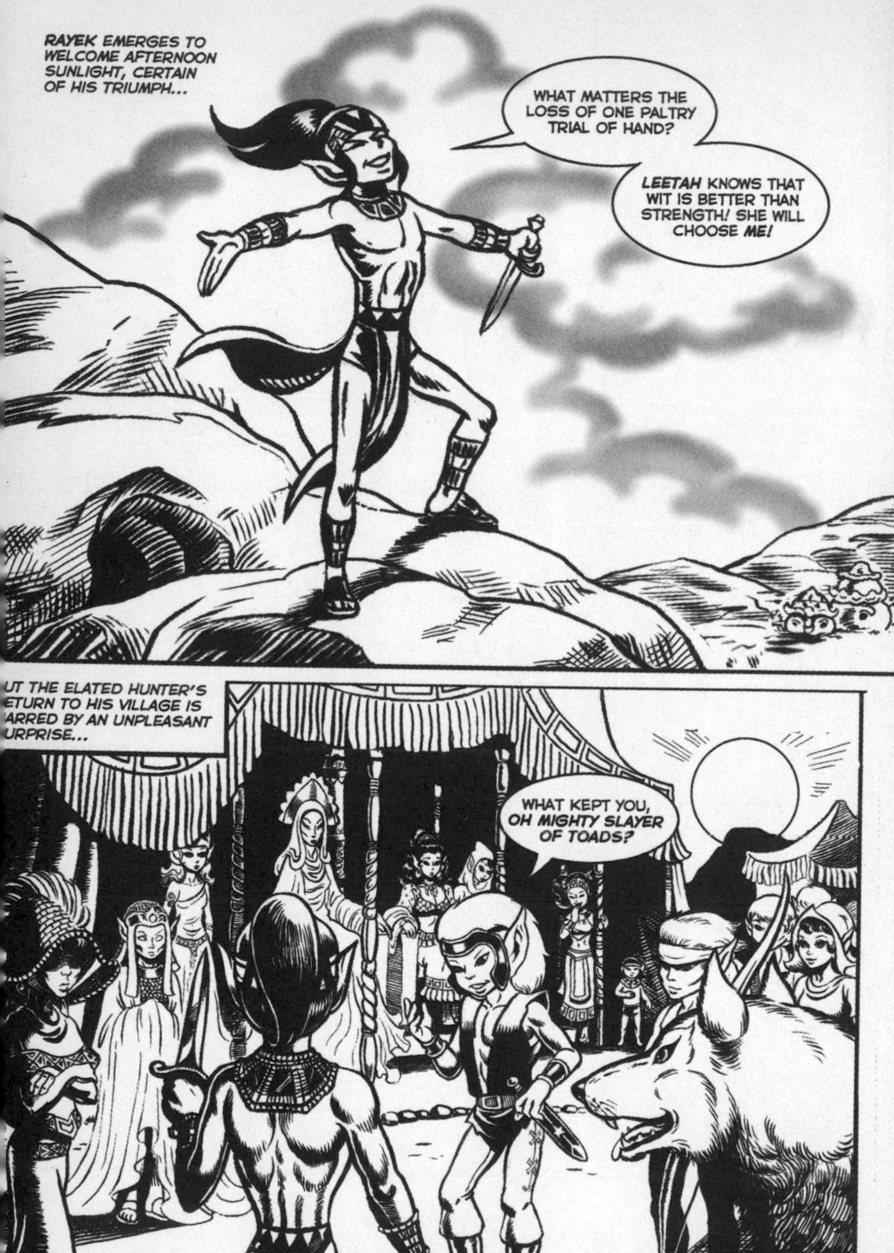
RAYEK EMERGES TO WELCOME AFTERNOON SUNLIGHT, CERTAIN OF HIS TRIUMPH...
WHAT MATTERS THE LOSS OF ONE PALTRY TRIAL OF HAND?
LEETAH KNOWS THAT WIT IS BETTER THAN STRENGTH! SHE WILL CHOOSE ME!
UT THE ELATED HUNTER'S ETURN TO HIS VILLAGE IS ARRED BY AN UNPLEASANT URPRISE...
WHAT KEPT YOU, OH MIGHTY SLAYER OF TOADS?

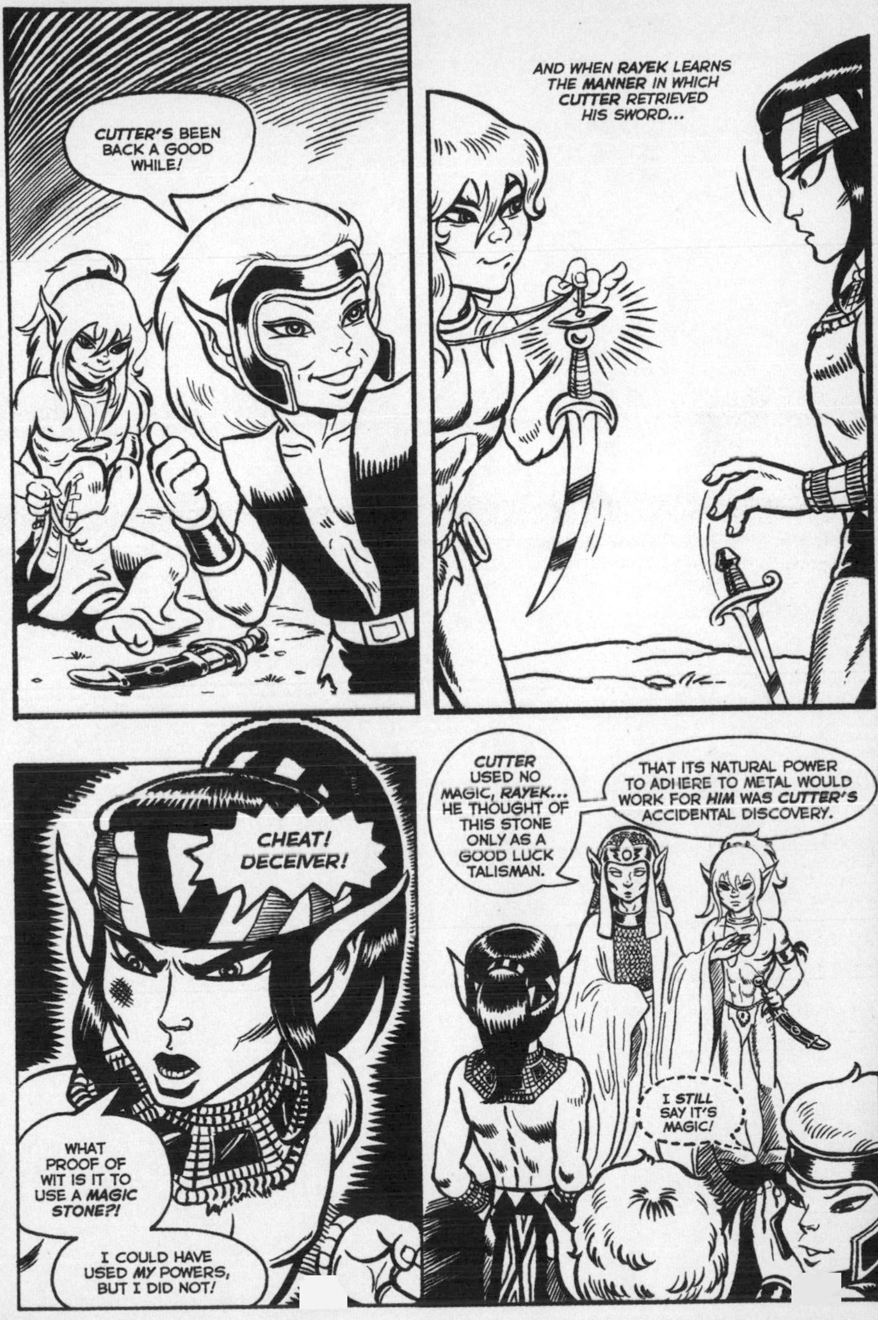
CUTTER'S BEEN BACK A GOOD WHILE!
AND WHEN RAYEK LEARNS THE MANNER IN WHICH CUTTER RETRIEVED HIS SWORD...
CHEAT! DECEIVER!
WHAT PROOF OF WIT IS IT TO USE A MAGIC STONE?!
I COULD HAVE USED MY POWERS, BUT I DID NOT!
CUTTER USED NO MAGIC, RAYEK... HE THOUGHT OF THIS STONE ONLY AS A GOOD LUCK TALISMAN.
THAT ITS NATURAL POWER TO ADHERE TO METAL WOULD WORK FOR HIM WAS CUTTER'S ACCIDENTAL DISCOVERY.
I STILL SAY IT'S MAGIC!

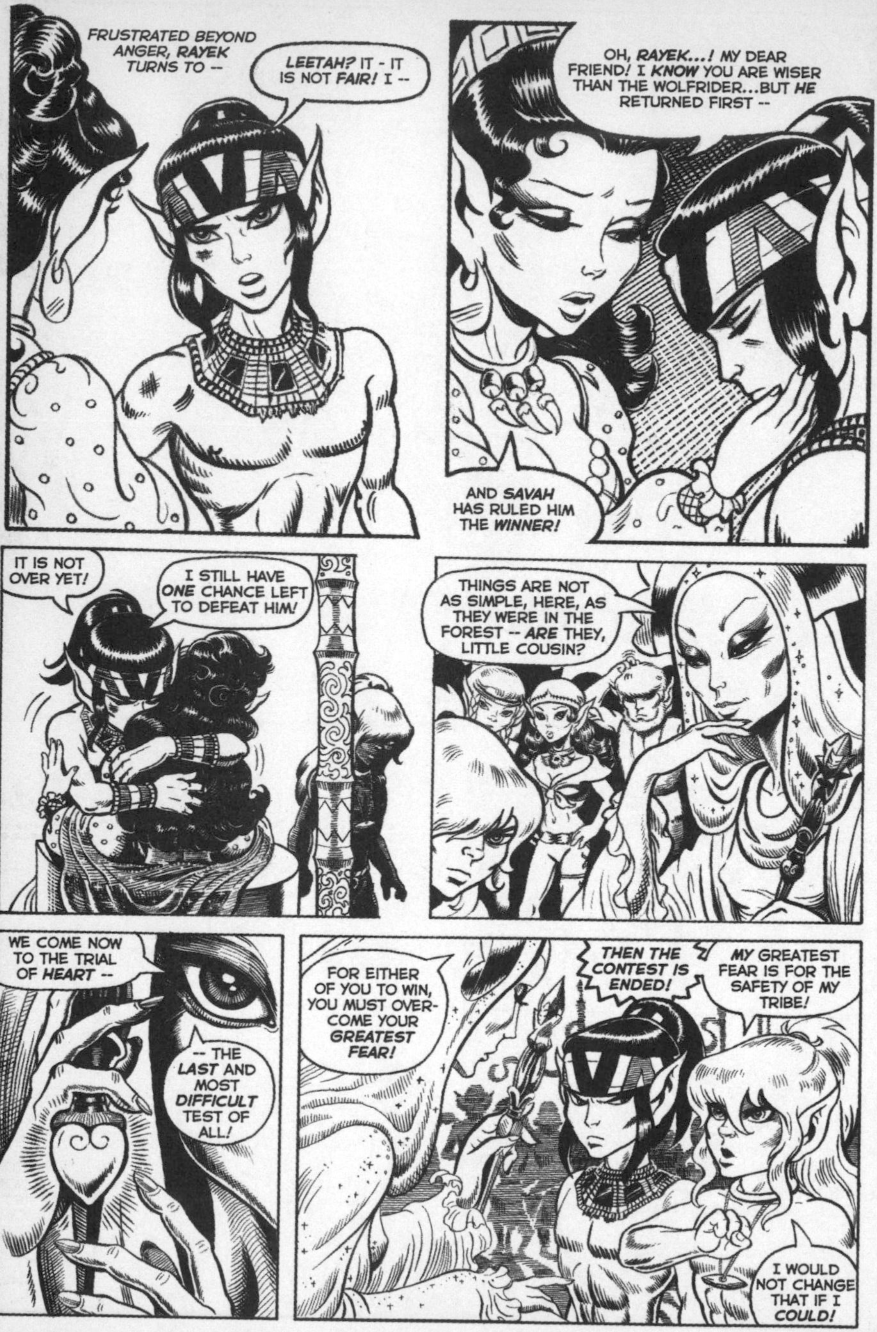

FRUSTRATED BEYOND ANGER, RAYEK TURNS TO --
LEETAH? IT - IT IS NOT FAIR! I --
OH, RAYEK...! MY DEAR FRIEND! I KNOW YOU ARE WISER THAN THE WOLFRIDER...BUT HE RETURNED FIRST --
AND SAVAH HAS RULED HIM THE WINNER!
IT IS NOT OVER YET!
I STILL HAVE ONE CHANCE LEFT TO DEFEAT HIM!
THINGS ARE NOT AS SIMPLE, HERE, AS THEY WERE IN THE FOREST -- ARE THEY, LITTLE COUSIN?
WE COME NOW TO THE TRIAL OF HEART --
-- THE LAST AND MOST DIFFICULT TEST OF ALL!
FOR EITHER OF YOU TO WIN, YOU MUST OVERCOME YOUR GREATEST FEAR!
THEN THE CONTEST IS ENDED!
MY GREATEST FEAR IS FOR THE SAFETY OF MY TRIBE!
I WOULD NOT CHANGE THAT IF I COULD!

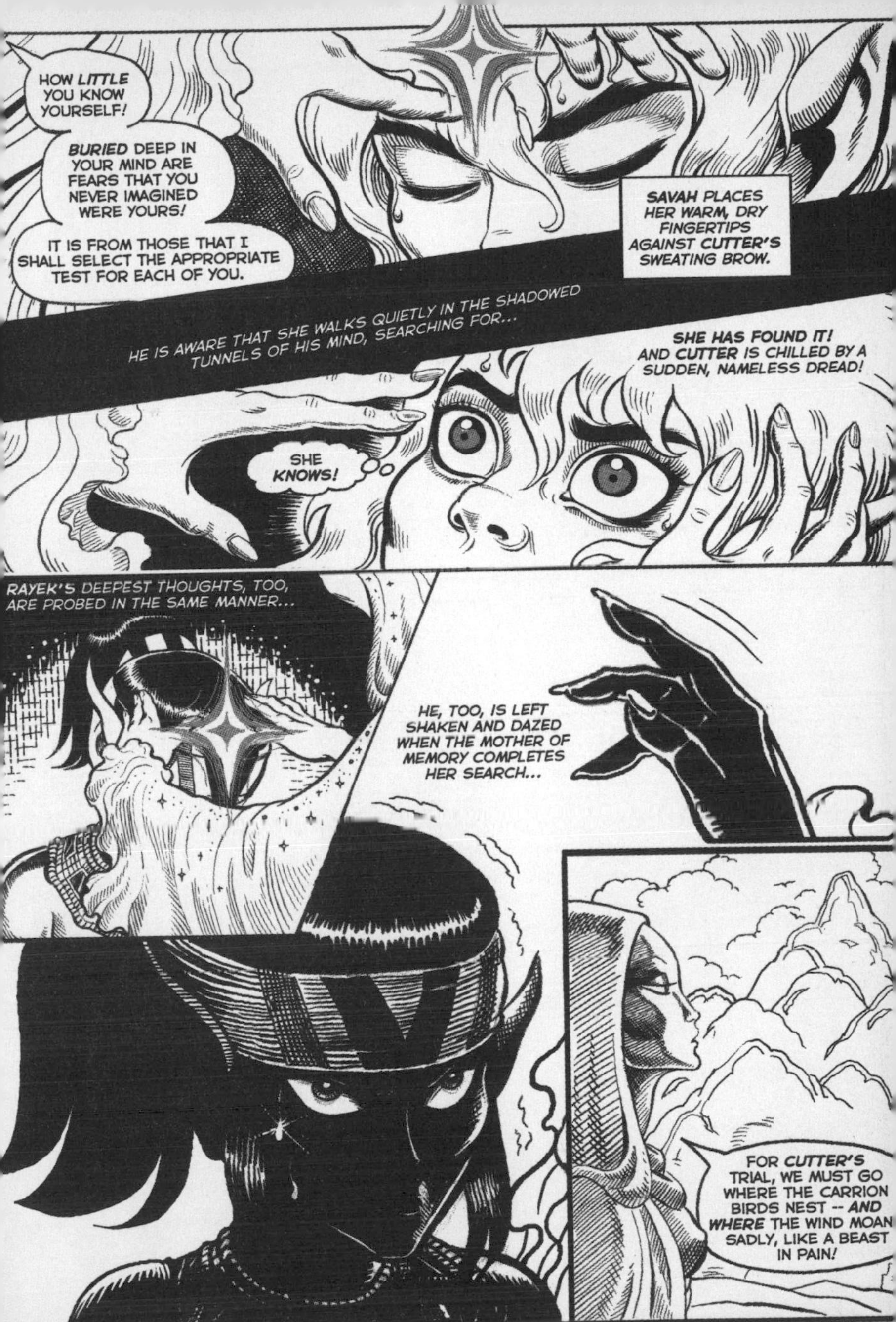

HOW LITTLE YOU KNOW YOURSELF!
BURIED DEEP IN YOUR MIND ARE FEARS THAT YOU NEVER IMAGINED WERE YOURS!
IT IS FROM THOSE THAT I SHALL SELECT THE APPROPRIATE TEST FOR EACH OF YOU.
SAVAH PLACES HER WARM, DRY FINGERTIPS AGAINST CUTTER'S SWEATING BROW.
HE IS AWARE THAT SHE WALKS QUIETLY IN THE SHADOWED TUNNELS OF HIS MIND, SEARCHING FOR...
SHE HAS FOUND IT! AND CUTTER IS CHILLED BY A SUDDEN, NAMELESS DREAD!
SHE KNOWS!
RAYEK'S DEEPEST THOUGHTS, TOO, ARE PROBED IN THE SAME MANNER...
HE, TOO, IS LEFT SHAKEN AND DAZED WHEN THE MOTHER OF MEMORY COMPLETES HER SEARCH...
FOR CUTTER'S TRIAL, WE MUST GO WHERE THE CARRION BIRDS NEST -- AND WHERE THE WIND MOAN SADLY, LIKE A BEAST IN PAIN!

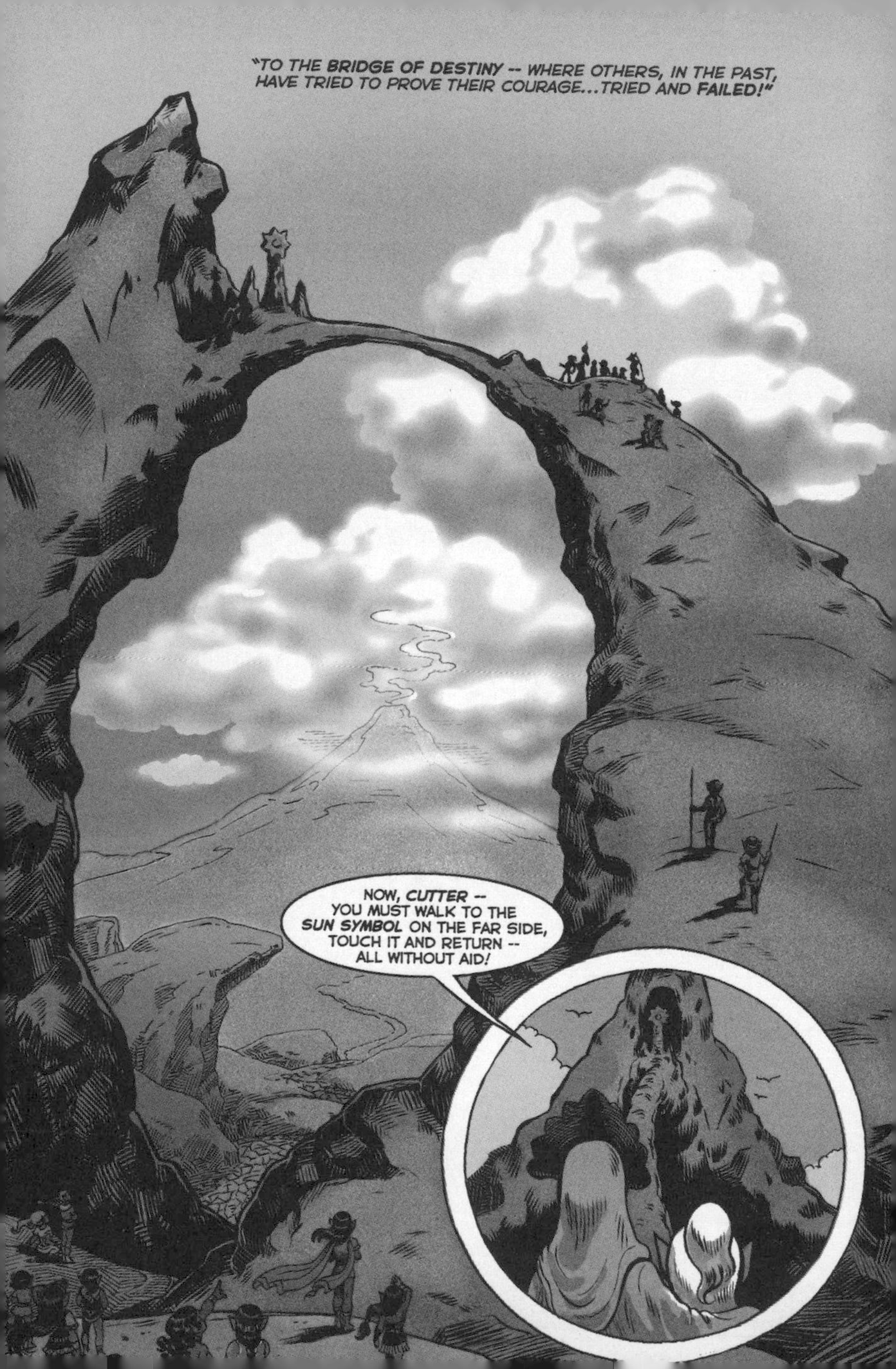
"TO THE BRIDGE OF DESTINY -- WHERE OTHERS, IN THE PAST, HAVE TRIED TO PROVE THEIR COURAGE...TRIED AND FAILED!"
NOW, CUTTER -- YOU MUST WALK TO THE SUN SYMBOL ON THE FAR SIDE, TOUCH IT AND RETURN -- ALL WITHOUT AID!

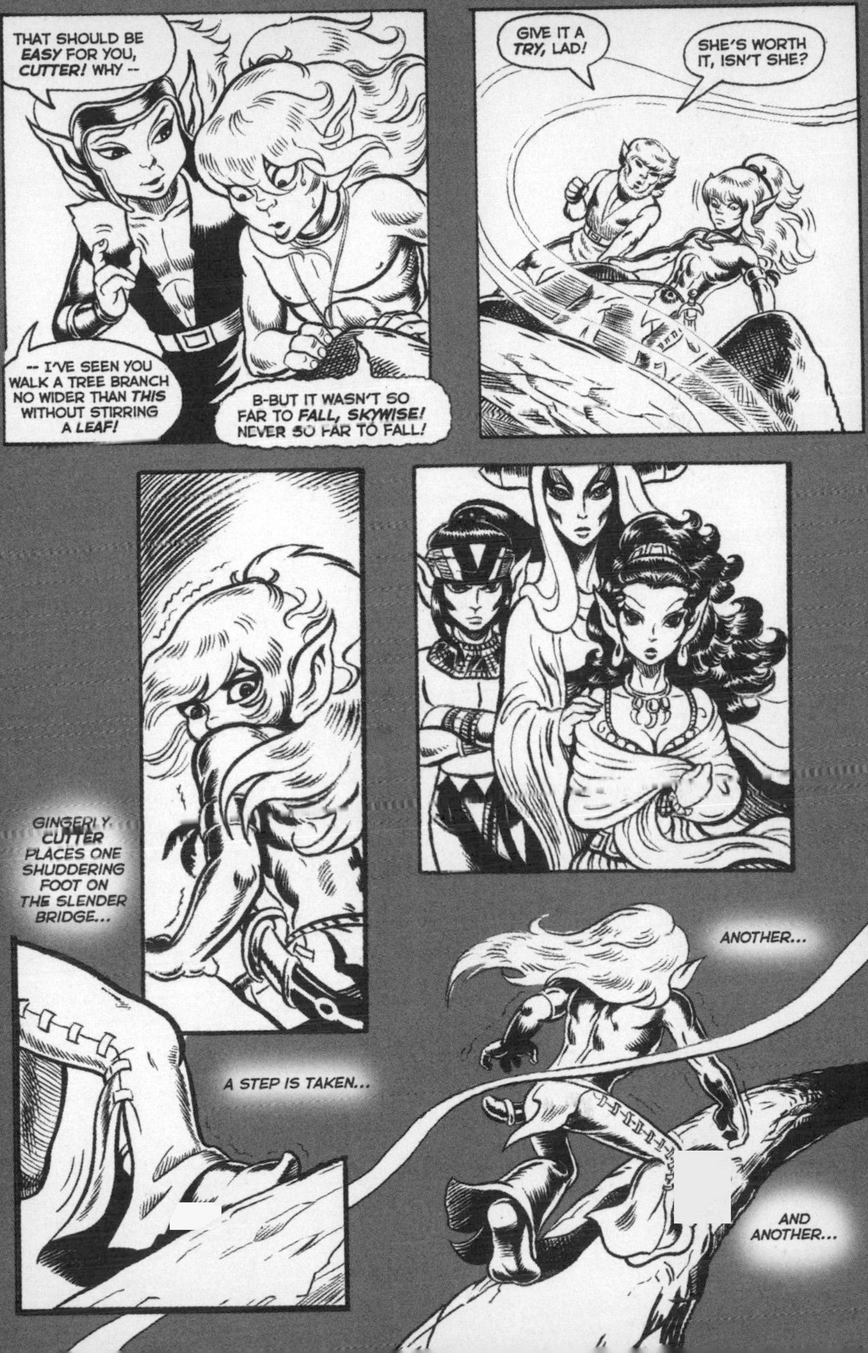
THAT SHOULD BE EASY FOR YOU, CUTTER! WHY --
-- I'VE SEEN YOU WALK A TREE BRANCH NO WIDER THAN THIS WITHOUT STIRRING A LEAF!
B-BUT IT WASN'T SO FAR TO FALL, SKYWISE! NEVER SO FAR TO FALL!
GIVE IT A TRY, LAD!
SHE'S WORTH IT, ISN'T SHE?
GINGERLY, CUTTER PLACES ONE SHUDDERING FOOT ON THE SLENDER BRIDGE...
A STEP IS TAKEN...
ANOTHER...
AND ANOTHER...

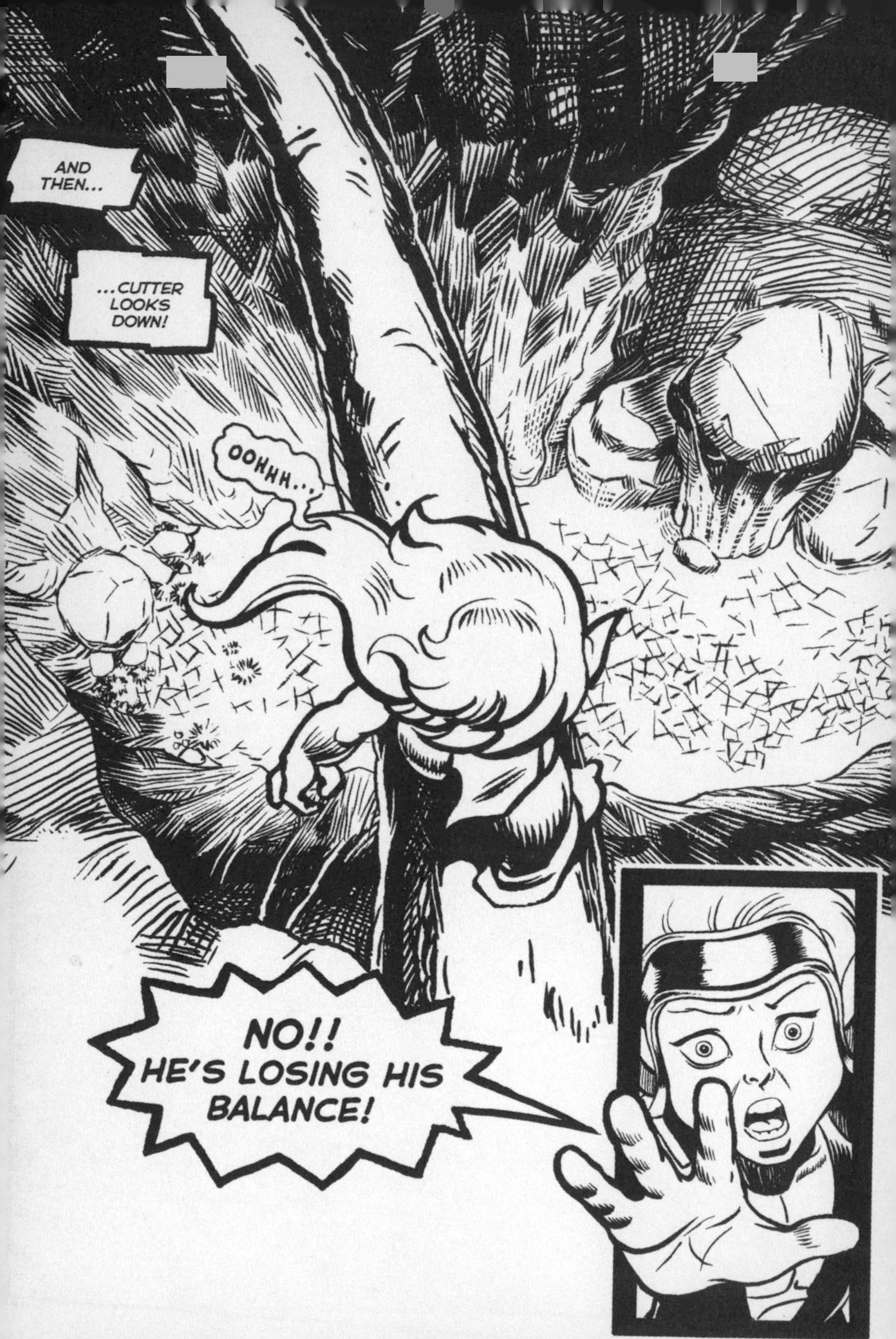
AND THEN...
...CUTTER LOOKS DOWN!
OOHHH...
NO!! HE'S LOSING HIS BALANCE!

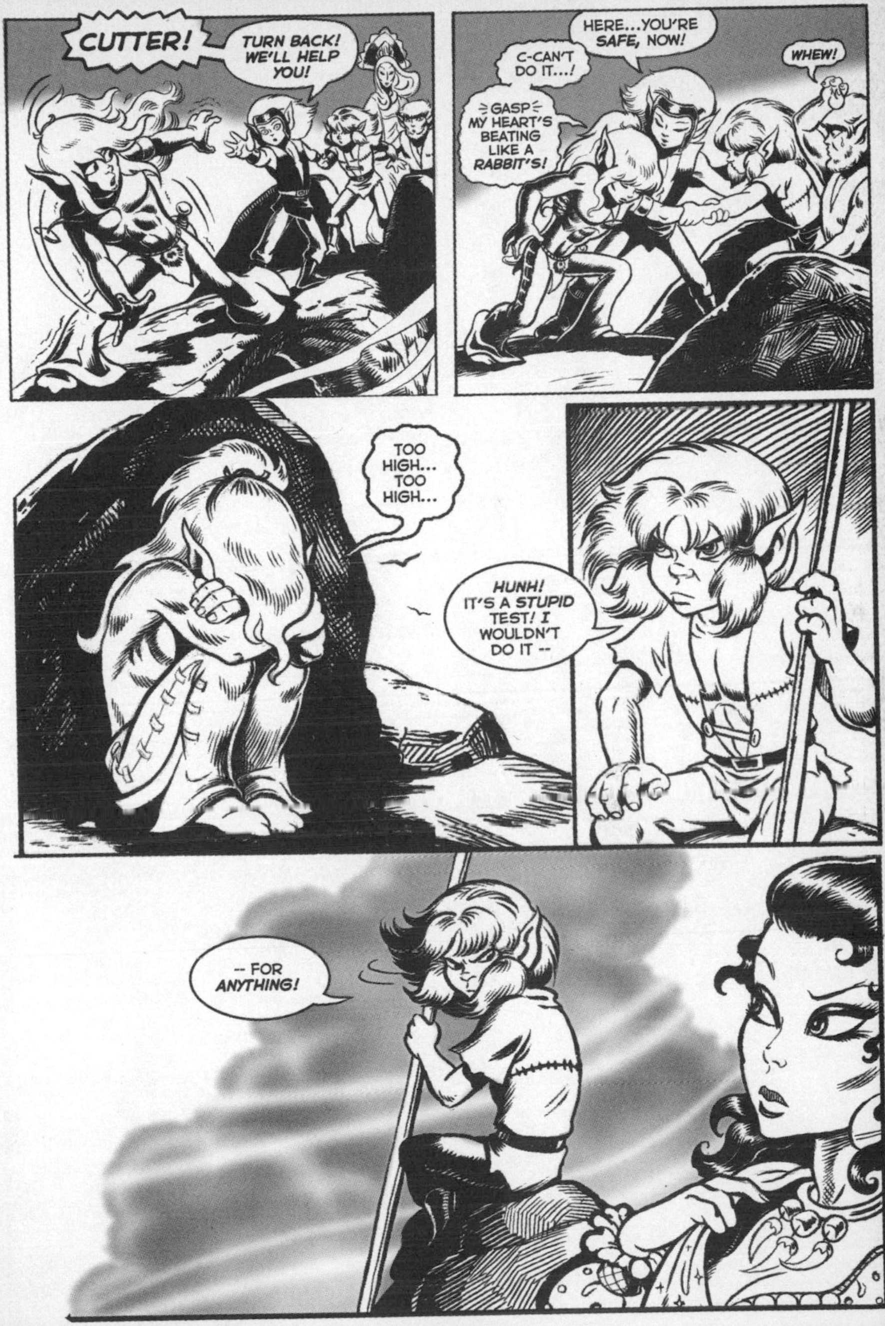
CUTTER!
TURN BACK! WE'LL HELP YOU!
HERE...YOU'RE SAFE, NOW!
C-CAN'T DO IT...!
WHEW!
GASP MY HEART'S BEATING LIKE A RABBIT'S!
TOO HIGH... TOO HIGH...
HUNH! IT'S A STUPID TEST! I WOULDN'T DO IT --
-- FOR ANYTHING!

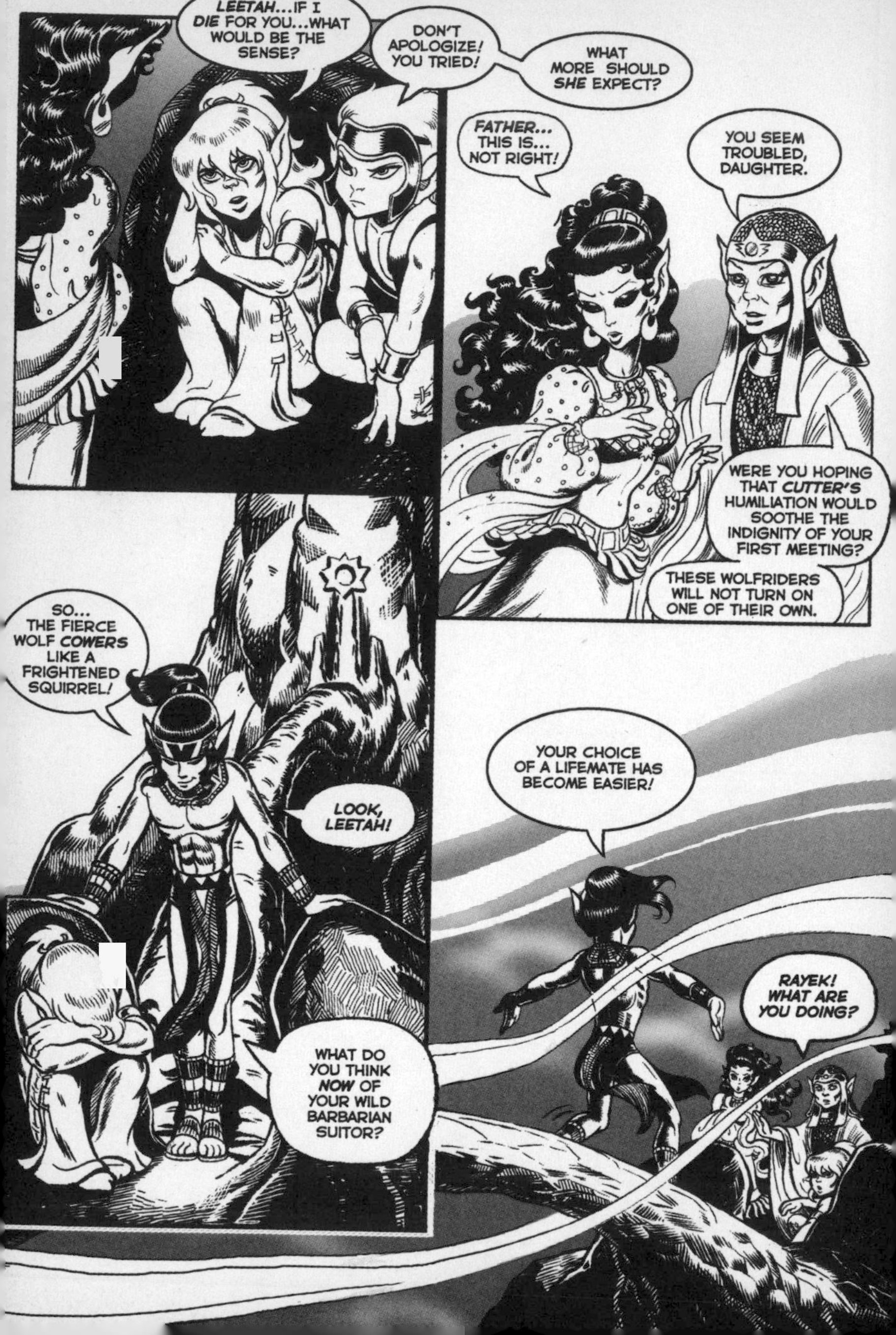
LEETAH...IF I DIE FOR YOU...WHAT WOULD BE THE SENSE?
DON'T APOLOGIZE! YOU TRIED!
WHAT MORE SHOULD SHE EXPECT?
FATHER... THIS IS... NOT RIGHT!
YOU SEEM TROUBLED, DAUGHTER.
WERE YOU HOPING THAT CUTTER'S HUMILIATION WOULD SOOTHE THE INDIGNITY OF YOUR FIRST MEETING?
THESE WOLFRIDERS WILL NOT TURN ON ONE OF THEIR OWN.
SO... THE FIERCE WOLF COWERS LIKE A FRIGHTENED SQUIRREL!
LOOK, LEETAH!
WHAT DO YOU THINK NOW OF YOUR WILD BARBARIAN SUITOR?
YOUR CHOICE OF A LIFEMATE HAS BECOME EASIER!
RAYEK! WHAT ARE YOU DOING?

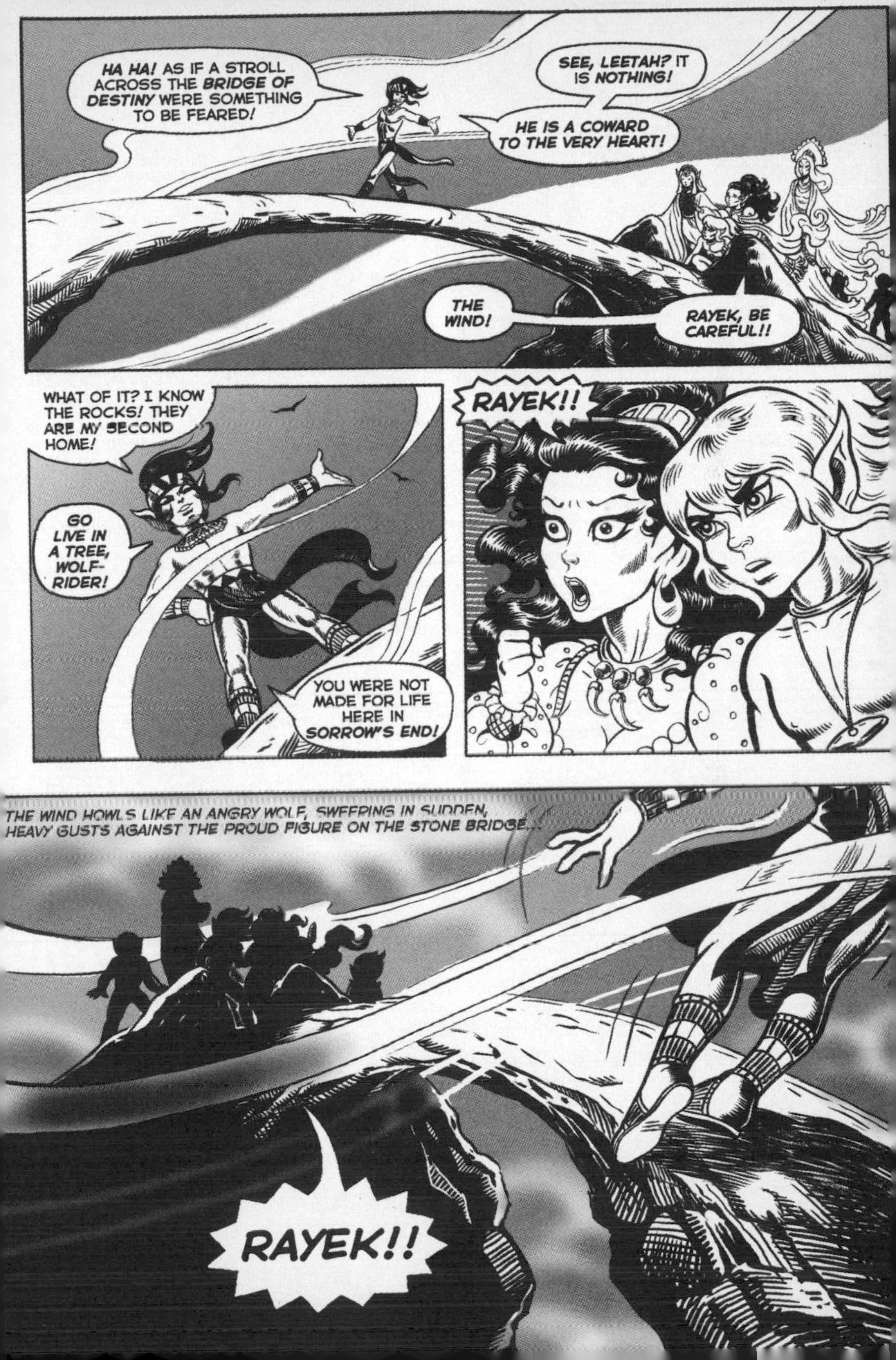
HA HA! AS IF A STROLL ACROSS THE BRIDGE OF DESTINY WERE SOMETHING TO BE FEARED!
SEE, LEETAH? IT IS NOTHING!
HE IS A COWARD TO THE VERY HEART!
THE WIND!
RAYEK, BE CAREFUL!!
WHAT OF IT? I KNOW THE ROCKS! THEY ARE MY SECOND HOME!
GO LIVE IN A TREE, WOLF-RIDER!
YOU WERE NOT MADE FOR LIFE HERE IN SORROW'S END!
RAYEK!!
THE WIND HOWLS LIKE AN ANGRY WOLF, SWEEPING IN SUDDEN, HEAVY GUSTS AGAINST THE PROUD FIGURE ON THE STONE BRIDGE...
RAYEK!!

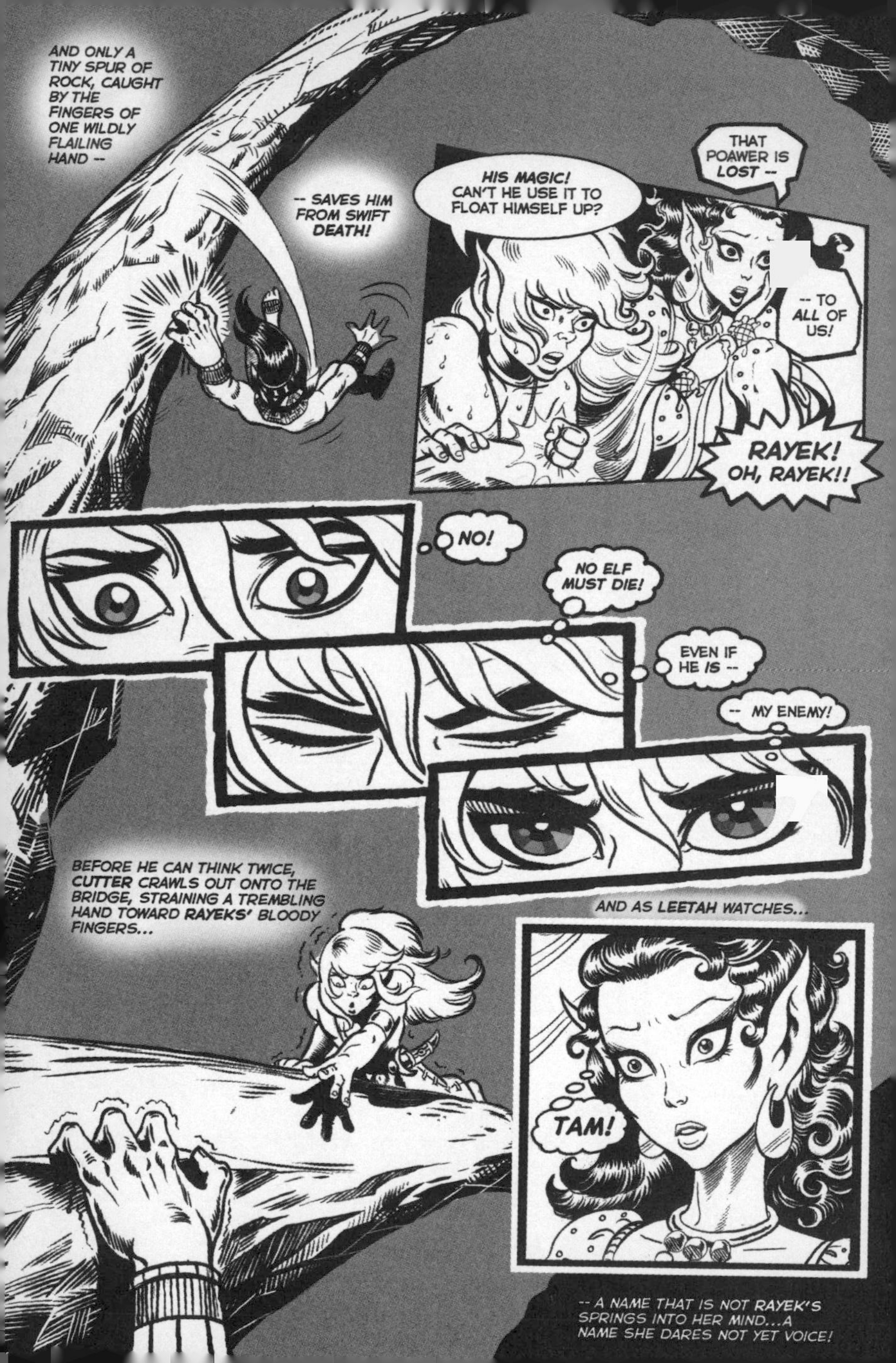
AND ONLY A TINY SPUR OF ROCK, CAUGHT BY THE FINGERS OF ONE WILDLY FLAILING HAND --
-- SAVES HIM FROM SWIFT DEATH!
HIS MAGIC! CAN'T HE USE IT TO FLOAT HIMSELF UP?
THAT POAWER IS LOST --
-- TO ALL OF US!
RAYEK! OH, RAYEK!!
NO!
NO ELF MUST DIE!
EVEN IF HE IS --
-- MY ENEMY!
BEFORE HE CAN THINK TWICE, CUTTER CRAWLS OUT ONTO THE BRIDGE, STRAINING A TREMBLING HAND TOWARD RAYEKS' BLOODY FINGERS...
AND AS LEETAH WATCHES...
TAM!
-- A NAME THAT IS NOT RAYEK'S SPRINGS INTO HER MIND...A NAME SHE DARES NOT YET VOICE!

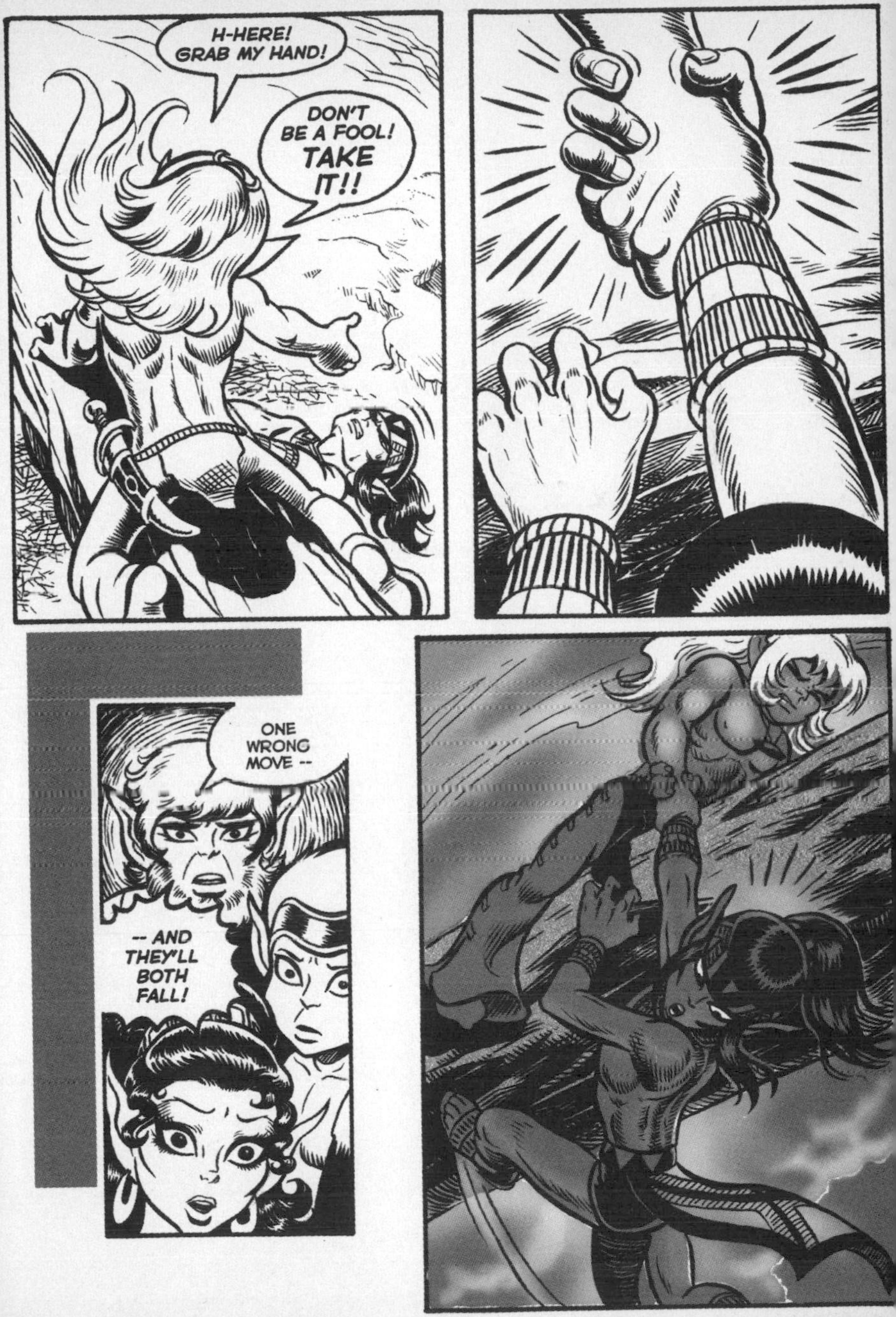
H-HERE! GRAB MY HAND!
DON'T BE A FOOL! TAKE IT!!
ONE WRONG MOVE --
-- AND THEY'LL BOTH FALL!

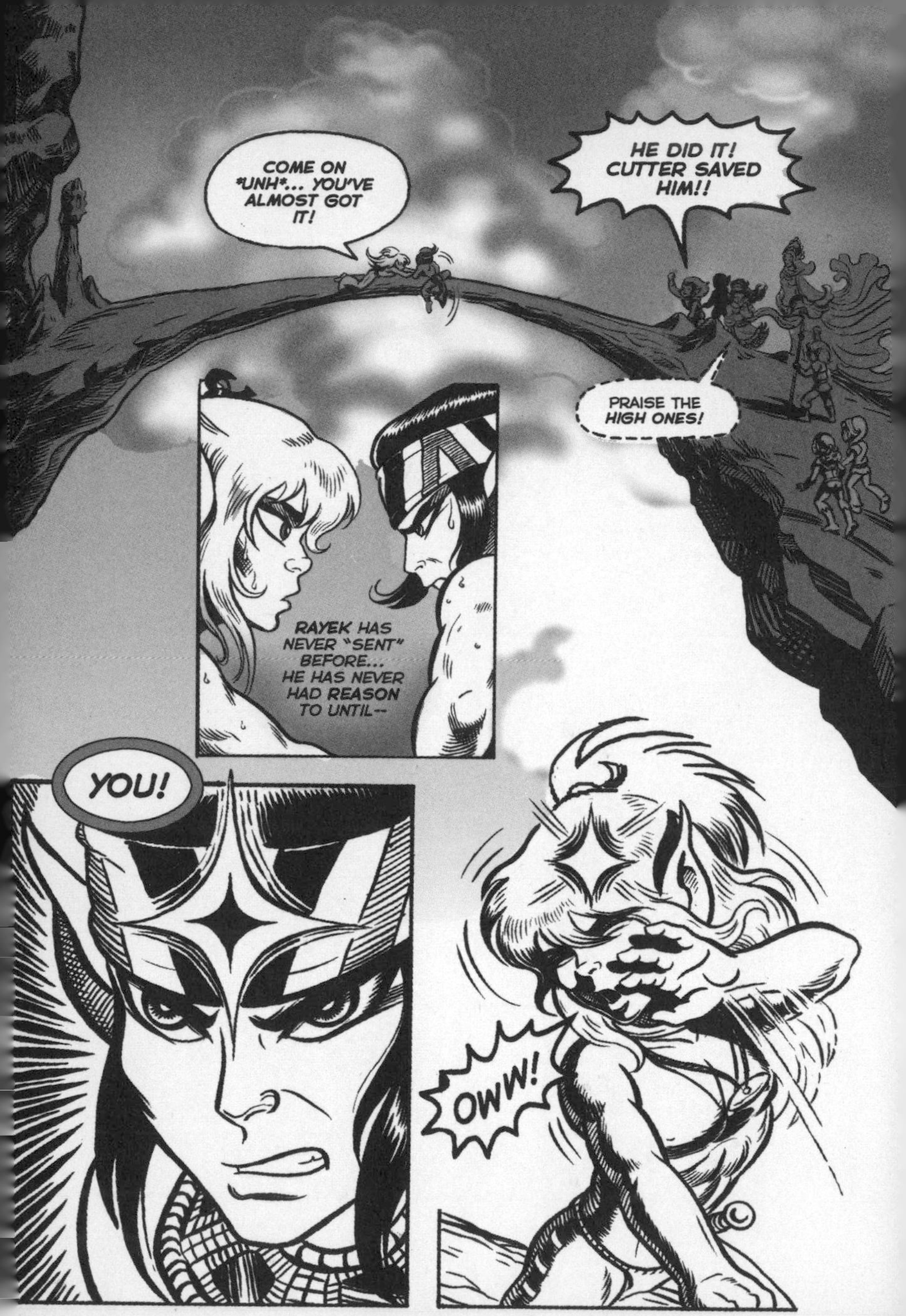

COME ON *UNH*... YOU'VE ALMOST GOT IT!
HE DID IT! CUTTER SAVED HIM!!
PRAISE THE HIGH ONES!
RAYEK HAS NEVER "SENT" BEFORE... HE HAS NEVER HAD REASON TO UNTIL--
YOU!
OWW!

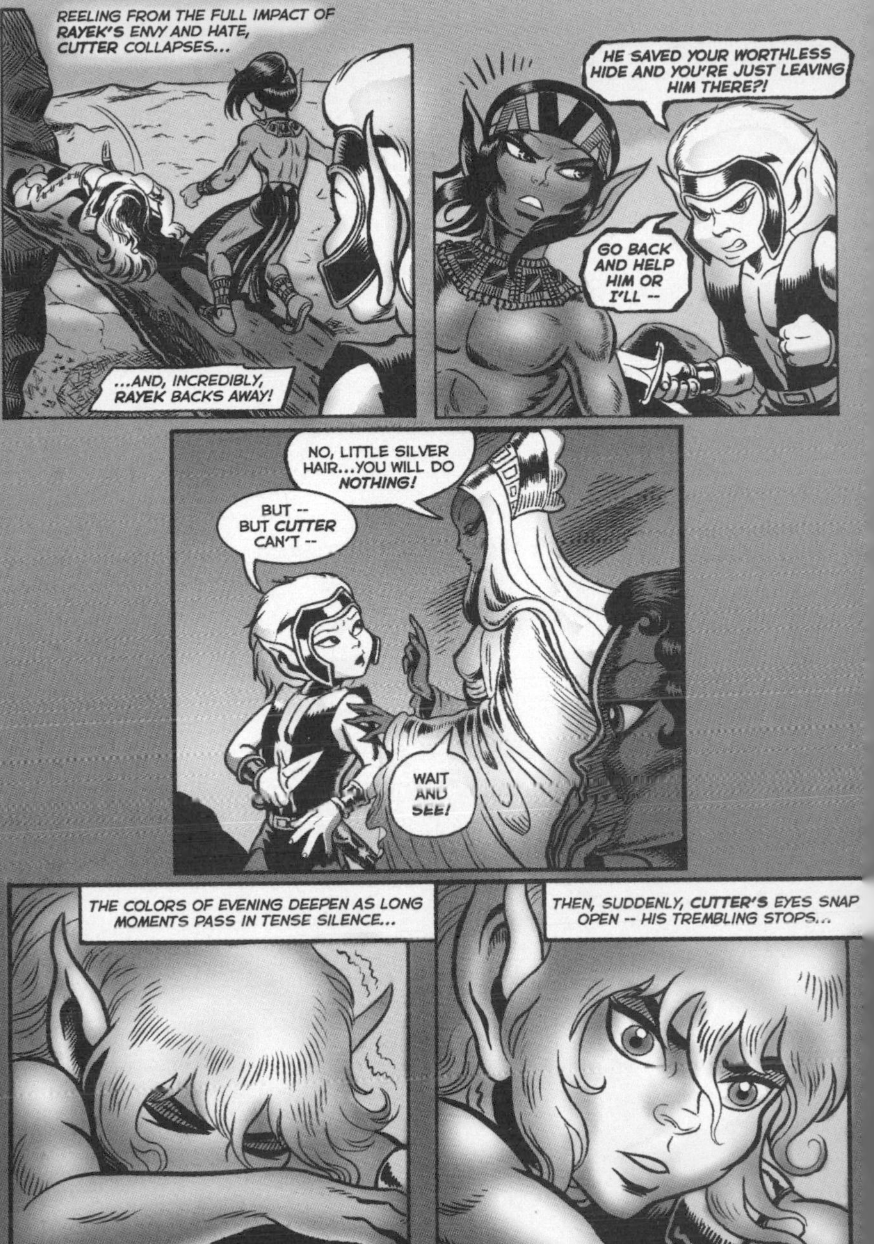
REELING FROM THE FULL IMPACT OF RAYEK'S ENVY AND HATE, CUTTER COLLAPSES...
...AND, INCREDIBLY, RAYEK BACKS AWAY!
HE SAVED YOUR WORTHLESS HIDE AND YOU'RE JUST LEAVING HIM THERE?!
GO BACK AND HELP HIM OR I'LL --
NO, LITTLE SILVER HAIR...YOU WILL DO NOTHING!
BUT -- BUT CUTTER CAN'T --
WAIT AND SEE!
THE COLORS OF EVENING DEEPEN AS LONG MOMENTS PASS IN TENSE SILENCE...
THEN, SUDDENLY, CUTTER'S EYES SNAP OPEN -- HIS TREMBLING STOPS...

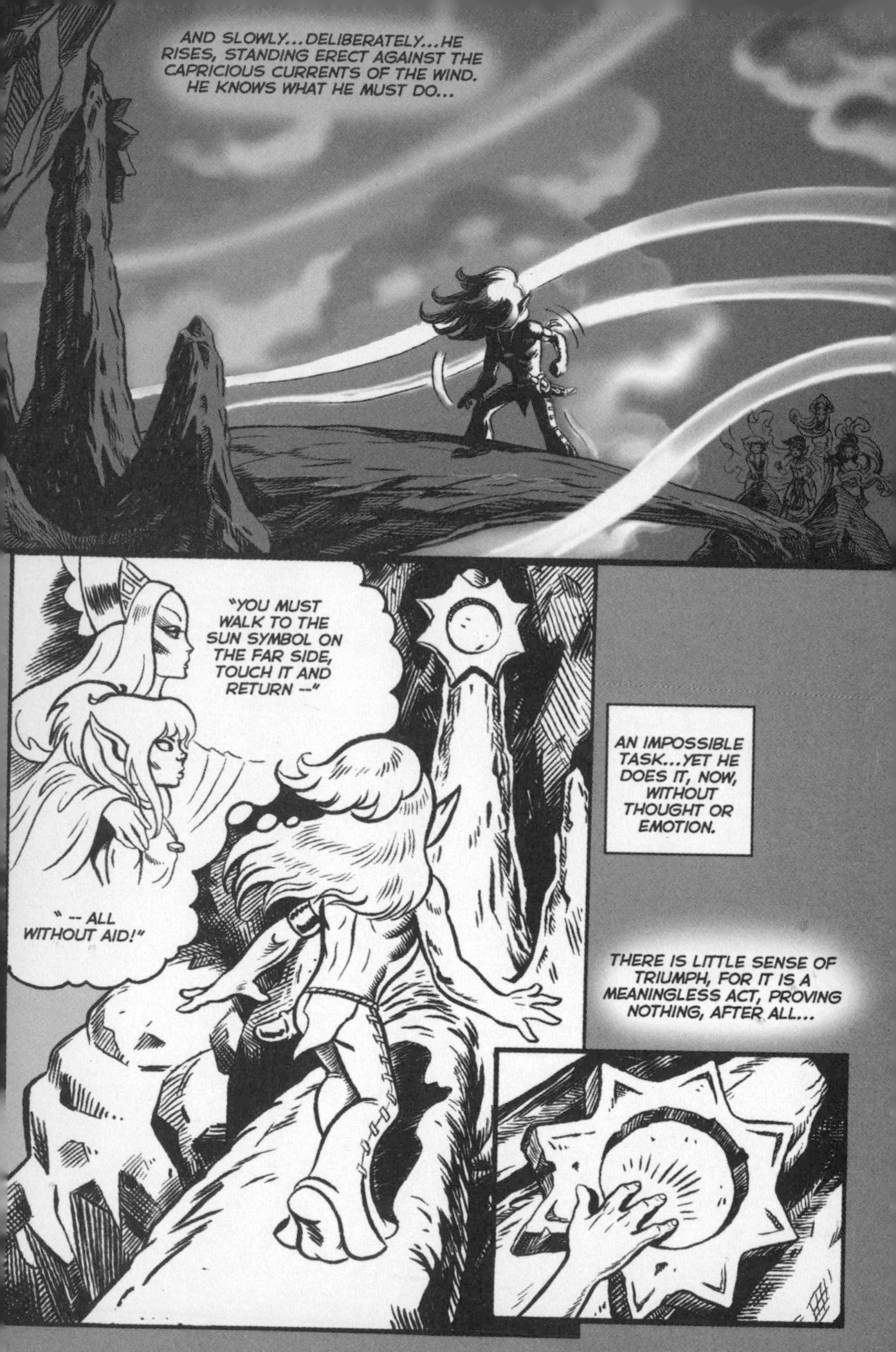
AND SLOWLY...DELIBERATELY...HE RISES, STANDING ERECT AGAINST THE CAPRICIOUS CURRENTS OF THE WIND. HE KNOWS WHAT HE MUST DO...
"YOU MUST WALK TO THE SUN SYMBOL ON THE FAR SIDE, TOUCH IT AND RETURN --"
" -- ALL WITHOUT AID!"
AN IMPOSSIBLE TASK...YET HE DOES IT, NOW, WITHOUT THOUGHT OR EMOTION.
THERE IS LITTLE SENSE OF TRIUMPH, FOR IT IS A MEANINGLESS ACT, PROVING NOTHING, AFTER ALL...

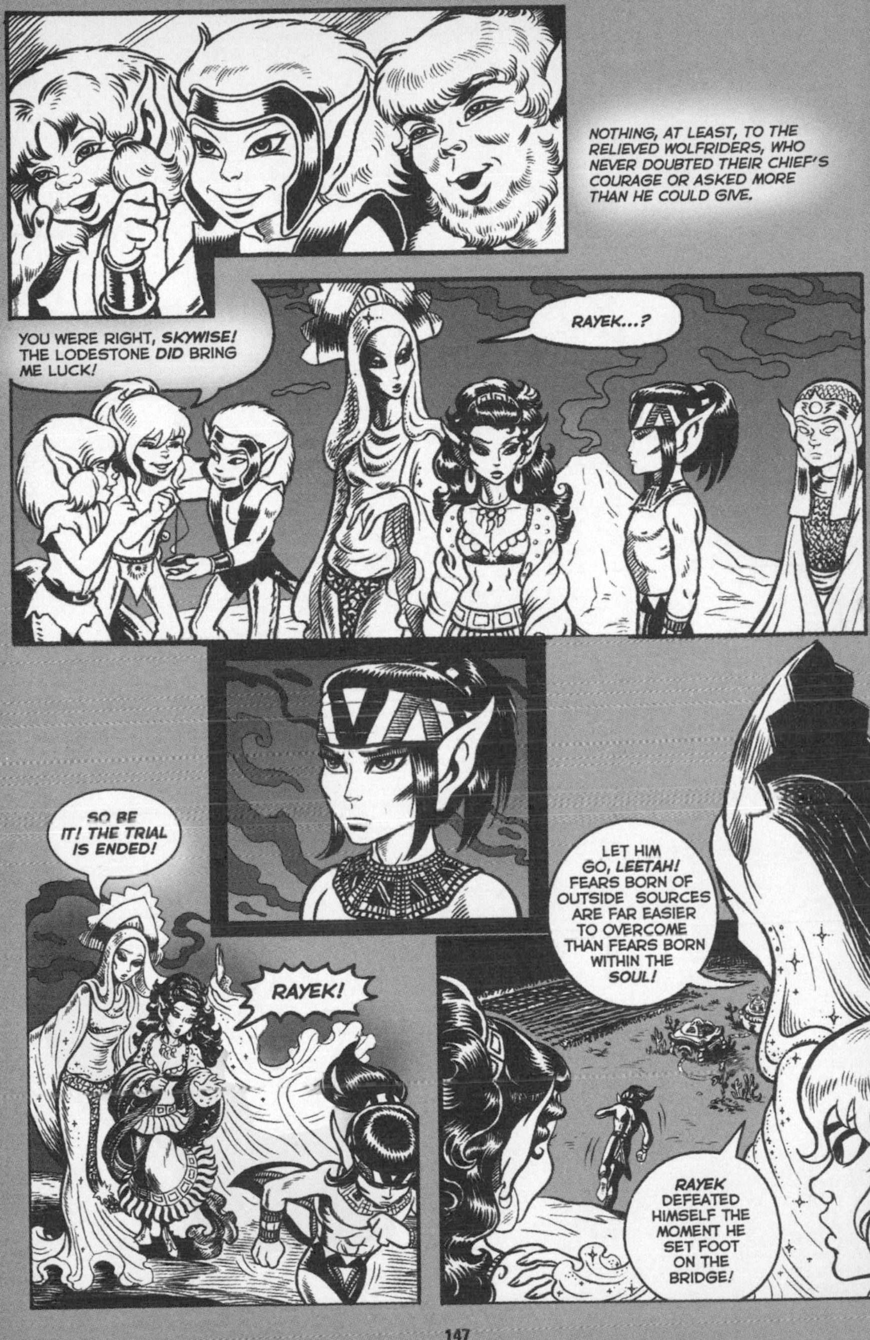
NOTHING, AT LEAST, TO THE RELIEVED WOLFRIDERS, WHO NEVER DOUBTED THEIR CHIEF'S COURAGE OR ASKED MORE THAN HE COULD GIVE.
YOU WERE RIGHT, SKYWISE! THE LODESTONE DID BRING ME LUCK!
RAYEK...?
SO BE IT! THE TRIAL IS ENDED!
RAYEK!
LET HIM GO, LEETAH! FEARS BORN OF OUTSIDE SOURCES ARE FAR EASIER TO OVERCOME THAN FEARS BORN WITHIN THE SOUL!
RAYEK DEFEATED HIMSELF THE MOMENT HE SET FOOT ON THE BRIDGE!

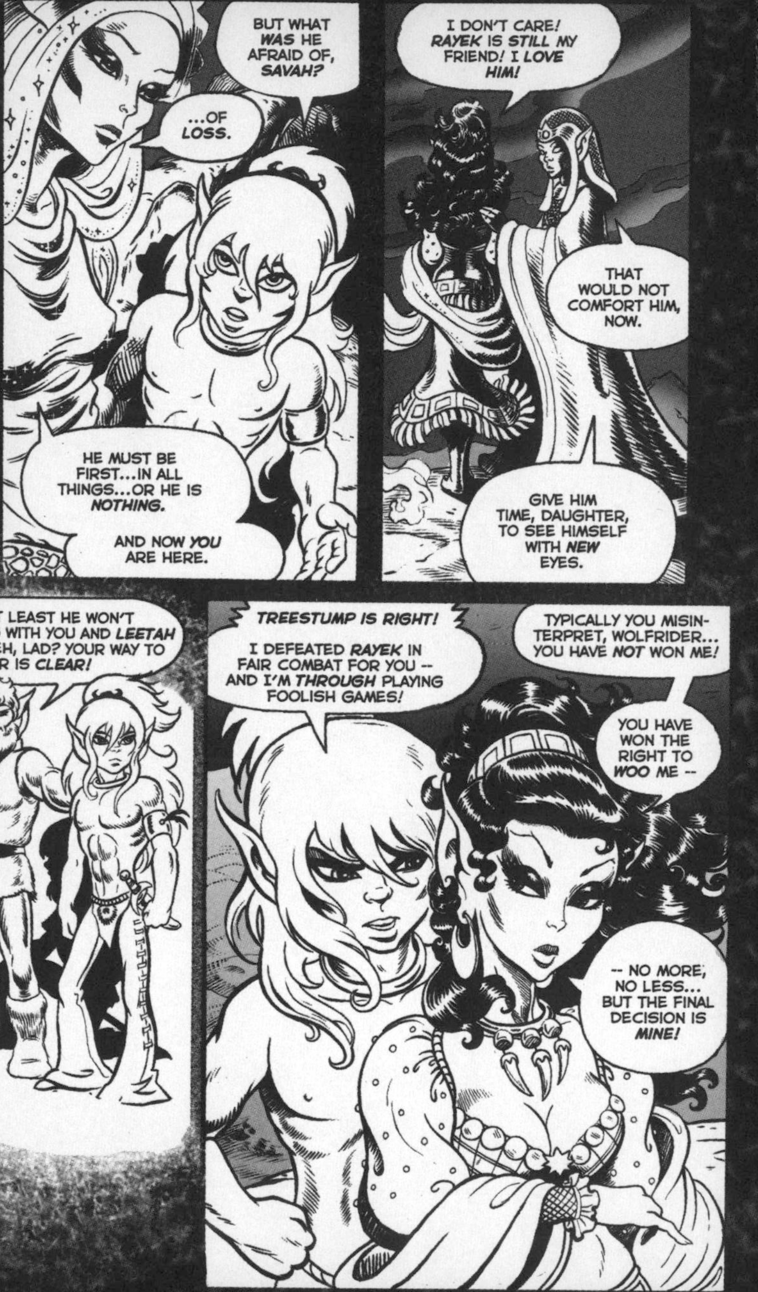

BUT WHAT WAS HE AFRAID OF, SAVAH?
...OF LOSS.
HE MUST BE FIRST...IN ALL THINGS...OR HE IS NOTHING.
AND NOW YOU ARE HERE.
I DON'T CARE! RAYEK IS STILL MY FRIEND! I LOVE HIM!
THAT WOULD NOT COMFORT HIM, NOW.
GIVE HIM TIME, DAUGHTER, TO SEE HIMSELF WITH NEW EYES.
WELL, AT LEAST HE WON'T BE MEDDLING WITH YOU AND LEETAH ANY MORE, EH, LAD? YOUR WAY TO HER IS CLEAR!
TREESTUMP IS RIGHT!
I DEFEATED RAYEK IN FAIR COMBAT FOR YOU -- AND I'M THROUGH PLAYING FOOLISH GAMES!
TYPICALLY YOU MISIN-TERPRET, WOLFRIDER... YOU HAVE NOT WON ME!
YOU HAVE WON THE RIGHT TO WOO ME --
-- NO MORE, NO LESS... BUT THE FINAL DECISION IS MINE!

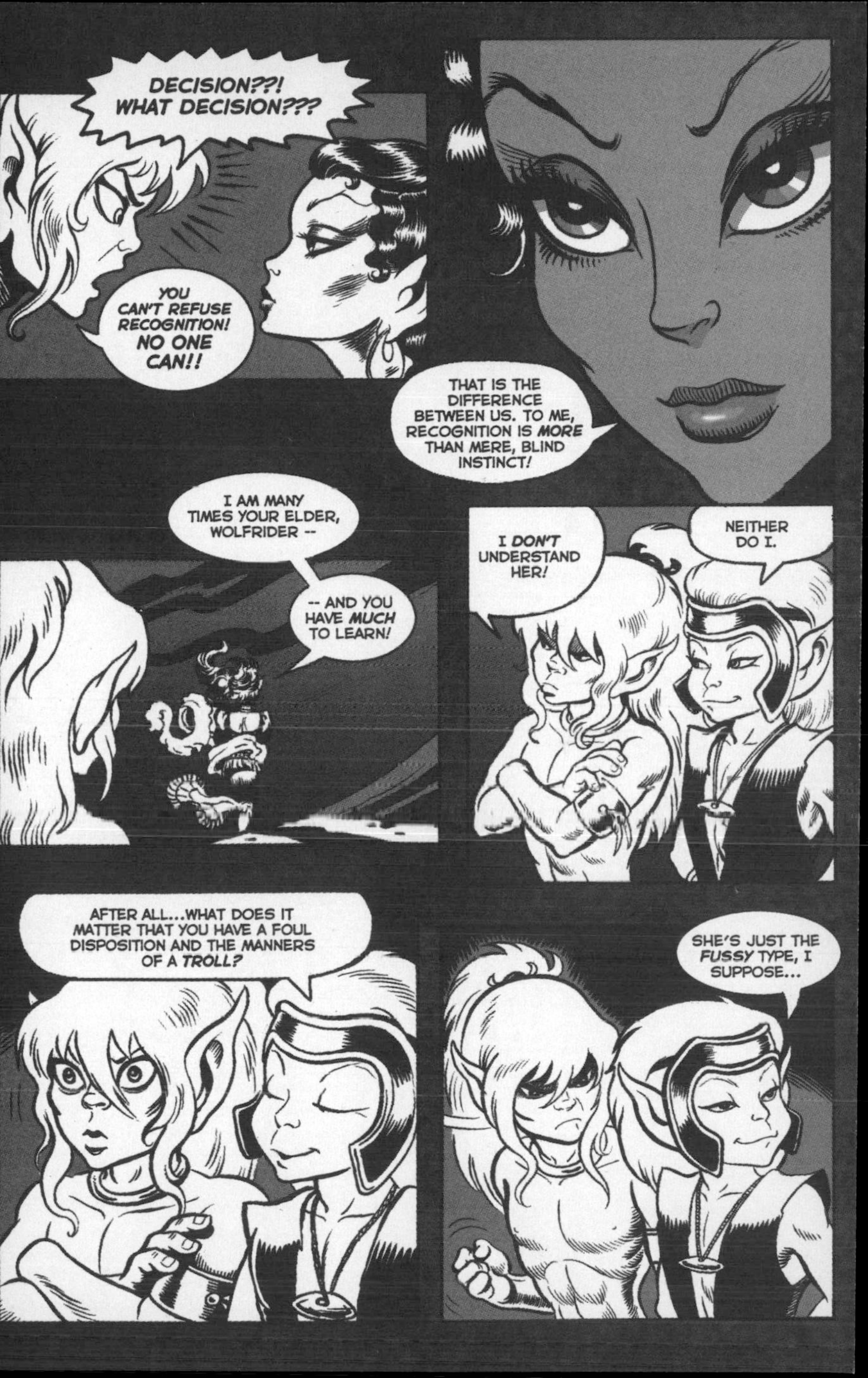
DECISION??! WHAT DECISION???
YOU CAN'T REFUSE RECOGNITION! NO ONE CAN!!
THAT IS THE DIFFERENCE BETWEEN US. TO ME, RECOGNITION IS MORE THAN MERE, BLIND INSTINCT!
I AM MANY TIMES YOUR ELDER, WOLFRIDER --
-- AND YOU HAVE MUCH TO LEARN!
I DON'T UNDERSTAND HER!
NEITHER DO I.
AFTER ALL...WHAT DOES IT MATTER THAT YOU HAVE A FOUL DISPOSITION AND THE MANNERS OF A TROLL?
SHE'S JUST THE FUSSY TYPE, I SUPPOSE...

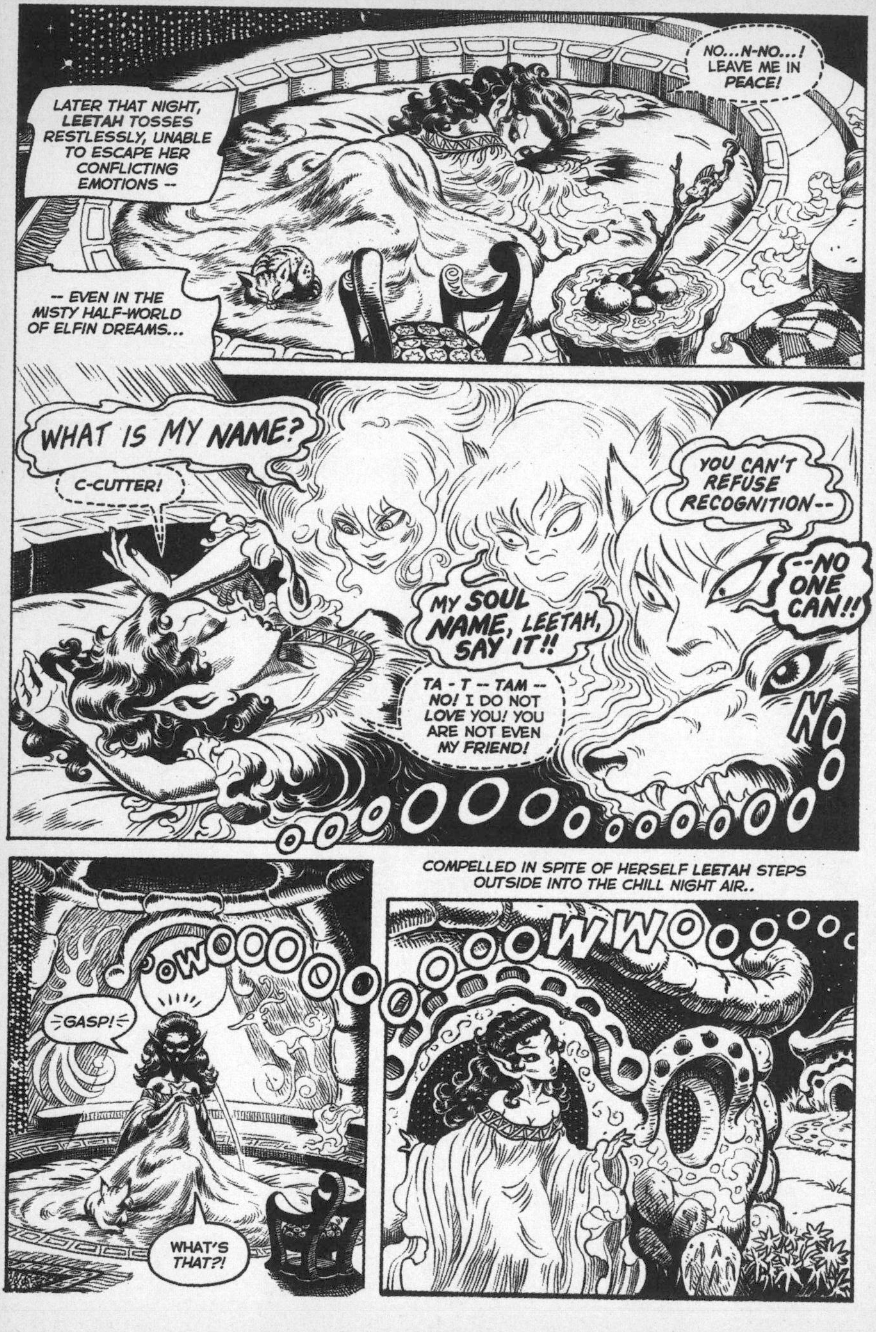

LATER THAT NIGHT, LEETAH TOSSES RESTLESSLY, UNABLE TO ESCAPE HER CONFLICTING EMOTIONS --
NO...N-NO...! LEAVE ME IN PEACE!
-- EVEN IN THE MISTY HALF-WORLD OF ELFIN DREAMS...
WHAT IS MY NAME?
C-CUTTER!
MY SOUL NAME, LEETAH, SAY IT!!
TA - T -- TAM -- NO! I DO NOT LOVE YOU! YOU ARE NOT EVEN MY FRIEND!
YOU CAN'T REFUSE RECOGNITION--
--NO ONE CAN!!
NOOOOOOOOOOOOOOOOOOOOO
=GASP!=
WHAT'S THAT?!
COMPELLED IN SPITE OF HERSELF LEETAH STEPS OUTSIDE INTO THE CHILL NIGHT AIR..
OOWOOOOOOOOOOOOWWOOOOOO

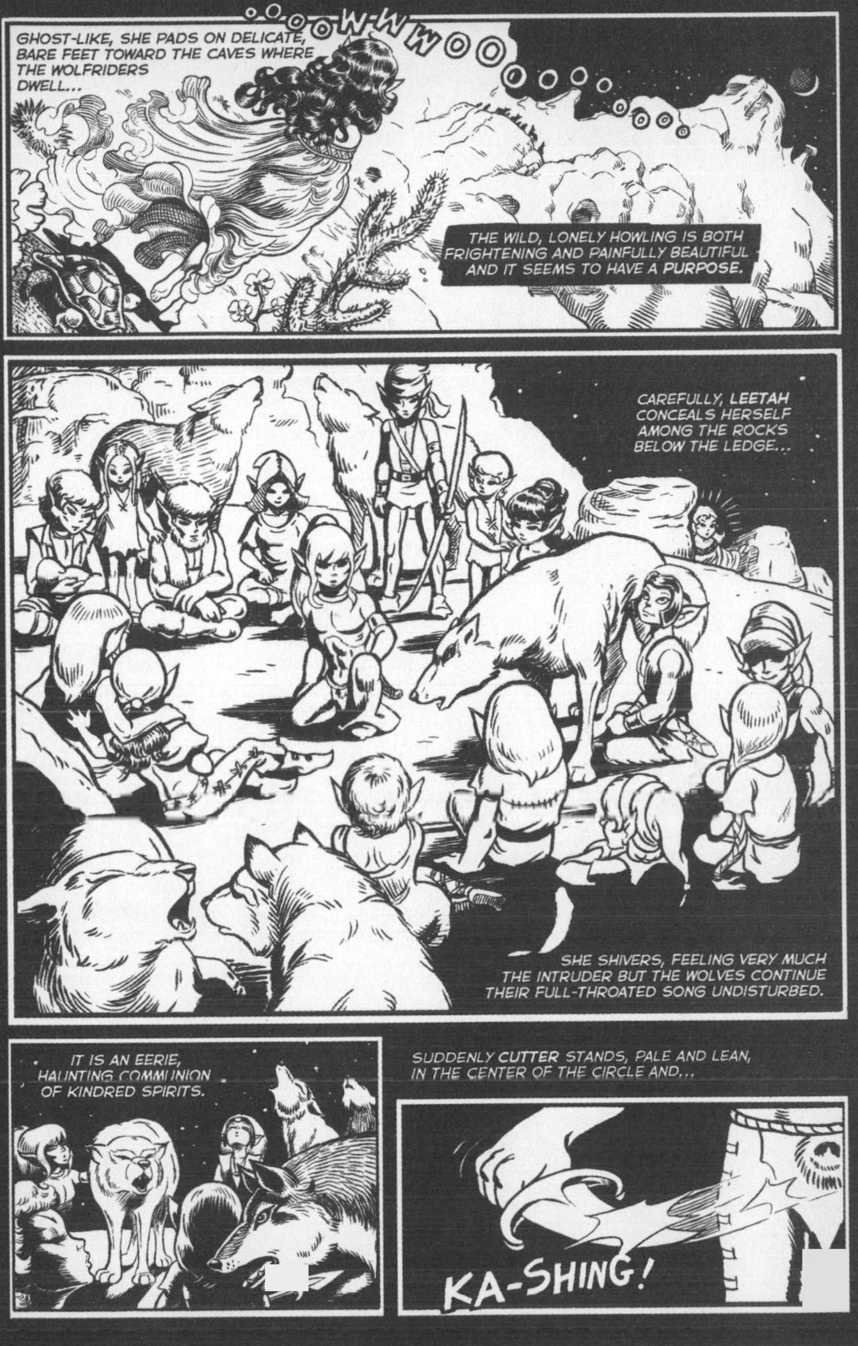
GHOST-LIKE, SHE PADS ON DELICATE, BARE FEET TOWARD THE CAVES WHERE THE WOLFRIDERS DWELL...
OOOOWWWWOOOOOOOOOOOO
THE WILD, LONELY HOWLING IS BOTH FRIGHTENING AND PAINFULLY BEAUTIFUL AND IT SEEMS TO HAVE A PURPOSE.
CAREFULLY, LEETAH CONCEALS HERSELF AMONG THE ROCKS BELOW THE LEDGE...
SHE SHIVERS, FEELING VERY MUCH THE INTRUDER BUT THE WOLVES CONTINUE THEIR FULL-THROATED SONG UNDISTURBED.
IT IS AN EERIE, HAUNTING COMMUNION OF KINDRED SPIRITS.
SUDDENLY CUTTER STANDS, PALE AND LEAN, IN THE CENTER OF THE CIRCLE AND...
KA-SHING!

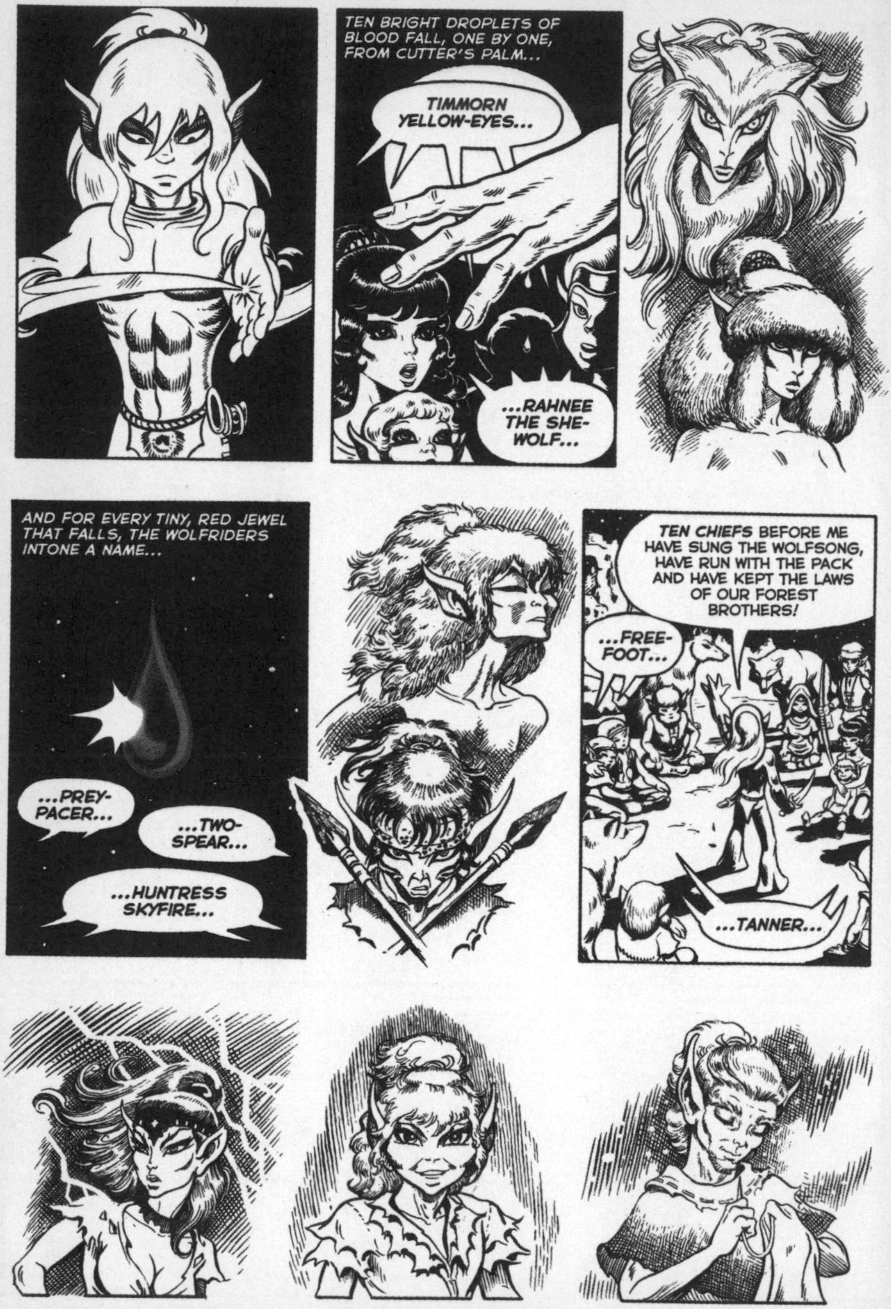

TEN BRIGHT DROPLETS OF BLOOD FALL, ONE BY ONE, FROM CUTTER'S PALM...
TIMMORN YELLOW-EYES...
...RAHNEE THE SHE-WOLF...
AND FOR EVERY TINY, RED JEWEL THAT FALLS, THE WOLFRIDERS INTONE A NAME...
...PREY-PACER...
...TWO-SPEAR...
...HUNTRESS SKYFIRE...
TEN CHIEFS BEFORE ME HAVE SUNG THE WOLFSONG, HAVE RUN WITH THE PACK AND HAVE KEPT THE LAWS OF OUR FOREST BROTHERS!
...FREE-FOOT...
...TANNER...

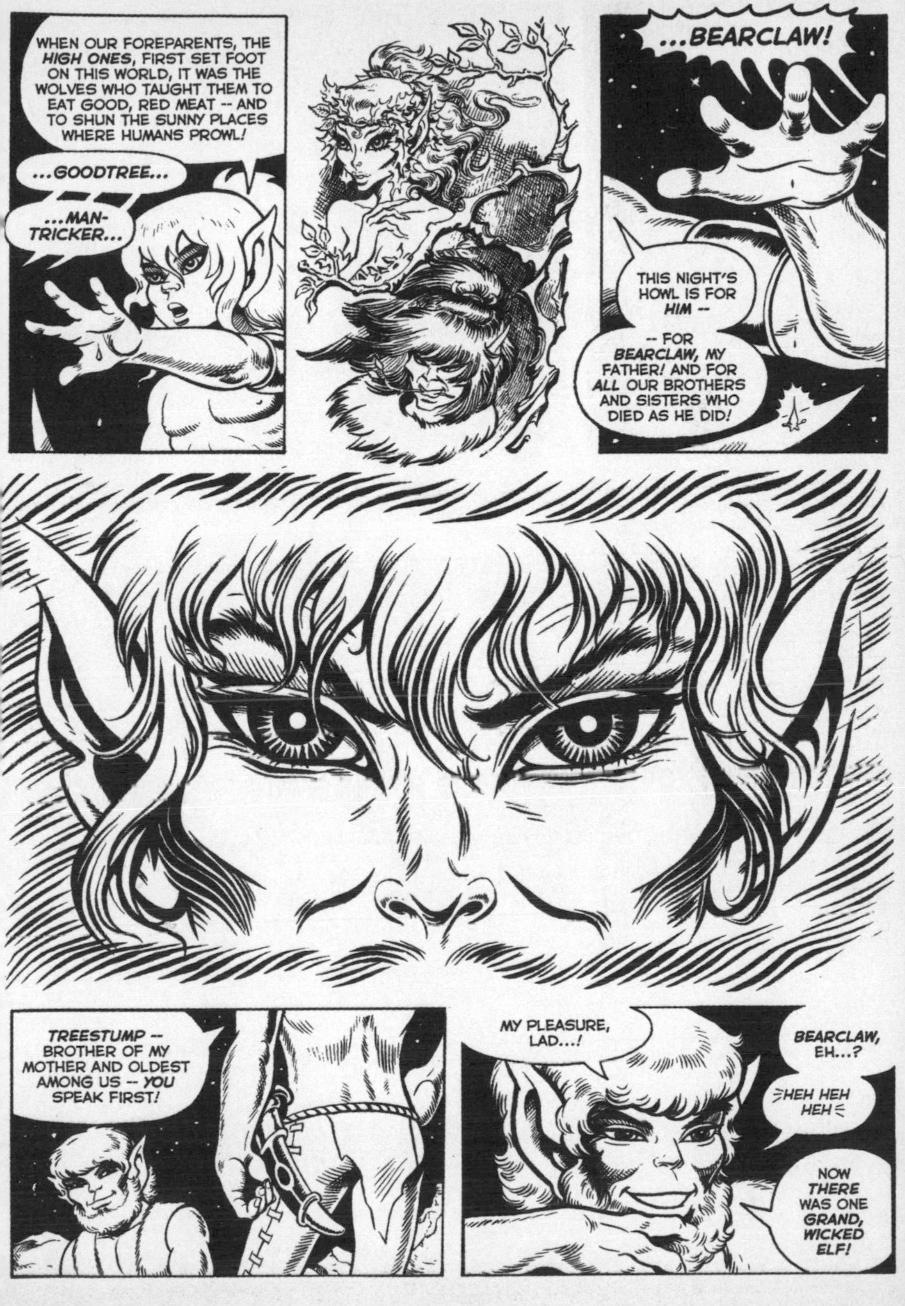
WHEN OUR FOREPARENTS, THE HIGH ONES, FIRST SET FOOT ON THIS WORLD, IT WAS THE WOLVES WHO TAUGHT THEM TO EAT GOOD, RED MEAT -- AND TO SHUN THE SUNNY PLACES WHERE HUMANS PROWL!
...GOODTREE...
...MAN-TRICKER...
...BEARCLAW!
THIS NIGHT'S HOWL IS FOR HIM --
-- FOR BEARCLAW, MY FATHER! AND FOR ALL OUR BROTHERS AND SISTERS WHO DIED AS HE DID!
TREESTUMP -- BROTHER OF MY MOTHER AND OLDEST AMONG US -- YOU SPEAK FIRST!
MY PLEASURE, LAD...!
BEARCLAW, EH...?
HEH HEH HEH
NOW THERE WAS ONE GRAND, WICKED ELF!

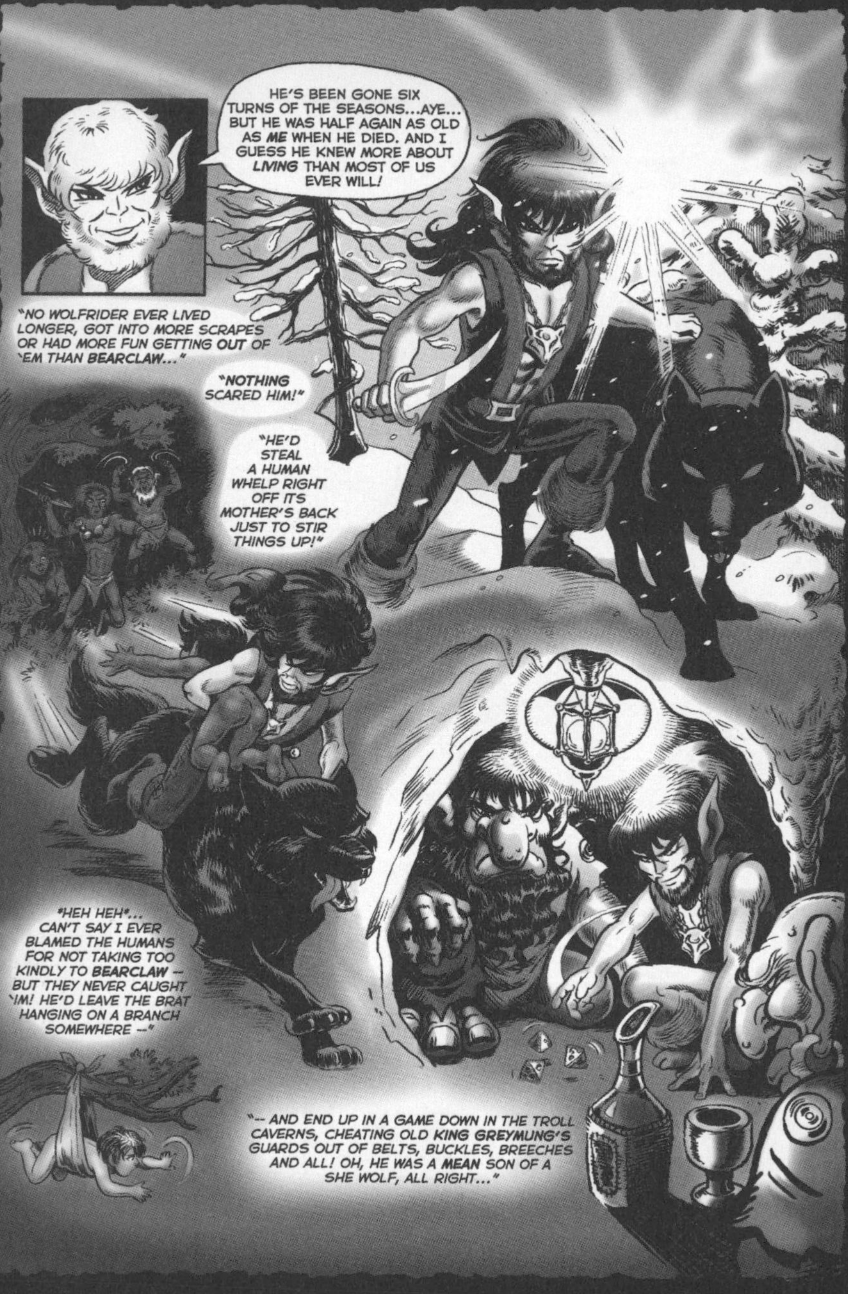

HE'S BEEN GONE SIX TURNS OF THE SEASONS...AYE... BUT HE WAS HALF AGAIN AS OLD AS ME WHEN HE DIED. AND I GUESS HE KNEW MORE ABOUT LIVING THAN MOST OF US EVER WILL!
"NO WOLFRIDER EVER LIVED LONGER, GOT INTO MORE SCRAPES OR HAD MORE FUN GETTING OUT OF 'EM THAN BEARCLAW..."
"NOTHING SCARED HIM!"
"HE'D STEAL A HUMAN WHELP RIGHT OFF ITS MOTHER'S BACK JUST TO STIR THINGS UP!"
HEH HEH... CAN'T SAY I EVER BLAMED THE HUMANS FOR NOT TAKING TOO KINDLY TO BEARCLAW -- BUT THEY NEVER CAUGHT 'IM! HE'D LEAVE THE BRAT HANGING ON A BRANCH SOMEWHERE --"
"-- AND END UP IN A GAME DOWN IN THE TROLL CAVERNS, CHEATING OLD KING GREYMUNG'S GUARDS OUT OF BELTS, BUCKLES, BREECHES AND ALL! OH, HE WAS A MEAN SON OF A SHE WOLF, ALL RIGHT..."

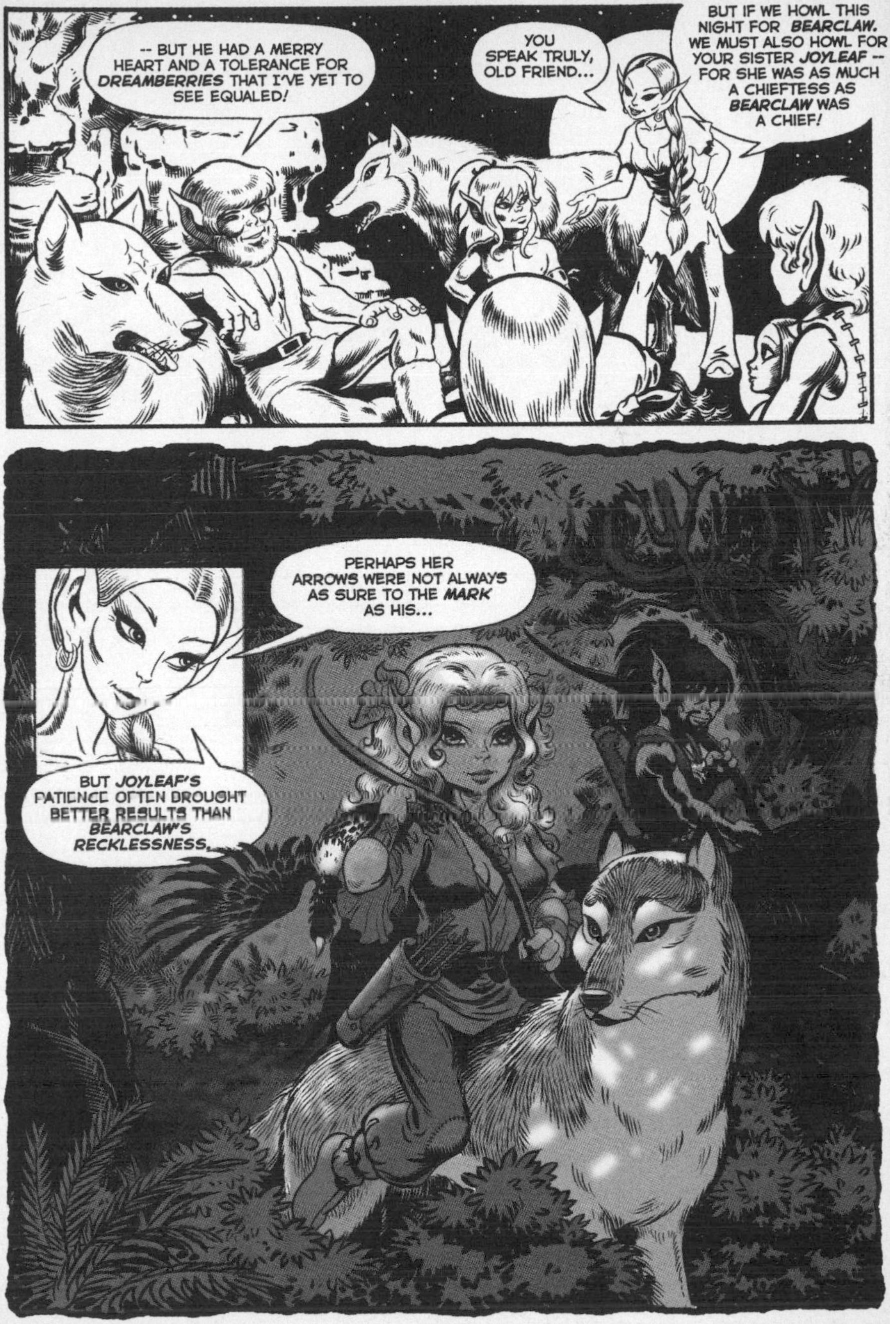
-- BUT HE HAD A MERRY HEART AND A TOLERANCE FOR DREAMBERRIES THAT I'VE YET TO SEE EQUALED!
YOU SPEAK TRULY, OLD FRIEND...
BUT IF WE HOWL THIS NIGHT FOR BEARCLAW. WE MUST ALSO HOWL FOR YOUR SISTER JOYLEAF -- FOR SHE WAS AS MUCH A CHIEFTESS AS BEARCLAW WAS A CHIEF!
PERHAPS HER ARROWS WERE NOT ALWAYS AS SURE TO THE MARK AS HIS...
BUT JOYLEAF'S PATIENCE OFTEN BROUGHT BETTER RESULTS THAN BEARCLAW'S RECKLESSNESS.

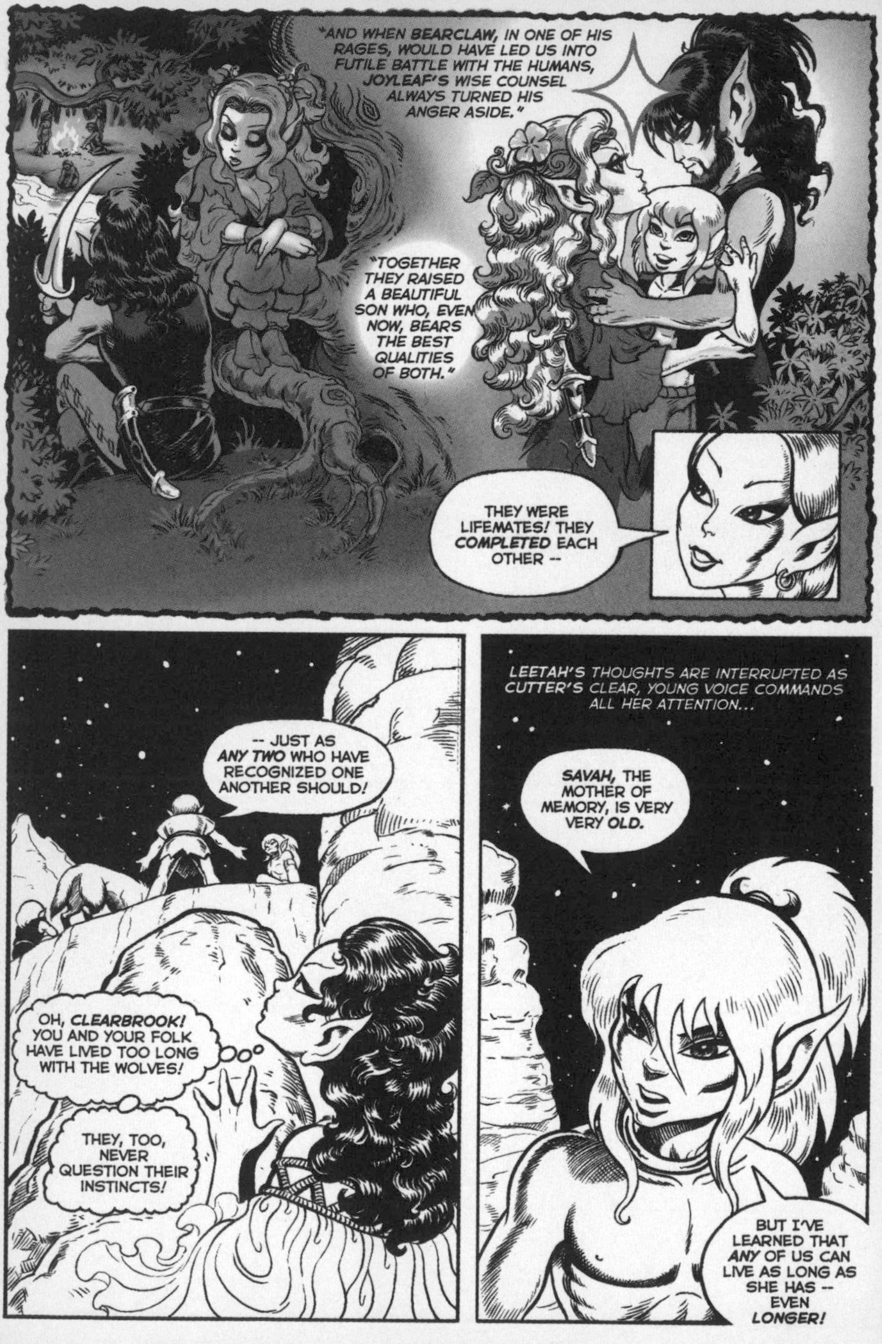
"AND WHEN BEARCLAW, IN ONE OF HIS RAGES, WOULD HAVE LED US INTO FUTILE BATTLE WITH THE HUMANS, JOYLEAF'S WISE COUNSEL ALWAYS TURNED HIS ANGER ASIDE."
"TOGETHER THEY RAISED A BEAUTIFUL SON WHO, EVEN NOW, BEARS THE BEST QUALITIES OF BOTH."
THEY WERE LIFEMATES! THEY COMPLETED EACH OTHER --
-- JUST AS ANY TWO WHO HAVE RECOGNIZED ONE ANOTHER SHOULD!
OH, CLEARBROOK! YOU AND YOUR FOLK HAVE LIVED TOO LONG WITH THE WOLVES!
THEY, TOO, NEVER QUESTION THEIR INSTINCTS!
LEETAH'S THOUGHTS ARE INTERRUPTED AS CUTTER'S CLEAR, YOUNG VOICE COMMANDS ALL HER ATTENTION...
SAVAH, THE MOTHER OF MEMORY, IS VERY VERY OLD.
BUT I'VE LEARNED THAT ANY OF US CAN LIVE AS LONG AS SHE HAS -- EVEN LONGER!

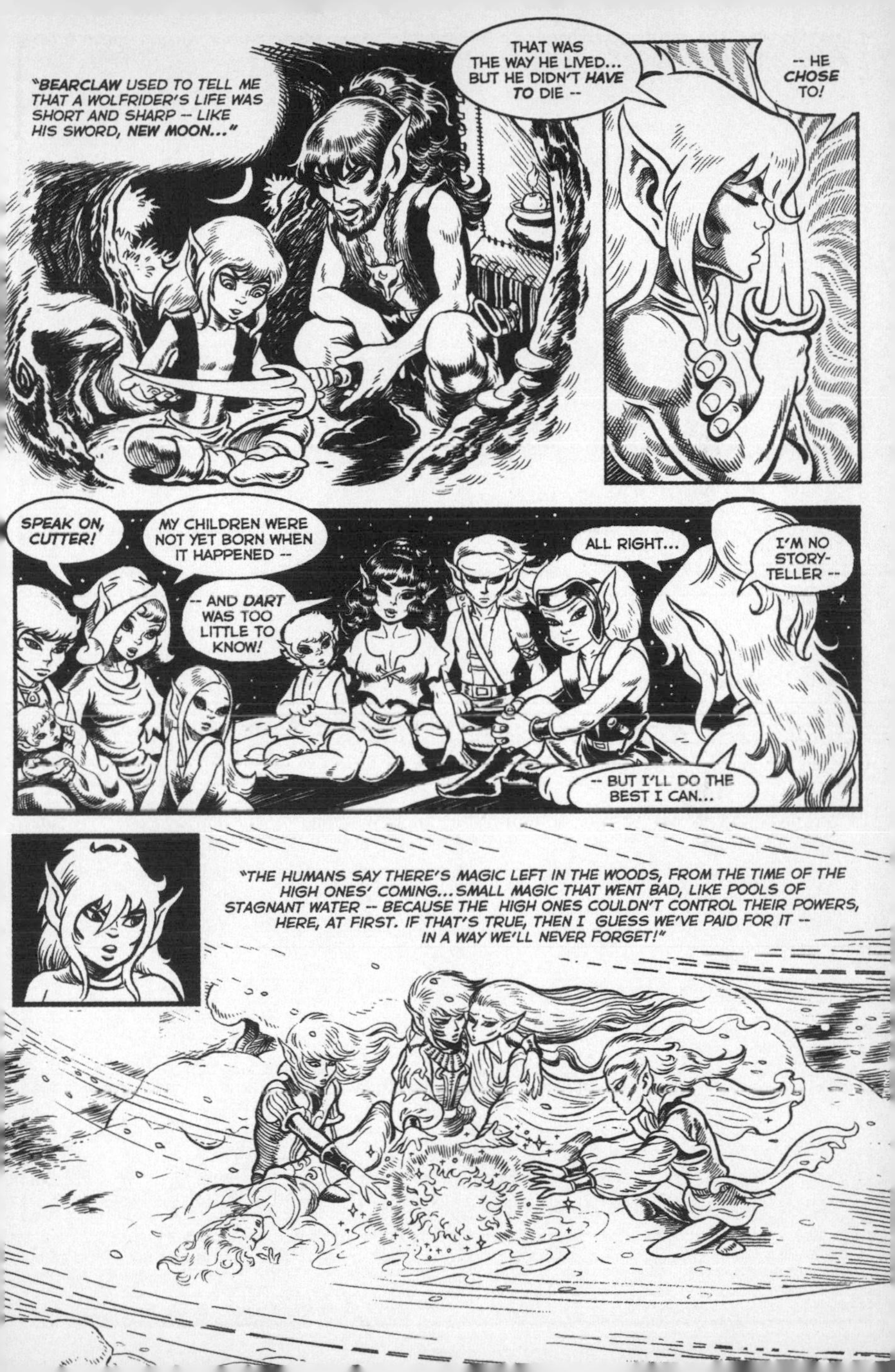
"BEARCLAW USED TO TELL ME THAT A WOLFRIDER'S LIFE WAS SHORT AND SHARP -- LIKE HIS SWORD, NEW MOON..."
THAT WAS THE WAY HE LIVED... BUT HE DIDN'T HAVE TO DIE --
-- HE CHOSE TO!
SPEAK ON, CUTTER!
MY CHILDREN WERE NOT YET BORN WHEN IT HAPPENED --
-- AND DART WAS TOO LITTLE TO KNOW!
ALL RIGHT...
I'M NO STORY-TELLER --
-- BUT I'LL DO THE BEST I CAN...
"THE HUMANS SAY THERE'S MAGIC LEFT IN THE WOODS, FROM THE TIME OF THE HIGH ONES' COMING... SMALL MAGIC THAT WENT BAD, LIKE POOLS OF STAGNANT WATER -- BECAUSE THE HIGH ONES COULDN'T CONTROL THEIR POWERS, HERE, AT FIRST. IF THAT'S TRUE, THEN I GUESS WE'VE PAID FOR IT -- IN A WAY WE'LL NEVER FORGET!"

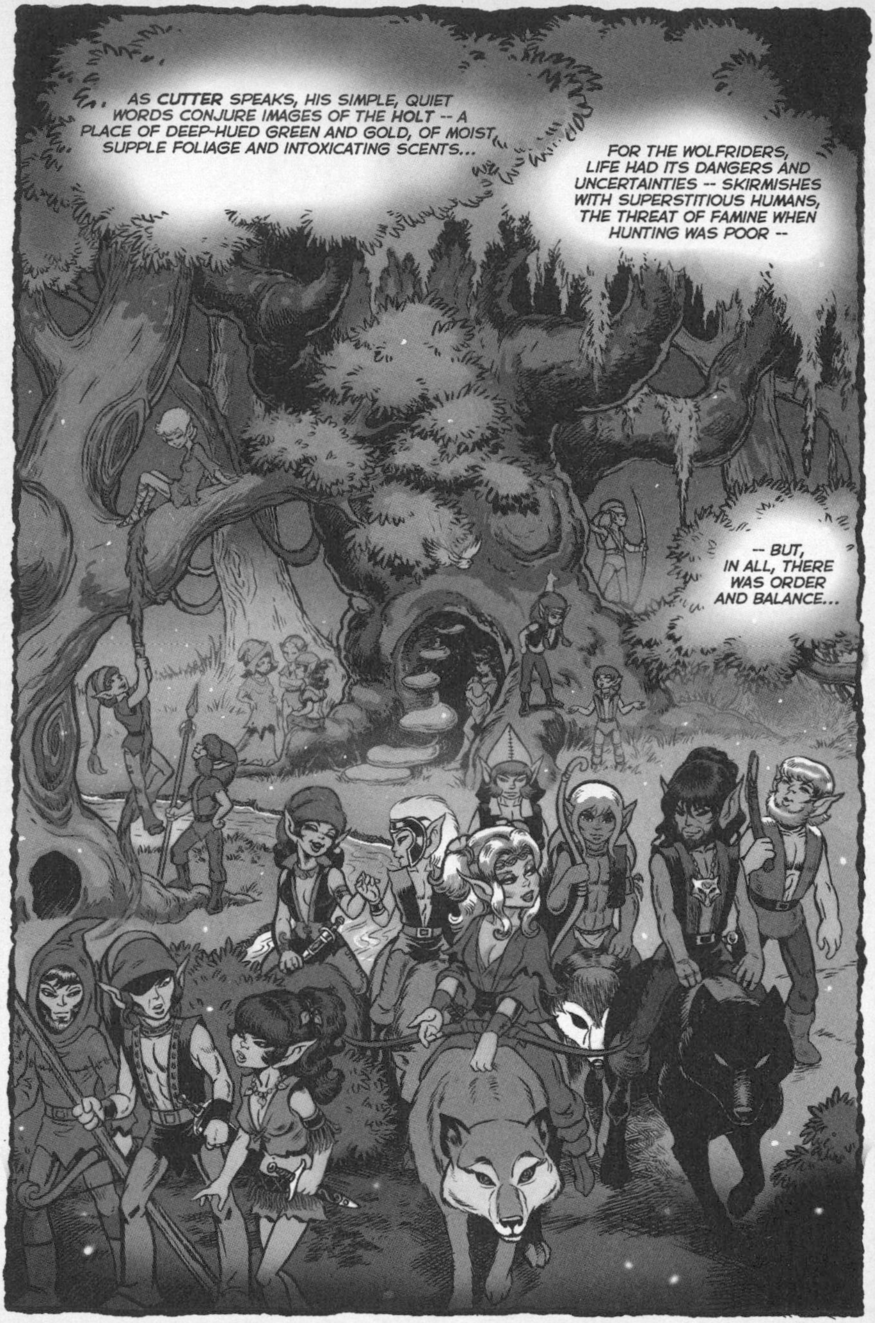
AS CUTTER SPEAKS, HIS SIMPLE, QUIET WORDS CONJURE IMAGES OF THE HOLT -- A PLACE OF DEEP-HUED GREEN AND GOLD, OF MOIST, SUPPLE FOLIAGE AND INTOXICATING SCENTS...
FOR THE WOLFRIDERS, LIFE HAD ITS DANGERS AND UNCERTAINTIES -- SKIRMISHES WITH SUPERSTITIOUS HUMANS, THE THREAT OF FAMINE WHEN HUNTING WAS POOR --
-- BUT, IN ALL, THERE WAS ORDER AND BALANCE...

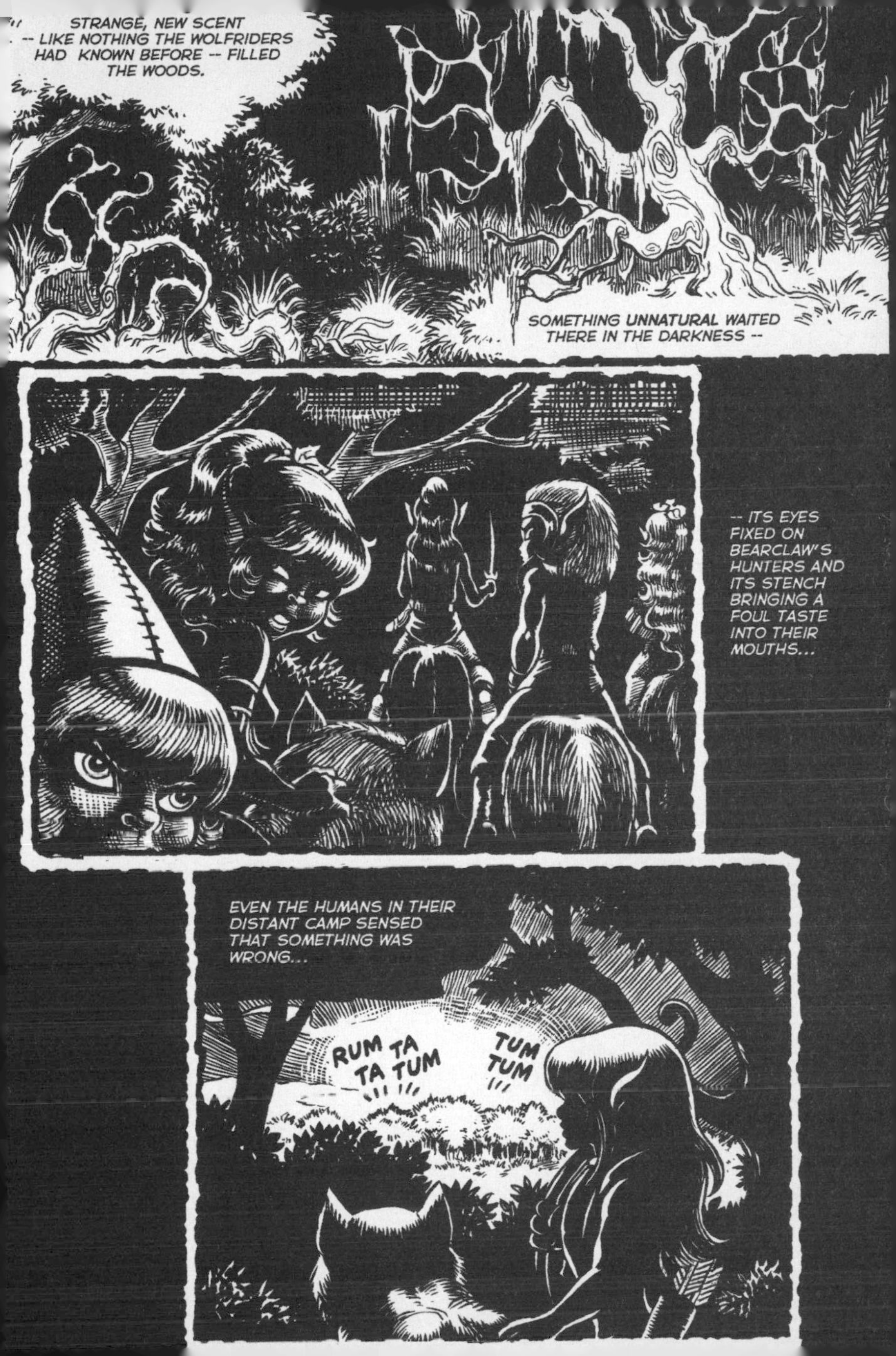
STRANGE, NEW SCENT -- LIKE NOTHING THE WOLFRIDERS HAD KNOWN BEFORE -- FILLED THE WOODS.
SOMETHING UNNATURAL WAITED THERE IN THE DARKNESS --
-- ITS EYES FIXED ON BEARCLAW'S HUNTERS AND ITS STENCH BRINGING A FOUL TASTE INTO THEIR MOUTHS...
EVEN THE HUMANS IN THEIR DISTANT CAMP SENSED THAT SOMETHING WAS WRONG...
RUM TA TA TUM
TUM TUM

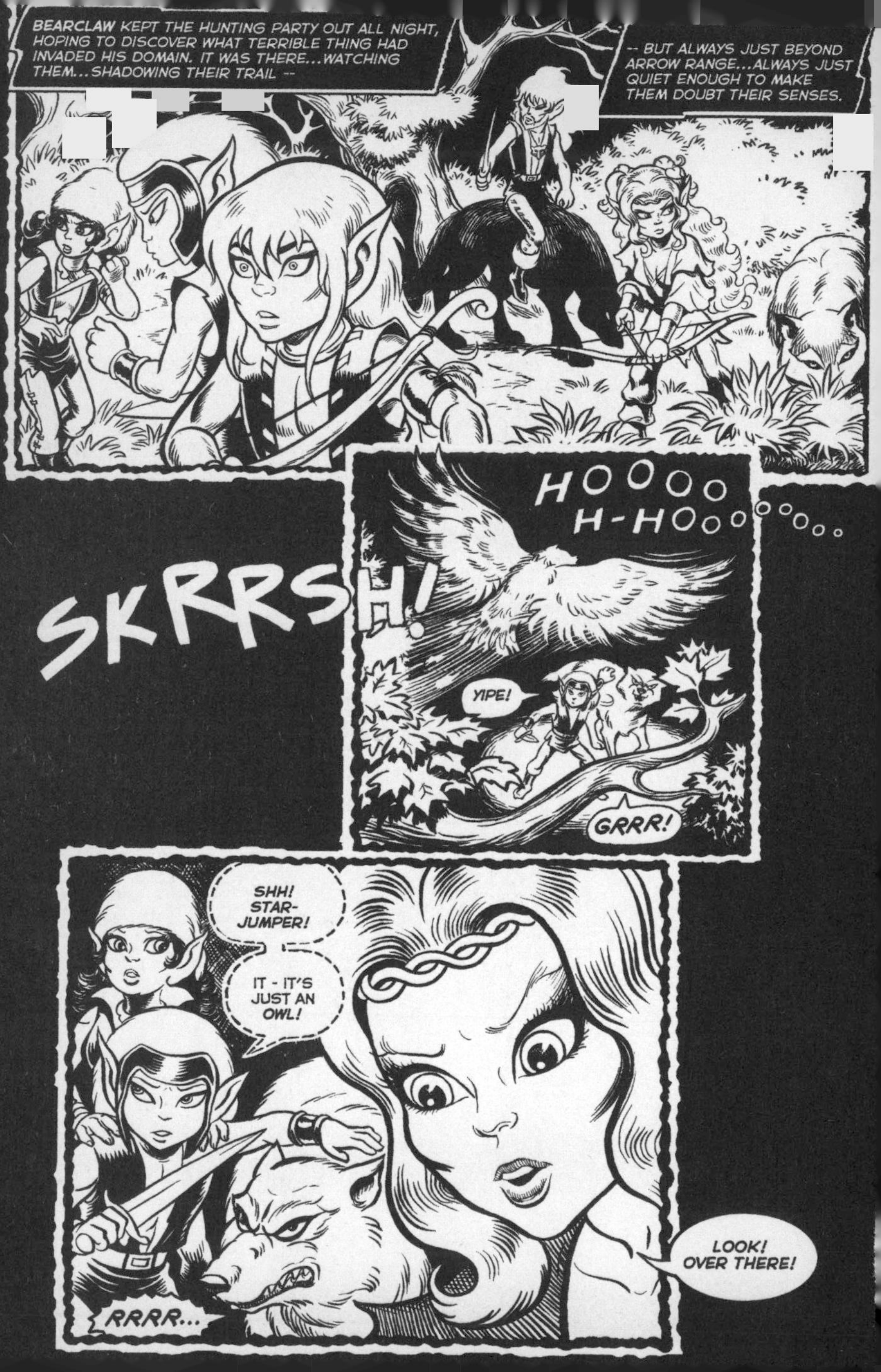
BEARCLAW KEPT THE HUNTING PARTY OUT ALL NIGHT, HOPING TO DISCOVER WHAT TERRIBLE THING HAD INVADED HIS DOMAIN. IT WAS THERE...WATCHING THEM...SHADOWING THEIR TRAIL --
-- BUT ALWAYS JUST BEYOND ARROW RANGE...ALWAYS JUST QUIET ENOUGH TO MAKE THEM DOUBT THEIR SENSES.
SKRRSH!
HOOOO H-HOOOOOOOO...
YIPE!
GRRR!
SHH! STAR-JUMPER!
IT - IT'S JUST AN OWL!
LOOK! OVER THERE!
RRRR...

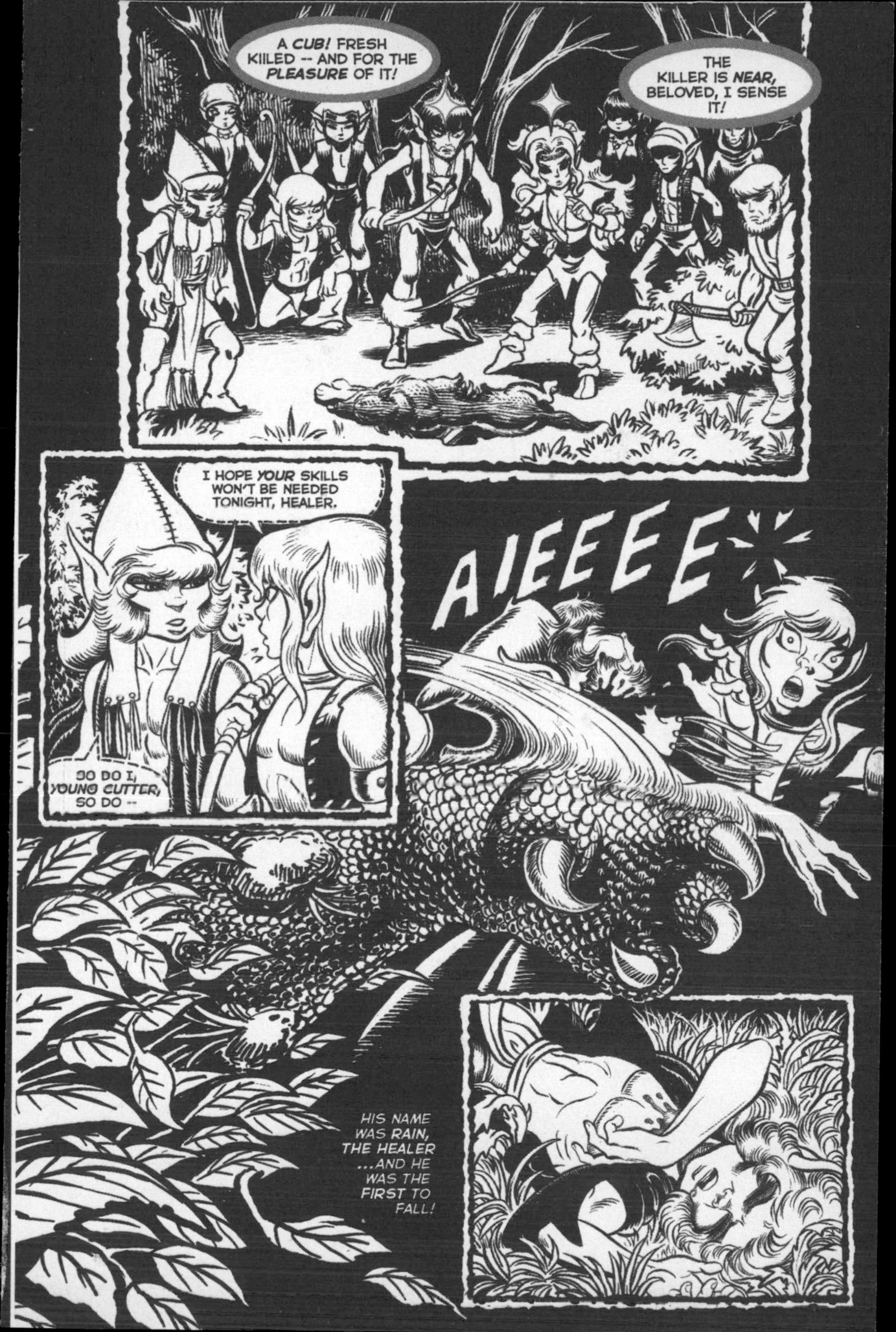
A CUB! FRESH KIILED -- AND FOR THE PLEASURE OF IT!
THE KILLER IS NEAR, BELOVED, I SENSE IT!
I HOPE YOUR SKILLS WON'T BE NEEDED TONIGHT, HEALER.
SO DO I, YOUNG CUTTER, SO DO --
AIEEEE!
HIS NAME WAS RAIN, THE HEALER ...AND HE WAS THE FIRST TO FALL!

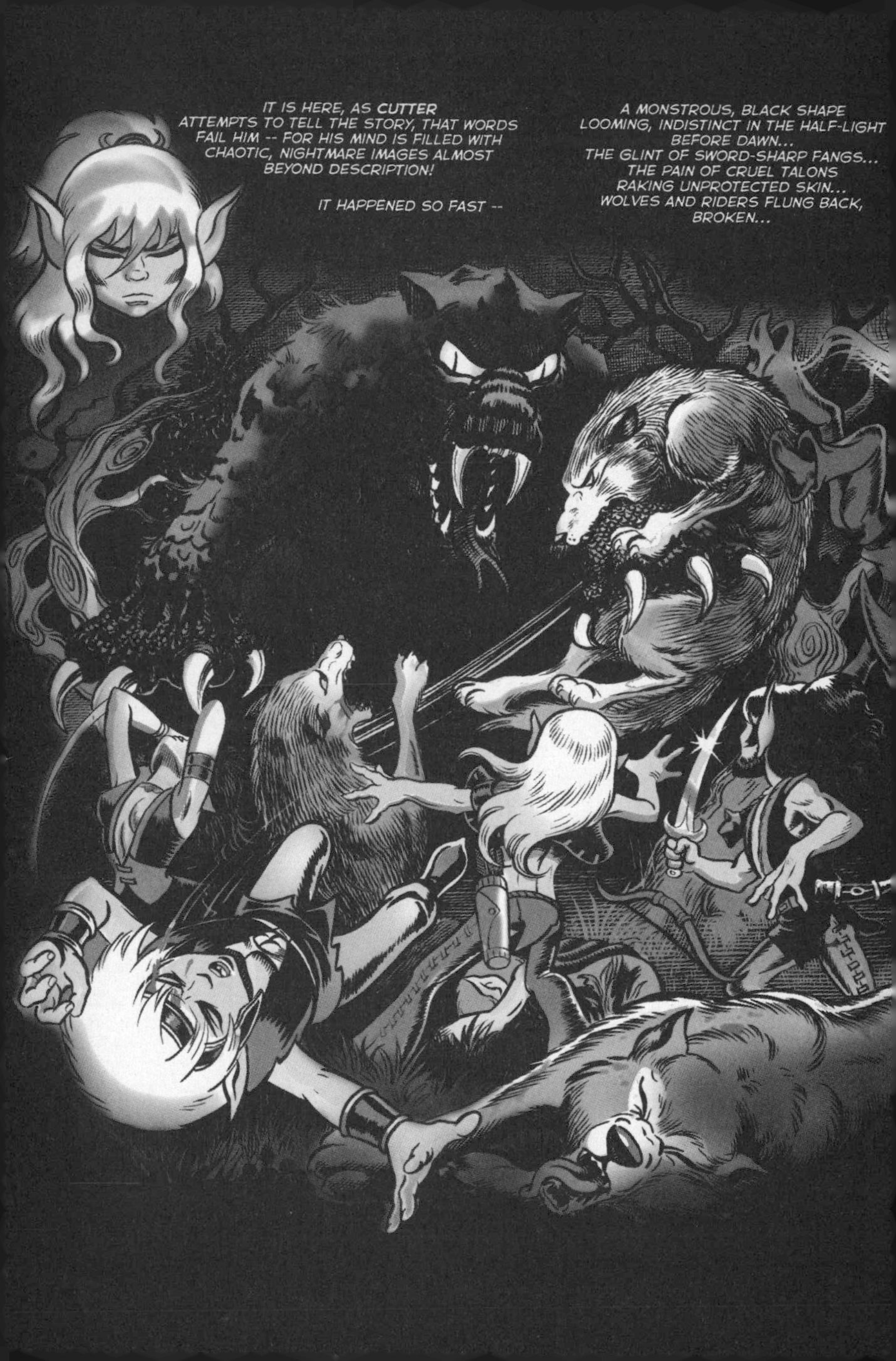
IT IS HERE, AS CUTTER ATTEMPTS TO TELL THE STORY, THAT WORDS FAIL HIM -- FOR HIS MIND IS FILLED WITH CHAOTIC, NIGHTMARE IMAGES ALMOST BEYOND DESCRIPTION!
IT HAPPENED SO FAST --
A MONSTROUS, BLACK SHAPE LOOMING, INDISTINCT IN THE HALF-LIGHT BEFORE DAWN... THE GLINT OF SWORD-SHARP FANGS... THE PAIN OF CRUEL TALONS RAKING UNPROTECTED SKIN... WOLVES AND RIDERS FLUNG BACK, BROKEN...

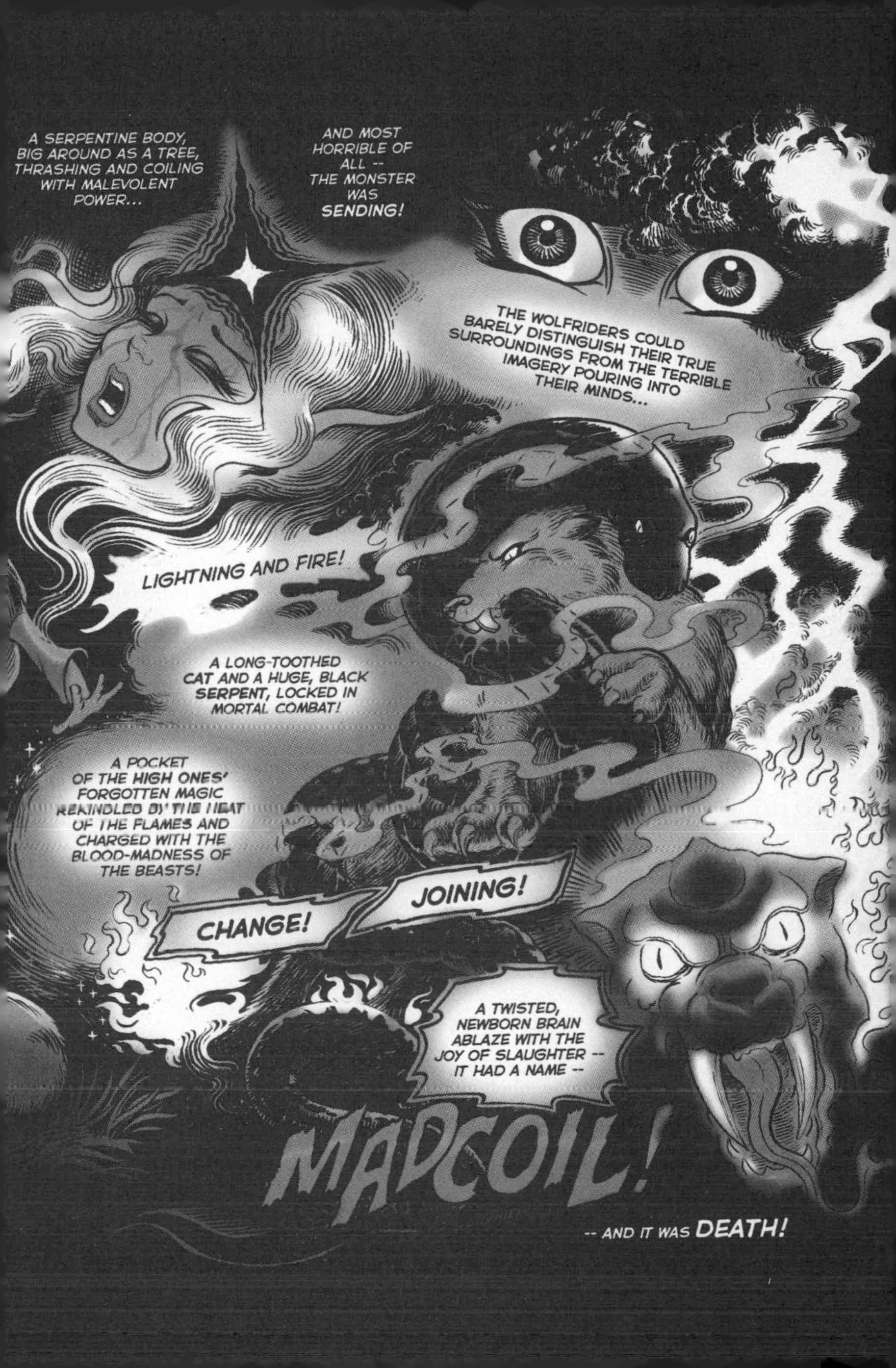
A SERPENTINE BODY, BIG AROUND AS A TREE, THRASHING AND COILING WITH MALEVOLENT POWER...
AND MOST HORRIBLE OF ALL -- THE MONSTER WAS SENDING!
THE WOLFRIDERS COULD BARELY DISTINGUISH THEIR TRUE SURROUNDINGS FROM THE TERRIBLE IMAGERY POURING INTO THEIR MINDS...
LIGHTNING AND FIRE!
A LONG-TOOTHED CAT AND A HUGE, BLACK SERPENT, LOCKED IN MORTAL COMBAT!
A POCKET OF THE HIGH ONES' FORGOTTEN MAGIC REKINDLED BY THE HEAT OF THE FLAMES AND CHARGED WITH THE BLOOD-MADNESS OF THE BEASTS!
CHANGE!
JOINING!
A TWISTED, NEWBORN BRAIN ABLAZE WITH THE JOY OF SLAUGHTER -- IT HAD A NAME --
MADCOIL!
-- AND IT WAS DEATH!

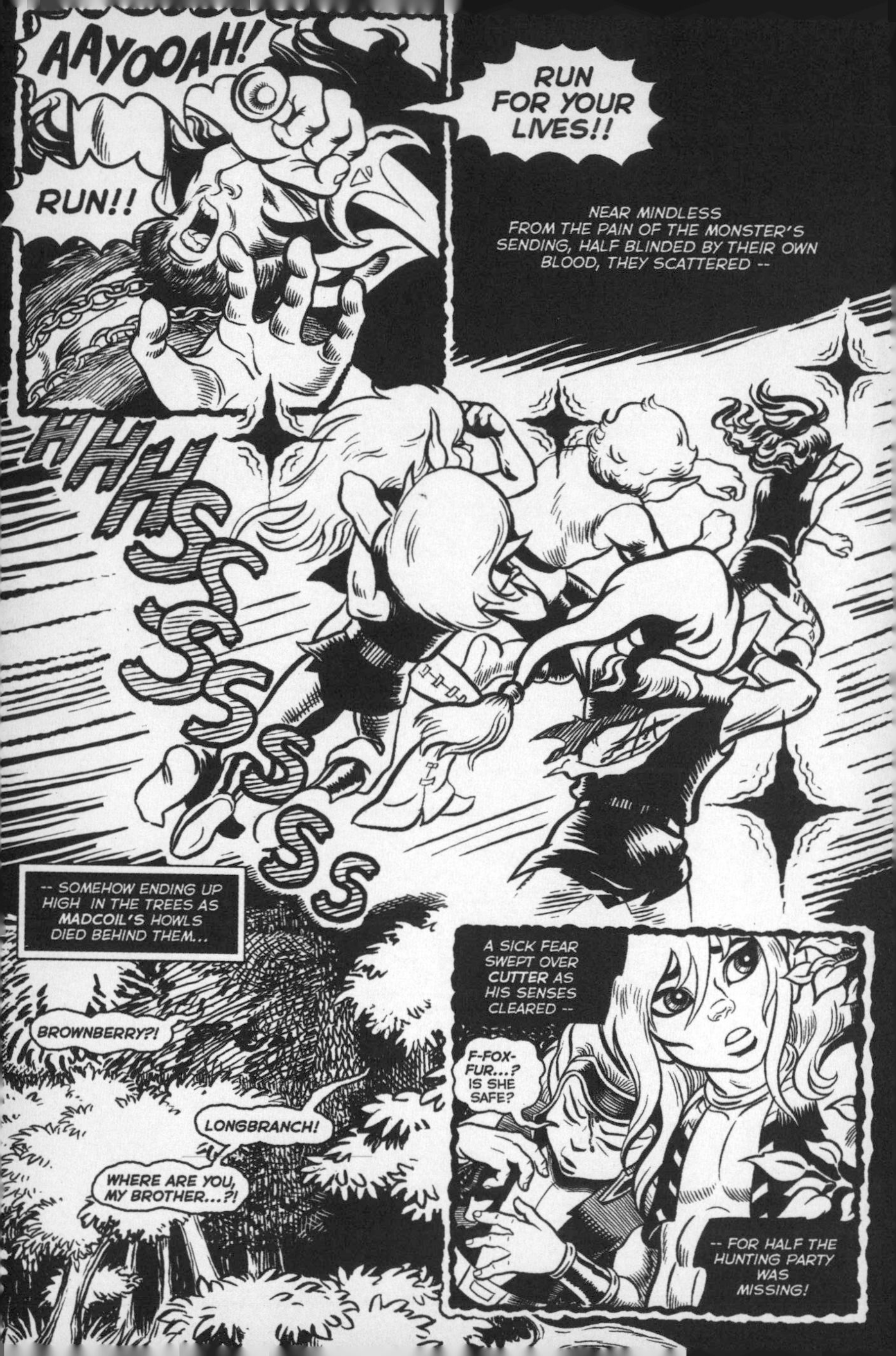
AAYOOAH!
RUN!!
RUN FOR YOUR LIVES!!
NEAR MINDLESS FROM THE PAIN OF THE MONSTER'S SENDING, HALF BLINDED BY THEIR OWN BLOOD, THEY SCATTERED --
HHHSSSSSSSSS
-- SOMEHOW ENDING UP HIGH IN THE TREES AS MADCOIL'S HOWLS DIED BEHIND THEM...
BROWNBERRY?!
LONGBRANCH!
WHERE ARE YOU, MY BROTHER...?!
A SICK FEAR SWEPT OVER CUTTER AS HIS SENSES CLEARED --
F-FOX-FUR...? IS SHE SAFE?
-- FOR HALF THE HUNTING PARTY WAS MISSING!

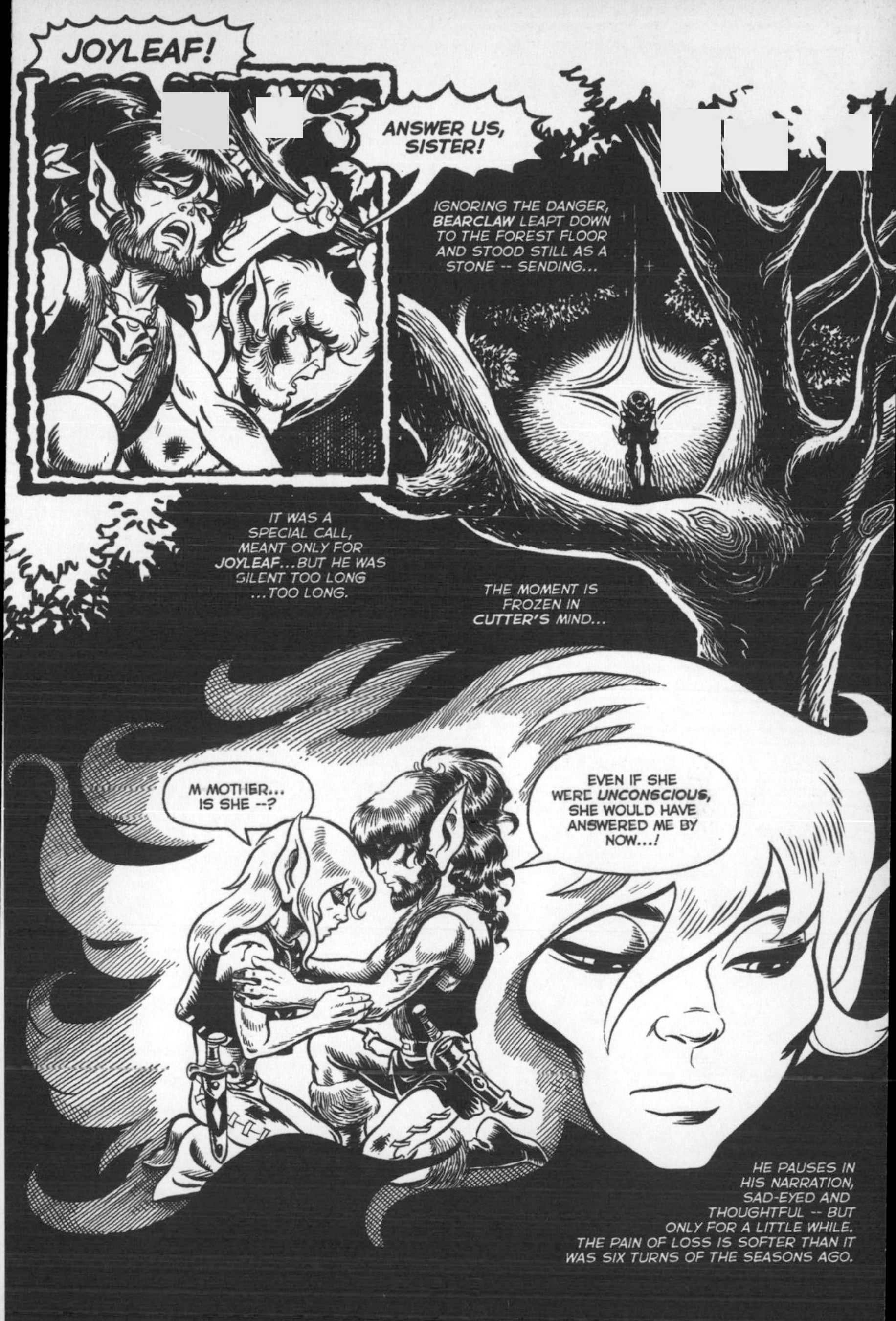
JOYLEAF!
ANSWER US, SISTER!
IGNORING THE DANGER, BEARCLAW LEAPT DOWN TO THE FOREST FLOOR AND STOOD STILL AS A STONE -- SENDING...
IT WAS A SPECIAL CALL, MEANT ONLY FOR JOYLEAF...BUT HE WAS SILENT TOO LONG ...TOO LONG.
THE MOMENT IS FROZEN IN CUTTER'S MIND...
M MOTHER... IS SHE --?
EVEN IF SHE WERE UNCONSCIOUS, SHE WOULD HAVE ANSWERED ME BY NOW...!
HE PAUSES IN HIS NARRATION, SAD-EYED AND THOUGHTFUL -- BUT ONLY FOR A LITTLE WHILE. THE PAIN OF LOSS IS SOFTER THAN IT WAS SIX TURNS OF THE SEASONS AGO.

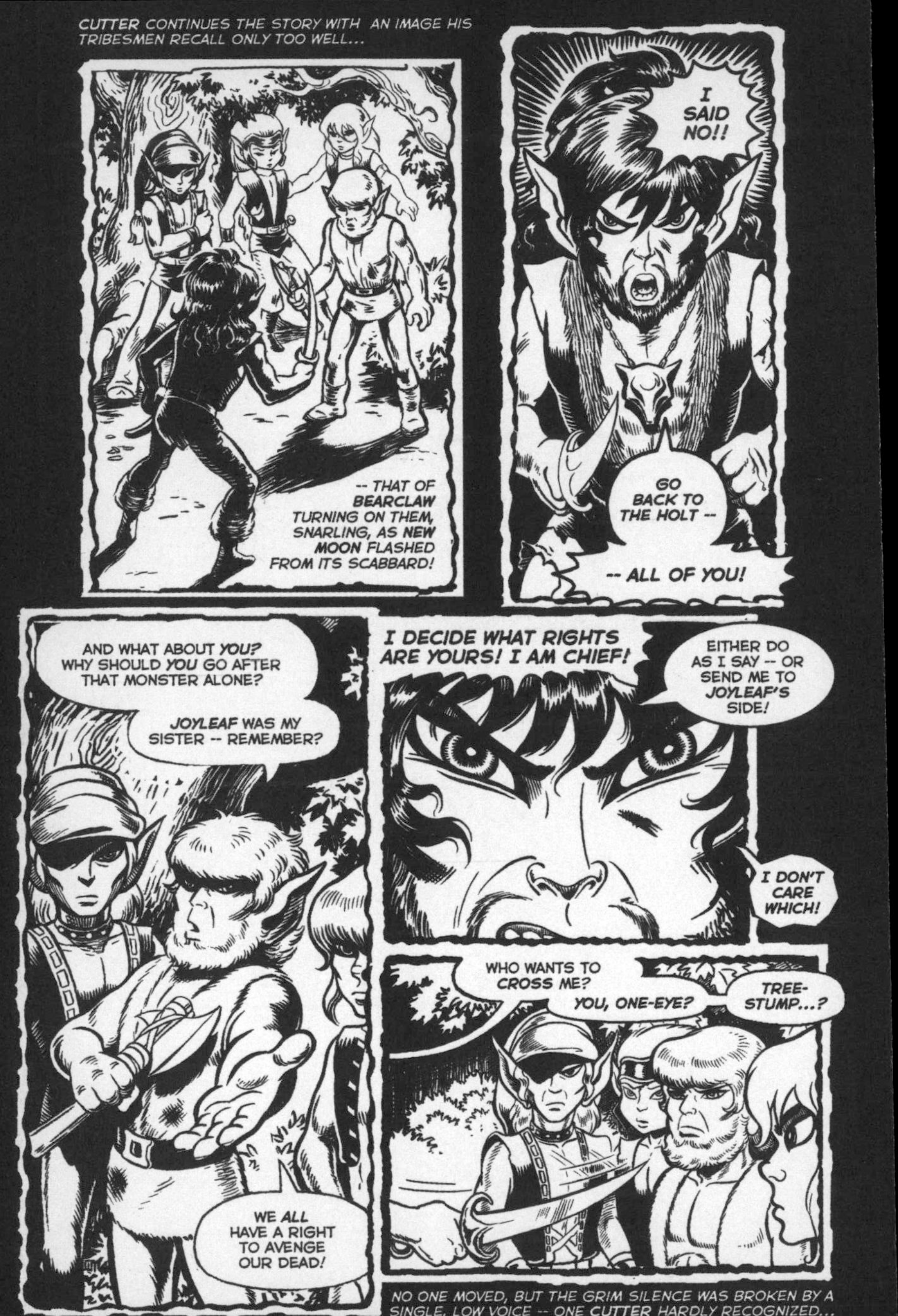
CUTTER CONTINUES THE STORY WITH AN IMAGE HIS TRIBESMEN RECALL ONLY TOO WELL...
-- THAT OF BEARCLAW TURNING ON THEM, SNARLING, AS NEW MOON FLASHED FROM ITS SCABBARD!
I SAID NO!!
GO BACK TO THE HOLT --
-- ALL OF YOU!
AND WHAT ABOUT YOU? WHY SHOULD YOU GO AFTER THAT MONSTER ALONE?
JOYLEAF WAS MY SISTER -- REMEMBER?
WE ALL HAVE A RIGHT TO AVENGE OUR DEAD!
I DECIDE WHAT RIGHTS ARE YOURS! I AM CHIEF!
EITHER DO AS I SAY -- OR SEND ME TO JOYLEAF'S SIDE!
I DON'T CARE WHICH!
WHO WANTS TO CROSS ME?
YOU, ONE-EYE?
TREE-STUMP...?
NO ONE MOVED, BUT THE GRIM SILENCE WAS BROKEN BY A SINGLE, LOW VOICE -- ONE CUTTER HARDLY RECOGNIZED...

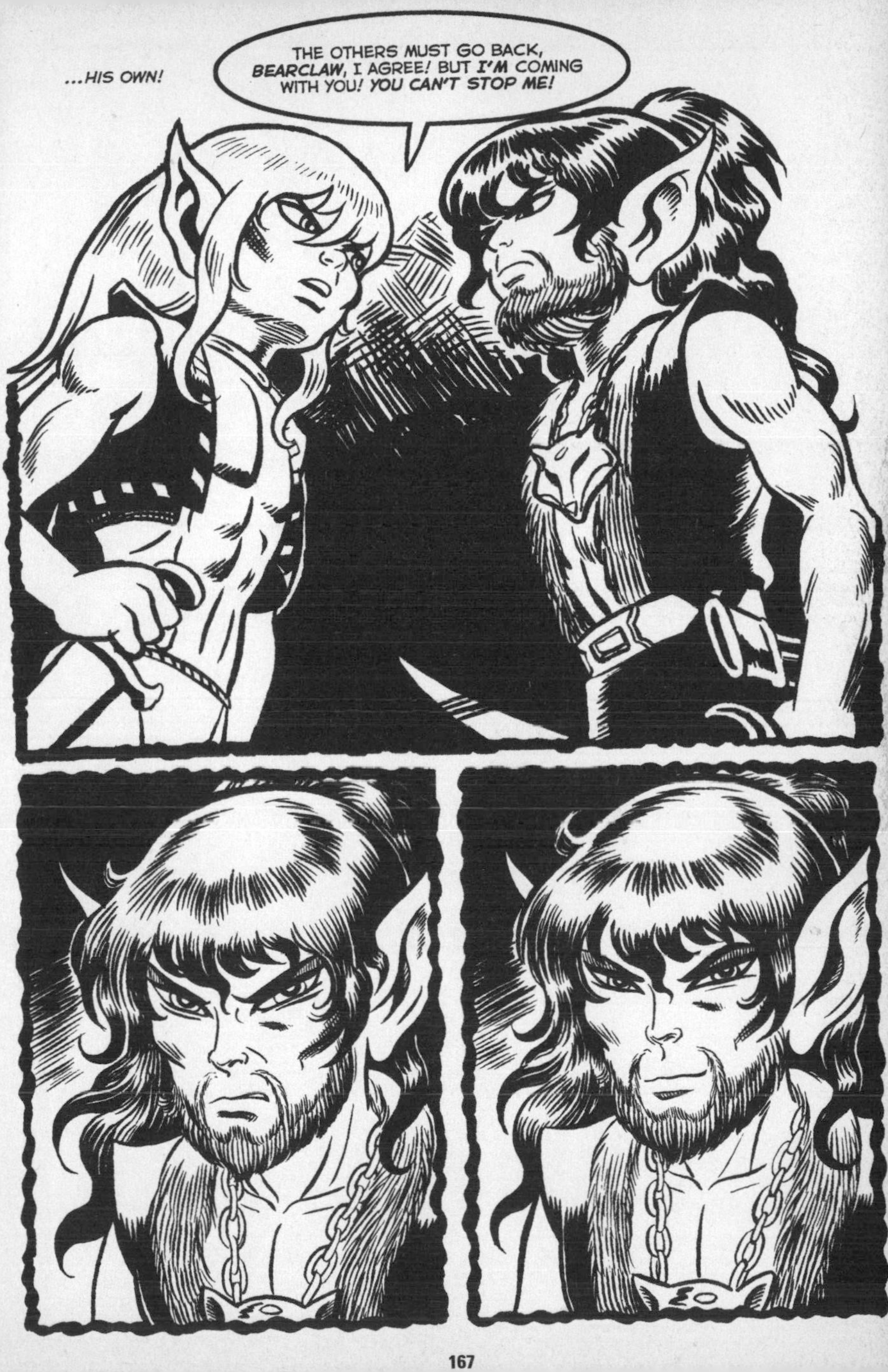

...HIS OWN!
THE OTHERS MUST GO BACK, BEARCLAW, I AGREE! BUT I'M COMING WITH YOU! YOU CAN'T STOP ME!

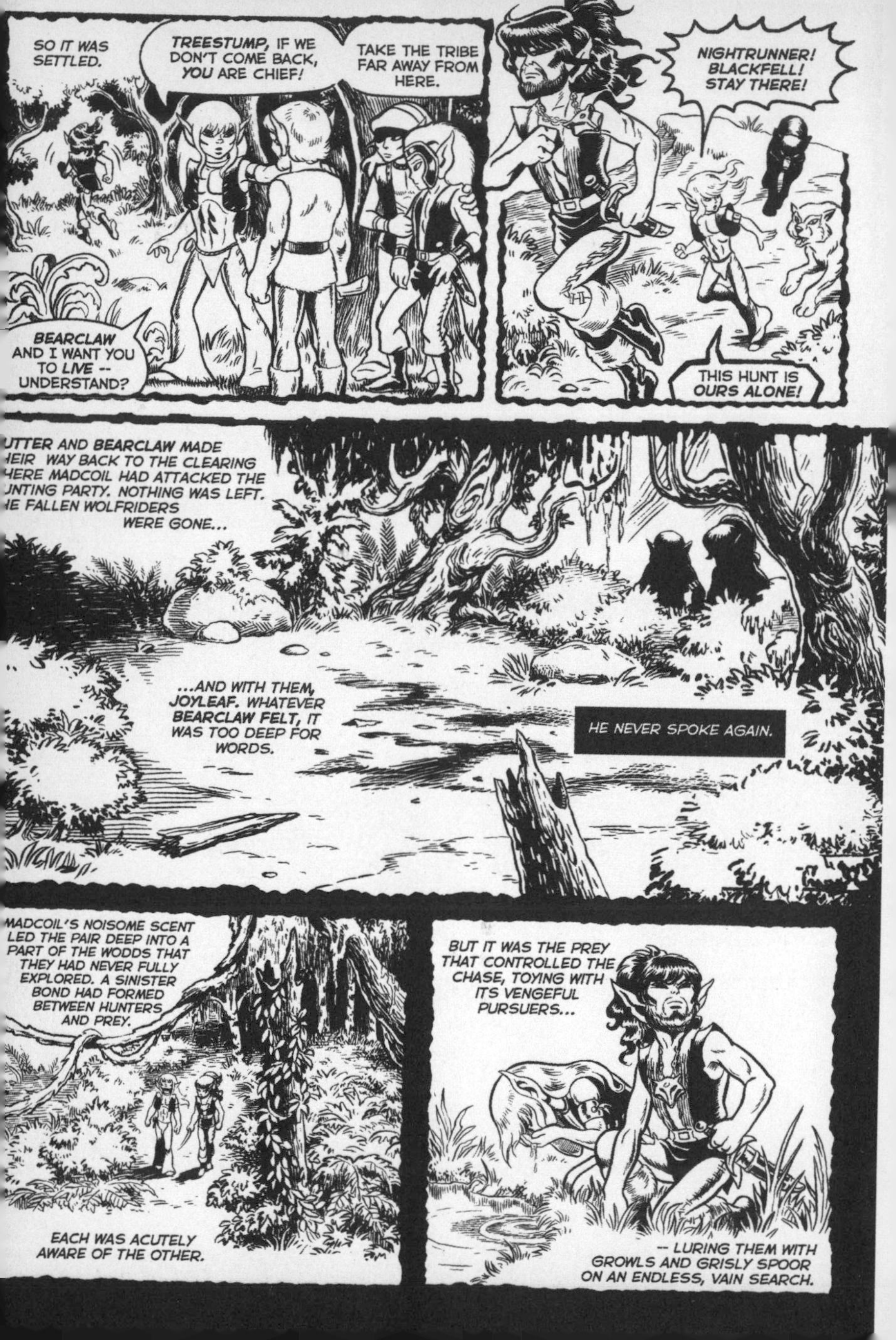
SO IT WAS SETTLED.
TREESTUMP, IF WE DON'T COME BACK, YOU ARE CHIEF!
TAKE THE TRIBE FAR AWAY FROM HERE.
BEARCLAW AND I WANT YOU TO LIVE -- UNDERSTAND?
NIGHTRUNNER! BLACKFELL! STAY THERE!
THIS HUNT IS OURS ALONE!
UTTER AND BEARCLAW MADE HEIR WAY BACK TO THE CLEARING HERE MADCOIL HAD ATTACKED THE UNTING PARTY. NOTHING WAS LEFT. HE FALLEN WOLFRIDERS WERE GONE...
...AND WITH THEM, JOYLEAF. WHATEVER BEARCLAW FELT, IT WAS TOO DEEP FOR WORDS.
HE NEVER SPOKE AGAIN.
MADCOIL'S NOISOME SCENT LED THE PAIR DEEP INTO A PART OF THE WODDS THAT THEY HAD NEVER FULLY EXPLORED. A SINISTER BOND HAD FORMED BETWEEN HUNTERS AND PREY.
EACH WAS ACUTELY AWARE OF THE OTHER.
BUT IT WAS THE PREY THAT CONTROLLED THE CHASE, TOYING WITH ITS VENGEFUL PURSUERS...
-- LURING THEM WITH GROWLS AND GRISLY SPOOR ON AN ENDLESS, VAIN SEARCH.

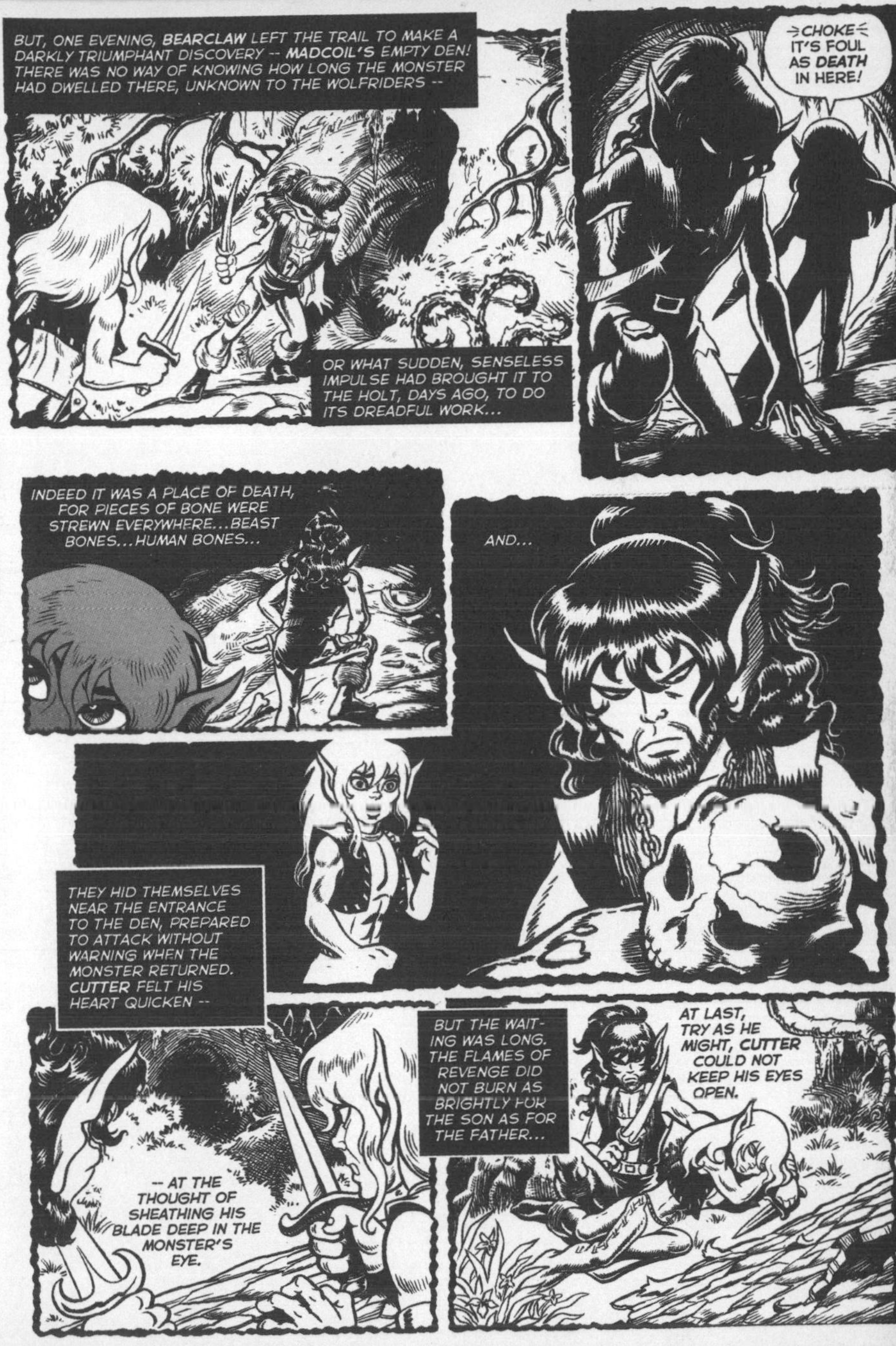

BUT, ONE EVENING, BEARCLAW LEFT THE TRAIL TO MAKE A DARKLY TRIUMPHANT DISCOVERY -- MADCOIL'S EMPTY DEN! THERE WAS NO WAY OF KNOWING HOW LONG THE MONSTER HAD DWELLED THERE, UNKNOWN TO THE WOLFRIDERS --
OR WHAT SUDDEN, SENSELESS IMPULSE HAD BROUGHT IT TO THE HOLT, DAYS AGO, TO DO ITS DREADFUL WORK...
CHOKE IT'S FOUL AS DEATH IN HERE!
INDEED IT WAS A PLACE OF DEATH, FOR PIECES OF BONE WERE STREWN EVERYWHERE...BEAST BONES...HUMAN BONES...
AND...
THEY HID THEMSELVES NEAR THE ENTRANCE TO THE DEN, PREPARED TO ATTACK WITHOUT WARNING WHEN THE MONSTER RETURNED. CUTTER FELT HIS HEART QUICKEN --
-- AT THE THOUGHT OF SHEATHING HIS BLADE DEEP IN THE MONSTER'S EYE.
BUT THE WAITING WAS LONG. THE FLAMES OF REVENGE DID NOT BURN AS BRIGHTLY FOR THE SON AS FOR THE FATHER...
AT LAST, TRY AS HE MIGHT, CUTTER COULD NOT KEEP HIS EYES OPEN.

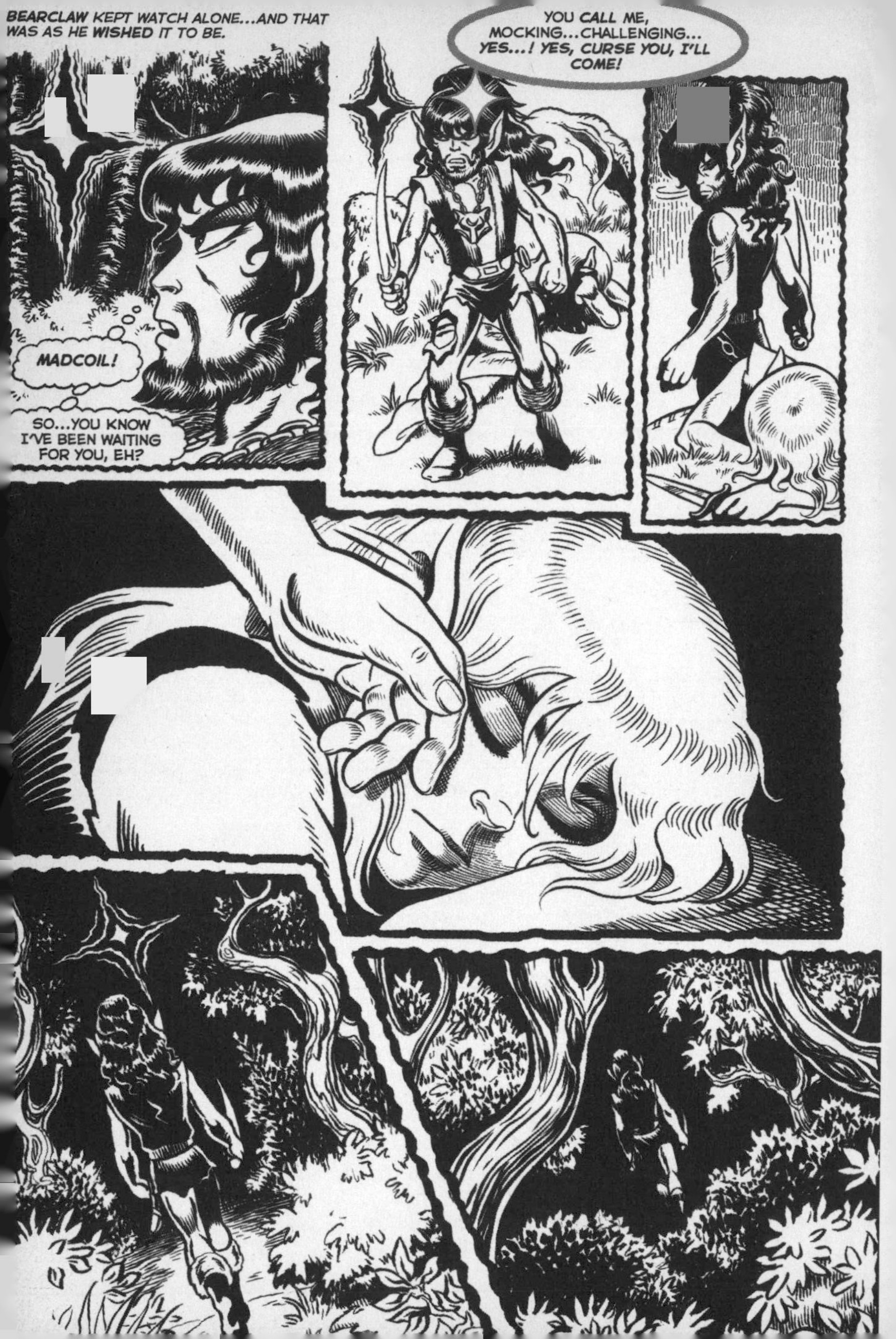
BEARCLAW KEPT WATCH ALONE...AND THAT WAS AS HE WISHED IT TO BE.
MADCOIL!
SO...YOU KNOW I'VE BEEN WAITING FOR YOU, EH?
YOU CALL ME, MOCKING...CHALLENGING... YES...! YES, CURSE YOU, I'LL COME!

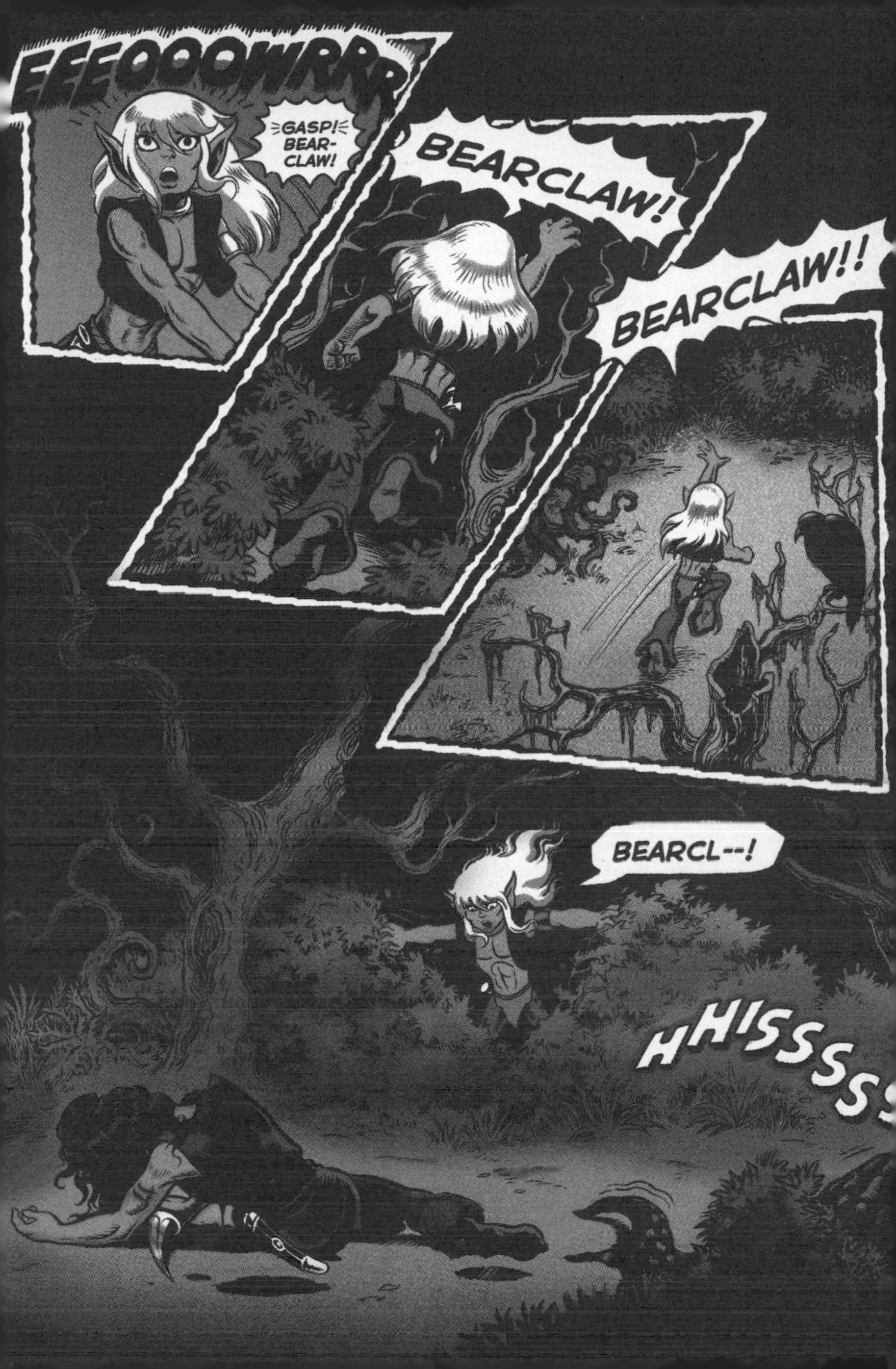
EEEOOOOWRRR
GASP! BEAR-CLAW!
BEARCLAW!
BEARCLAW!!
BEARCL--!
HHISSSSS

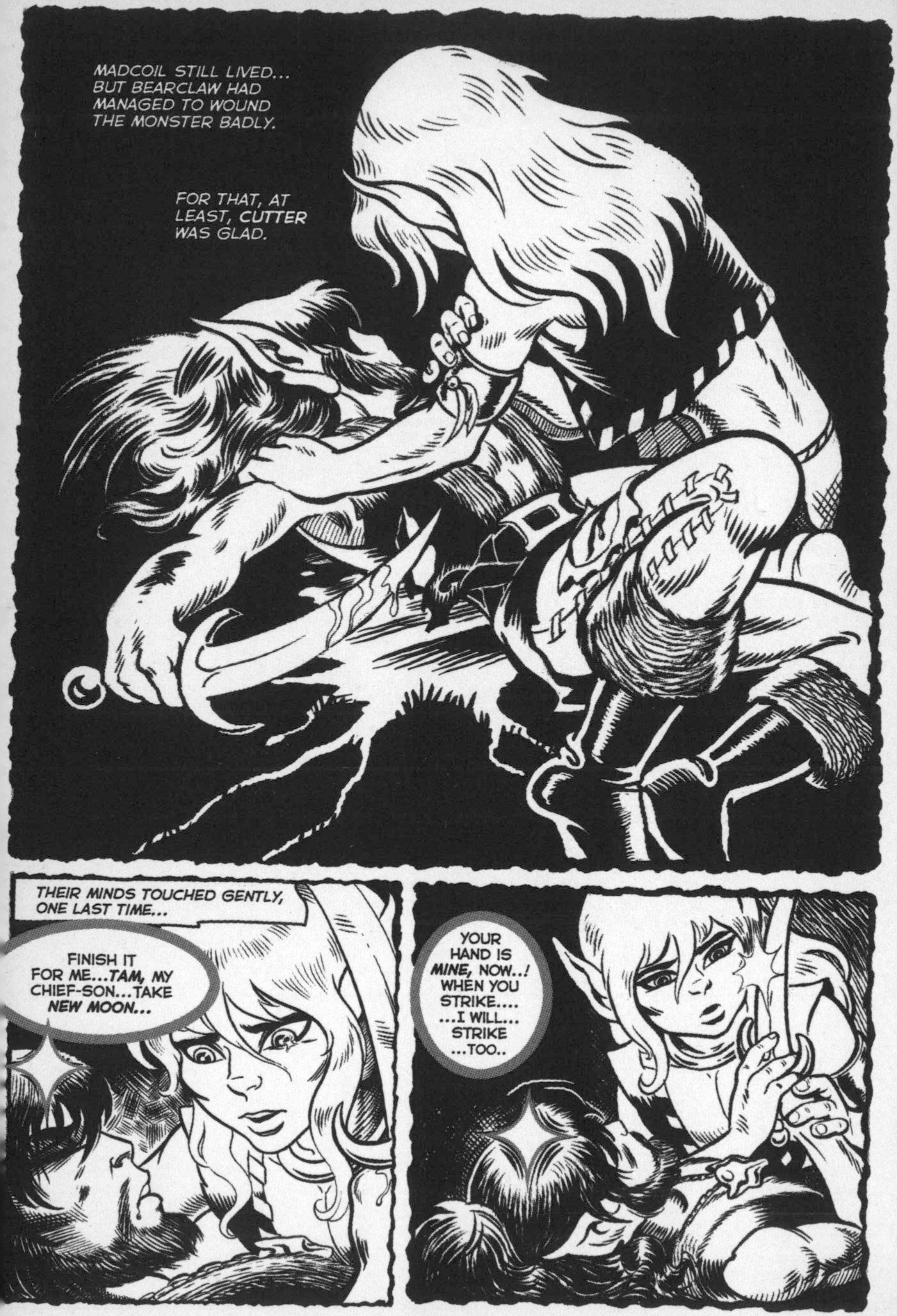
MADCOIL STILL LIVED... BUT BEARCLAW HAD MANAGED TO WOUND THE MONSTER BADLY.
FOR THAT, AT LEAST, CUTTER WAS GLAD.
THEIR MINDS TOUCHED GENTLY, ONE LAST TIME...
FINISH IT FOR ME...TAM, MY CHIEF-SON...TAKE NEW MOON...
YOUR HAND IS MINE, NOW...! WHEN YOU STRIKE.... ...I WILL... STRIKE ...TOO..

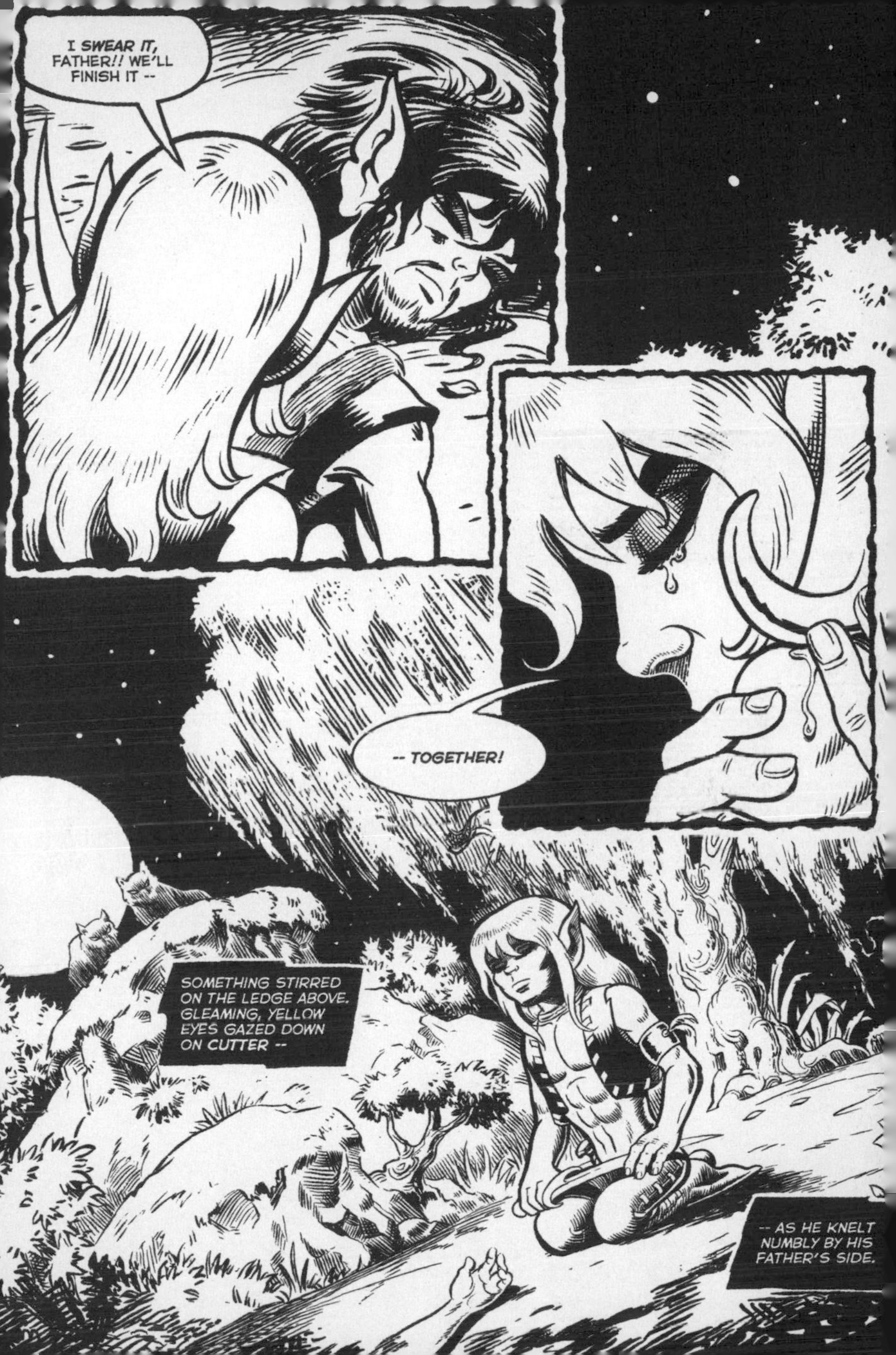
I SWEAR IT, FATHER!! WE'LL FINISH IT --
-- TOGETHER!
SOMETHING STIRRED ON THE LEDGE ABOVE. GLEAMING, YELLOW EYES GAZED DOWN ON CUTTER --
-- AS HE KNELT NUMBLY BY HIS FATHER'S SIDE.

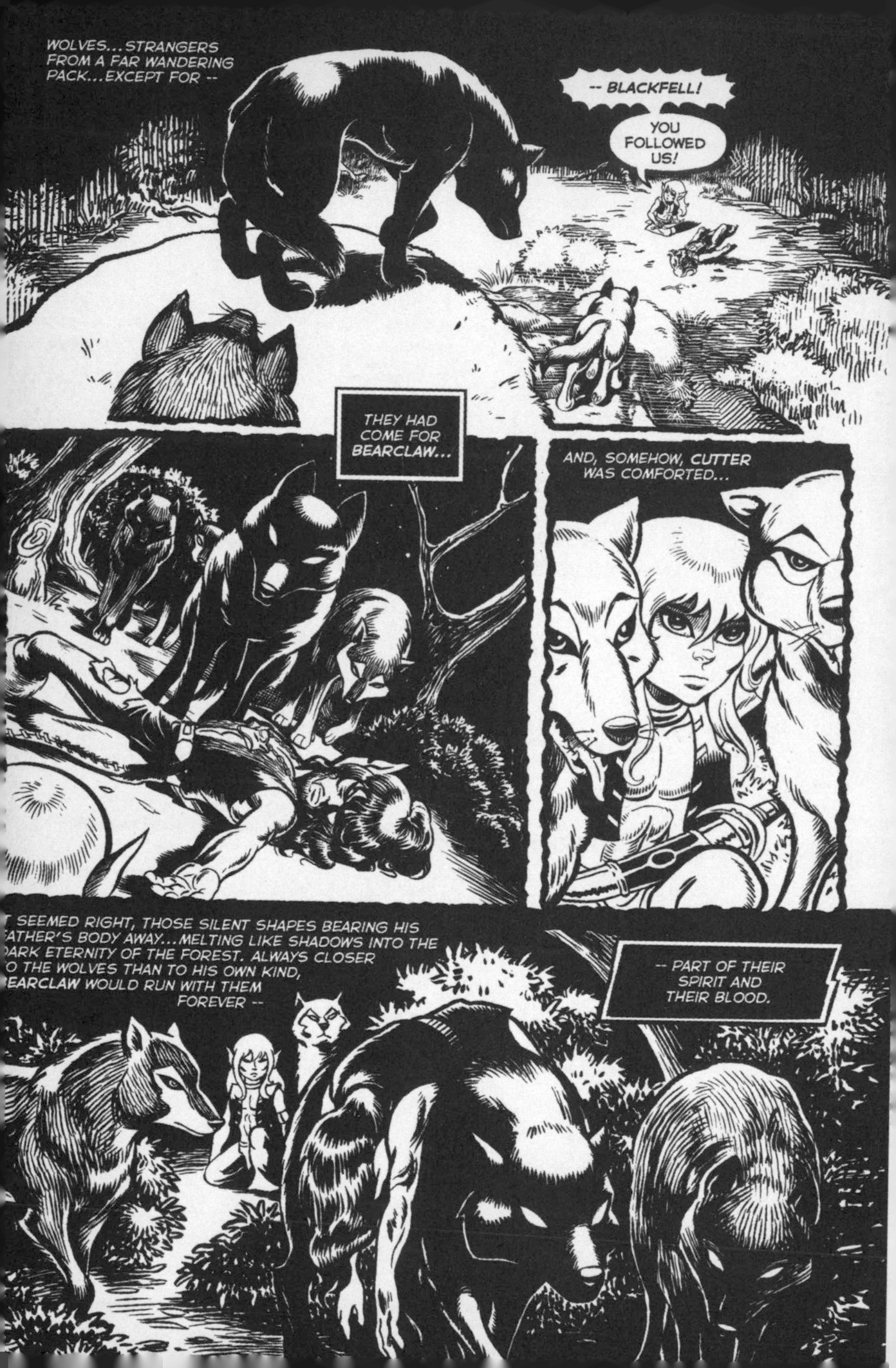
WOLVES...STRANGERS FROM A FAR WANDERING PACK...EXCEPT FOR --
-- BLACKFELL!
YOU FOLLOWED US!
THEY HAD COME FOR BEARCLAW...
AND, SOMEHOW, CUTTER WAS COMFORTED...
T SEEMED RIGHT, THOSE SILENT SHAPES BEARING HIS ATHER'S BODY AWAY...MELTING LIKE SHADOWS INTO THE ARK ETERNITY OF THE FOREST. ALWAYS CLOSER O THE WOLVES THAN TO HIS OWN KIND, EARCLAW WOULD RUN WITH THEM FOREVER --
-- PART OF THEIR SPIRIT AND THEIR BLOOD.

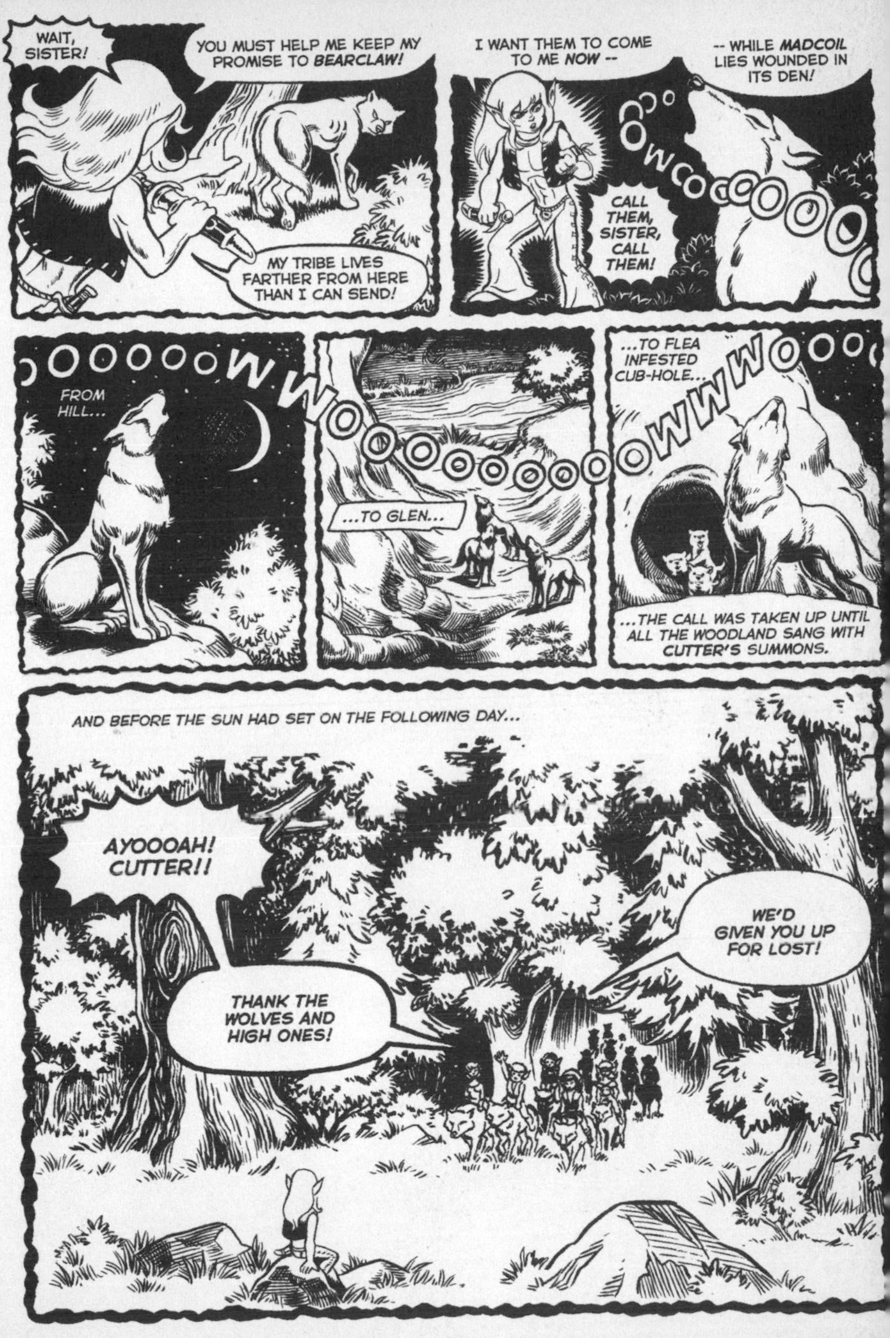
WAIT, SISTER!
YOU MUST HELP ME KEEP MY PROMISE TO BEARCLAW!
MY TRIBE LIVES FARTHER FROM HERE THAN I CAN SEND!
I WANT THEM TO COME TO ME NOW --
-- WHILE MADCOIL LIES WOUNDED IN ITS DEN!
CALL THEM, SISTER, CALL THEM!
OOOWOOOOOOOOO
OOOOOOOWWWOOOOOOOOOOOOOWWWWOOOO
FROM HILL...
...TO GLEN...
...TO FLEA INFESTED CUB-HOLE...
...THE CALL WAS TAKEN UP UNTIL ALL THE WOODLAND SANG WITH CUTTER'S SUMMONS.
AND BEFORE THE SUN HAD SET ON THE FOLLOWING DAY...
AYOOOAH! CUTTER!!
WE'D GIVEN YOU UP FOR LOST!
THANK THE WOLVES AND HIGH ONES!

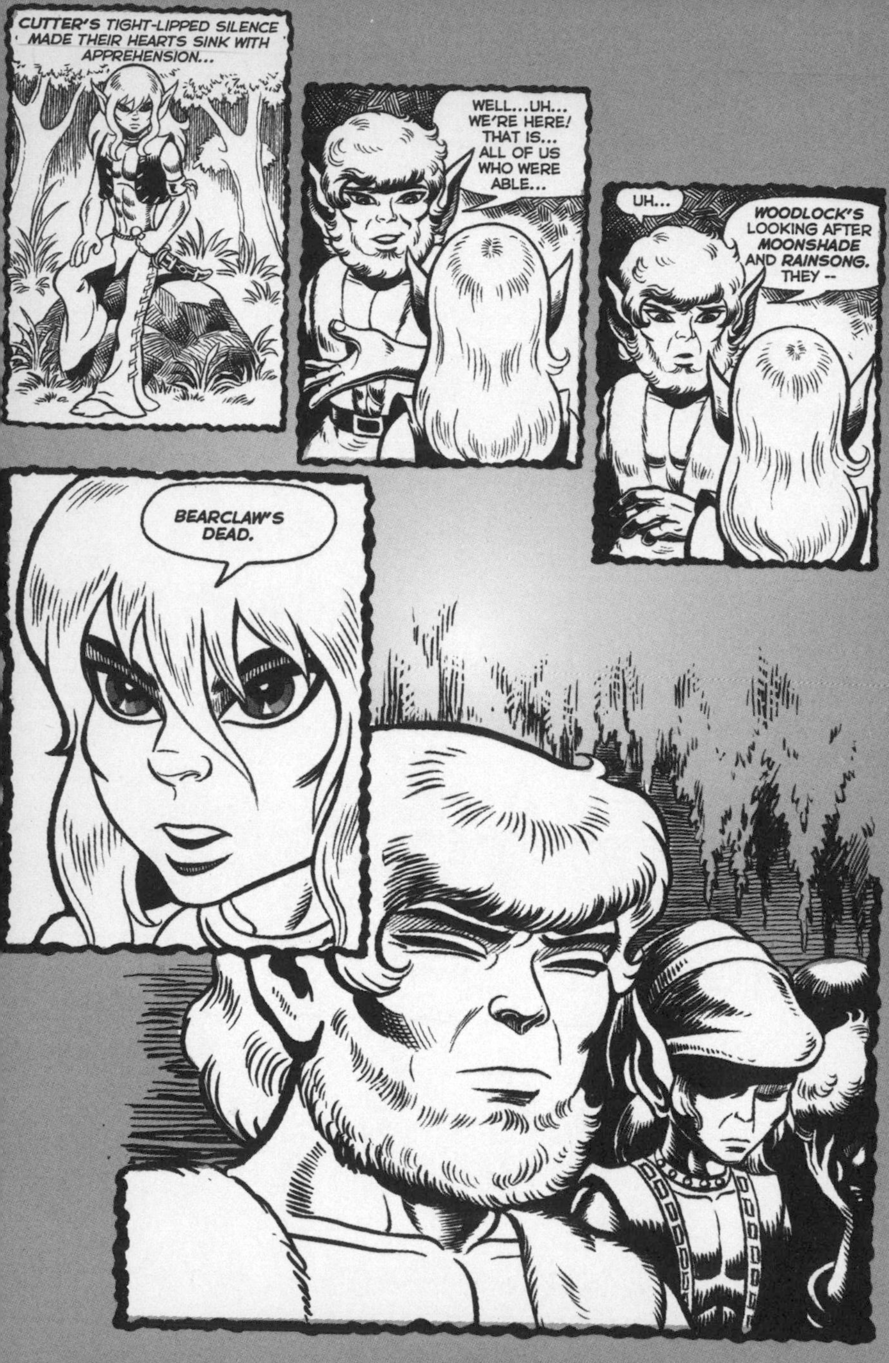
CUTTER'S TIGHT-LIPPED SILENCE MADE THEIR HEARTS SINK WITH APPREHENSION...
WELL...UH... WE'RE HERE! THAT IS... ALL OF US WHO WERE ABLE...
UH...
WOODLOCK'S LOOKING AFTER MOONSHADE AND RAINSONG. THEY --
BEARCLAW'S DEAD.

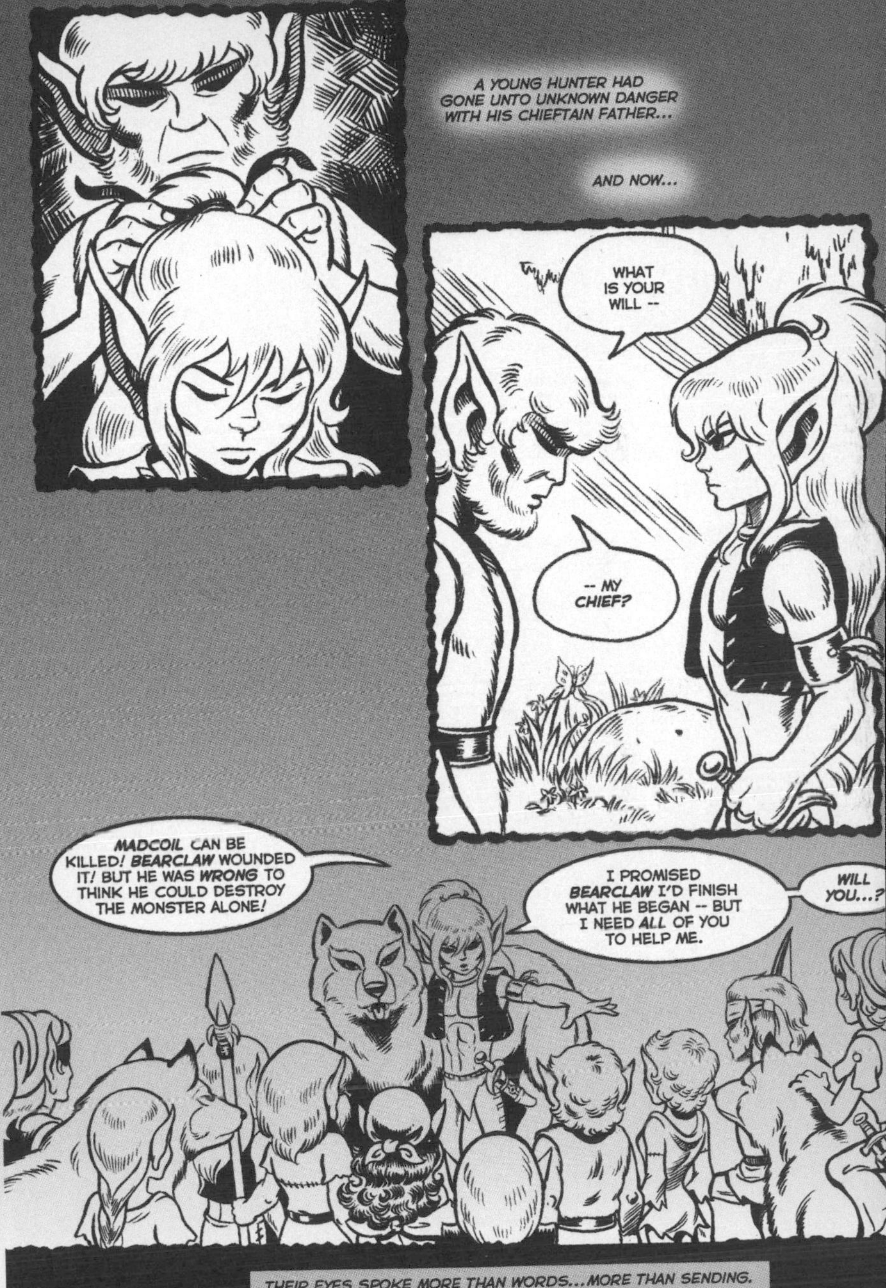
A YOUNG HUNTER HAD GONE UNTO UNKNOWN DANGER WITH HIS CHIEFTAIN FATHER...
AND NOW...
WHAT IS YOUR WILL --
-- MY CHIEF?
MADCOIL CAN BE KILLED! BEARCLAW WOUNDED IT! BUT HE WAS WRONG TO THINK HE COULD DESTROY THE MONSTER ALONE!
I PROMISED BEARCLAW I'D FINISH WHAT HE BEGAN -- BUT I NEED ALL OF YOU TO HELP ME.
WILL YOU...?
THEIR EYES SPOKE MORE THAN WORDS...MORE THAN SENDING. CUTTER SIGHED, SMILED AND TOLD THEM HIS PLAN...

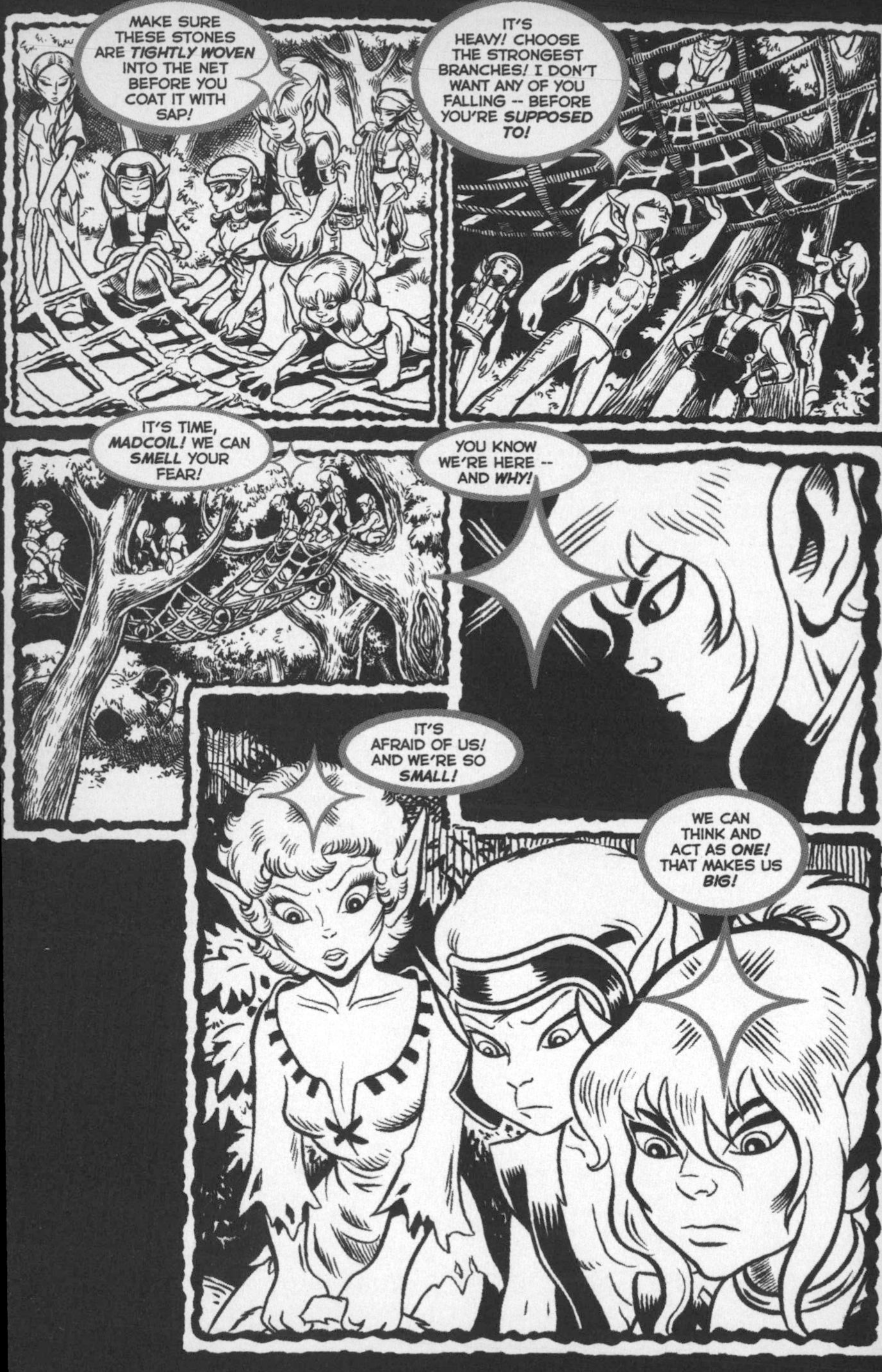
MAKE SURE THESE STONES ARE TIGHTLY WOVEN INTO THE NET BEFORE YOU COAT IT WITH SAP!
IT'S HEAVY! CHOOSE THE STRONGEST BRANCHES! I DON'T WANT ANY OF YOU FALLING -- BEFORE YOU'RE SUPPOSED TO!
IT'S TIME, MADCOIL! WE CAN SMELL YOUR FEAR!
YOU KNOW WE'RE HERE -- AND WHY!
IT'S AFRAID OF US! AND WE'RE SO SMALL!
WE CAN THINK AND ACT AS ONE! THAT MAKES US BIG!

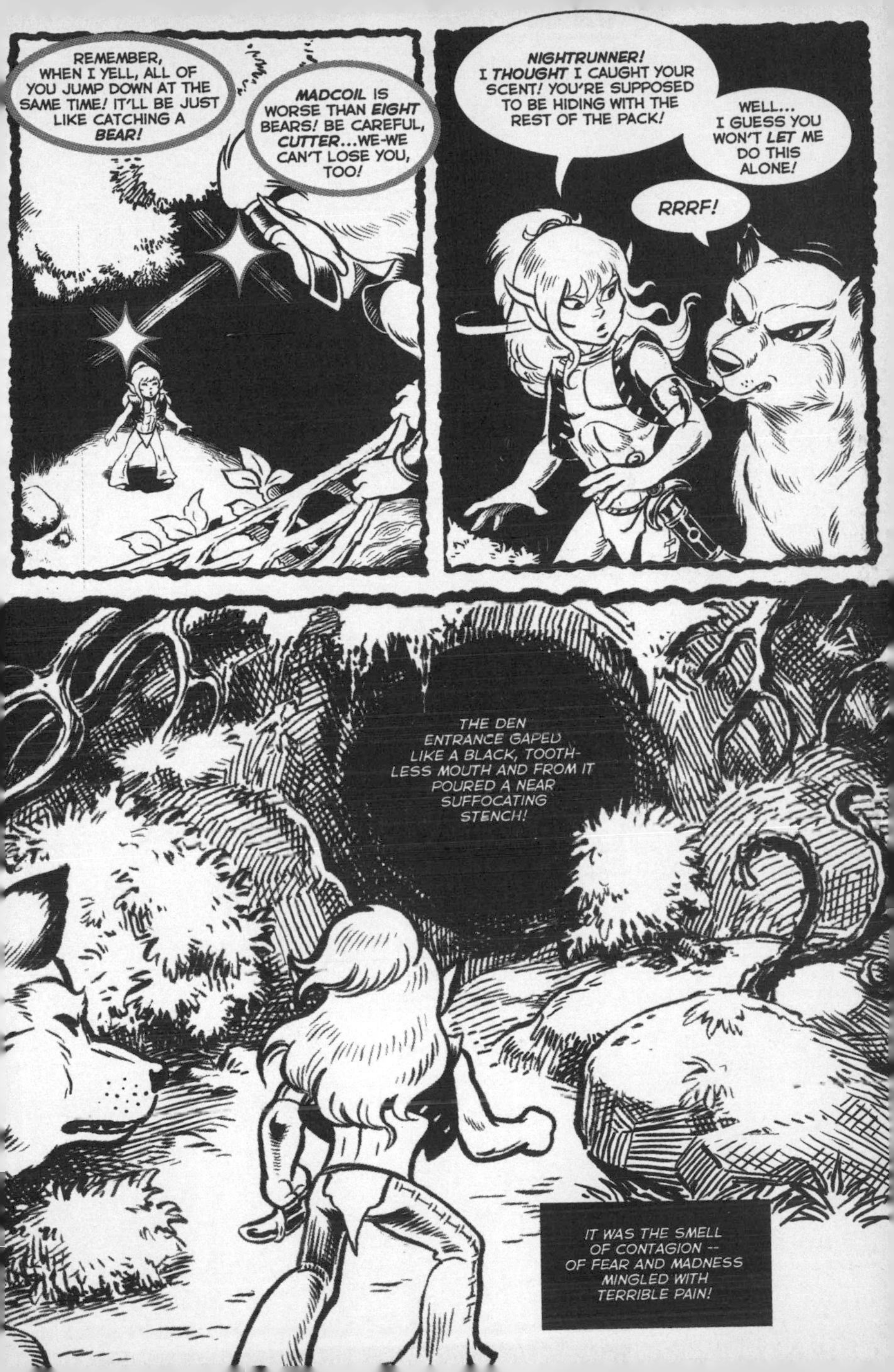
REMEMBER, WHEN I YELL, ALL OF YOU JUMP DOWN AT THE SAME TIME! IT'LL BE JUST LIKE CATCHING A BEAR!
MADCOIL IS WORSE THAN EIGHT BEARS! BE CAREFUL, CUTTER...WE-WE CAN'T LOSE YOU, TOO!
NIGHTRUNNER! I THOUGHT I CAUGHT YOUR SCENT! YOU'RE SUPPOSED TO BE HIDING WITH THE REST OF THE PACK!
RRRF!
WELL... I GUESS YOU WON'T LET ME DO THIS ALONE!
THE DEN ENTRANCE GAPED LIKE A BLACK, TOOTH-LESS MOUTH AND FROM IT POURED A NEAR SUFFOCATING STENCH!
IT WAS THE SMELL OF CONTAGION -- OF FEAR AND MADNESS MINGLED WITH TERRIBLE PAIN!

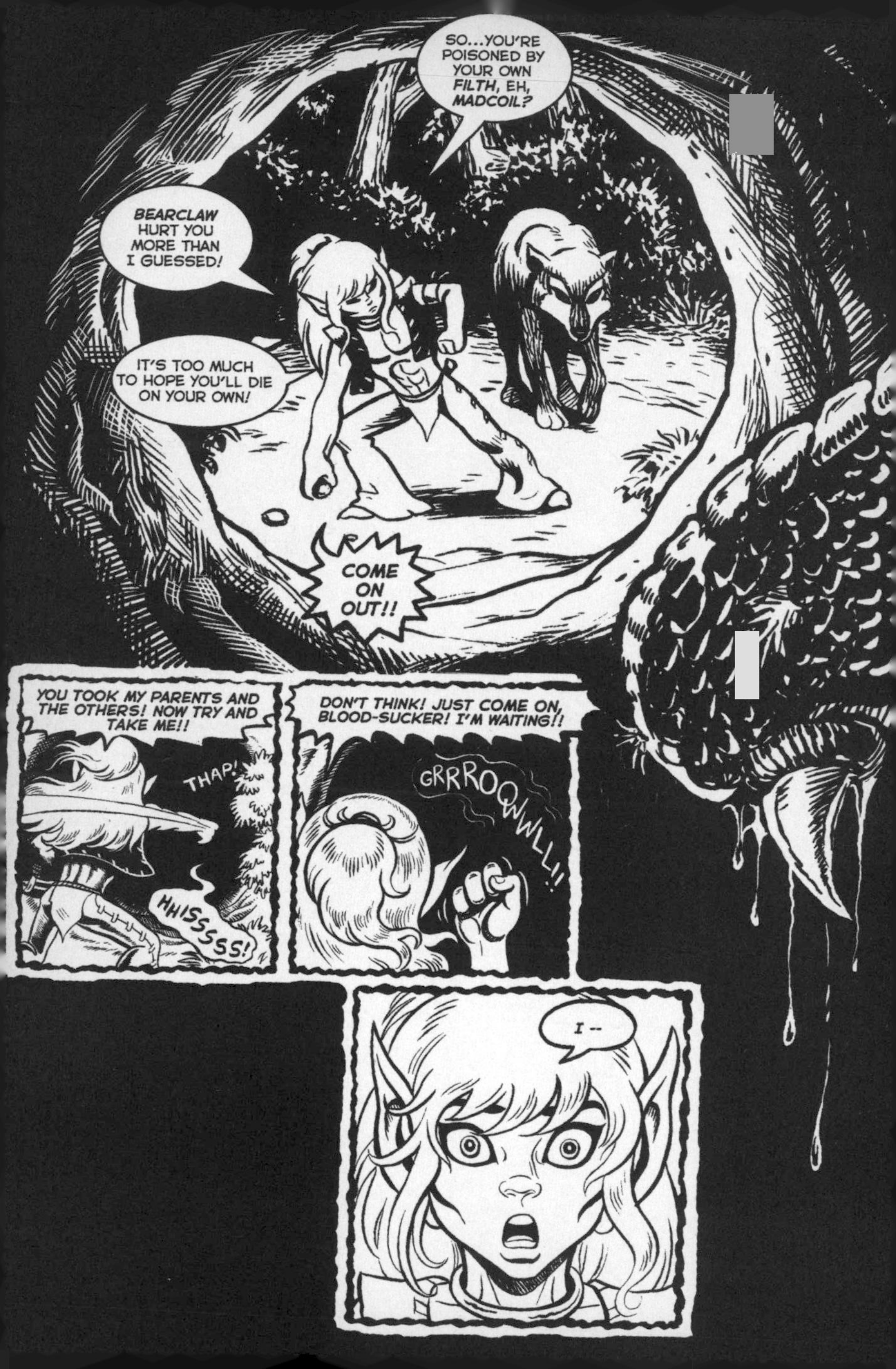
SO...YOU'RE POISONED BY YOUR OWN *FILTH*, EH, *MADCOIL?*
BEARCLAW HURT YOU MORE THAN I GUESSED!
IT'S TOO MUCH TO HOPE YOU'LL DIE ON YOUR OWN!
COME ON OUT!!
YOU TOOK MY PARENTS AND THE OTHERS! NOW TRY AND TAKE ME!!
THAP!
HHISSSSSS!
DON'T THINK! JUST COME ON, BLOOD-SUCKER! I'M WAITING!!
GRRROOWWLLL!!
I --

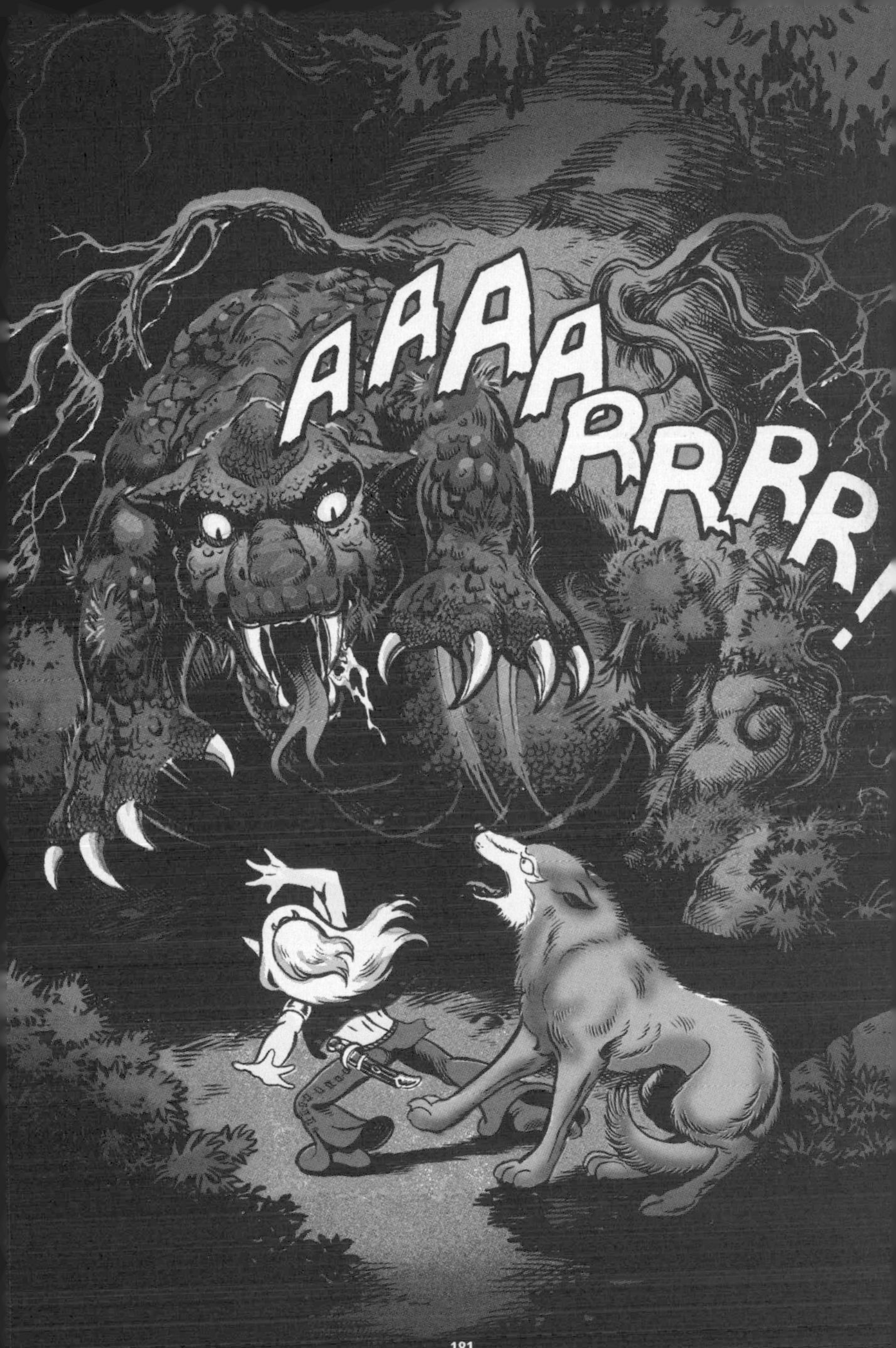
AAAAARRRRR!!

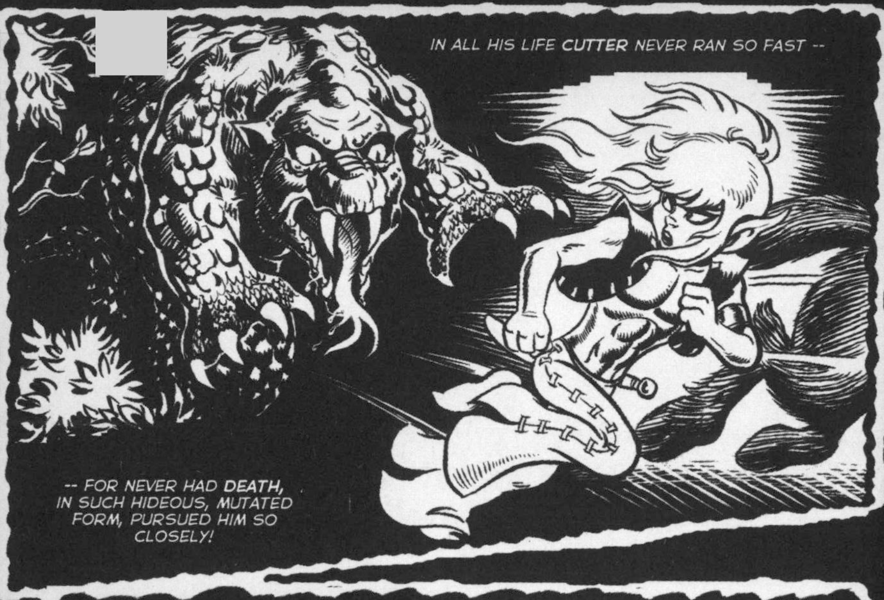
IN ALL HIS LIFE CUTTER NEVER RAN SO FAST --
-- FOR NEVER HAD DEATH, IN SUCH HIDEOUS, MUTATED FORM, PURSUED HIM SO CLOSELY!

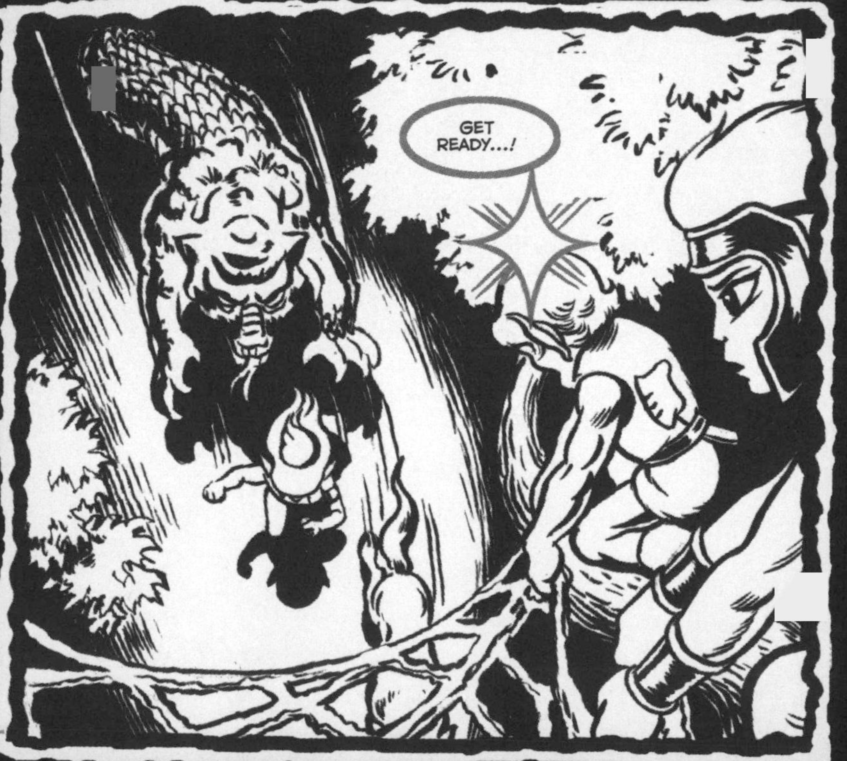
GET READY...!

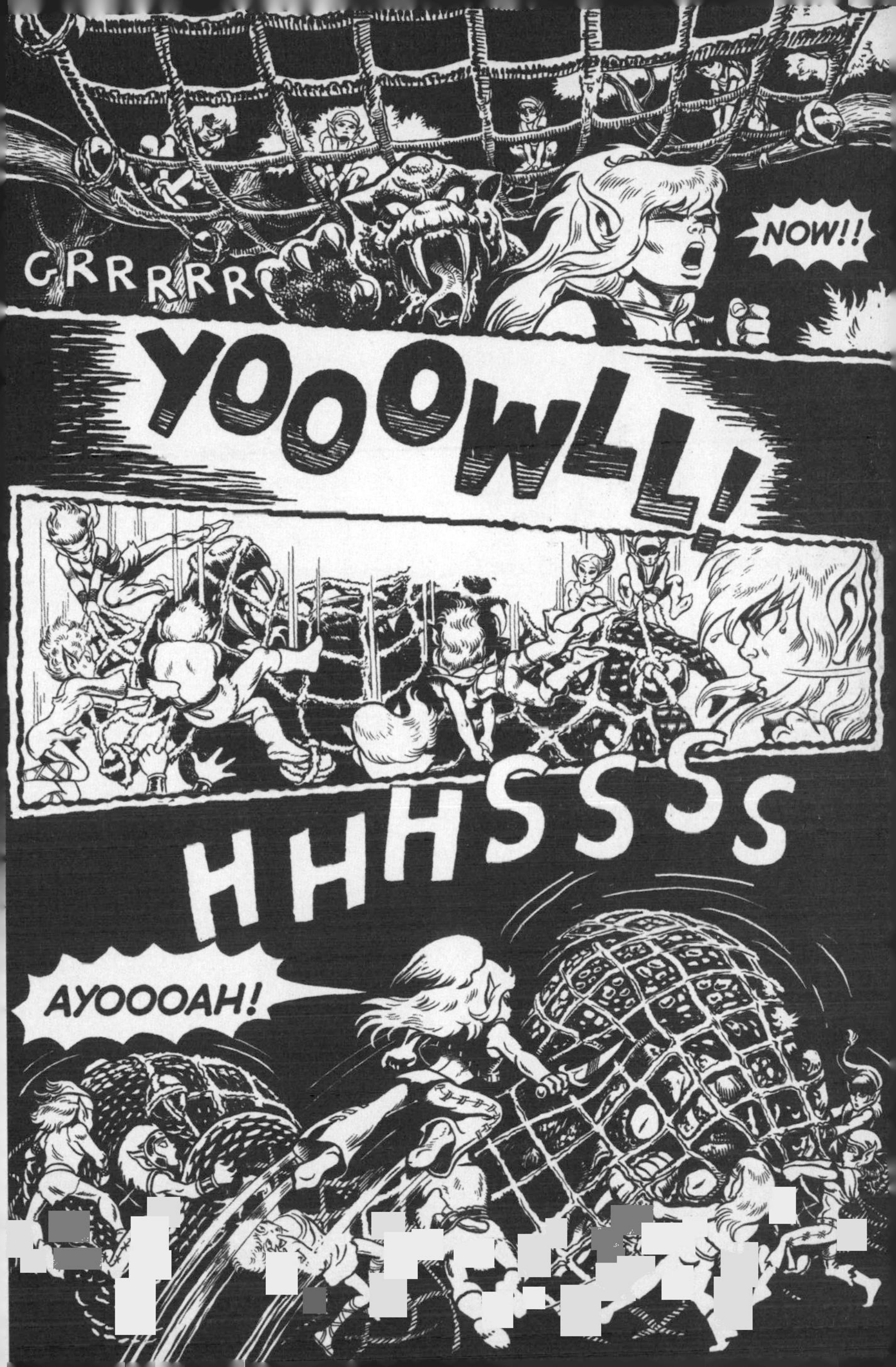

GRRRRRR
NOW!!
YOOOWLL!
HHSSSS
AYOOOAH!

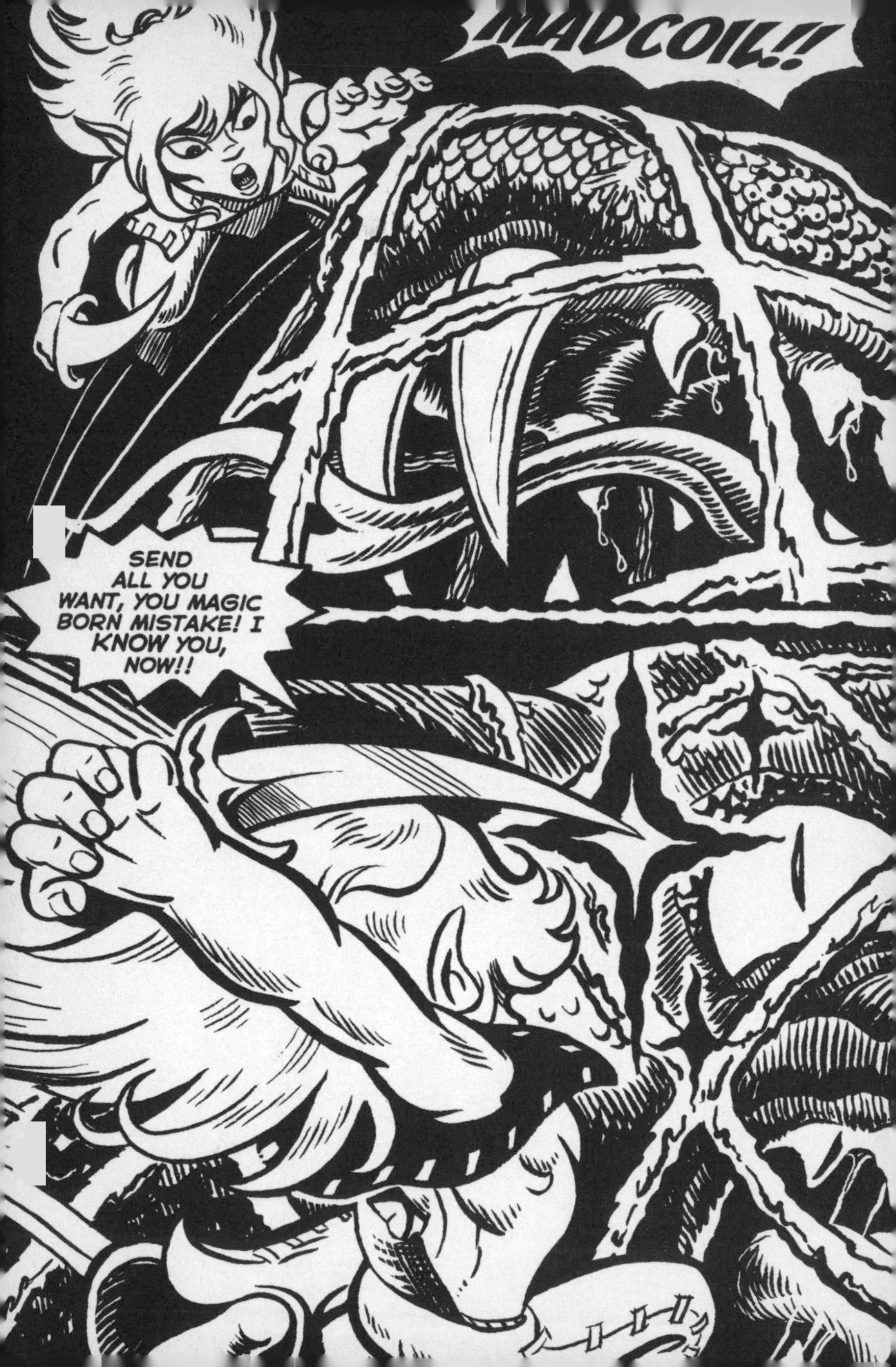
MADCOIL!!
SEND ALL YOU WANT, YOU MAGIC BORN MISTAKE! I KNOW YOU, NOW!!

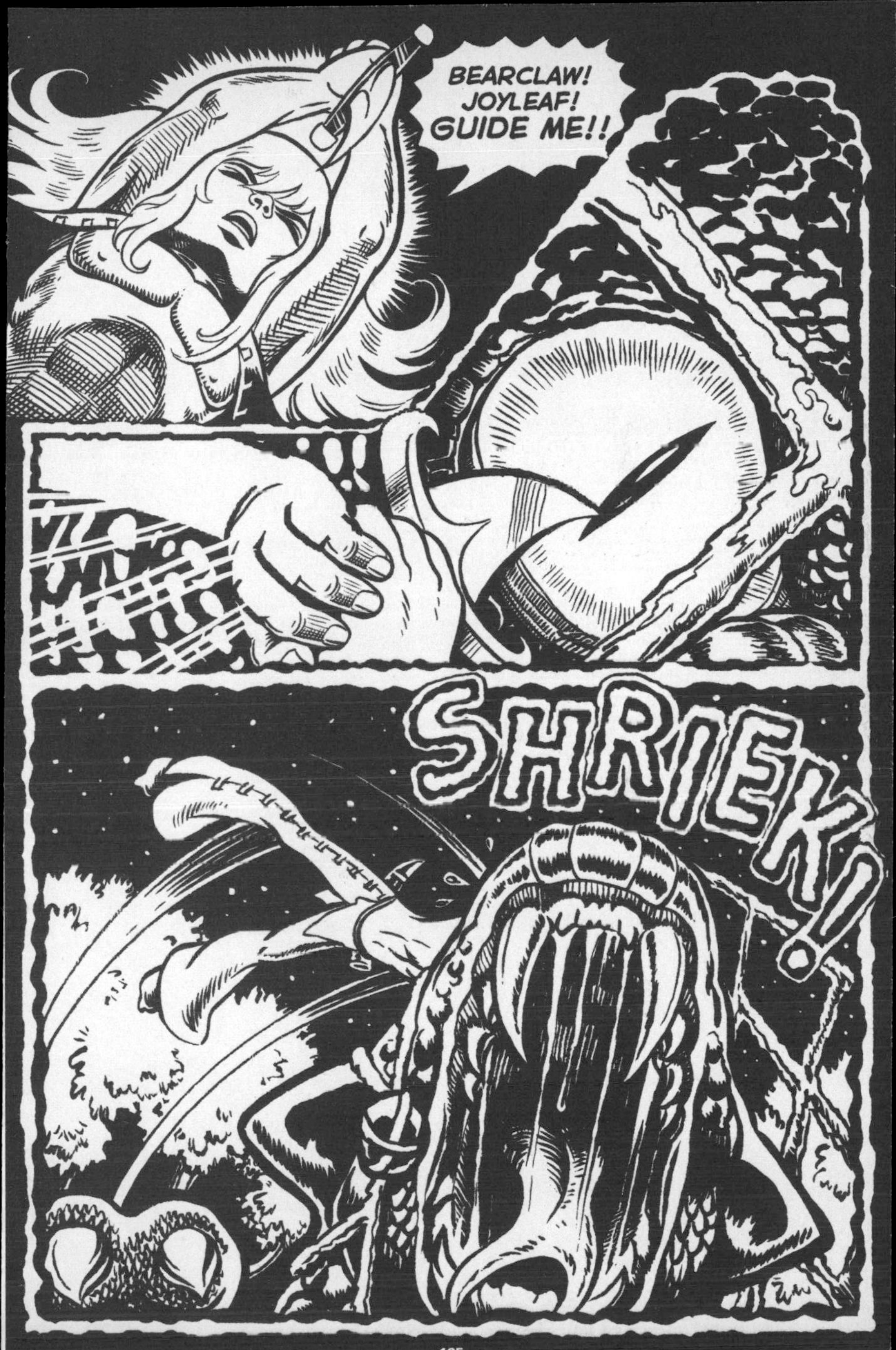
BEARCLAW! JOYLEAF! GUIDE ME!!
SHRIEK!

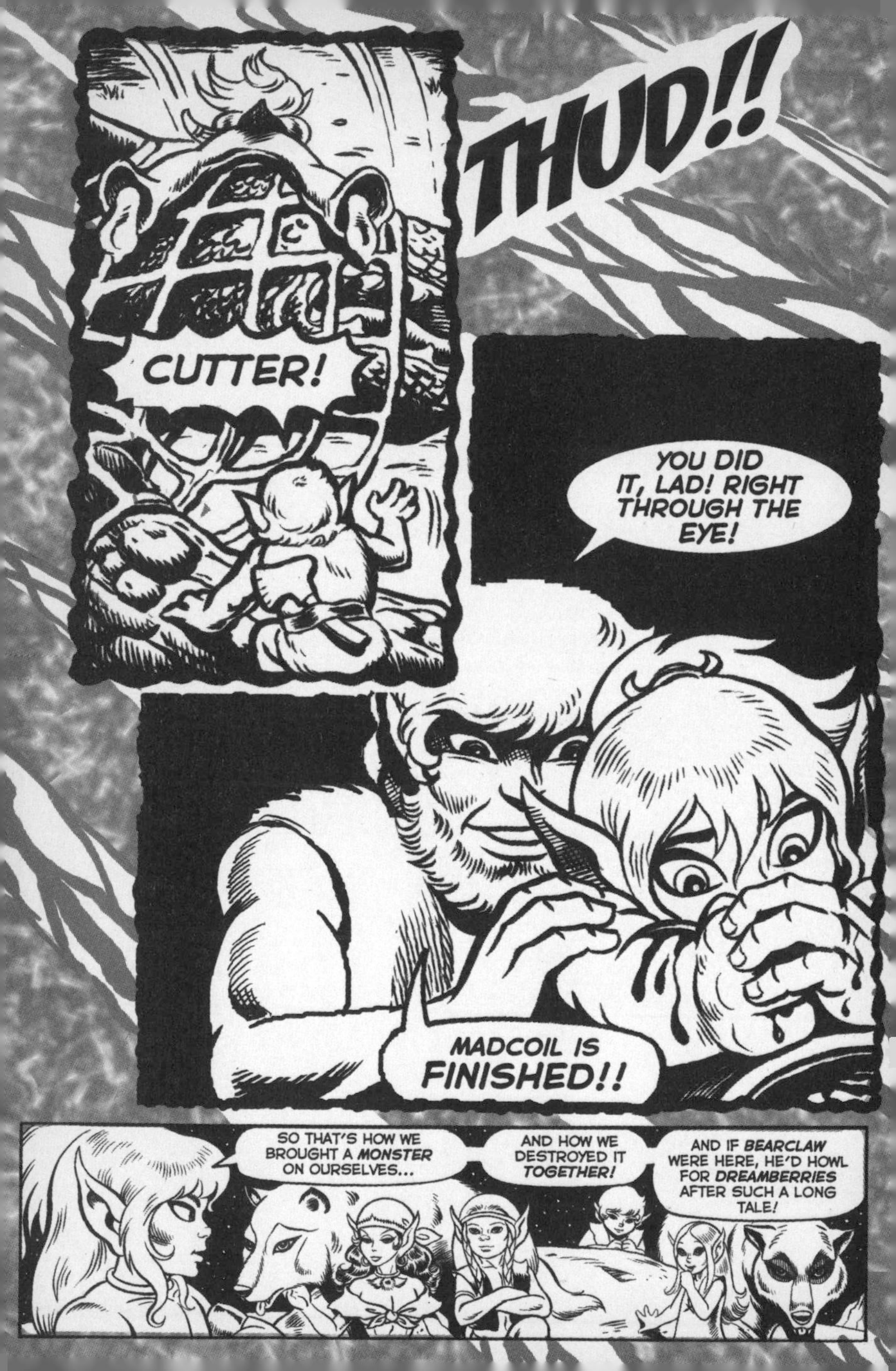
THUD!!
CUTTER!
YOU DID IT, LAD! RIGHT THROUGH THE EYE!
MADCOIL IS FINISHED!!
SO THAT'S HOW WE BROUGHT A MONSTER ON OURSELVES...
AND HOW WE DESTROYED IT TOGETHER!
AND IF BEARCLAW WERE HERE, HE'D HOWL FOR DREAMBERRIES AFTER SUCH A LONG TALE!

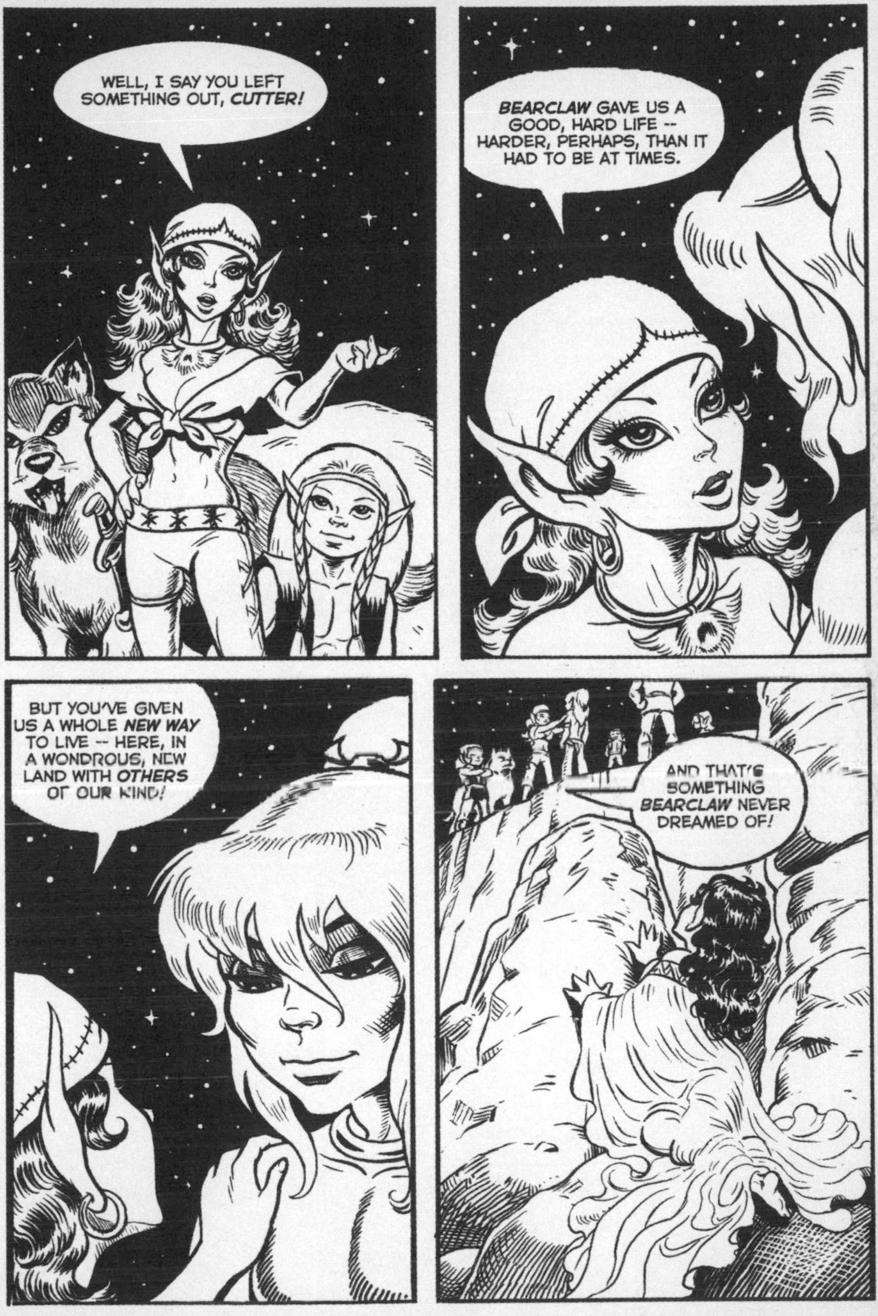
WELL, I SAY YOU LEFT SOMETHING OUT, CUTTER!
BEARCLAW GAVE US A GOOD, HARD LIFE -- HARDER, PERHAPS, THAN IT HAD TO BE AT TIMES.
BUT YOU'VE GIVEN US A WHOLE NEW WAY TO LIVE -- HERE, IN A WONDROUS, NEW LAND WITH OTHERS OF OUR KIND!
AND THAT'S SOMETHING BEARCLAW NEVER DREAMED OF!

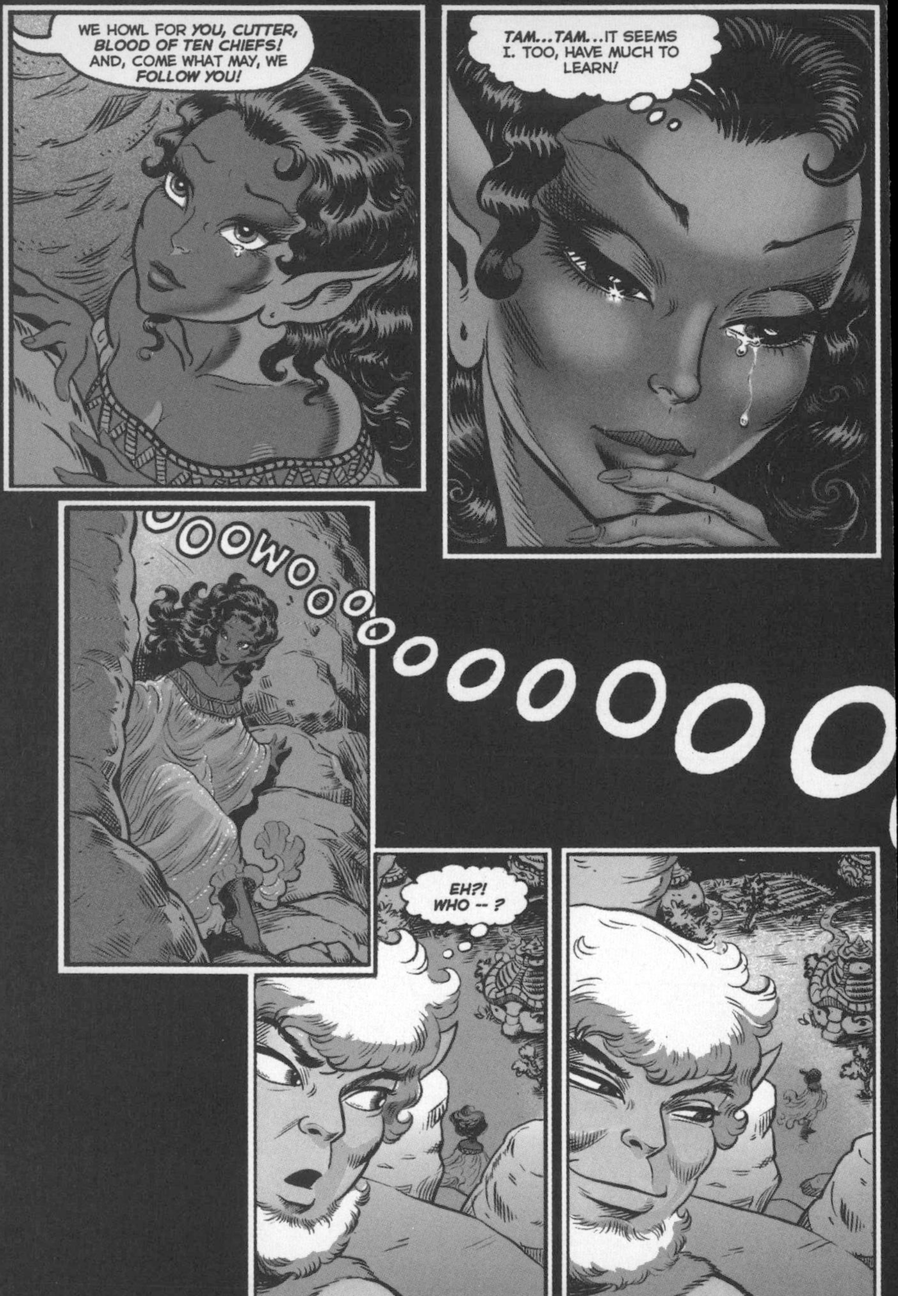
WE HOWL FOR YOU, CUTTER, BLOOD OF TEN CHIEFS! AND, COME WHAT MAY, WE FOLLOW YOU!
TAM...TAM...IT SEEMS I, TOO, HAVE MUCH TO LEARN!
OOOWOOOOOOOOOOO
EH?! WHO -- ?

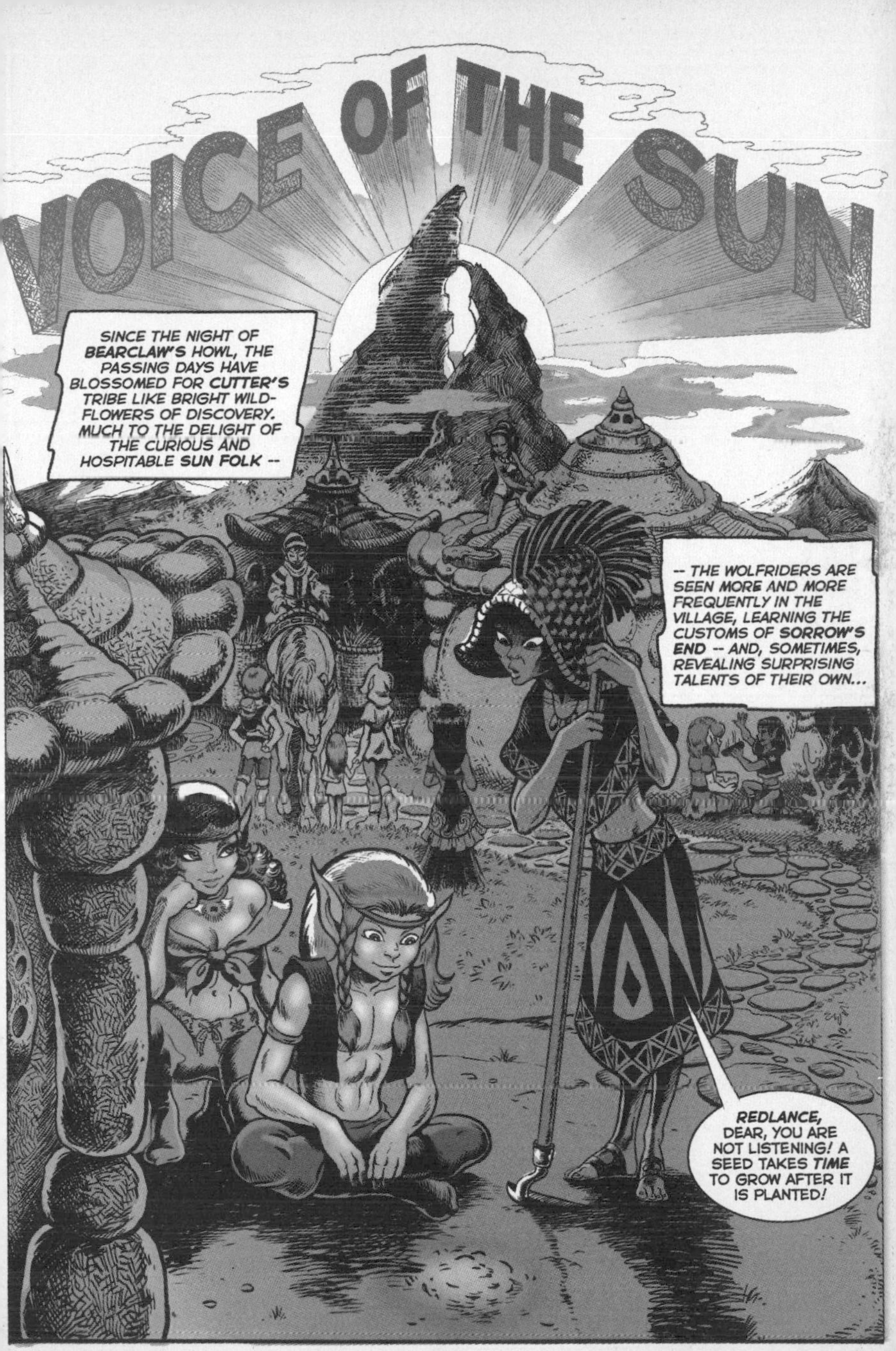
VOICE OF THE SUN
SINCE THE NIGHT OF BEARCLAW'S HOWL, THE PASSING DAYS HAVE BLOSSOMED FOR CUTTER'S TRIBE LIKE BRIGHT WILD-FLOWERS OF DISCOVERY. MUCH TO THE DELIGHT OF THE CURIOUS AND HOSPITABLE SUN FOLK --
-- THE WOLFRIDERS ARE SEEN MORE AND MORE FREQUENTLY IN THE VILLAGE, LEARNING THE CUSTOMS OF SORROW'S END -- AND, SOMETIMES, REVEALING SURPRISING TALENTS OF THEIR OWN...
REDLANCE, DEAR, YOU ARE NOT LISTENING! A SEED TAKES TIME TO GROW AFTER IT IS PLANTED!

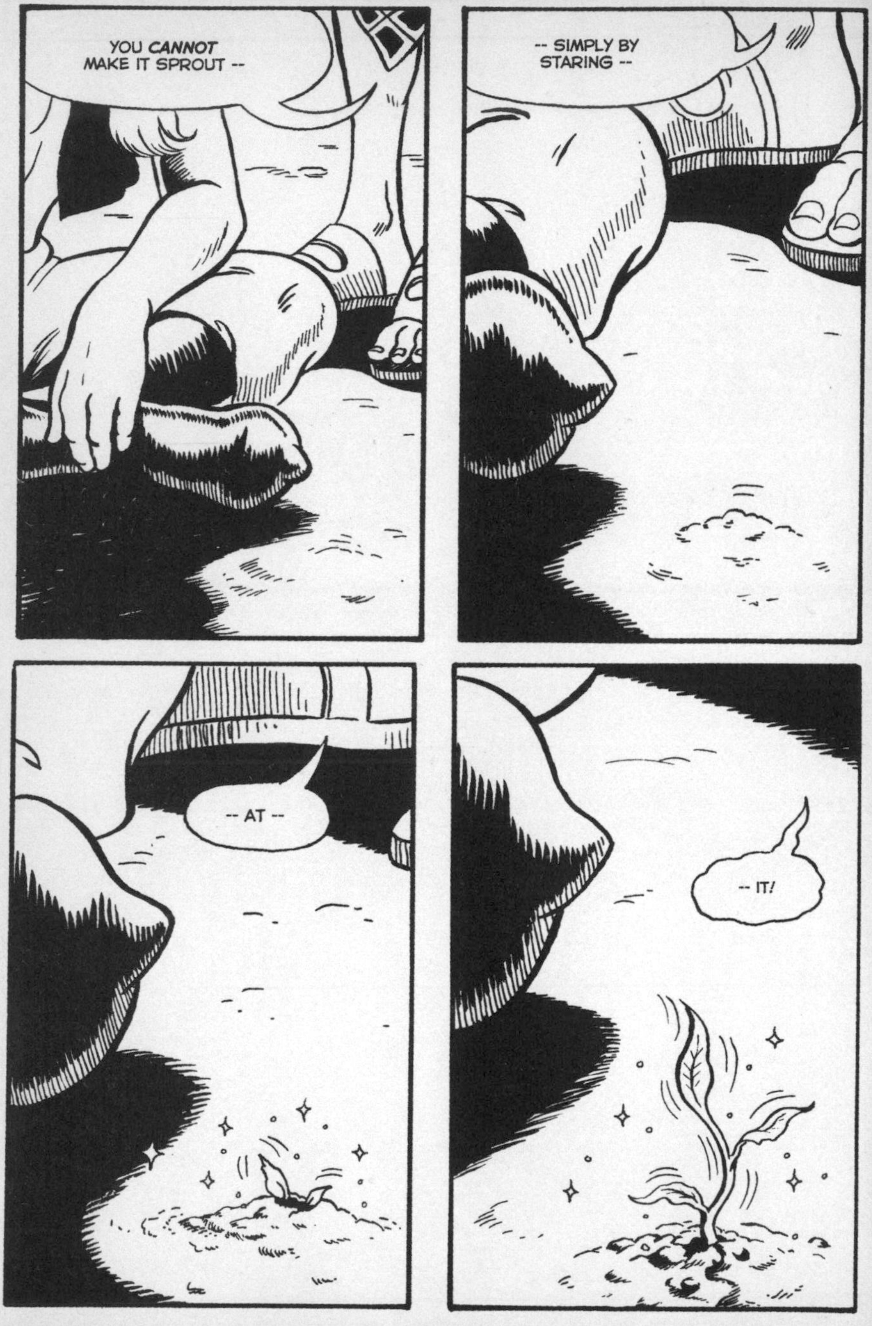
YOU CANNOT MAKE IT SPROUT --
-- SIMPLY BY STARING --
-- AT --
-- IT!

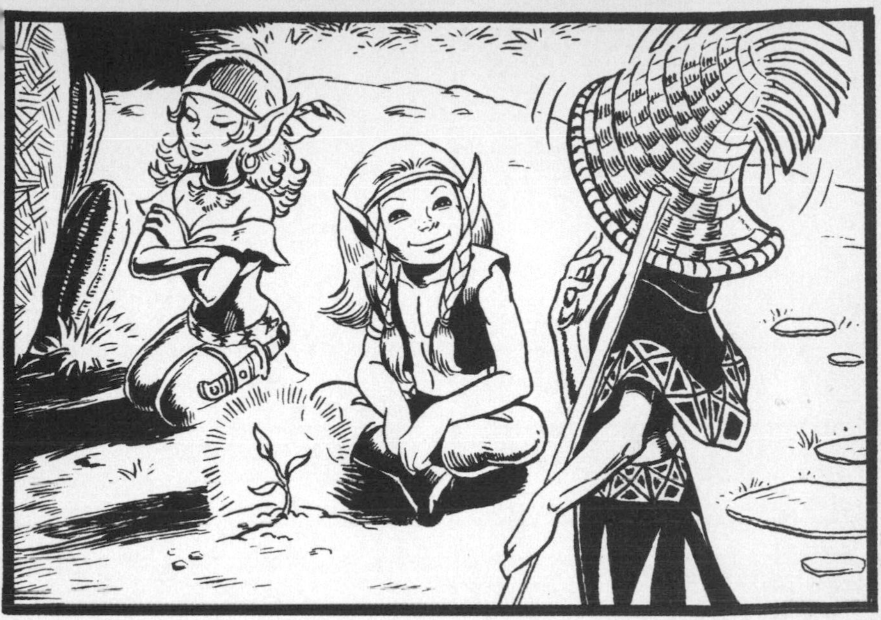

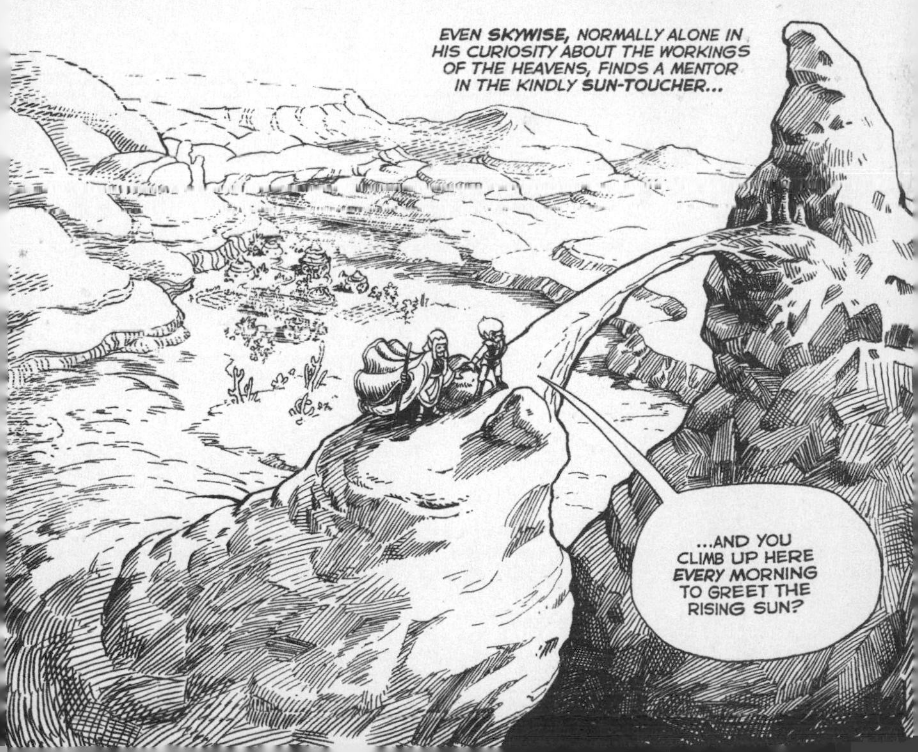
EVEN SKYWISE, NORMALLY ALONE IN HIS CURIOSITY ABOUT THE WORKINGS OF THE HEAVENS, FINDS A MENTOR IN THE KINDLY SUN-TOUCHER...
...AND YOU CLIMB UP HERE EVERY MORNING TO GREET THE RISING SUN?

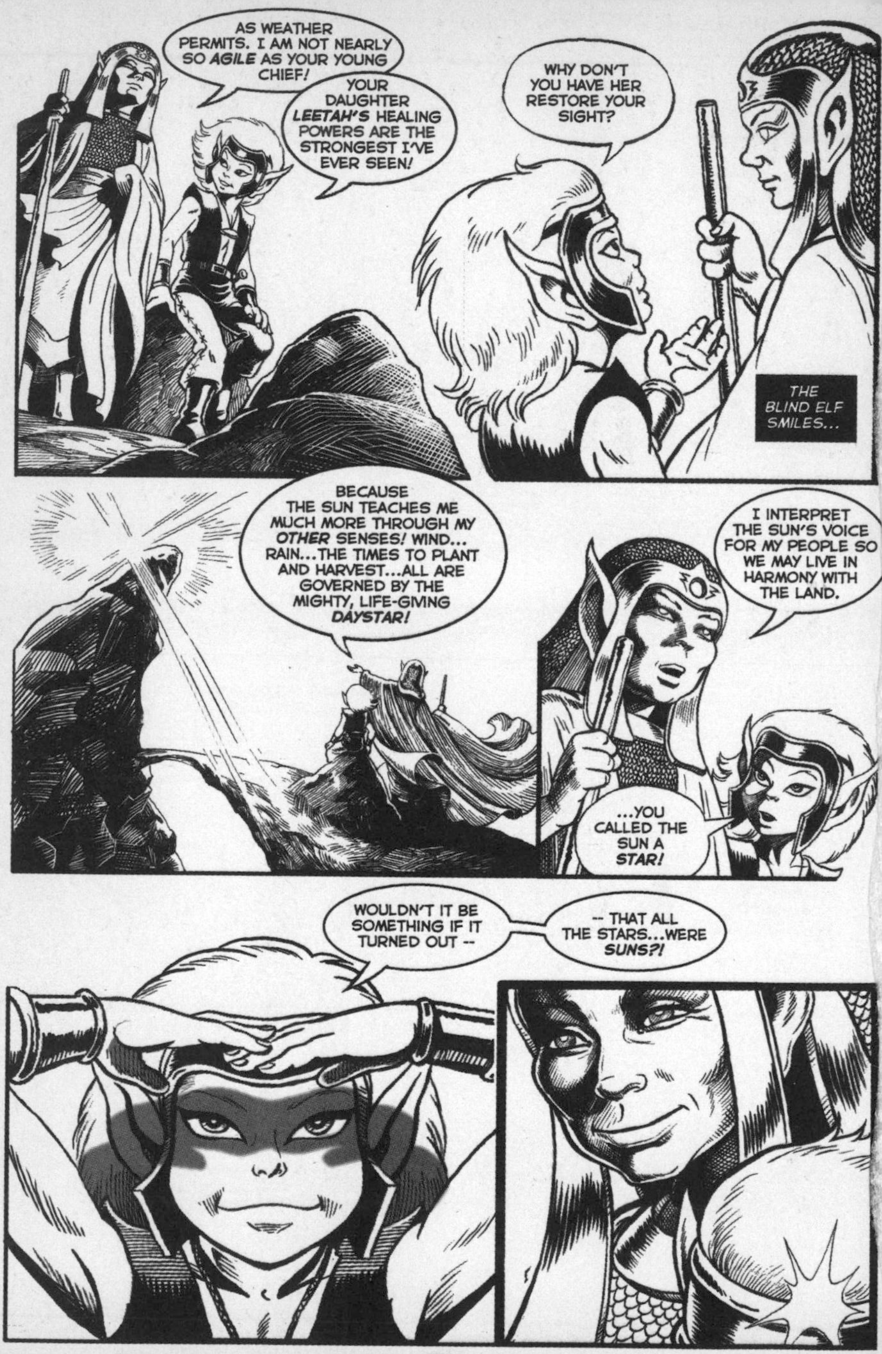
AS WEATHER PERMITS. I AM NOT NEARLY SO AGILE AS YOUR YOUNG CHIEF!
YOUR DAUGHTER LEETAH'S HEALING POWERS ARE THE STRONGEST I'VE EVER SEEN!
WHY DON'T YOU HAVE HER RESTORE YOUR SIGHT?
THE BLIND ELF SMILES...
BECAUSE THE SUN TEACHES ME MUCH MORE THROUGH MY OTHER SENSES! WIND... RAIN...THE TIMES TO PLANT AND HARVEST...ALL ARE GOVERNED BY THE MIGHTY, LIFE-GIVING DAYSTAR!
I INTERPRET THE SUN'S VOICE FOR MY PEOPLE SO WE MAY LIVE IN HARMONY WITH THE LAND.
...YOU CALLED THE SUN A STAR!
WOULDN'T IT BE SOMETHING IF IT TURNED OUT --
-- THAT ALL THE STARS...WERE SUNS?!

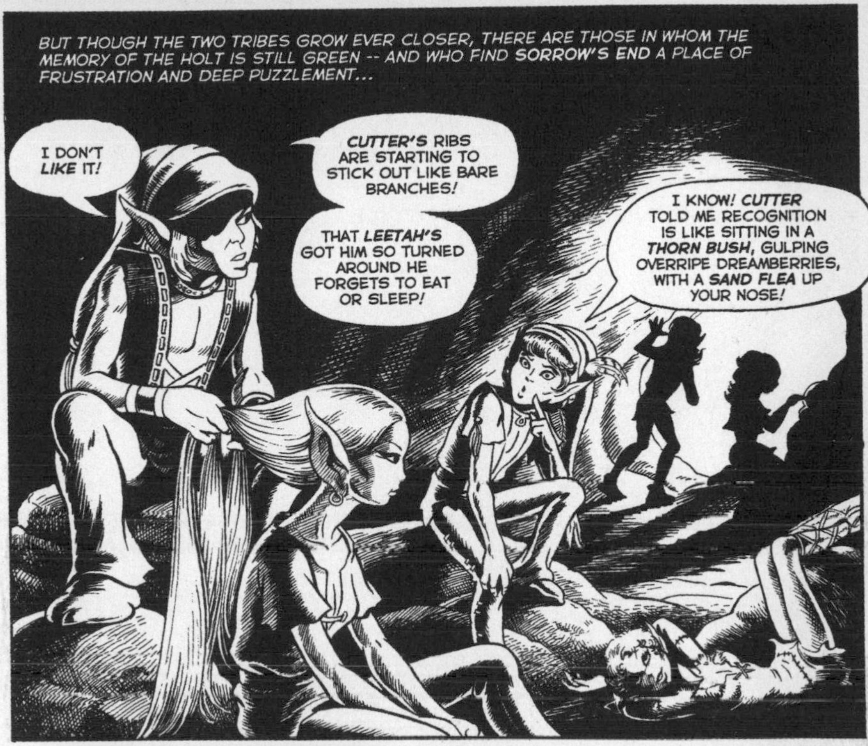
BUT THOUGH THE TWO TRIBES GROW EVER CLOSER, THERE ARE THOSE IN WHOM THE MEMORY OF THE HOLT IS STILL GREEN -- AND WHO FIND SORROW'S END A PLACE OF FRUSTRATION AND DEEP PUZZLEMENT...
I DON'T LIKE IT!
CUTTER'S RIBS ARE STARTING TO STICK OUT LIKE BARE BRANCHES!
THAT LEETAH'S GOT HIM SO TURNED AROUND HE FORGETS TO EAT OR SLEEP!
I KNOW! CUTTER TOLD ME RECOGNITION IS LIKE SITTING IN A THORN BUSH, GULPING OVERRIPE DREAMBERRIES, WITH A SAND FLEA UP YOUR NOSE!

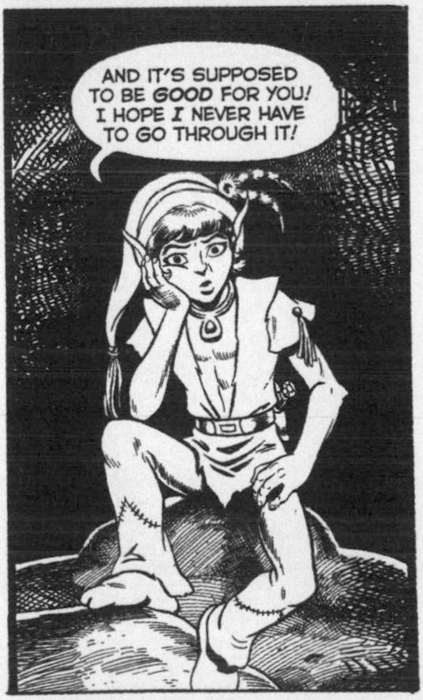
AND IT'S SUPPOSED TO BE GOOD FOR YOU! I HOPE I NEVER HAVE TO GO THROUGH IT!

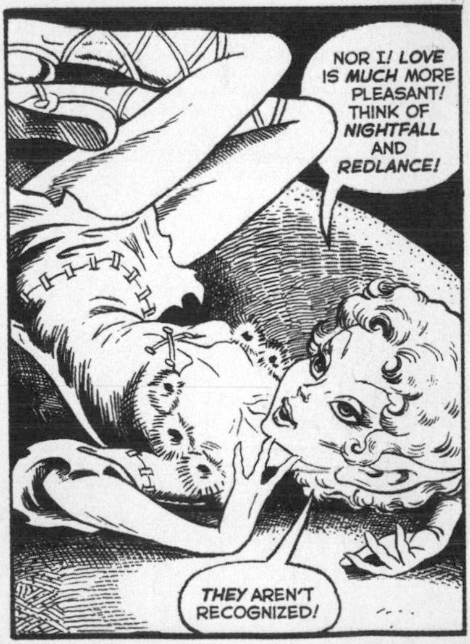
NOR I! LOVE IS MUCH MORE PLEASANT! THINK OF NIGHTFALL AND REDLANCE!
THEY AREN'T RECOGNIZED!

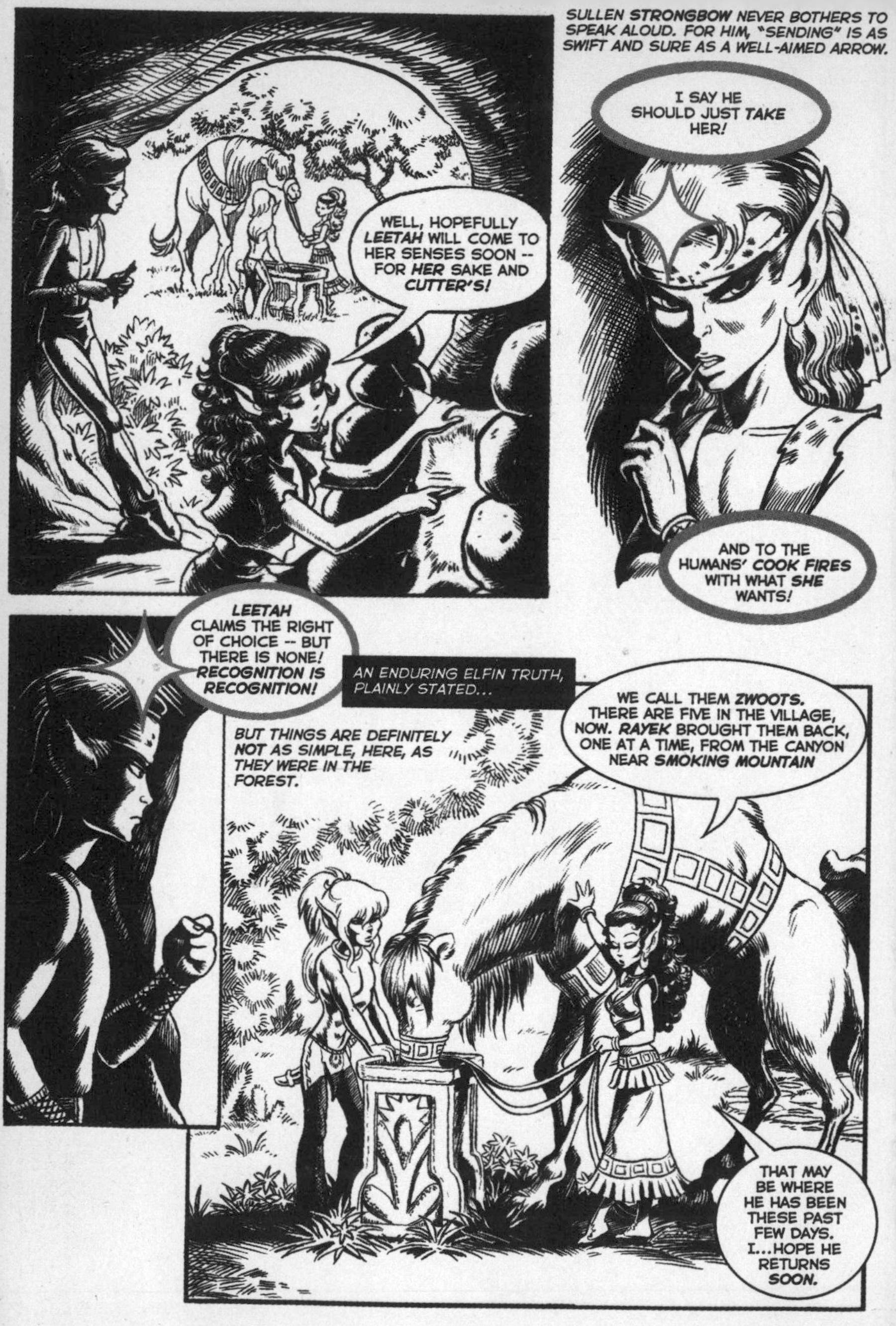
WELL, HOPEFULLY LEETAH WILL COME TO HER SENSES SOON -- FOR HER SAKE AND CUTTER'S!
SULLEN STRONGBOW NEVER BOTHERS TO SPEAK ALOUD. FOR HIM, "SENDING" IS AS SWIFT AND SURE AS A WELL-AIMED ARROW.
I SAY HE SHOULD JUST TAKE HER!
AND TO THE HUMANS' COOK FIRES WITH WHAT SHE WANTS!
LEETAH CLAIMS THE RIGHT OF CHOICE -- BUT THERE IS NONE! RECOGNITION IS RECOGNITION!
AN ENDURING ELFIN TRUTH, PLAINLY STATED...
BUT THINGS ARE DEFINITELY NOT AS SIMPLE, HERE, AS THEY WERE IN THE FOREST.
WE CALL THEM ZWOOTS. THERE ARE FIVE IN THE VILLAGE, NOW. RAYEK BROUGHT THEM BACK, ONE AT A TIME, FROM THE CANYON NEAR SMOKING MOUNTAIN
THAT MAY BE WHERE HE HAS BEEN THESE PAST FEW DAYS. I...HOPE HE RETURNS SOON.

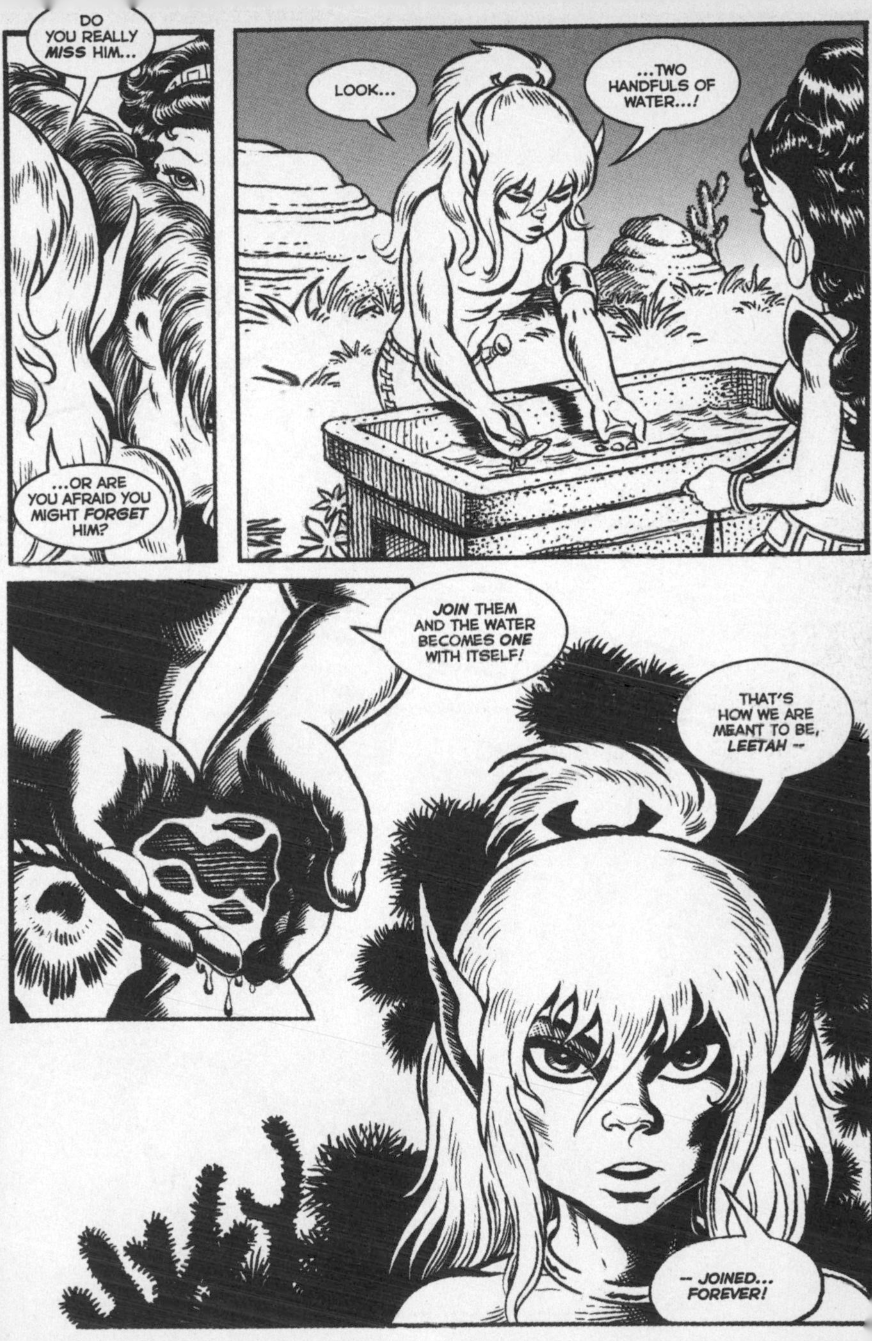
DO YOU REALLY MISS HIM...
...OR ARE YOU AFRAID YOU MIGHT FORGET HIM?
LOOK...
...TWO HANDFULS OF WATER...!
JOIN THEM AND THE WATER BECOMES ONE WITH ITSELF!
THAT'S HOW WE ARE MEANT TO BE, LEETAH --
-- JOINED... FOREVER!

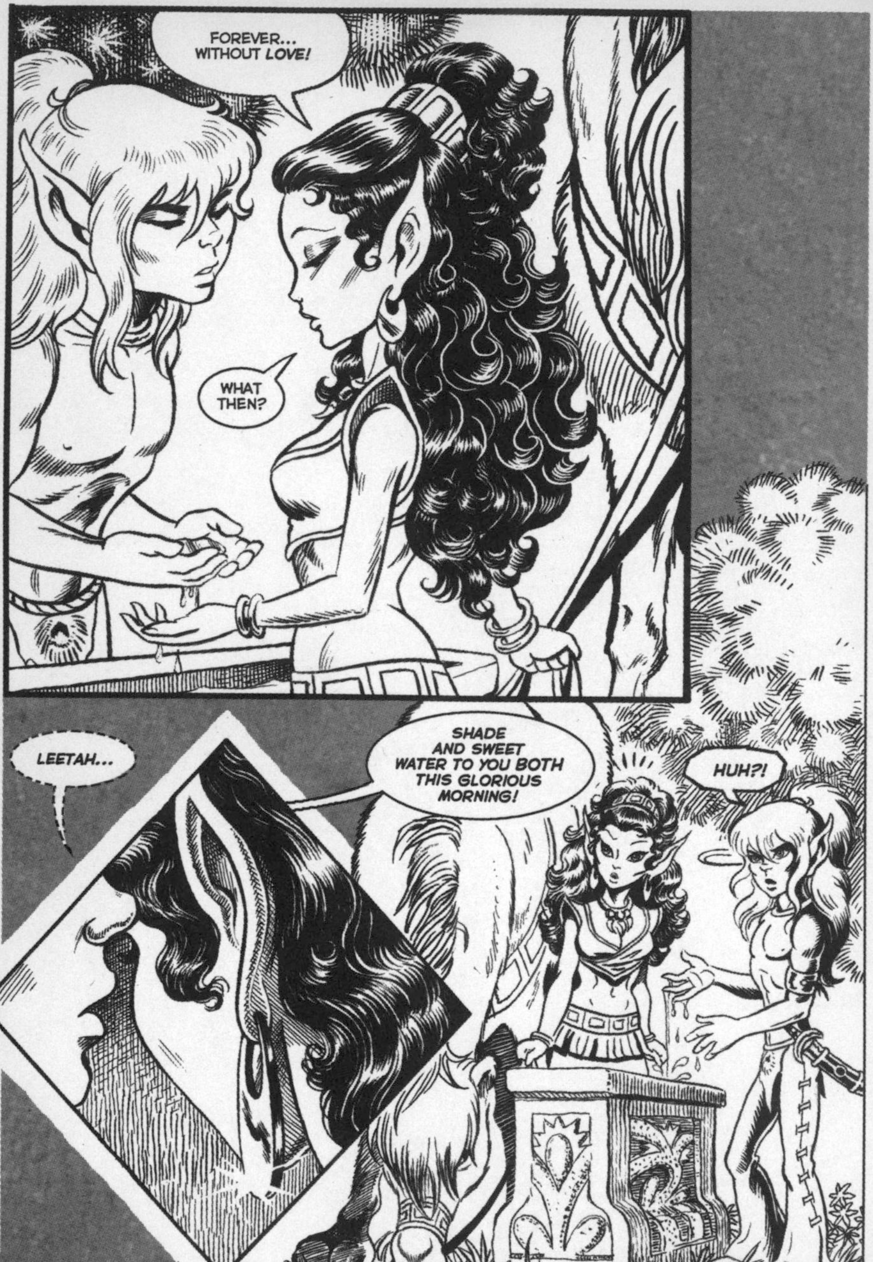

FOREVER... WITHOUT LOVE!
WHAT THEN?
LEETAH...
SHADE AND SWEET WATER TO YOU BOTH THIS GLORIOUS MORNING!
HUH?!

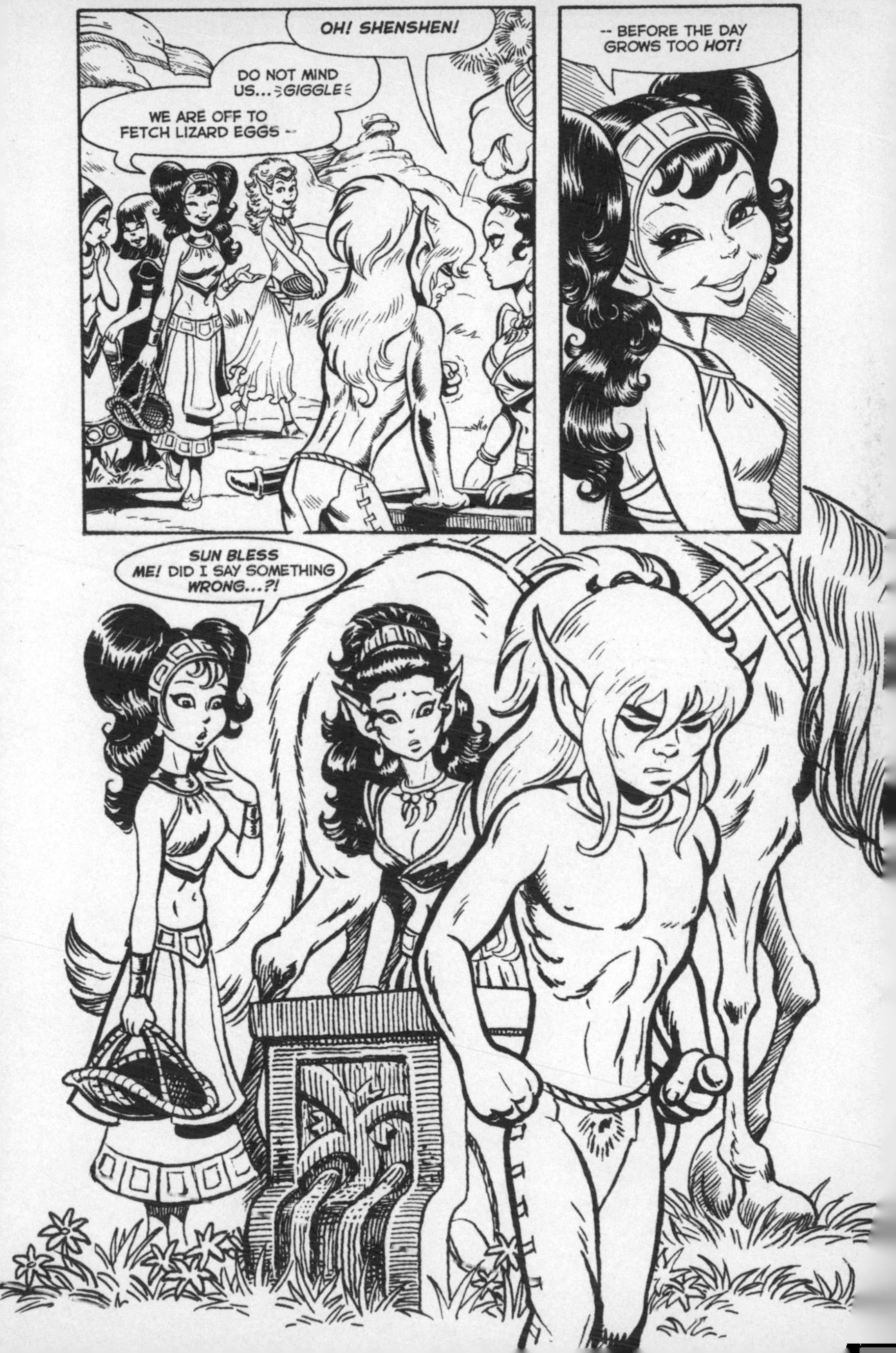
WE ARE OFF TO FETCH LIZARD EGGS --
DO NOT MIND US... ≷GIGGLE≶
OH! SHENSHEN!
-- BEFORE THE DAY GROWS TOO HOT!
SUN BLESS ME! DID I SAY SOMETHING WRONG...?!

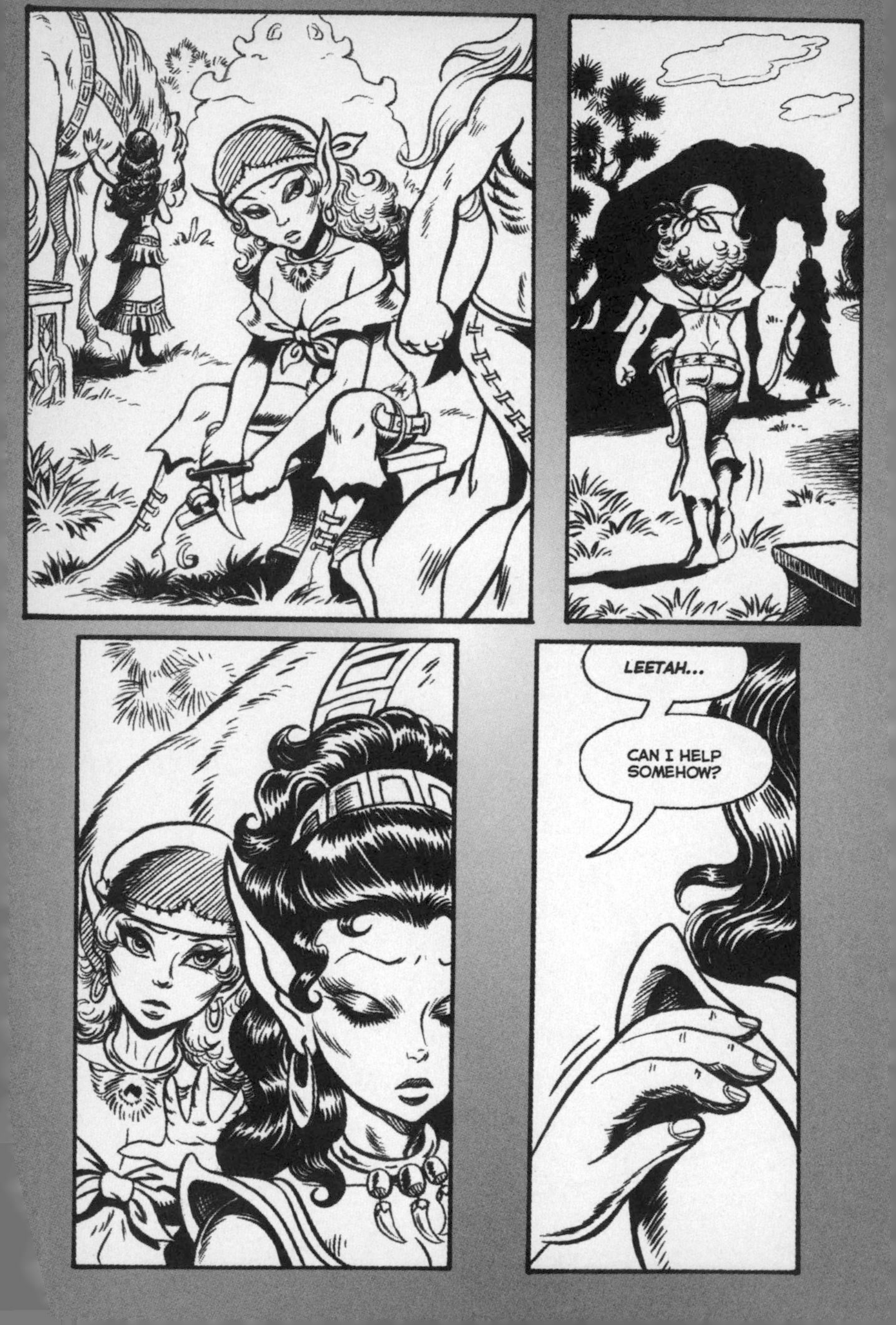
LEETAH...
CAN I HELP SOMEHOW?

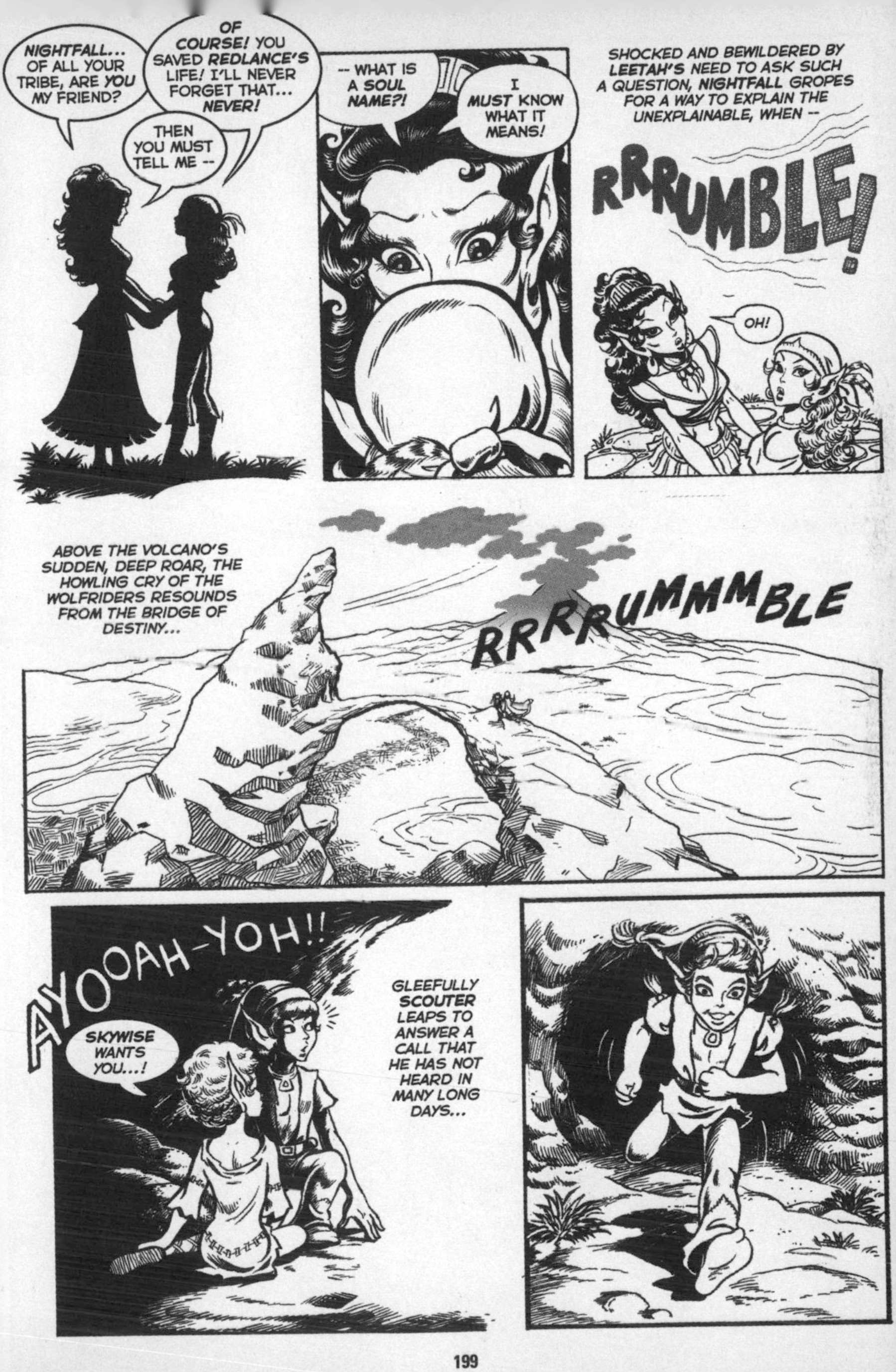
NIGHTFALL... OF ALL YOUR TRIBE, ARE YOU MY FRIEND?
OF COURSE! YOU SAVED REDLANCE'S LIFE! I'LL NEVER FORGET THAT... NEVER!
THEN YOU MUST TELL ME --
-- WHAT IS A SOUL NAME?!
I MUST KNOW WHAT IT MEANS!
SHOCKED AND BEWILDERED BY LEETAH'S NEED TO ASK SUCH A QUESTION, NIGHTFALL GROPES FOR A WAY TO EXPLAIN THE UNEXPLAINABLE, WHEN --
RRRUMBLE!
OH!
ABOVE THE VOLCANO'S SUDDEN, DEEP ROAR, THE HOWLING CRY OF THE WOLFRIDERS RESOUNDS FROM THE BRIDGE OF DESTINY...
RRRRUMMMMBLE
AYOOAH-YOH!!
SKYWISE WANTS YOU...!
GLEEFULLY SCOUTER LEAPS TO ANSWER A CALL THAT HE HAS NOT HEARD IN MANY LONG DAYS...

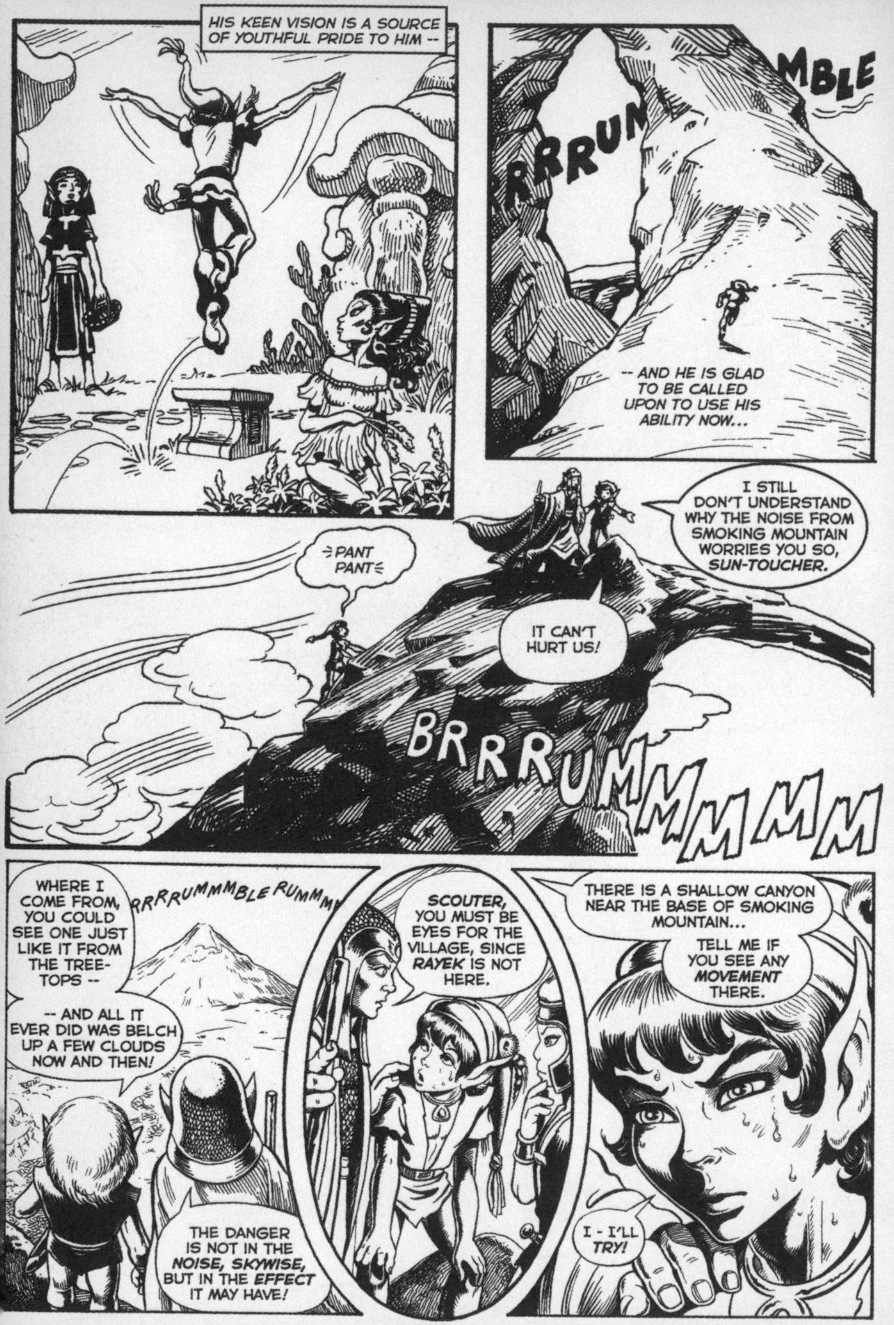
HIS KEEN VISION IS A SOURCE OF YOUTHFUL PRIDE TO HIM --
RRRRUMBLE
-- AND HE IS GLAD TO BE CALLED UPON TO USE HIS ABILITY NOW...
PANT PANT
I STILL DON'T UNDERSTAND WHY THE NOISE FROM SMOKING MOUNTAIN WORRIES YOU SO, SUN-TOUCHER.
IT CAN'T HURT US!
BRRRUMMMMMM
WHERE I COME FROM, YOU COULD SEE ONE JUST LIKE IT FROM THE TREE-TOPS --
RRRRUMMMBLE RUMMM
-- AND ALL IT EVER DID WAS BELCH UP A FEW CLOUDS NOW AND THEN!
THE DANGER IS NOT IN THE NOISE, SKYWISE, BUT IN THE EFFECT IT MAY HAVE!
SCOUTER, YOU MUST BE EYES FOR THE VILLAGE, SINCE RAYEK IS NOT HERE.
THERE IS A SHALLOW CANYON NEAR THE BASE OF SMOKING MOUNTAIN...
TELL ME IF YOU SEE ANY MOVEMENT THERE.
I - I'LL TRY!

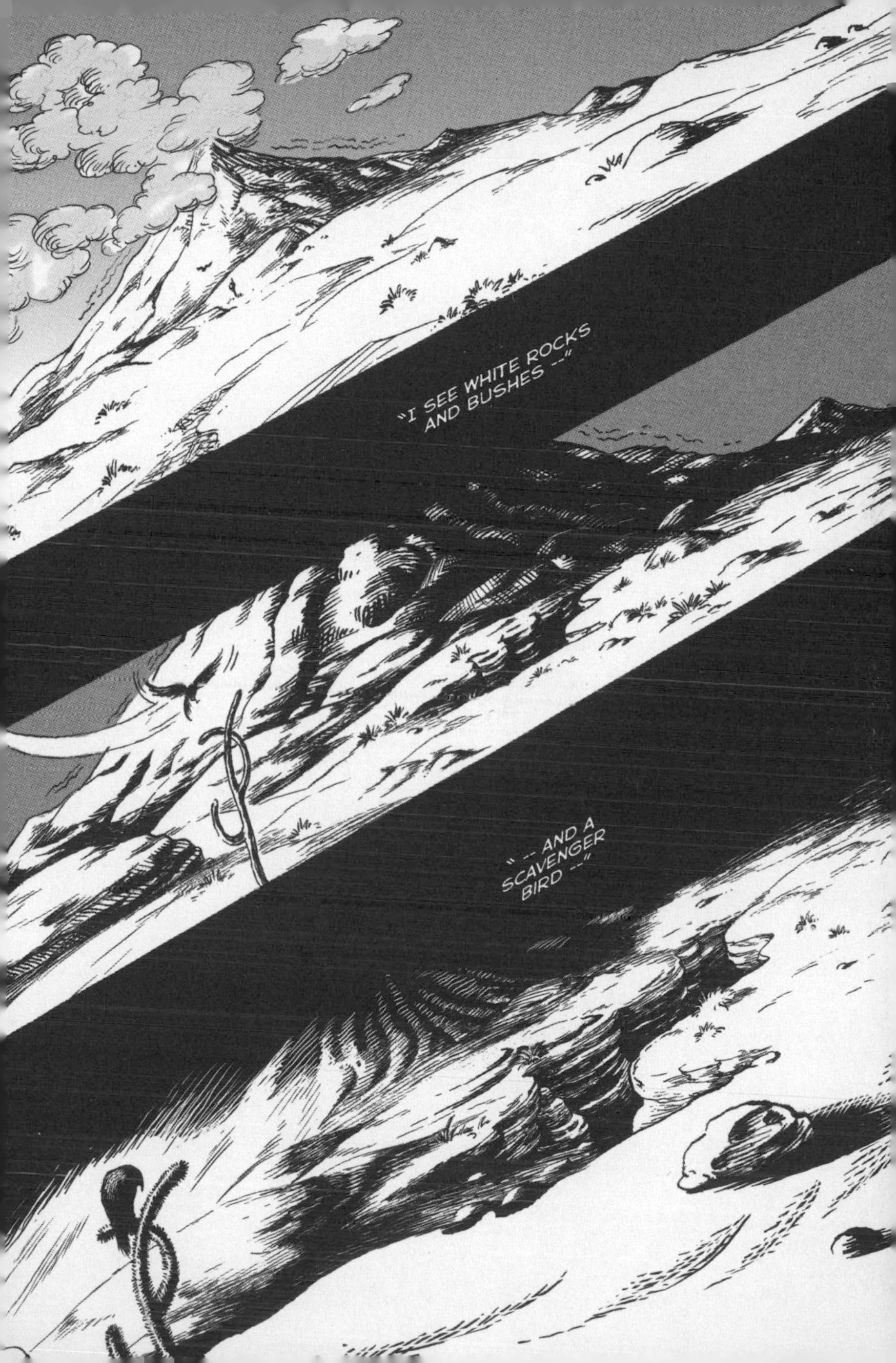
"I SEE WHITE ROCKS AND BUSHES --"
"-- AND A SCAVENGER BIRD --"

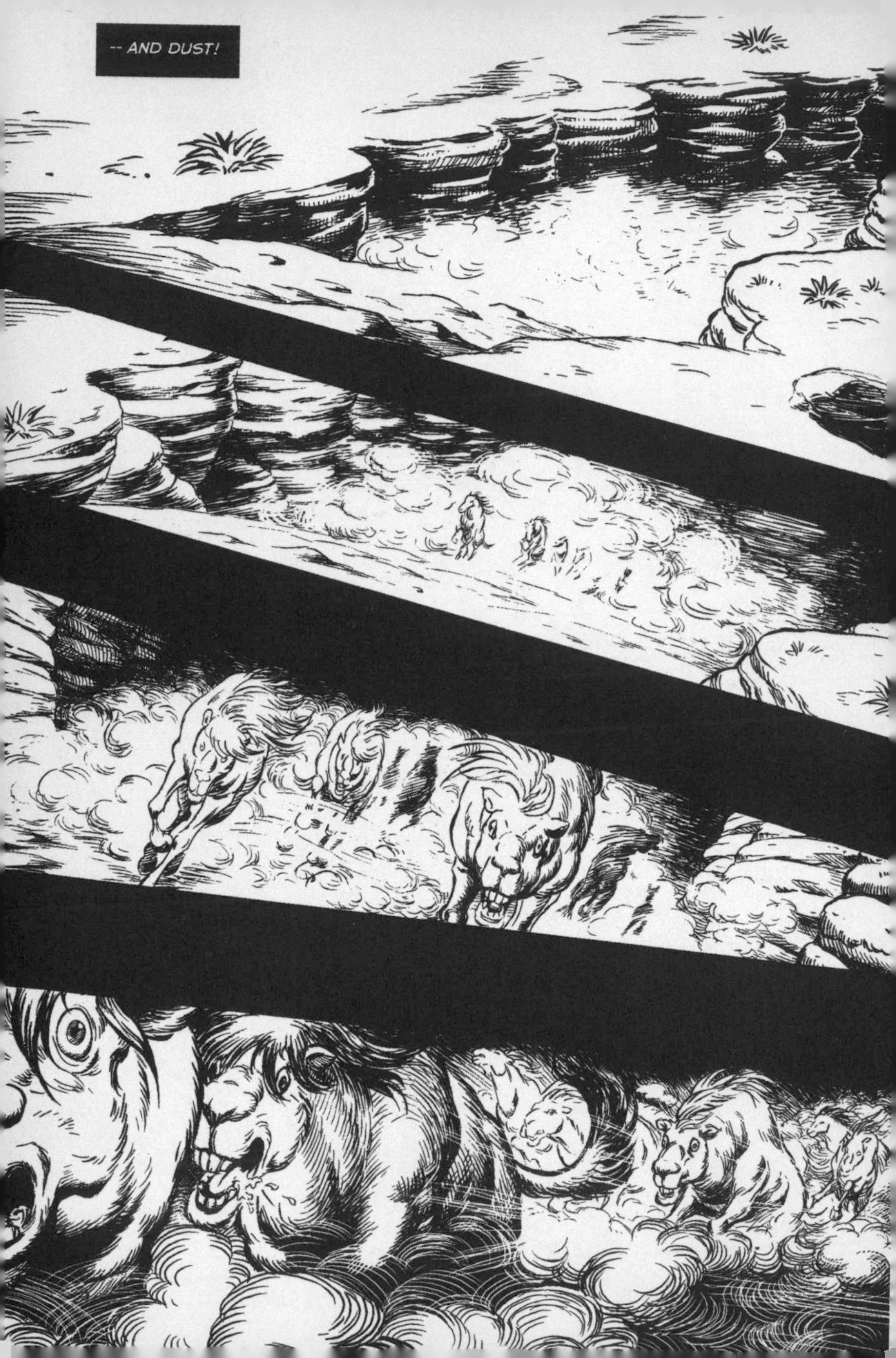
-- AND DUST!

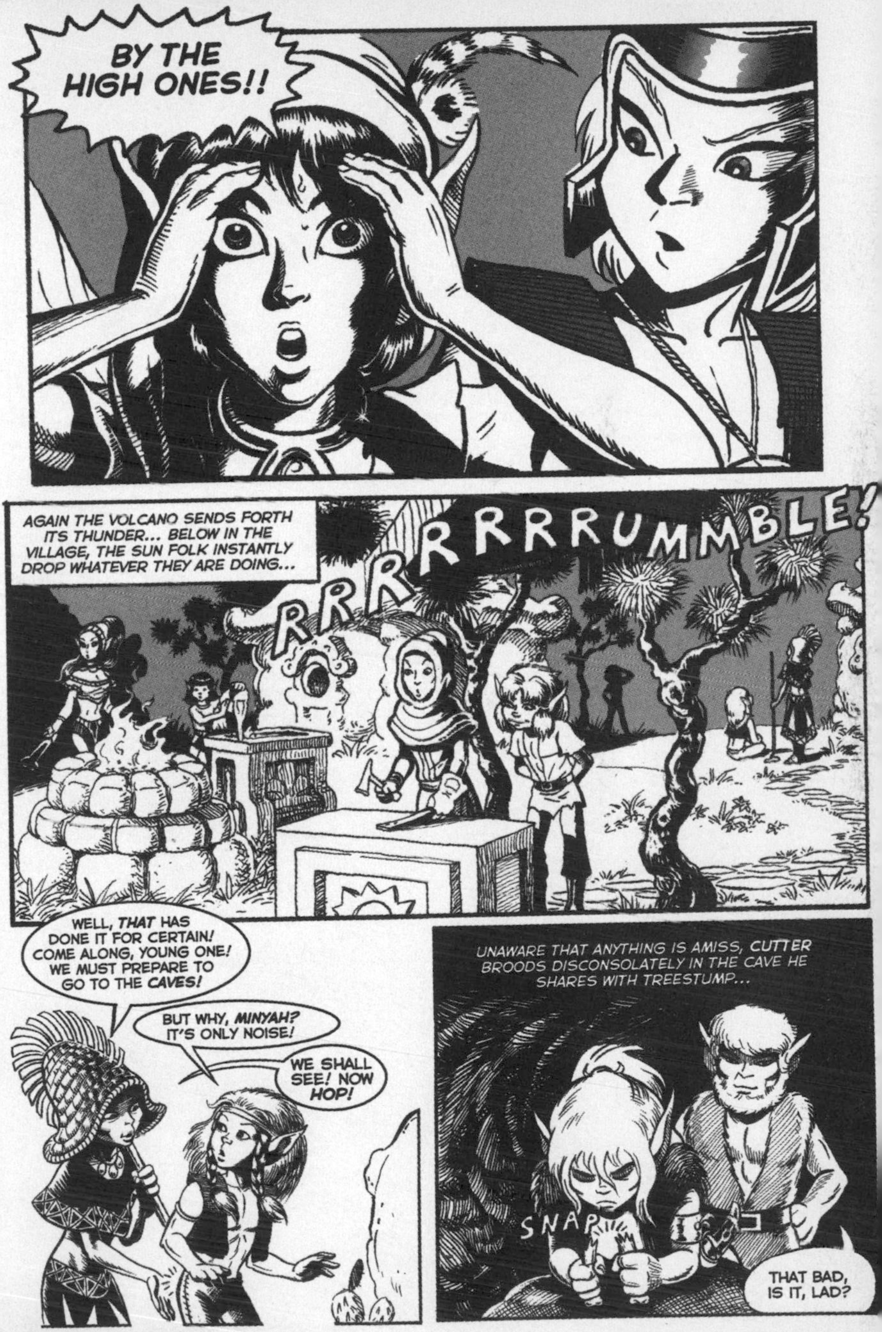
BY THE HIGH ONES!!
AGAIN THE VOLCANO SENDS FORTH ITS THUNDER... BELOW IN THE VILLAGE, THE SUN FOLK INSTANTLY DROP WHATEVER THEY ARE DOING...
RRRRRRRRUMMBLE!
WELL, THAT HAS DONE IT FOR CERTAIN! COME ALONG, YOUNG ONE! WE MUST PREPARE TO GO TO THE CAVES!
BUT WHY, MINYAH? IT'S ONLY NOISE!
WE SHALL SEE! NOW HOP!
UNAWARE THAT ANYTHING IS AMISS, CUTTER BROODS DISCONSOLATELY IN THE CAVE HE SHARES WITH TREESTUMP...
SNAP
THAT BAD, IS IT, LAD?

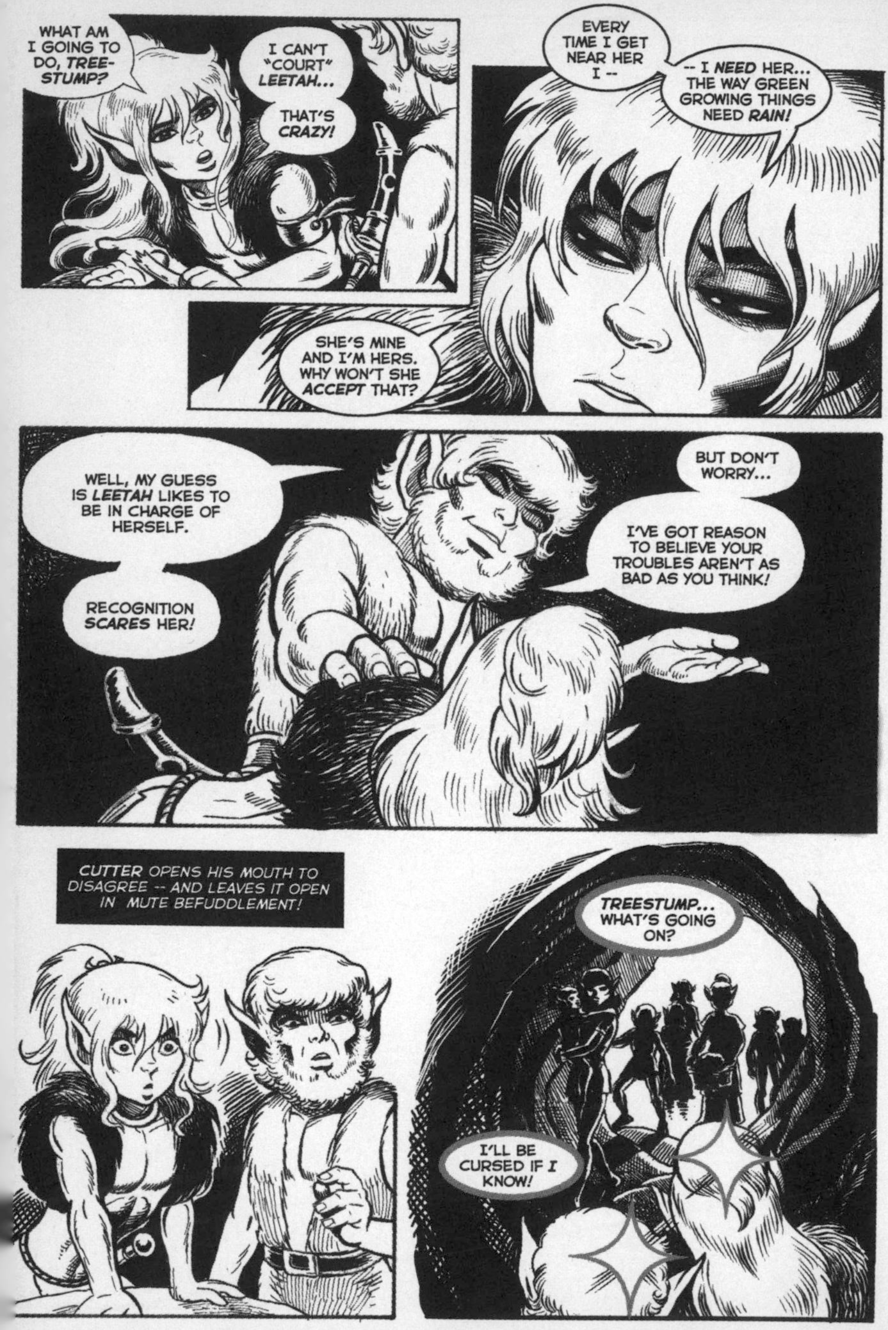
WHAT AM I GOING TO DO, TREE-STUMP?
I CAN'T "COURT" LEETAH...
THAT'S CRAZY!
EVERY TIME I GET NEAR HER I --
-- I NEED HER... THE WAY GREEN GROWING THINGS NEED RAIN!
SHE'S MINE AND I'M HERS. WHY WON'T SHE ACCEPT THAT?
WELL, MY GUESS IS LEETAH LIKES TO BE IN CHARGE OF HERSELF.
RECOGNITION SCARES HER!
BUT DON'T WORRY...
I'VE GOT REASON TO BELIEVE YOUR TROUBLES AREN'T AS BAD AS YOU THINK!
CUTTER OPENS HIS MOUTH TO DISAGREE -- AND LEAVES IT OPEN IN MUTE BEFUDDLEMENT!
TREESTUMP... WHAT'S GOING ON?
I'LL BE CURSED IF I KNOW!

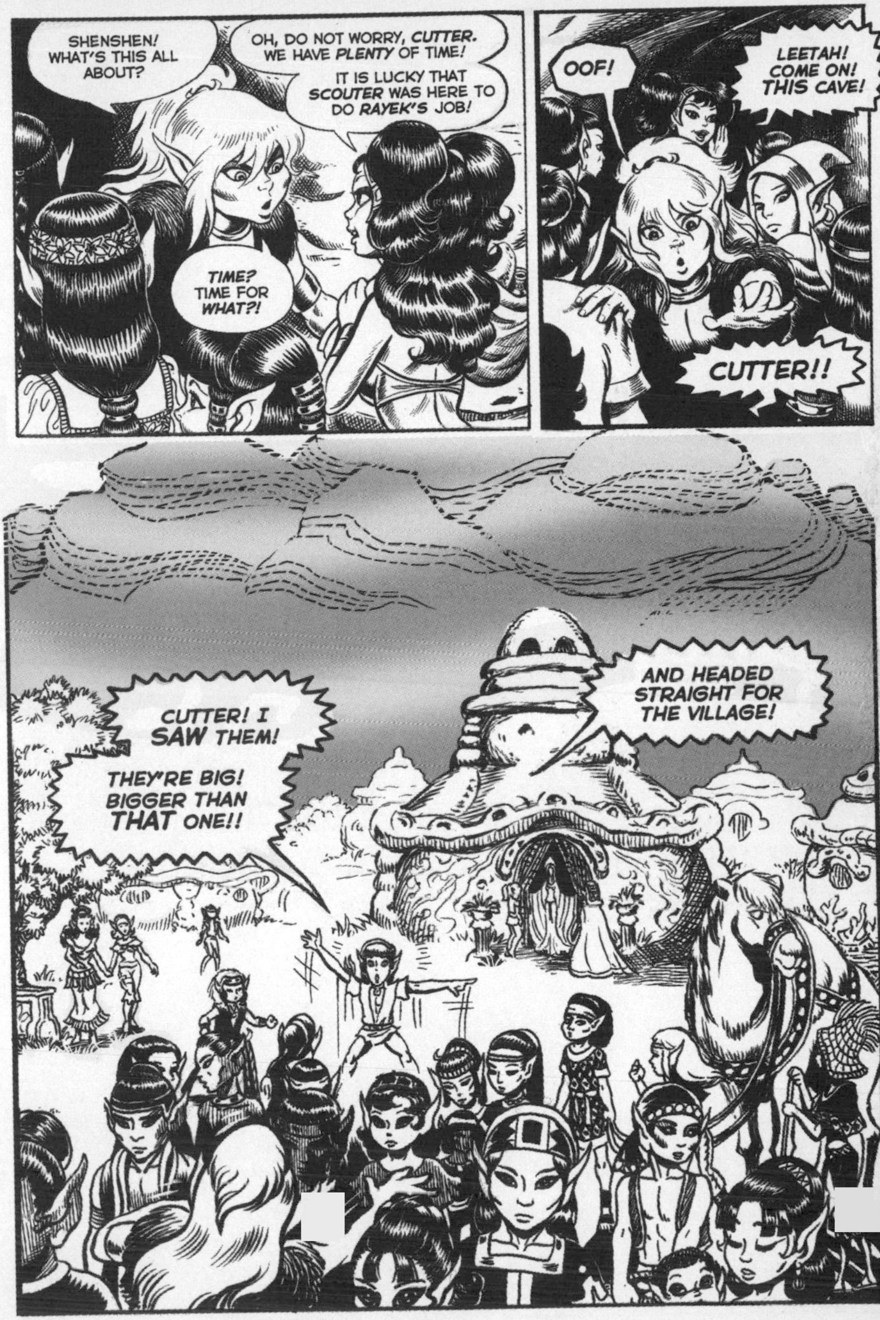
SHENSHEN! WHAT'S THIS ALL ABOUT?
OH, DO NOT WORRY, CUTTER. WE HAVE PLENTY OF TIME!
IT IS LUCKY THAT SCOUTER WAS HERE TO DO RAYEK'S JOB!
TIME? TIME FOR WHAT?!
OOF!
LEETAH! COME ON! THIS CAVE!
CUTTER!!
CUTTER! I SAW THEM!
THEY'RE BIG! BIGGER THAN THAT ONE!!
AND HEADED STRAIGHT FOR THE VILLAGE!

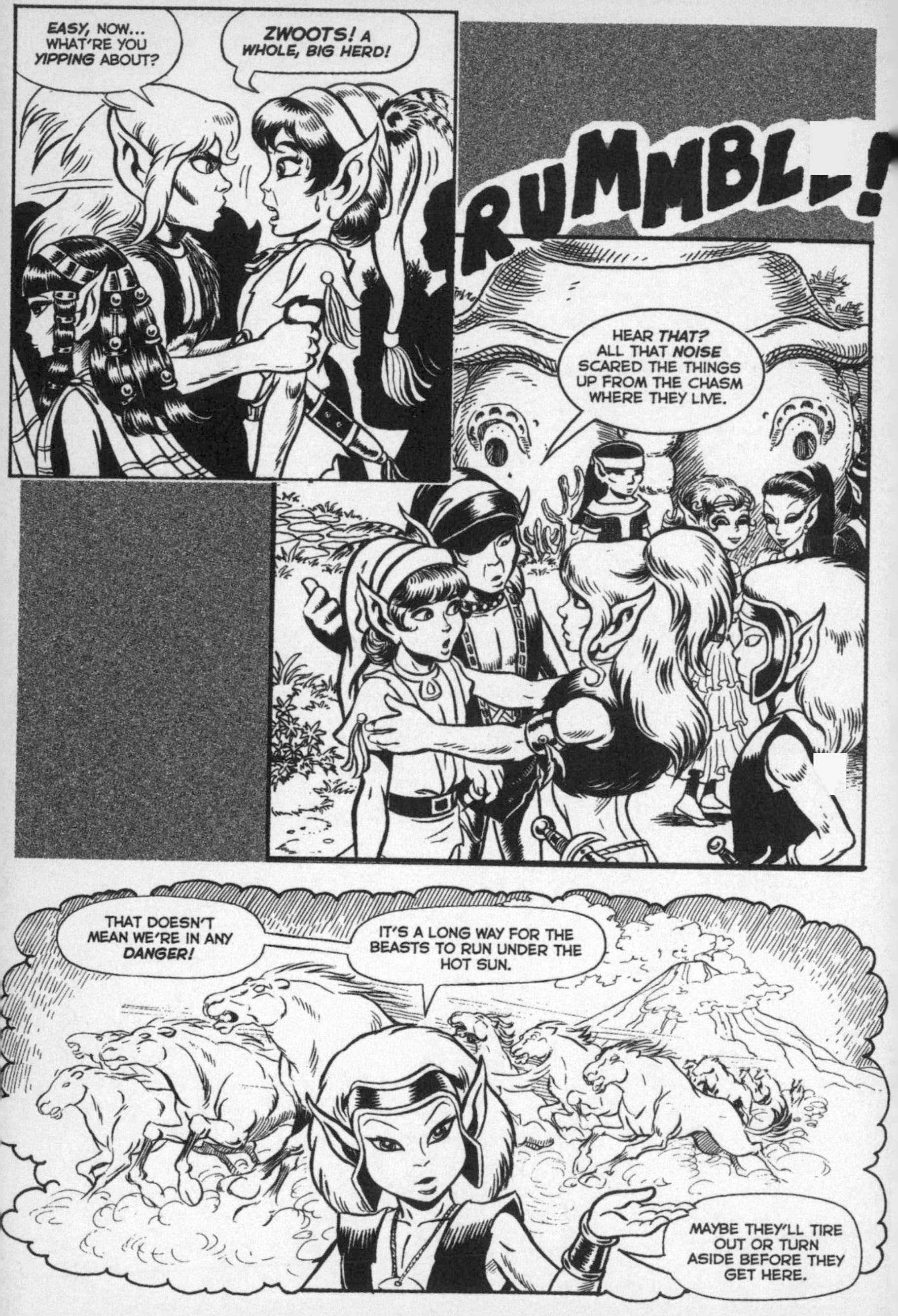
EASY, NOW... WHAT'RE YOU YIPPING ABOUT?
ZWOOTS! A WHOLE, BIG HERD!
RUMMBL
HEAR THAT? ALL THAT NOISE SCARED THE THINGS UP FROM THE CHASM WHERE THEY LIVE.
THAT DOESN'T MEAN WE'RE IN ANY DANGER!
IT'S A LONG WAY FOR THE BEASTS TO RUN UNDER THE HOT SUN.
MAYBE THEY'LL TIRE OUT OR TURN ASIDE BEFORE THEY GET HERE.

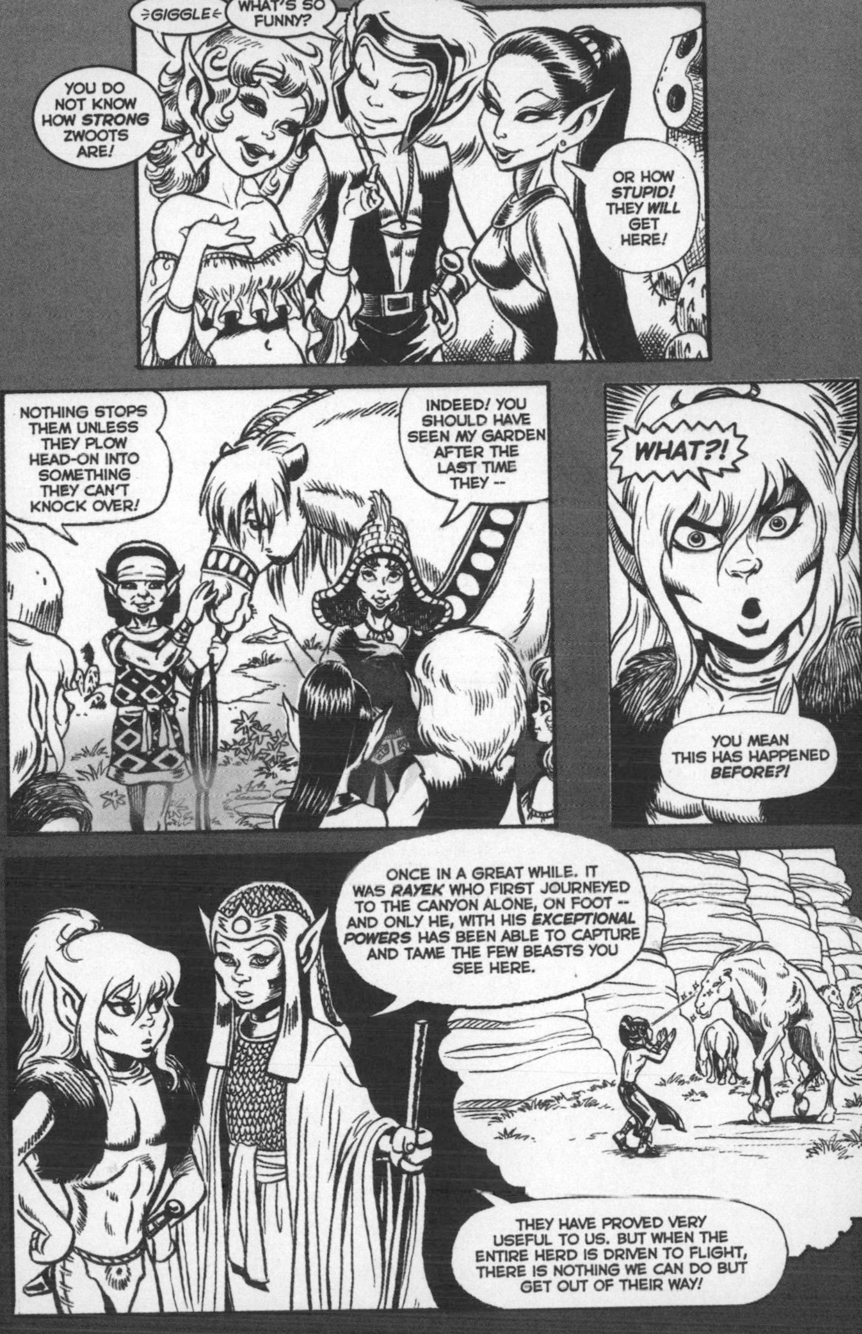

~GIGGLE~
WHAT'S SO FUNNY?
YOU DO NOT KNOW HOW *STRONG* ZWOOTS ARE!
OR HOW *STUPID!* THEY *WILL* GET HERE!
NOTHING STOPS THEM UNLESS THEY PLOW HEAD-ON INTO SOMETHING THEY CAN'T KNOCK OVER!
INDEED! YOU SHOULD HAVE SEEN MY GARDEN AFTER THE LAST TIME THEY --
WHAT?!
YOU MEAN THIS HAS HAPPENED *BEFORE?!*
ONCE IN A GREAT WHILE. IT WAS *RAYEK* WHO FIRST JOURNEYED TO THE CANYON ALONE, ON FOOT -- AND ONLY HE, WITH HIS *EXCEPTIONAL POWERS* HAS BEEN ABLE TO CAPTURE AND TAME THE FEW BEASTS YOU SEE HERE.
THEY HAVE PROVED VERY USEFUL TO US. BUT WHEN THE ENTIRE HERD IS DRIVEN TO FLIGHT, THERE IS NOTHING WE CAN DO BUT GET OUT OF THEIR WAY!

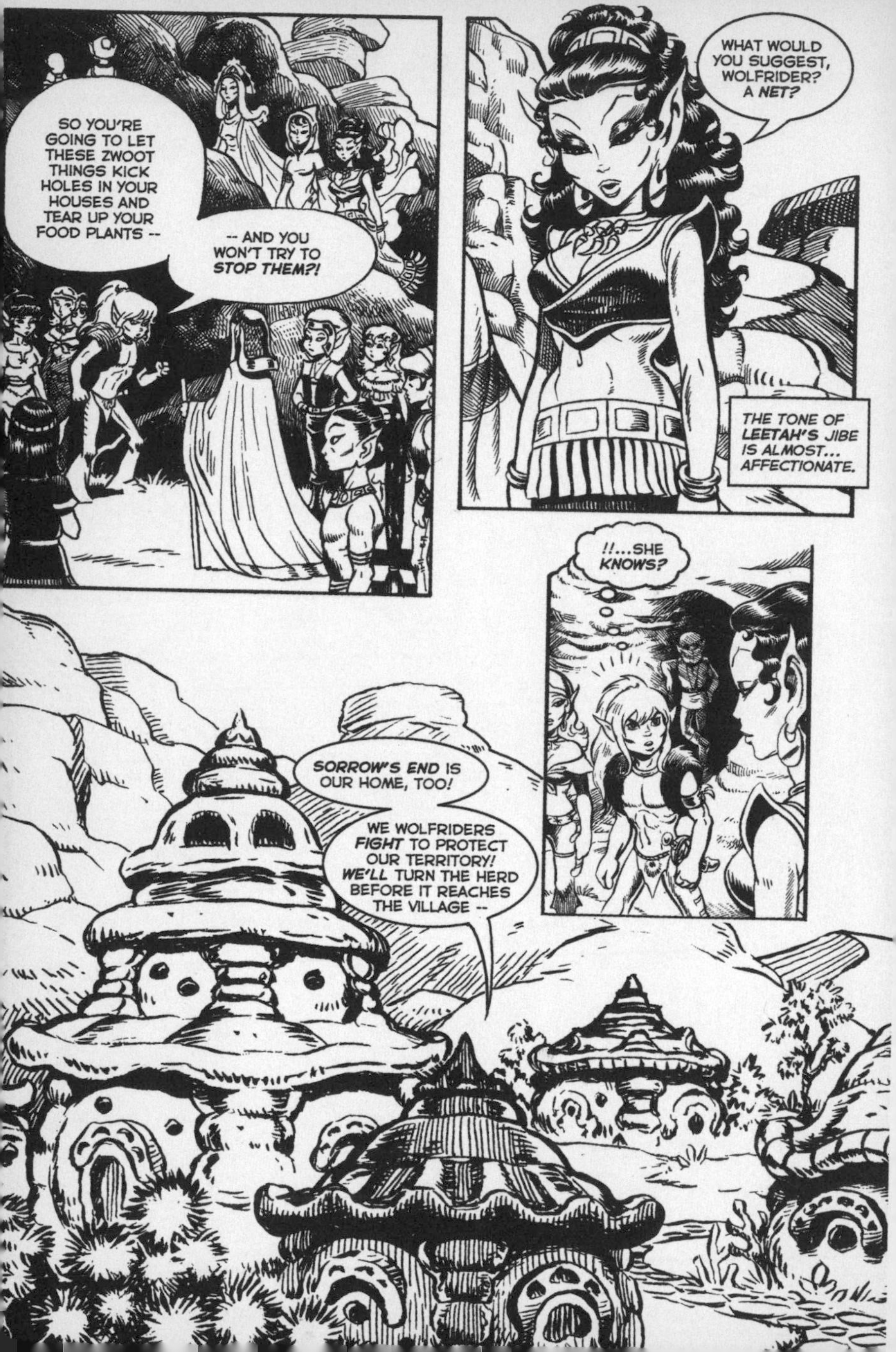
SO YOU'RE GOING TO LET THESE ZWOOT THINGS KICK HOLES IN YOUR HOUSES AND TEAR UP YOUR FOOD PLANTS --
-- AND YOU WON'T TRY TO *STOP THEM?!*
WHAT WOULD YOU SUGGEST, WOLFRIDER? A *NET?*
THE TONE OF LEETAH'S JIBE IS ALMOST... AFFECTIONATE.
!!...SHE KNOWS?
SORROW'S END IS OUR HOME, TOO!
WE WOLFRIDERS *FIGHT* TO PROTECT OUR TERRITORY! *WE'LL* TURN THE HERD BEFORE IT REACHES THE VILLAGE --

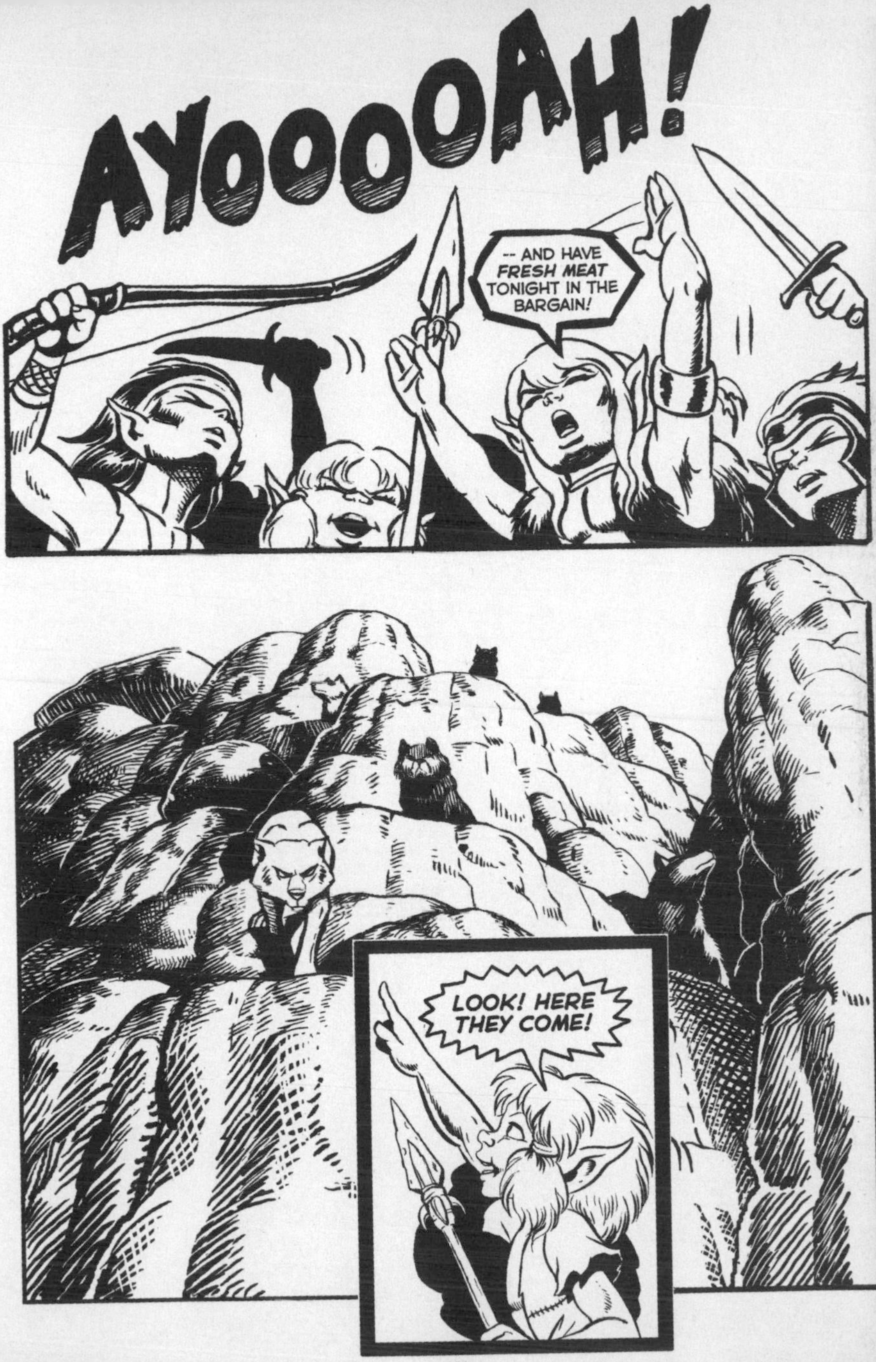
AYOOOOAH!
-- AND HAVE *FRESH MEAT* TONIGHT IN THE BARGAIN!
LOOK! HERE THEY COME!

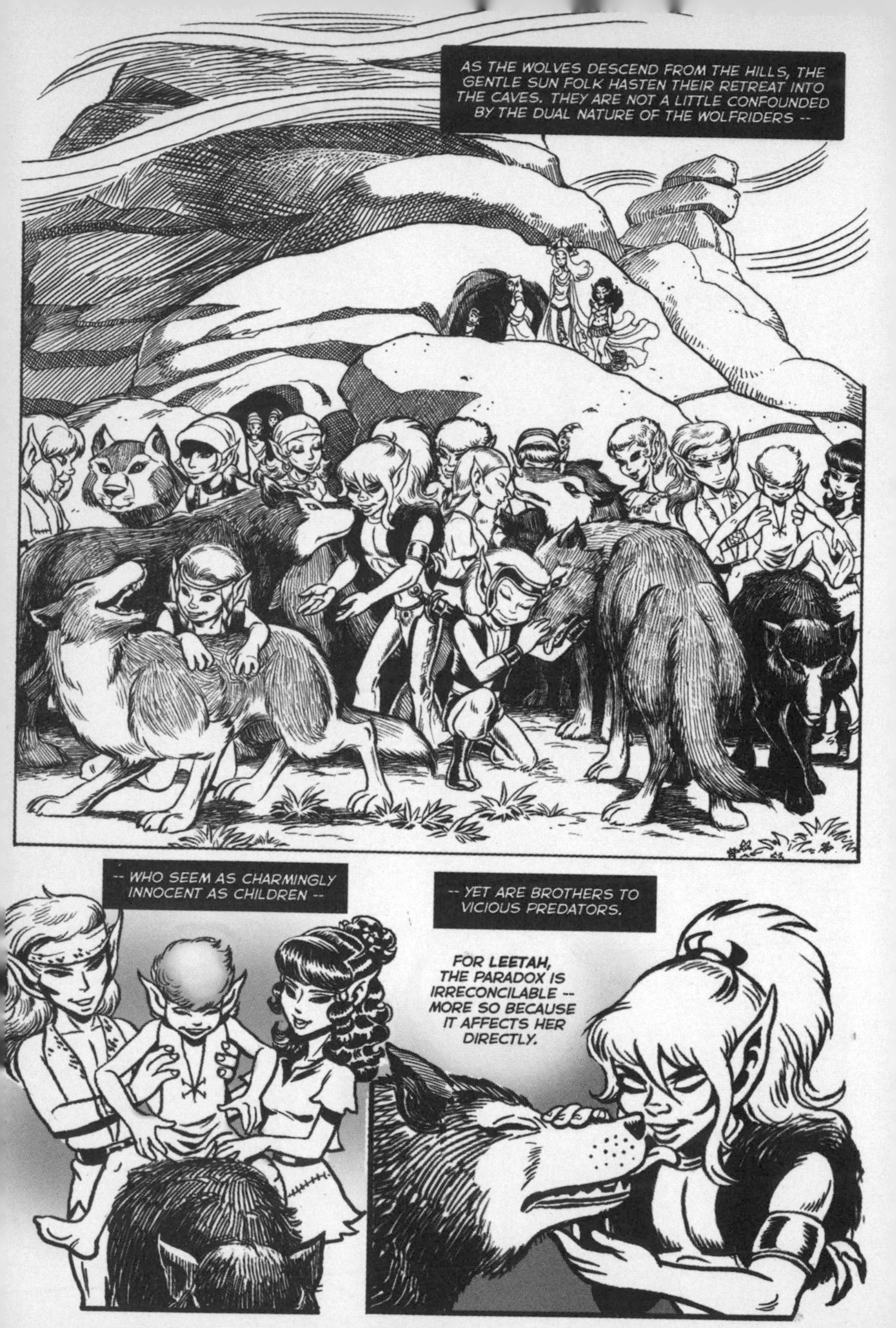
AS THE WOLVES DESCEND FROM THE HILLS, THE GENTLE SUN FOLK HASTEN THEIR RETREAT INTO THE CAVES. THEY ARE NOT A LITTLE CONFOUNDED BY THE DUAL NATURE OF THE WOLFRIDERS --
-- WHO SEEM AS CHARMINGLY INNOCENT AS CHILDREN --
-- YET ARE BROTHERS TO VICIOUS PREDATORS.
FOR LEETAH, THE PARADOX IS IRRECONCILABLE -- MORE SO BECAUSE IT AFFECTS HER DIRECTLY.

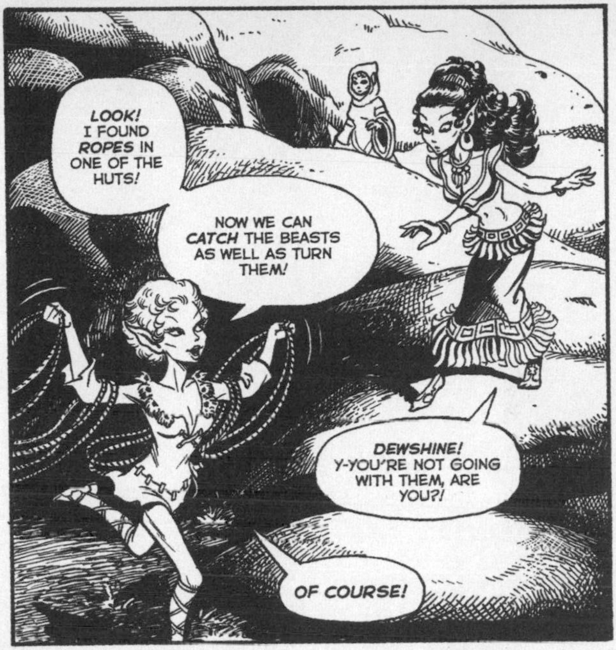
LOOK! I FOUND ROPES IN ONE OF THE HUTS!
NOW WE CAN CATCH THE BEASTS AS WELL AS TURN THEM!
DEWSHINE! Y-YOU'RE NOT GOING WITH THEM, ARE YOU?!
OF COURSE!

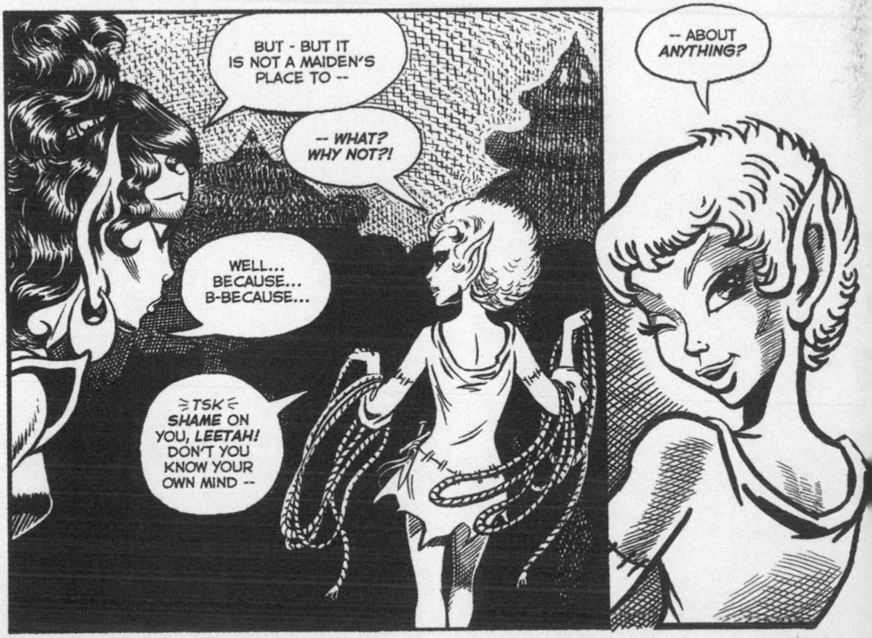
BUT - BUT IT IS NOT A MAIDEN'S PLACE TO --
-- WHAT? WHY NOT?!
WELL... BECAUSE... B-BECAUSE...
TSK SHAME ON YOU, LEETAH! DON'T YOU KNOW YOUR OWN MIND --
-- ABOUT ANYTHING?

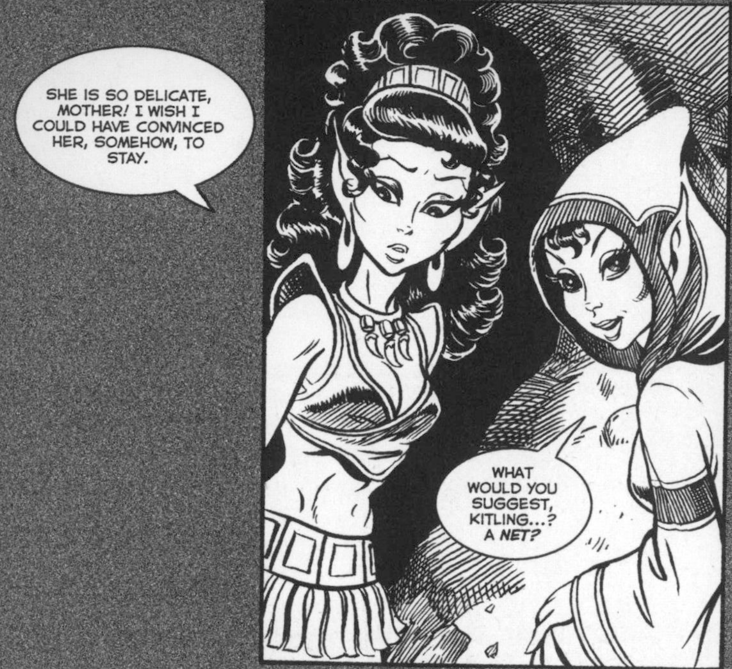
SHE IS SO DELICATE, MOTHER! I WISH I COULD HAVE CONVINCED HER, SOMEHOW, TO STAY.
WHAT WOULD YOU SUGGEST, KITLING...? A NET?

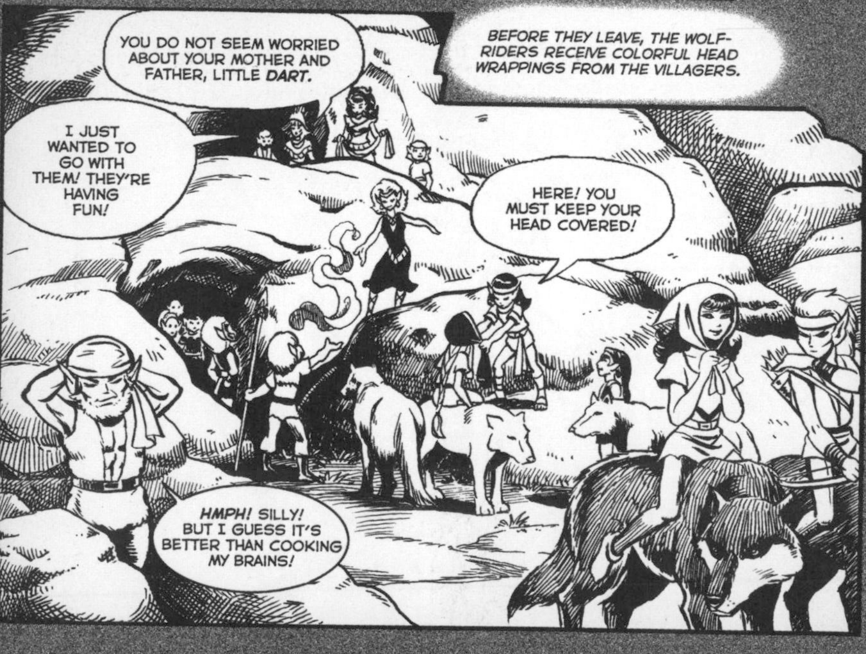
BEFORE THEY LEAVE, THE WOLF-RIDERS RECEIVE COLORFUL HEAD WRAPPINGS FROM THE VILLAGERS.
YOU DO NOT SEEM WORRIED ABOUT YOUR MOTHER AND FATHER, LITTLE DART.
I JUST WANTED TO GO WITH THEM! THEY'RE HAVING FUN!
HERE! YOU MUST KEEP YOUR HEAD COVERED!
HMPH! SILLY! BUT I GUESS IT'S BETTER THAN COOKING MY BRAINS!

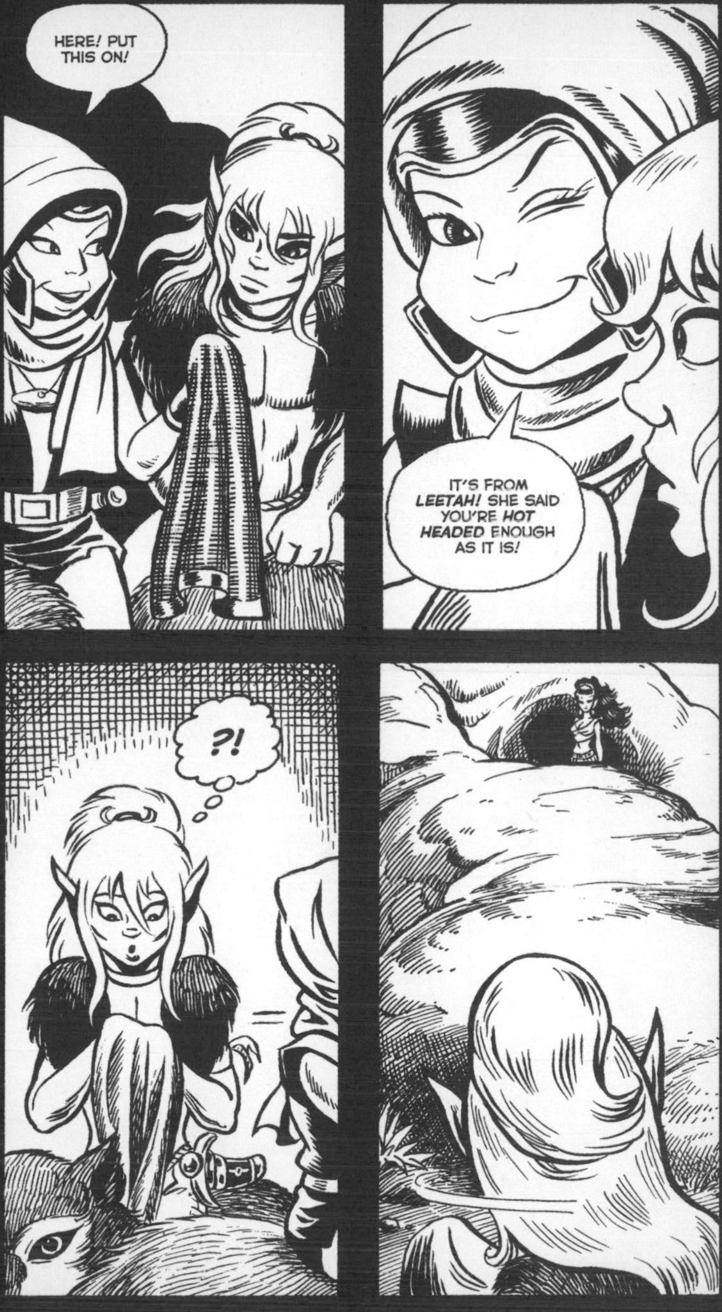
HERE! PUT THIS ON!
IT'S FROM *LEETAH!* SHE SAID YOU'RE *HOT HEADED* ENOUGH AS IT IS!
?!

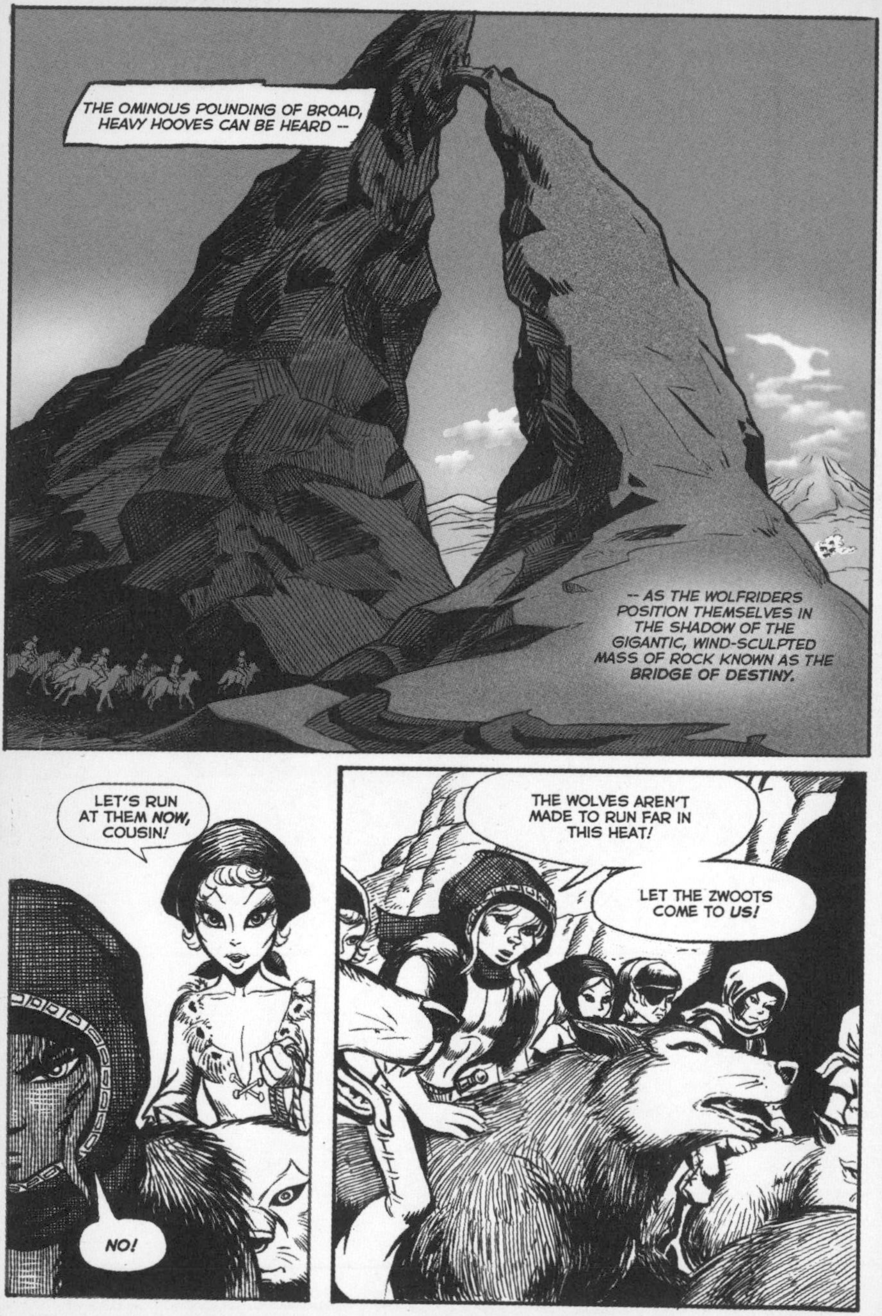
THE OMINOUS POUNDING OF BROAD, HEAVY HOOVES CAN BE HEARD --
-- AS THE WOLFRIDERS POSITION THEMSELVES IN THE SHADOW OF THE GIGANTIC, WIND-SCULPTED MASS OF ROCK KNOWN AS THE BRIDGE OF DESTINY.
LET'S RUN AT THEM NOW, COUSIN!
NO!
THE WOLVES AREN'T MADE TO RUN FAR IN THIS HEAT!
LET THE ZWOOTS COME TO US!

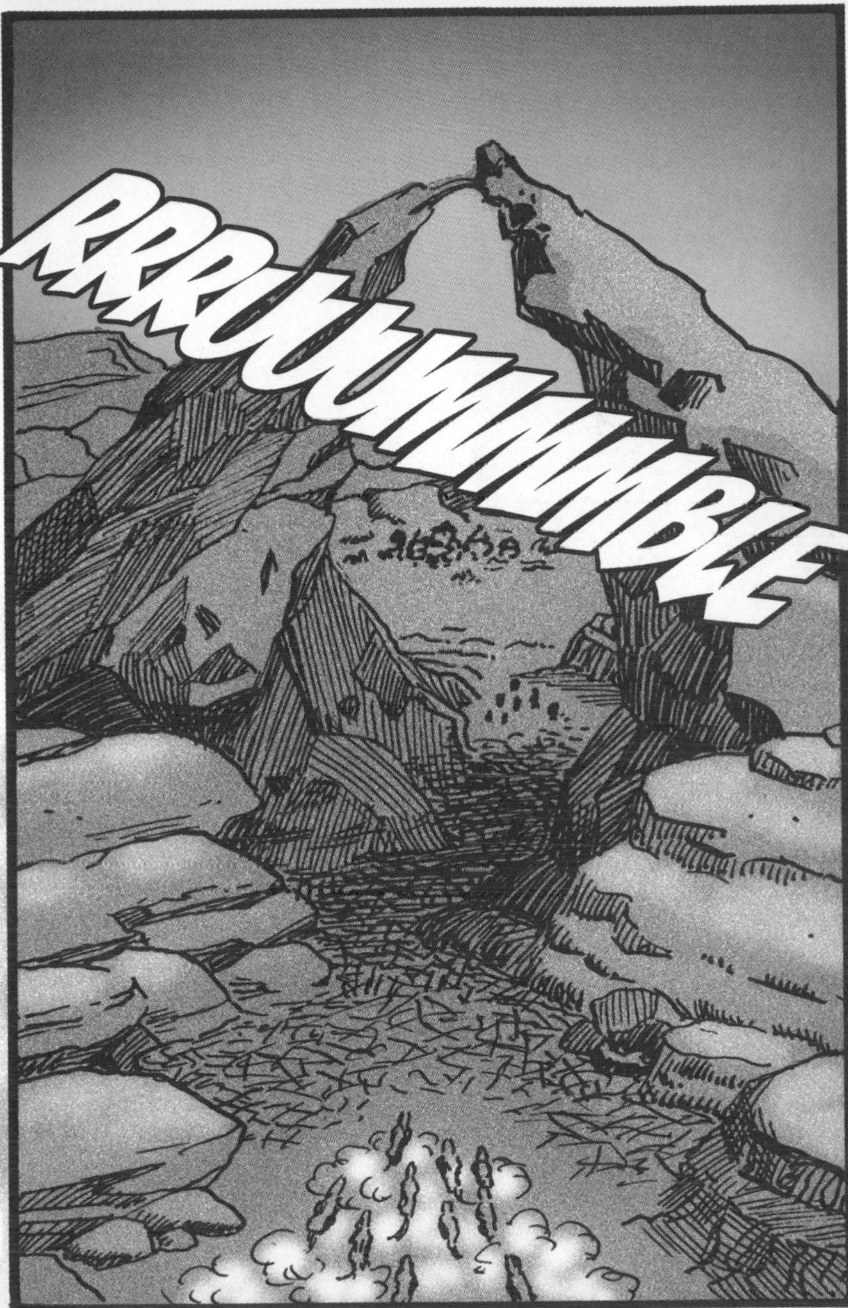
RRRRUUMMMBLE

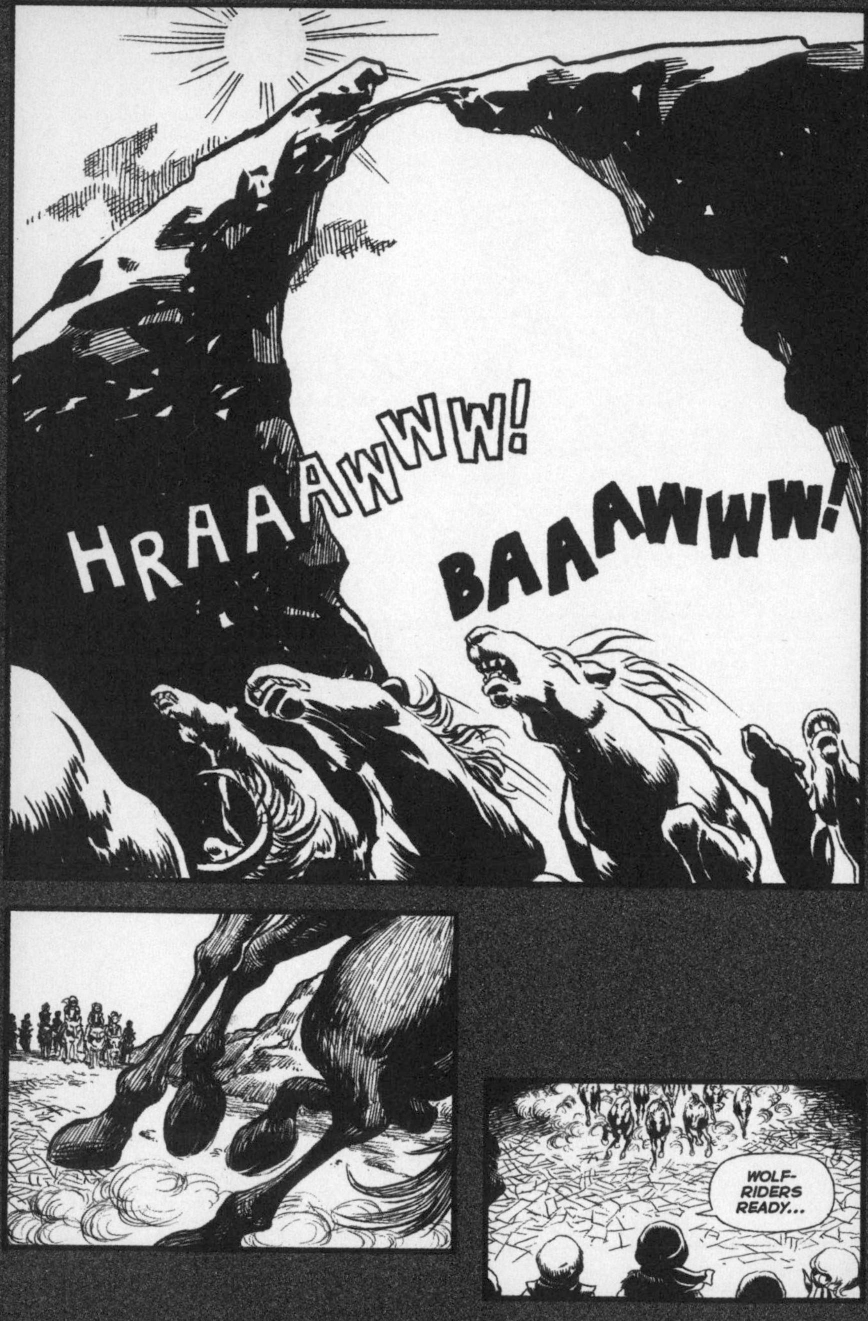
HRAAAWWW!
BAAAWWWW!
WOLF-RIDERS READY...

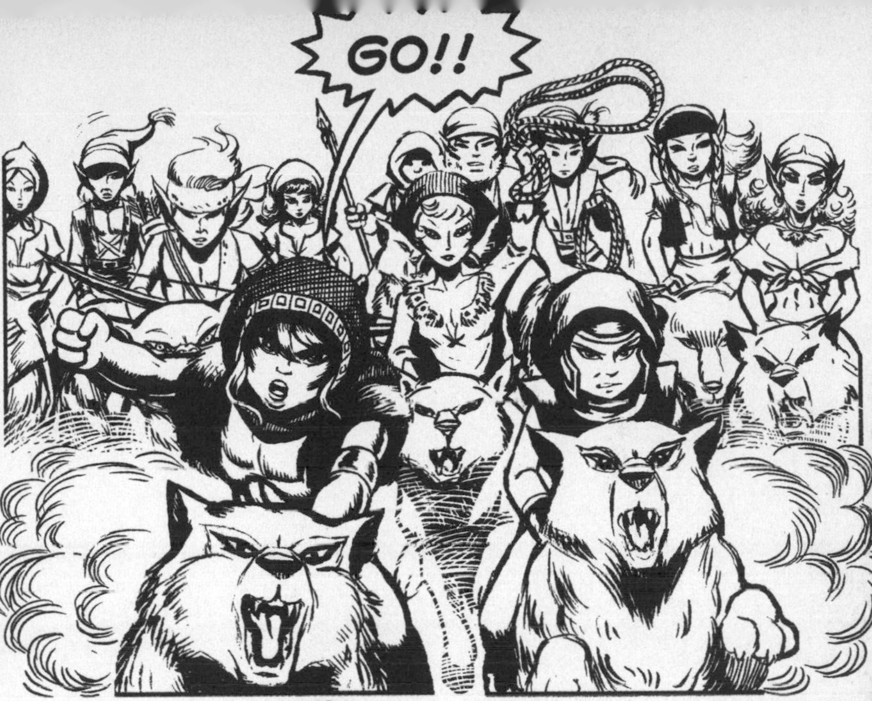
GO!!

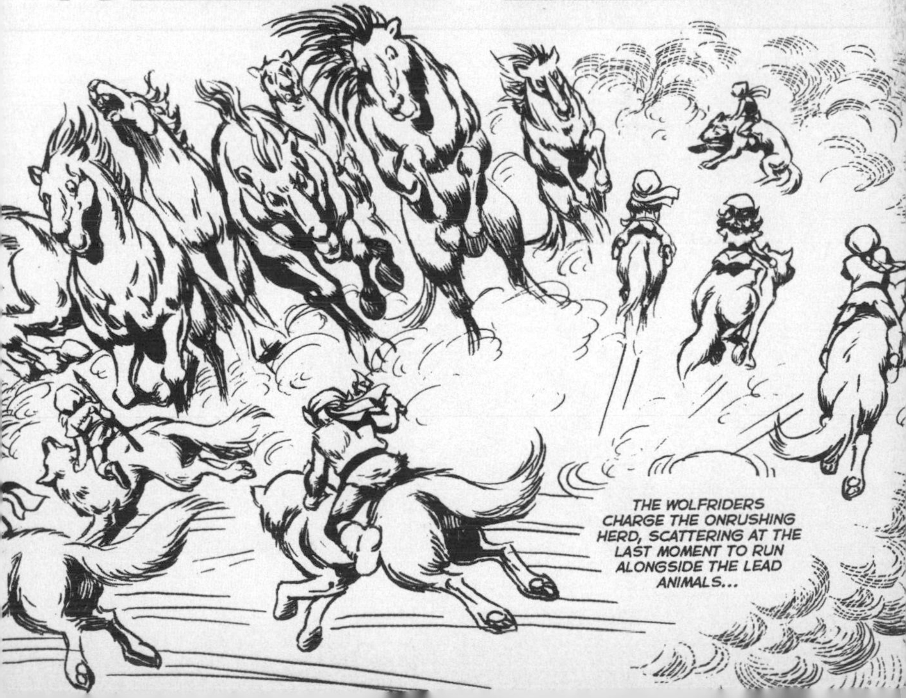
THE WOLFRIDERS CHARGE THE ONRUSHING HERD, SCATTERING AT THE LAST MOMENT TO RUN ALONGSIDE THE LEAD ANIMALS...

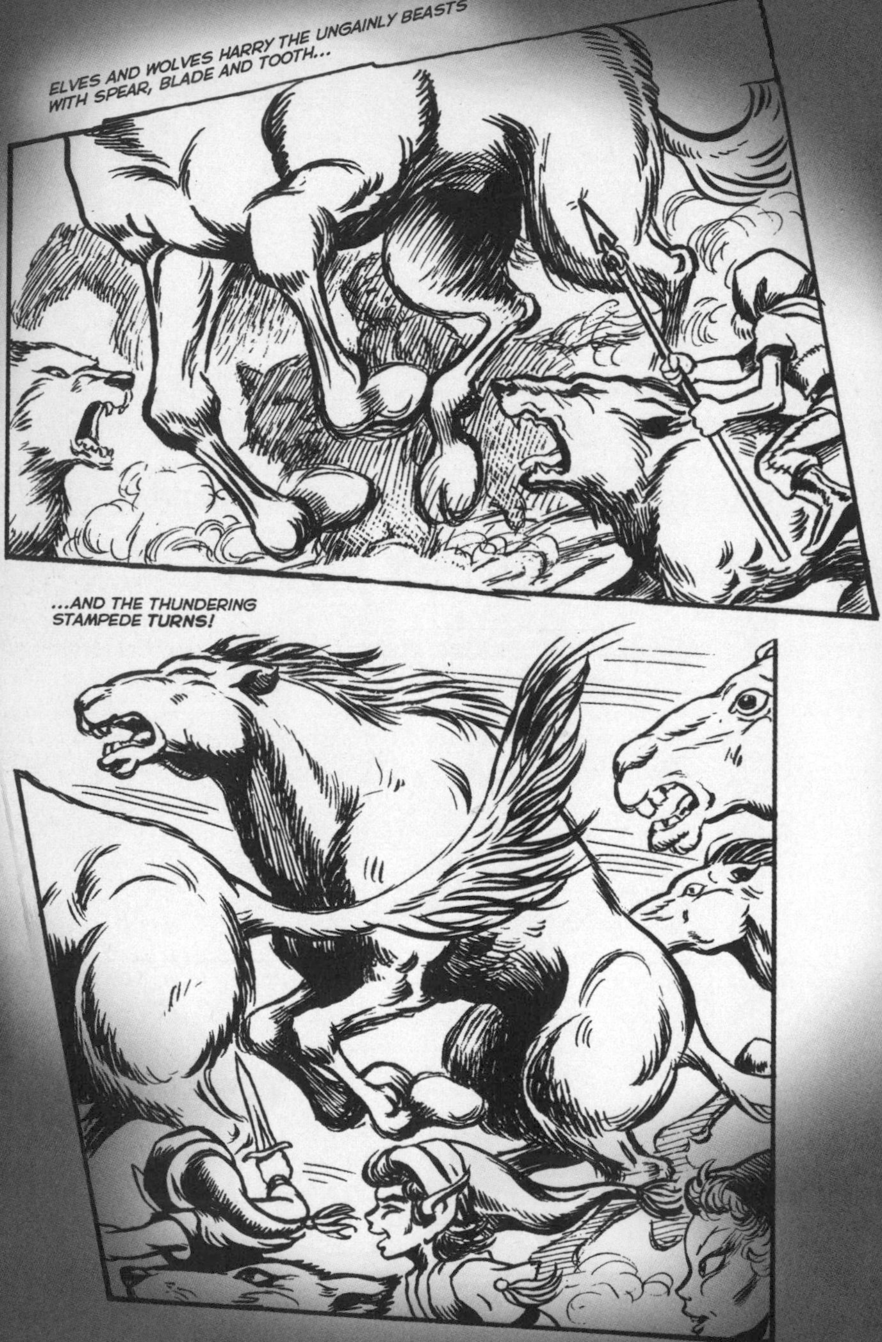
ELVES AND WOLVES HARRY THE UNGAINLY BEASTS WITH SPEAR, BLADE AND TOOTH...
...AND THE THUNDERING STAMPEDE TURNS!

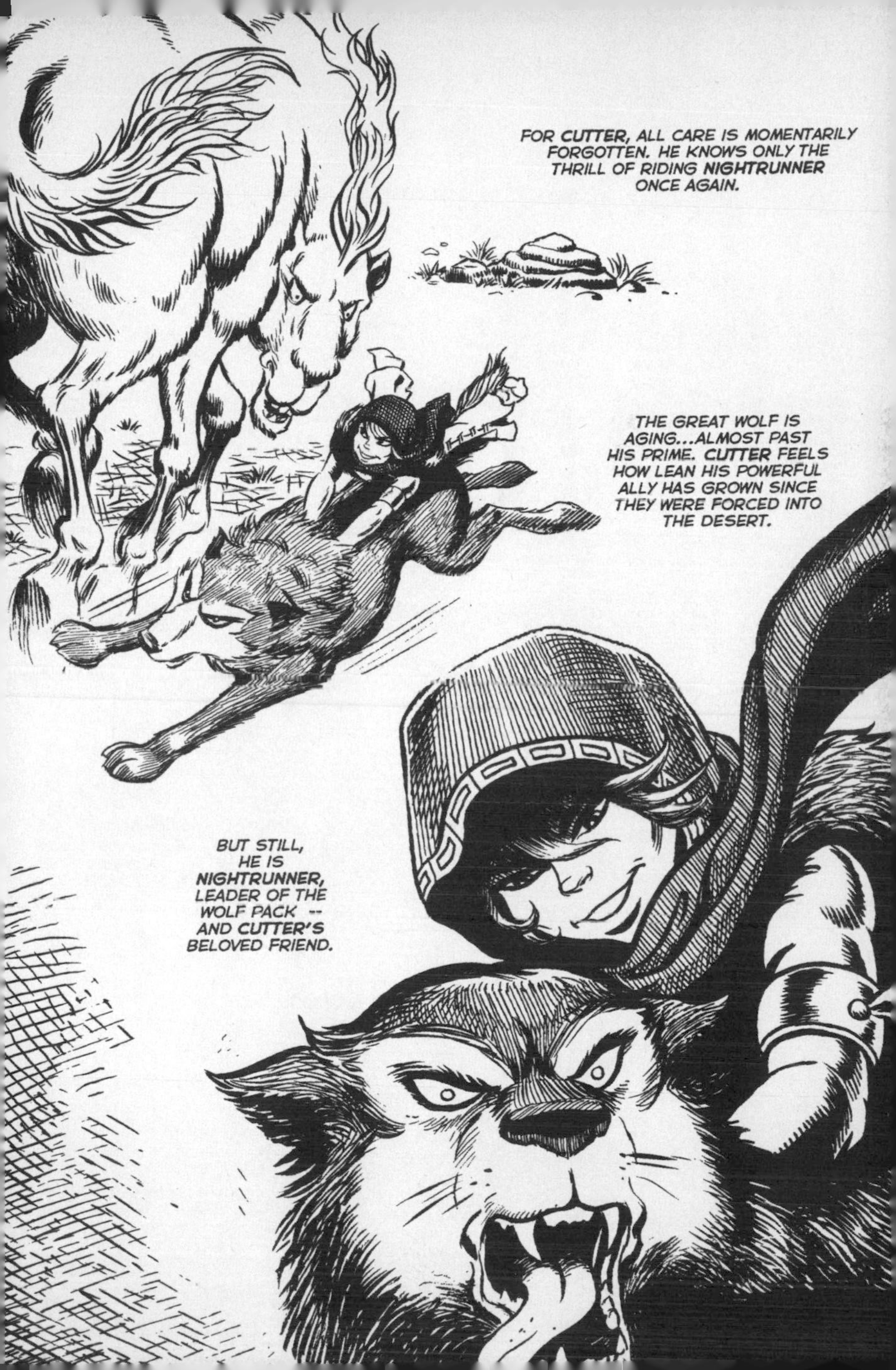
FOR CUTTER, ALL CARE IS MOMENTARILY FORGOTTEN. HE KNOWS ONLY THE THRILL OF RIDING NIGHTRUNNER ONCE AGAIN.
THE GREAT WOLF IS AGING...ALMOST PAST HIS PRIME. CUTTER FEELS HOW LEAN HIS POWERFUL ALLY HAS GROWN SINCE THEY WERE FORCED INTO THE DESERT.
BUT STILL, HE IS NIGHTRUNNER, LEADER OF THE WOLF PACK -- AND CUTTER'S BELOVED FRIEND.

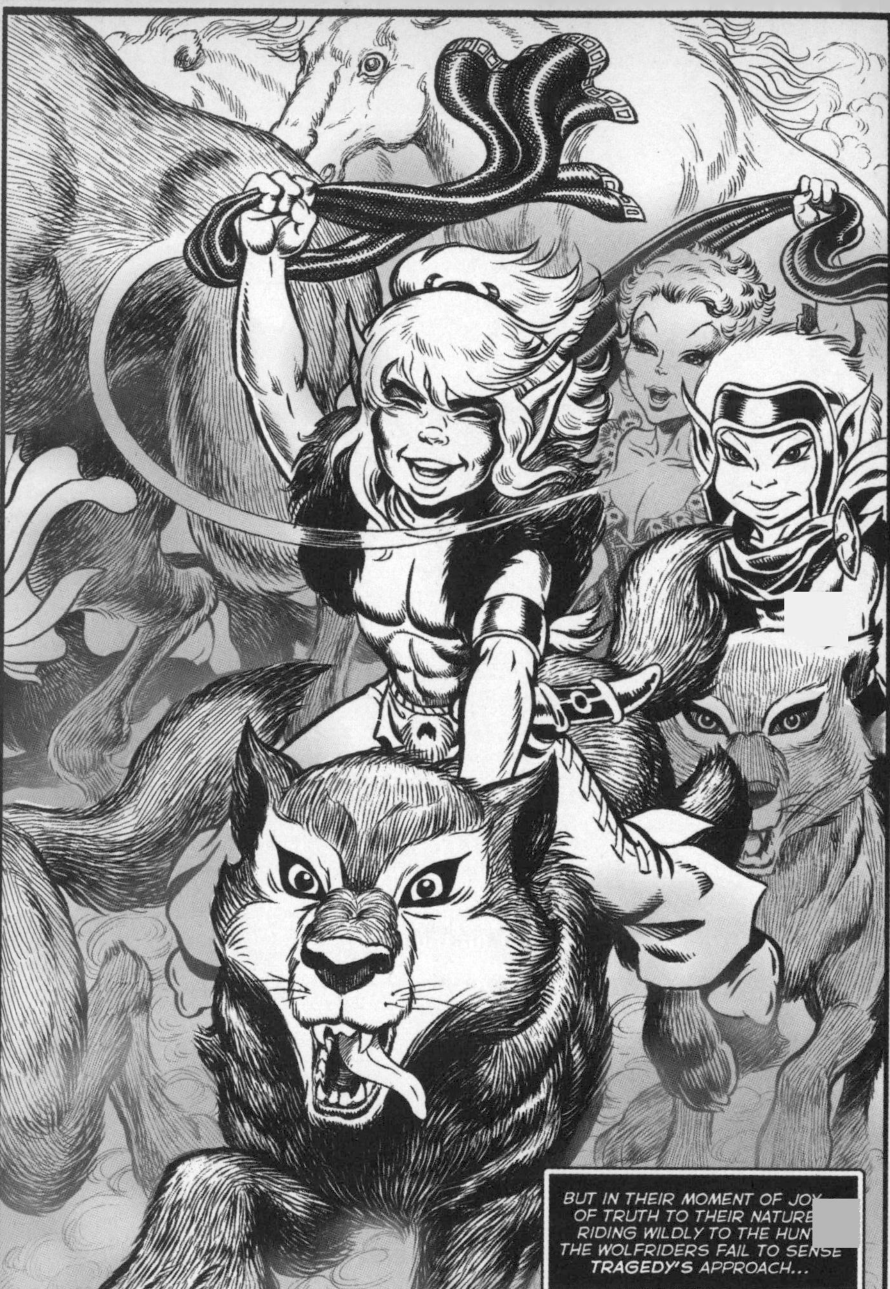
BUT IN THEIR MOMENT OF JOY
OF TRUTH TO THEIR NATURE
RIDING WILDLY TO THE HUNT
THE WOLFRIDERS FAIL TO SENSE
TRAGEDY'S APPROACH...
TO BE CONTINUED...

IN THE NEXT VOLUME

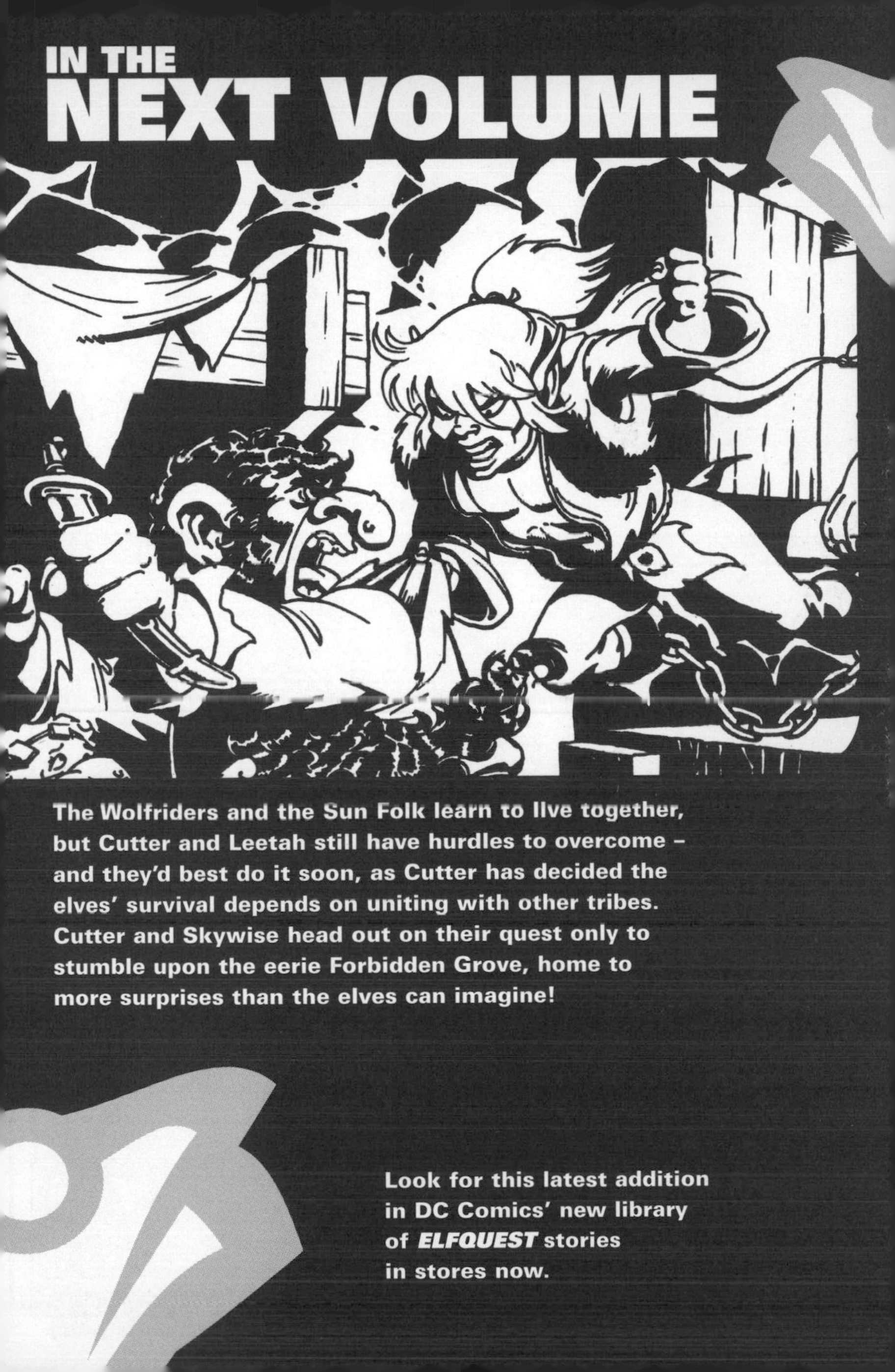

The Wolfriders and the Sun Folk learn to live together, but Cutter and Leetah still have hurdles to overcome – and they'd best do it soon, as Cutter has decided the elves' survival depends on uniting with other tribes. Cutter and Skywise head out on their quest only to stumble upon the eerie Forbidden Grove, home to more surprises than the elves can imagine!

Look for this latest addition in DC Comics' new library of *ELFQUEST* stories in stores now.

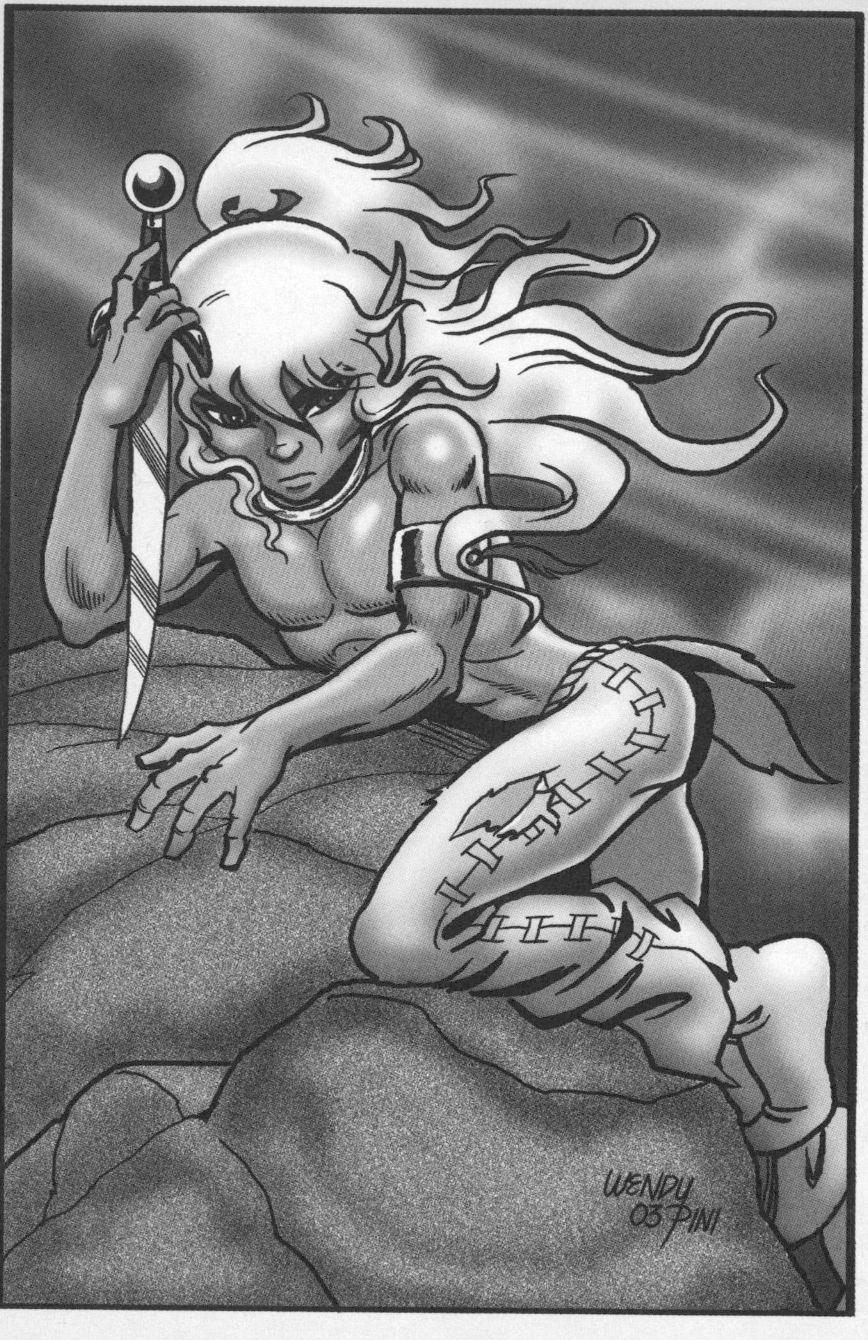
WENDY
03 PINI

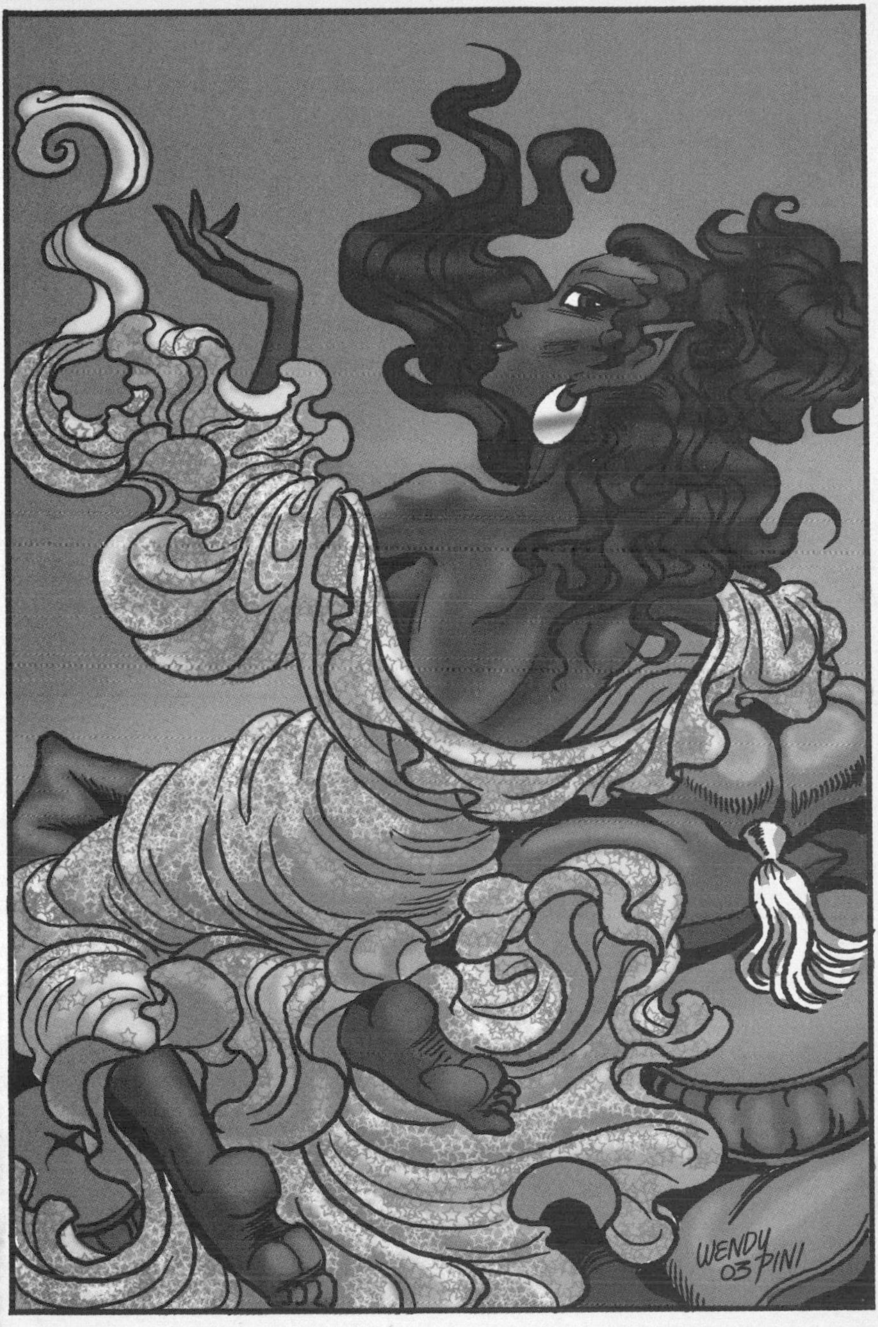
WENDY
03 PINI

THE *ELFQUEST* LIBRARY

FROM DC COMICS